Teacher's Resources for

From School to Work

Publisher
The Goodheart-Willcox Company, Inc.
Tinley Park, Illinois

ontents

Introduction

Using the Text. 5

Using the *Student Activity Guide* 6

Using the *Teacher's Annotated Edition*. 6

Using the *Teacher's Resource Guide* 6

Using the *Teacher's Resource Binder*. 7

Using the *GW Test Creation Software* 7

The Secretary's Commission on Achieving
Necessary Skills (SCANS) 8

Assessment Techniques 9

Using Other Resources 9

Evaluation of Individual Participation 17

Evaluation of Individual Report. 18

Evaluation of Group Participation 19

Scope and Sequence Chart 21

SCANS Correlation Chart. 29

Bulletin Boards or Displays 36

		Teacher's Resource Guide/Binder	Text	Student Activity Guide
Part 1	**Work-Based Learning**			
Chapter 1	Making the Transition from School to Work	43	19	7
Chapter 2	Understanding Work-Based Learning	53	31	15
Chapter 3	What Your Employer Expects	65	45	23
Part 2	**Skills for Success**			
Chapter 4	Teamwork and Problem-Solving Skills	75	63	29
Chapter 5	Communicating on the Job	85	81	37
Chapter 6	Math in the Workplace	99	109	45
Chapter 7	Computer and Internet Skills	109	125	51
Chapter 8	Looking Good on the Job	123	149	57
Chapter 9	Safety on the Job	131	163	63
Chapter 10	Leadership and Group Dynamics	141	183	69
Chapter 11	Participating in Meetings	149	195	75

			Teacher's Resource Guide/Binder	Text	Student Activity Guide

Part 3   Career Planning

Chapter 12	Learning About Yourself	159	209	81
Chapter 13	Learning About Careers	169	223	89
Chapter 14	Researching Careers	181	263	93
Chapter 15	Making Career Decisions	189	279	99

Part 4   The Job Hunt

Chapter 16	Applying for Jobs	203	293	105
Chapter 17	Taking Pre-Employment Tests	213	317	113
Chapter 18	Interviewing for Jobs	221	329	119

Part 5   Job Satisfaction

Chapter 19	Succeeding on the Job	231	345	129
Chapter 20	Diversity and Rights in the Workplace	243	365	137
Chapter 21	Succeeding in Our Economic System	255	387	145
Chapter 22	Entrepreneurship: A Business of Your Own	265	401	151

Part 6   Managing Your Income

Chapter 23	Understanding Income and Taxes	275	425	159
Chapter 24	Managing Spending	289	445	165
Chapter 25	Using Credit	301	469	175
Chapter 26	Banking, Saving, and Investing	313	489	183
Chapter 27	Insurance	325	517	191
Chapter 28	Managing Family, Work, and Citizenship Roles	335	533	199

Introduction

From School to Work is a comprehensive text designed to help students in career and technical education programs make smooth transitions from classrooms to meaningful careers. In addition to the student text, the *From School to Work* learning package includes the *Student Activity Guide, Teacher's Annotated Edition, Teacher's Resource Guide, Teacher's Resource Binder,* and *GW Test Creation Software.* Using these products can help you develop an effective career education program tailored to your students' unique needs.

Using the Text

The text, *From School to Work,* is designed to help your students develop career awareness. They will learn how to develop the skills they need to succeed on the job, both now and in the future.

The text is divided into six parts with a total of 28 chapters. The material is organized and presented in a logical sequence of topics. Although the text was written to be studied in its entirety, individual chapters and sections are complete enough to be studied independently.

The text is straightforward and easy to read. Hundreds of photographs and charts attract student interest and emphasize key concepts. References to the illustrations are included in the copy to help students associate the visual images with the written material. This helps reinforce learning.

The text includes a glossary at the back of the book to help students learn terms related to career education and occupational awareness. A complete index helps them find information they want quickly and easily. Each chapter also includes several features designed to help students study effectively and review what they have learned.

Objectives. A set of behavioral objectives appear at the beginning of each chapter. These are performance goals that students will be expected to achieve after studying the chapter. Review the objectives in each chapter with students to help make them aware of the skills they will be building as they read the chapter material. SCANS competencies reinforced by the chapter content are clearly identified.

Terms to Know. A list of vocabulary terms appears at the beginning of each chapter. Terms are listed in the order in which they appear in the chapter. These terms are in bold type throughout the text so students can recognize them while reading. Discussing these words with students will help them learn concepts to which they are being introduced. To help students become familiar with these terms, you may want to ask them to

- relate each term to the topic being studied.
- look up, define, and explain each term.
- match terms with their definitions.
- find examples of how the terms are used in current newspapers and magazines, reference books, and other related materials.

Think more about it.... Thought-provoking questions appear throughout each chapter to encourage class discussion and students' use of higher-level thinking skills. The questions require students to apply their knowledge of chapter content as well as critical thinking skills.

Case Studies. Each chapter includes at least one case study. These provide life-like situations that help students apply information from the chapter. Discussion questions guide student analysis.

Summary. A chapter summary is located at the end of each chapter. This section is a review of the major concepts covered in the entire chapter.

Facts in Review. Review questions at the end of each chapter are included to cover the basic information presented. This section consists primarily of short answer and essay questions. It is designed to help students recall, organize, and use the information presented in the text. Answers to these questions appear beside the questions in the *Teacher's Annotated Edition,* but are also provided in the *Teacher's Resource Guide* and *Teacher's Resource Binder.*

Applying Your Skills. Suggested activities at the end of each chapter offer students opportunities to increase knowledge through firsthand experiences. These activities encourage students to apply many of the concepts learned in the chapter to real-life situations. Suggestions for both individual and group work are provided in varying degrees of difficulty. Therefore, you may choose and assign activities according to students' interests and abilities.

Developing SCANS Workplace Competencies. Each chapter ends with a suggested activity that will help develop the SCANS Competencies stated in the chapter objectives. These are more involved activities, usually group projects that promote the development of workplace know-how.

Using the *Student Activity Guide*

The *Student Activity Guide* designed for use with *From School to Work* helps students recall and review material presented in the text. It also helps them apply what they have learned as they participate in career education experiences.

The activities in the guide are divided into chapters that correspond to the chapters in the text. The text provides the information students will need to complete many of the activities. Other activities will require creative thinking and research beyond the textbook.

You may want to use the exercises in the *Student Activity Guide* that are directly related to textual material as introductory, review, or evaluation tools. Ask students to do the exercises without looking in the book. Then they can use the text to check their answers and to answer questions they could not complete. The pages of the *Student Activity Guide* are perforated so students can easily remove pages and give completed activities to you for evaluation.

The *Student Activity Guide* includes different types of activities. Some have specific answers related to text material. Students can use these activities to review as they study for tests and quizzes. Answers to these activities appear in the *Teacher's Resource Guide* and the *Teacher's Resource Binder.*

Other activities, such as case studies and surveys, ask for students' thoughts or opinions. Answers to these activities cannot be judged as right or wrong. These activities allow students to form their own ideas by considering alternatives and evaluating situations thoughtfully. These thought-provoking exercises can often be used as a basis for classroom discussion by asking students to justify their answers and conclusions.

Using the *Teacher's Annotated Edition*

The *Teacher's Annotated Edition* for *From School to Work* is a special edition of the student text. It is designed to help you more effectively coordinate materials in the *Student Activity Guide,* the *Teacher's Resource Guide,* and the *Teacher's Resource Binder* with text concepts. It also provides you with additional suggestions to help you add variety to your classroom teaching.

Annotations are located throughout the text. Numbers are placed in the margins that correspond with annotations located at the side or bottom of each page.

In addition to annotations placed throughout the student text, the *Teacher's Annotated Edition* includes a special introductory section. It begins with an explanation of the various components in the teaching package for *From School to Work*. The introduction continues with several sections that provide useful background information in teaching career education

courses, such as suggestions for teaching learners with special needs. Ideas for marketing your program are also provided.

Next is a *Lesson Planning Guide* for each chapter in the text. A chapter outline is provided to help you see the organization of the chapter. The resources that are available for teaching each section of the chapter are then listed. Each guide also has two special sections:

- **Technology Applications** are activities and projects that focus on the use of technology, particularly the Internet and computer software programs.
- **Academic Connections** are ideas for relating the chapter content to other curriculum areas, such as math, history, social studies, and science.

Using the *Teacher's Resource Guide*

The *Teacher's Resource Guide* for *From School to Work* suggests many methods of presenting the text concepts to students. It includes helpful information in the introduction, a *Scope and Sequence Chart,* a *SCANS Correlation Chart,* and a section on bulletin board and display ideas for each part of the text.

Scope and Sequence Chart

The *Scope and Sequence Chart,* located at the end of this introduction, identifies the major concepts presented in each chapter of the text. It also shows where information related to the SCANS Foundation Skills and Workplace Competencies can be found in the text. This special resource is provided to help you select for study those topics that meet your curriculum needs.

SCANS Correlation Chart

Another feature of this *Teacher's Resource Guide* is the *SCANS Correlation Chart.* This chart has been designed to identify those activities in the *From School to Work* text and supplements that specifically encourage the development of the SCANS competencies and foundation skills. The section of the chart titled "SCANS Foundation Skills" lists activities in five categories: reading, writing, arithmetic/math/science, speaking/listening, and thinking skills. (Thinking skills involve the higher-order skills needed for thinking creatively, making decisions, solving problems, visualizing information, reasoning, and knowing how to learn.) The chart includes activities from the "Applying Your Skills" section of the text, activities from the *Student Activity Guide,* and strategies from the *Teacher's Resource Guide* and *Teacher's Resource Binder.* Incorporating a variety of these activities into your daily lesson plans will provide your students with vital practice in the development of SCANS competencies and foundation skills. Also, if you find that students in your classes are weak in a specific skill, you can select activities to strengthen that area.

Chapter-by-Chapter Resources

Like the *Student Activity Guide,* the *Teacher's Resource Guide* is divided into chapters that match the chapters in the text. Each chapter contains the following features:

Objectives. These are the objectives that students will be able to accomplish after reading the chapter and completing the suggested activities.

Teaching Materials. A list of materials available to supplement each chapter in the text is provided. The list includes the names of all the activities contained in the *Student Activity Guide* and all the masters contained in the *Teacher's Resource Guide* and *Teacher's Resource Binder.*

Activities to Introduce the Chapter. These motivational exercises are designed to stimulate your students' interest in the topics they will be studying. The activities help create a sense of curiosity that students will want to satisfy by reading the chapter.

Instructional Concepts and Student Learning Experiences. A variety of student learning strategies are described for teaching each of the major concepts discussed in the text. Each major concept appears in the guide in bold type. The student learning experiences for each concept follow. Activities from the *Student Activity Guide* are listed for your convenience in planning daily lessons. They are identified with the title and letter of the activity followed by the letters *SAG* (for example, *Measuring Distances,* Activity E, SAG).

Activities to Enrich and Extend Learning. These additional activities include diverse experiences— role-playing, field trips, speakers, research topics, etc. Many activities promote critical thinking, problem solving, and decision-making skills.

Answer Key. This section provides answers for review questions at the end of each chapter in the text and for activities in the *Student Activity Guide.* Answers for the reproducible masters in the *Teacher's Resource Guide/Binder* and chapter tests are also included here.

Reproducible Masters. Several reproducible masters are included for each chapter. These masters are designed to enhance the presentation of concepts in the text. Some of the masters are designated as *transparency masters* for use with an overhead projector. These are often charts or graphs that can serve as a basis for class discussion of important concepts. They can also be used as student handouts. Some of the masters are designed as *reproducible masters.* Each student can be given a copy of the activity. These activities encourage creative and critical thinking. They can also serve as a basis for class discussion. Some masters provide material not contained in the text that you may want students to know.

A reproducible "Review and Study Guide" is provided for each chapter. These study guides can be used by those students who find the review questions in the text too difficult. Special needs students may find these more objective review sheets easier to use.

Chapter Test Masters. Individual tests with clear, specific questions that cover all the chapter topics are provided. True/false, multiple choice, and matching questions are used to measure student learning about facts and definitions. Essay questions are also provided in the chapter tests. Some of these require students to list information, while others encourage students to express their answers in their own words. You may wish to modify the tests and tailor the questions to your classroom needs.

Using the *Teacher's Resource Binder*

The *Teacher's Resource Binder* for *From School to Work* includes all the resources from the *Teacher's Resource Guide* plus a set of color transparencies. All of the materials are included in a convenient three-ring binder. Reproducible materials can be removed easily. You can also insert additional resource materials of your own. Handy dividers included with the binder help you organize materials so you can quickly find the items you need.

The color transparencies found in the *Teacher's Resource Binder* can help you add variety to your classroom discussions. You will find some transparencies useful in illustrating and reinforcing information presented in the text. Others will provide you with an opportunity to extend learning beyond the scope of the text. Attractive colors are visually appealing and hold students' attention. Suggestions for how the transparencies can be used in the classroom are included among the teaching strategies listed for each chapter.

Using the *GW Test Creation Software*

In addition to the printed supplements designed to support *From School to Work, GW Test Creation Software* is available. The database for this software package includes all the test master questions from the *Teacher's Resource Guide/Binder* plus an additional 25 percent new questions prepared just for this product. You can choose to have the computer generate a test for you with randomly selected questions. You can also opt to choose specific questions from the database and, if you wish, add your own questions to create customized tests to meet your classroom needs. You may want to make different versions of the same test to use during different class periods. Answer keys are generated automatically to simplify grading.

The Secretary's Commission on Achieving Necessary Skills (SCANS)

You will find frequent mention of SCANS in this edition of *From School to Work.* The following is additional background information on SCANS that you may find informative.

In 1989, the U.S. Secretary of Labor convened a blue ribbon panel to identify the work-readiness competencies needed for success in the changing workplace. This panel was named the Secretary's Commission on Achieving Necessary Skills (SCANS). The SCANS Commission was composed of representatives of education, business, labor, and management. They spoke with jobholders in both the public and private sectors. Following their study, the Commission identified five workplace competencies and a three-part foundation of skills and personal qualities that workers need in order to perform effectively on the job. These are listed in a chart on page 25 of the text and described in more detail here.

The three-part foundation of skills and personal qualities include the following:

- **Basic skills** involve expressing thoughts and communicating. They include reading, writing, arithmetic/math, speaking, and listening.
- **Thinking skills** involve developing ideas and solving problems. The key skills are thinking creatively, making decisions, solving problems, visualizing ideas, knowing how to learn, and reasoning.
- **Personal qualities** include individual responsibility, self-esteem, sociability, self-management, and integrity.

The necessary skills needed for the new world of work are called SCANS competencies. They are the basis of the modern workplace and the hallmarks of today's expert worker. The SCANS competencies bridge the span between school and work. Whether students go directly to work after high school or continue their education, the SCANS competencies are considered essential preparation for all avenues of life. The SCANS competencies focus on the following five areas:

- **competence with resources**
- **competence with interpersonal skills**
- **competence with information**
- **competence with systems**
- **competence with technology**

Some ways to identify the successful development of these related skills are described below.

1. A student who has **competence with resources** is able to identify, organize, plan, and allocate them as follows:
   - Time—Selects goal-relevant activities, ranks them, allocates time, and prepares and follows schedules.
   - Money—Uses or prepares budgets, makes forecasts, keeps records, and makes adjustments to meet objectives.
   - Materials and facilities—Acquires, stores, allocates, and uses materials or space efficiently.
   - Human resources—Assesses skills and distributes work accordingly, evaluates performance, and provides feedback.

2. A student who has **competence with interpersonal skills** works well with others:
   - Participates as a member of a team—Contributes to a group effort.
   - Teaches others new skills.
   - Serves clients/customers—Works to satisfy customers' expectations.
   - Exercises leadership—Communicates ideas to justify positions, persuades and convinces others, and responsibly challenges existing procedures and policies.
   - Negotiates—Works toward agreements involving the exchange of resources and resolves divergent interests.
   - Works with diversity—Works well with students from diverse backgrounds.

3. A student who has **competence with information** knows how to get and use information effectively.
   - Acquires and evaluates information.
   - Organizes and maintains data.
   - Interprets and communicates information.
   - Uses computers to process information.

4. A student who has **competence with systems** understands complex interrelationships.
   - Understands systems—Knows how social, organizational, and technological systems work and operates effectively with them.
   - Monitors and corrects performance—Distinguishes trends, predicts impacts on systems operations, diagnoses systems' performance, and corrects malfunctions.
   - Improves or designs systems—Suggests modifications to existing systems and develops new or alternative systems to improve performance.

5. A student who has **competence with technology** works well with a variety of technologies.
   - Selects technology—Chooses procedures, tools, or equipment, including computers and related technologies.
   - Applies technology to the task—Understands the overall intent and proper procedures for setup and operation of equipment.

- Maintains and troubleshoots equipment—Prevents, identifies, or solves problems with equipment, including computers and other technologies.

Because the SCANS competencies interrelate, it is almost impossible to focus on just one at a time in your teaching. Therefore, the complex activities that end each chapter generally involve the development of three or more SCANS competencies.

Assessment Techniques

Various forms of assessment need to be used with students in order to evaluate their achievement. Written tests have traditionally been used to evaluate performance. This method of evaluation is good to use when assessing knowledge and comprehension. Other methods of assessment are preferable for measuring the achievement of the higher-level skills of application, analysis, synthesis, and evaluation.

Included in this *Teacher's Resource Guide/Binder* are two means of assessing learning. For each chapter in the text there is a reproducible "Review and Study Guide." These are especially helpful for students who have difficulty drawing important information from their reading. Also included for each chapter is an objective test.

The *Facts in Review* sections in the text can be used to evaluate students' recall of key concepts. The activities in *Applying Your Skills* and *Developing SCANS Workplace Competencies* will provide opportunities for you to assess your students' abilities to use critical thinking, problem solving, and application.

Performance Assessment

When you assign students some of the projects described in the text, a different form of assessing mastery or achievement is required. One method that teachers have successfully used is a rubric. A rubric consists of a set of criteria that includes specific descriptors or standards that can be used to arrive at performance scores for students. A point value is given for each set of descriptors, leading to a range of possible points to be assigned, usually from 1 to 5. The criteria can also be weighted. This method of assessment reduces the guesswork involved in grading, leading to fair and consistent scoring. The standards clearly indicate to students the various levels of mastery of a task. Students are even able to assess their own achievement based on the criteria.

When using rubrics, students should see the criteria at the beginning of the assignment. Then they can focus their effort on what needs to be done to reach a certain level of performance or quality of project. They have a clear understanding of your expectations of achievement.

Though you will want to design many of your own rubrics, three generic versions are included in this *Teacher's Resource Guide/Binder.* These are designed to assess the following:

- **Individual Participation**
- **Individual Reports**
- **Group Participation**

These rubrics allow you to assess a student's performance and arrive at a performance score. Students can see what levels they have surpassed and what levels they can still strive to reach.

If your students are involved in work-based learning, you will probably have their supervisors use a form of rubric to evaluate their trainees' performance on the job. A sample of such an evaluation form is shown in *From School to Work.* Some of the criteria for evaluation included on this form include cooperation, initiative, courtesy, job knowledge, punctuality, etc. The performance standards are described in detail so students know exactly what they need to do to improve their work performance.

Using Other Resources

Student learning in your class can be reinforced and expanded by exposing your students to a variety of viewpoints. Information may be obtained through various government offices and trade and professional organizations. Local sources of information might include cooperative extension offices, state departments of labor, and employment agencies.

The following is a list of various trade and professional organizations, government resources, and companies that may be able to provide you with resources for use in your classroom. Names, addresses, phone numbers, and Web site addresses are included. Please note these addresses may have changed since publication of this resource book.

Trade and Professional Organizations*

American Arbitration Association
    1633 Broadway
    New York, NY 10019
    (212) 484-4000

American Association of Family and Consumer Sciences (AAFCS)
    1555 King St.
    Alexandria, VA 22314
    (703) 706-4600
    www.aafcs.org

American Association for Vocational Instructional Materials
    735 Gaines School Rd.
    Athens, GA 30605

American Bankers Association
   1120 Connecticut Ave., NW
   Washington, DC 20036 (202) 663-5000

American Bar Association
   750 North Lake Shore Dr.
   Chicago, IL 60611
   (312) 988-5000

American Council of Life Insurance
   1001 Pennsylvania Ave., NW
   Suite 500 South
   Washington, DC 20004
   (202) 624-2000

American Council on Consumer Interests
   240 Stanley Hall
   University of Missouri
   Columbia, MO 65211-0001
   (573) 882-3817

American Dietetic Association
   216 W. Jackson Blvd.
   Chicago, IL 60606-6995
   (800) 366-1655
   www.eatright.org

American Educational Research Association (AERA)
   1230 17th St., NW
   Washington, DC 20036

American Medical Association
   515 N. State St.
   Chicago, IL 60610
   (312) 464-5000
   www.ama-assn.org

American Savings Education Council
   www.asec.org

American Stock Exchange, Inc.
   86 Trinity Place
   New York, NY 10006
   (212) 306-1000

Association for Career and Technical Education
   1410 King St.
   Alexandria, VA 22314

Automotive Consumer Action Program
   8400 West Park Dr.
   McLean, VA 22102
   (703) 821-7144

Center for Science in the Public Interest (CSPI)
   1875 Connecticut Ave., NW, Suite 300
   Washington, DC 20009
   (202) 332-9110

Chamber of Commerce of the United States of America
   1615 H St., NW
   Washington, DC 20062

Chicago Board of Trade
   141 W. Jackson Blvd.
   Chicago, IL 60604
   (312) 435-3500

Concord Coalition
   Citizens for America's Future
   1019 19th St., NW, Suite 810
   Washington, DC 20036
   (202) 467-6222

Consumer Federation of America
   1424 16th St., NW, Suite 604
   Washington, DC 20036
   (202) 387-6121

Consumers Union
   www.consumerreports.org

Crafted with Pride in the USA Council, Inc.
   1045 Avenue of the Americas
   New York, NY 10018
   (212) 819-4397

Credit Union National Association, Inc.
   PO Box 431
   Madison, WI 53701
   (608) 231-4000

Food and Agricultural Organization of the United Nations
   www.fao.org

Insurance Information Institute
   110 William St.
   New York, NY 10038
   (212) 669-9200

Mayo Health Oasis
   www.mayo.ivi.com

National Academy of Sciences
   www.nas.edu

National Business Education Association
   1914 Association Drive
   Reston, VA 20191-1596
   (703) 860-8300

National Center for Research in Vocational Education (NCRVE)
   www.vocserve.berkeley.edu

National Consumer Law Center
18 Tremont St., Suite 400
Boston, MA 02108
(617) 523-8010

National Consumers League
1701 K St., NW, Suite 1201
Washington, DC 20006
(202) 835-3323
www.natlconsumersleague.org

National Council of Better Business Bureaus
4200 Wilson Blvd., Suite 800
Arlington, VA 22203-1838
(703) 276-0100

National Council on Economics Education
1140 Avenue of the Americas,
Second Floor
New York, NY 10036
(212) 730-7007

National Foundation for Consumer Credit, Inc.
8611 Second Ave., Suite 100
Silver Spring, MD 20910
(301) 589-5600

National Fraud Information Center
Consumer Fraud Hot Line
(800) 876-7060

National Institute for Automotive Service Excellence
13505 Dulles Technology Dr.
Herndon, VA 20171-3421
(703) 713-3800

National Institute for Consumer Education
www.emich.edu/public/coe/nice

National Insurance Consumer Helpline
(800) 942-4242

National Safety Council
1121 Spring Lake Dr.
Itasca, IL 60143-3201
(630) 285-1121

National Taxpayers' Union
108 N. Alfred St.
Alexandria, VA 22314
www.ntu.org

New York Stock Exchange
11 Wall St.
New York, NY 10005
(212) 656-3000

Public Voice for Food and Health Policy
1101 14th St., NW, Suite 710
Washington, DC 20005
(202) 371-1840

Tax Foundation
1250 H St., Suite 750
Washington, DC 20005
(202) 783-2760

World Agricultural Outlook Board
Public Information Office
(202) 720-5447

World Health Organization
www.who.ch

Government Resources*

Sources of General Information

The Consumer Information Center (CIC) publishes the free *Consumer Information Catalog*, which lists more than 200 free and low-cost government booklets on a wide variety of consumer topics. Copies of the catalog can be obtained by contacting the Web address *www.pueblo.gsa.gov*, writing to *Consumer Information Catalog*, Pueblo, CO 81009, or calling (719) 948-4000.

The Federal Information Center (FIC), which is administered by the General Services Administration (GSA), can help you find information about United States government agencies, services, and programs. The FIC can also tell you which office to contact for help with problems. You can contact the FIC online or by calling (800) 688-9889.

Specific Federal Agencies and Services

Centers for Disease Control and Prevention (CDC)
Public Inquiries—(404) 639-3534
www.cdc.gov

Consumer Education for Teens
www.wa.gov/ago/youth

Office of Consumer Affairs
Department of Commerce
14th & Constitution Ave., NW
Washington, DC 20230
(202) 482-5001

Office of Public Affairs
Department of Education
400 Maryland Ave., SW
Washington, DC 20202
(800) 872-5327

Office of Consumer and Public Liaison
Department of Energy
Washington, DC 20585
(202) 586-5373
www.eren.doe.gov

National Health Information Center
Department of Health and Human Services
PO Box 1133
Washington, DC 20013-1133
(800) 336-4797

Office of Fair Housing and Equal Opportunity
Department of Housing and Urban Development
451 7th St., SW, Room 5100
Washington, DC 20410
(202) 708-4252

Office of the Secretary
Department of the Interior
1849 C St., NW
Washington, DC 20240
(202) 208-3100

Coordinator of Consumer Affairs
Department of Labor
200 Constitution Ave., NW
Washington, DC 20210
(202) 693-4650

Auto Safety Hotline
National Highway Traffic Safety Administration
(NHTSA) (NEF-11)
Department of Transportation
Washington, DC 20590
(800) 424-9393

Bureau of the Public Debt
Public Affairs Officer
Office of the Commissioner
Department of the Treasury
999 E St., NW, Room 553
Washington, DC 20239-0001
(202) 691-3502

Public Information Center PIC
(PM-211B)
Environmental Protection Agency
Washington, DC 20007
(202) 342-3338

Consumer Assistance Branch
Federal Communications Commission
1919 M St., NW, Room 254
Washington, DC 20554
(202) 418-0200

Office of Consumer Affairs
Federal Deposit Insurance Corporation
550 17th St., NW
Washington, DC 20429
(800) 934-3342

Board of Governors of the Federal Reserve System
20th & C Streets, NW
Washington, DC 20551
(202) 452-3000

Regional Federal Reserve Banks:
Atlanta, GA 30303
Boston, MA 02106
Chicago, IL 60604
Cleveland, OH 44114
Dallas, TX 75201
Kansas City, MO 64198
Minneapolis, MN 55480-0291
New York, NY 10045
Philadelphia, PA 19106
Richmond, VA 23219
St. Louis, MO 63102
San Francisco, CA 94105

Federal Trade Commission (FTC)
CRC-240
Washington, DC 20580
www.ftc.gov

Food and Nutrition Information Center of the National Agricultural Library
www.nalusda.gov/fnic

Consumer Affairs and Information
Food and Drug Administration (FDA)
Department of Health and Human Services
5600 Fishers Lane, Room 16-63
Rockville, MD 20857
(301) 443-3170
www.fda.gov

Internal Revenue Service
1111 Constitution Ave., NW
Washington, DC 20224
(800) 829-1040
www.irs.ustreas.gov

National Center for Educational Statistics
www.nces.ed.gov

National Center for Health Statistics
www.cdc.gov/nchswww/default.htm

National Center for Injury Prevention & Control
www.cdc.gov/ncipc

National Institute on Aging
www.nih.gov/hia

National Institutes of Health
www.nih.gov/od/odp.whi

Securities and Exchange Commission
Office of Filings, Information, and Consumer
Services
450 5th St., NW
(Mail Stop 2-6)
Washington, DC 20549
(202) 942-7040

Small Business Administration
www.sba.gov

Social Security Administration
www.ssa.gov

Product Safety Hotline
U.S. Consumer Product Safety Commission
1111 18th St., NW
Washington, DC 20207
(800) 638-2772
www.cpsc.gov

USDA Economic Research Service (ERS)
(800) 999-6779

USDA Food and Consumer Services
Consumer Affairs
(703) 305-2281

USDA Information
(202) 720-2791

U.S. Government Printing Office
Publications Office
(202) 512-1800

U.S. House of Representatives
www.house.gov

Consumer Advocate
U.S. Postal Service
475 L' Enfant Plaza, SW
Washington, DC 20260-6720
(202) 268-2284

U.S. Senate
www.senate.gov

Other Resources*

The following is a list of various companies, associations, and groups that may serve as resources for additional teaching materials. Most provide videos and/or computer software. Many provide printed materials. Contact these organizations for their latest catalogs.

American Association for Vocational Instructional
Materials (AAVIM)
220 Smithonia Rd.
Winterville, GA 30683
(800) 228-4689
(software, videos, and publications)

AGC Educational Media
1560 Sherman Ave., Suite 100
Evanston, IL 60201
(800) 323-9084
FAX: (708) 328-6706

Bergwall Productions, Inc.
540 Baltimore Pk.
PO Box 2400
Chadds Ford, PA 19317

Cambridge Educational
PO Box 2153
Charleston, WV 25328-2153
(800) 468-4227
(videos, software, CD-ROM, printed materials)

Concept Media
2493 Dubridge Ave.
Irvine, CA 92606
(800) 233-7078

Creative Educational Video
PO Box 65265
Lubbock, TX 79464-5265
(800) 922-9965

Distinctive Home Video Productions
391 El Portal Rd.
San Mateo, CA 94402
(415) 344-7756

Durrin Productions
1748 Kaorama Rd., NW
Washington, DC 20009
(800) 536-6843

Films for the Humanities and Sciences
PO Box 2053
Princeton, NJ 08543
(800) 257-5126

The Health Connection
55 W. Oak Ridge Dr.
Hagerstown, MD 21740
(800) 548-8700
(pamphlets, books, teaching aids, posters, and
audiovisual aids)

Human Relations Media Video (HRM)
175 Tompkins Ave.
Pleasantville, NY 10570
(800) 431-2050
(videos for guidance, health, and conflict
resolution)

Internet Fraud Watch
(800) 876-7060
www.fraud.org

Mail Order Action Line
    1120 Avenue of the Americas
    New York, NY 10036
    (212) 768-7277

Meridian Education Corp.
    236 E. Front St.
    Bloomington, IL 61701
    (800) 727-5507
    (videos/multimedia)

NIMCO, Inc.
    PO Box 9102, Highway 81 North
    Calhoun, KY 42327
    (800) 962-6662
    (textbooks, videos, and slides)

RMI Media Productions
    2807 West 47th St.
    Shawnee Mission, KS 66205
    (800) 821-5480
    (educational videos)

Teaching Aids, Inc.
    PO Box 1798
    Costa Mesa, CA 92628-0798

Teenager's Guide to the Real World: Money Really
Matters
    www.bygpub.com

Teen-Aid
    723 E. Jackson
    Spokane, WA 99207-2647
    (509) 482-2868
    FAX: (509) 482-7994
    (videos, teaching modules, lesson plans,
    pamphlets, overheads, and posters)

Career-Related Web Sites*

100 Hot Jobs
    www.100hot.com/jobs

America's Career InfoNet
    www.acinet.org

America's Job Bank (AJB)
    www.ajb.org

America's Learning Exchange
    www.alx.org

America's Talent Bank (ATB)
    www.atb.org

The Armed Services Vocational Aptitude Battery
(ASVAB)
    www.dmdc.osd.mil/asvab/careerexplorationprogram

Bureau of Apprenticeship and Training (BAT)
    www.doleta.gov/individ/apprent.htm

Bureau of Labor Statistics
    http:\\stats.bls.gov/k12/html/edu_over.htm

Career City
    www.careercity.com

Career Magazine
    www.careermag.com

Career Mosaic
    www.careermosaic.com

Career Path
    www.careerpath.com

Career Resource Center
    www.careers.org

Department of Labor's Employment and Training
Administration
    www.doleta.gov

The Equal Employment Opportunity Commission
(EEOC)
    www.eeoc.gov

Exploring Careers (Cornell University)
    www.explore.cornell.edu/careers/explorin.htm

Guide for Occupational Exploration
    www.doi.gov/octc/occupat2.htm

JOBTRAK
    www.jobtrak.com

Mapping Your Future
    www.mapping-your-future.org

Monster Board
    www.monster.com

My Future
    www.myfuture.com

National Association of Colleges and Employers
JobWeb
    www.jobweb.org

Occupational Information Network (O*NET)
    www.doleta.gov/programs/onet

One-Stop Career Centers
    www.ttrc.doleta.gov/onestop

The Secretary's Commission on Achieving Necessary
Skills (SCANS)
    www.scans.jhu.edu

USTA Career Services
www.jobbank.usta.edu/cpguide.html

Vocational Student Organization Web Sites

Business Professionals of America (BPA)
www.bpa.org

DECA—An Association of Marketing Students
www.deca.org

Family, Career and Community Leaders of America (FCCLA)
www.fhahero.org

Future Business Leaders of America–Phi Beta Lambda
www.fbla-pbl.org

Health Occupations Students of America (HOSA)
www.hosa.org

National FFA Organization
www.ffa.org

SkillsUSA–VICA
www.vica.org

Technology Student Association (TSA)
www.tsawww.org

---

*Note: The addresses, phone numbers, FAX numbers, and Web site addresses listed may have changed since the publication of this *Teacher's Resource Guide/Binder.*

Goodheart-Willcox Welcomes Your Comments

We welcome your comments or suggestions regarding *From School to Work* and its ancillaries as we are continually striving to publish better educational materials. Please send any comments you may have to:
Editorial Department
Goodheart-Willcox Publishers
18604 West Creek Drive
Tinley Park, IL 60477-6243
or e-mail
www.goodheartwillcox.com

Reproducible Master

Evaluation of Individual Participation

Name _____ **Date** _____ **Period** _____

The rating scale below shows an evaluation of your class participation. It indicates what levels you have passed and what levels you can continue to try to reach.

Criteria:

1. Attentiveness

1	2	3	4	5
Completely inattentive.	Seldom attentive.	Somewhat attentive.	Usually attentive.	Extremely attentive.

2. Contribution to Discussion

1	2	3	4	5
Never contributes to class discussion.	Rarely contributes to class discussion.	Occasionally contributes to class discussion.	Regularly contributes to class discussion.	Frequently contributes to class discussion.

3. Interaction with Peers

1	2	3	4	5
Often distracts others.	Shows little interaction with others.	Follows leadership of other students.	Sometimes assumes leadership role.	Respected by peers for ability.

4. Response to Teacher

1	2	3	4	5
Unable to respond when called on.	Often unable to support or justify answers when called on.	Supports answers based on class information, but seldom offers new ideas.	Able to offer new ideas with prompting.	Often offers new ideas without prompting.

Total Points: _____ out of 20

Comments: _____

_____

_____

Evaluation of Individual Report

Name_____ Date _____ Period _____

The rating scale below shows an evaluation of your oral or written report. It indicates what levels you have passed and what levels you can try to reach on future reports.

Report title_____ Oral _____ Written _____

Criteria:

1. Choice of Topic

1	2	3	4	5
Slow to choose topic.	Chooses topic with indifference.	Chooses topic as assigned, seeks suggestions.	Chooses relevant topic without assistance.	Chooses creative topic.

2. Use of Resources

1	2	3	4	5
Unable to find resources.	Needs direction to find resources.	Uses fewer than assigned number of resources.	Uses assigned number of resources from typical sources.	Uses additional resources from a variety of sources.

3. Oral Presentation

1	2	3	4	5
Uses no notes or reads completely. Poor subject coverage.	Has few good notes. Limited subject coverage.	Uses notes somewhat effectively. Adequate subject coverage.	Uses notes effectively. Good subject coverage.	Uses notes very effectively. Complete coverage.

4. Written Presentation

1	2	3	4	5
Many grammar and spelling mistakes. No organization.	Several grammar and spelling mistakes. Poor organization.	Some grammar and spelling mistakes. Fair organization.	A few grammar and spelling mistakes. Good organization.	No grammar or spelling mistakes. Excellent organization.

Total Points: _____ **out of 15**

Reproducible Master

Evaluation of Group Participation

Group _____

Members _____   _____

_____   _____

_____   _____

The rating scale below shows an evaluation of the efforts of your group. It indicates what levels you have passed and what levels you can try to reach on future group projects.

Criteria:

1. Teamwork

1	2	3	4	5
Passive membership. Failed to identify what tasks needed to be completed.	Argumentative membership. Unable to designate who should complete each task.	Independent membership. All tasks completed individually.	Helpful membership. Completed individual tasks and then assisted others.	Cooperative membership. Worked together to complete all tasks.

2. Leadership

1	2	3	4	5
No attempt at leadership.	No effective leadership.	Sought leadership from outside group.	One member assumed primary leadership role for the group.	Leadership responsibilities shared by several group members.

3. Goal Achievement

1	2	3	4	5
Did not attempt to achieve goal.	Were unable to achieve goal.	Achieved goal with outside assistance.	Achieved assigned goal.	Achieved goal using added materials to enhance total effort.

Total Points: _____ **out of 15**

Members cited for excellent contributions to group's effort are:

_____   _____

_____   _____

Members failing to contribute to group's effort are:

_____   _____

_____   _____

Scope and Sequence

Including SCANS Foundation Skills and Workplace Competencies

In planning your course, you may want to use the *Scope and Sequence Chart* below. This chart is organized by parts of the book. Chapter numbers are listed, followed by the main headings in that chapter. For each part, the chart lists the major topics by chapter that relate to the SCANS Foundation Skills and Workplace Competencies. In addition, it identifies chapter topics related to the following content areas, which are often included in courses using this book:

- Health and Safety
- Government and Consumer Economics
- Career Exploration and Planning

You will find this chart helpful as you plan your course and integrate *From School to Work* into your curriculum.

Part 1: Work-Based Learning

SCANS Foundation Skills

Basic Skills
1: Learning how to work
2: Abide by the training agreement; study and learn

Thinking Skills
1: Benefits of learning on the job; study and learn

Personal Qualities
2: Practice good study habits
3: Personal qualities as SCANS foundation elements; Personal qualities needed on the job; positive attitude; good attendance; punctuality; performance; initiative; cooperation; accepting criticism; courtesy; personal appearance; good health and fitness; ethics in the workplace

SCANS Workplace Competencies

Resources
2: Your training station

Interpersonal Skills
3: Cooperation; accepting criticism; courtesy

Information
1: Exploring the world of work; opportunities to learn on the job
2: Know the law; study and learn

Systems
2: Take notes

Health and Safety

3: Health and fitness

Government and Consumer Economics

2: Get a social security number and a work permit; know the law

Career Exploration and Planning

1: Exploring the world of work; opportunities to learn on the job; benefits of learning on the job; learning how to work

2: Abide by the training agreement; follow the training plan

Part 2: Skills for Success

SCANS Foundation Skills

Basic Skills

5: Effective communication; listening skills; reading and comprehension skills; writing and keyboarding skills; business letters; memos; business reports; nonverbal communication; speaking skills

6: Making change; using a calculator; using fractions, decimals, and percentages; taking measurements; using the metric system

Thinking Skills

4: Problem solving

6: Analyzing data

11: Why have meetings?

Personal Qualities

4: Characteristics of an effective team; managing conflict

8: Good health; good grooming

10: Skills and qualities of a good leader

SCANS Workplace Competencies

Resources

4: Teams in the workplace

6: Making change

7: Computer software; the Internet; personal organizers

8: Dressing for the job

11: Committees

Interpersonal Skills

4: Changing nature of the workplace; teams in the workplace; characteristics of an effective team; managing conflict

5: Informal communication channels

10: Leaders and authority; skills and qualities of a good leader; dynamics and groups; leadership and group dynamics in school; leadership and group dynamics in the workplace

11: Why have meetings?; committees

Information 5: Effective communication; listening skills; reading and comprehension skills; writing and keyboarding skills; business letters; memos; business reports; nonverbal communication; speaking skills; communication technology

6: Analyzing data

8: Caring for clothes; care labels

11: Order of business; motions

Systems 4: Teams in the workplace; stages of team development

5: Informal communication channels

6: Using the metric system

7: Computer systems; the Internet; the World Wide Web; computer applications in school

10: Dynamics in groups; leadership

11: Order of business; committees; electing officers

Technology 5: Keyboarding skills; communication technology

6: Using a calculator; digital instruments

7: Computer systems; methods of storing data; computer software; the Internet; the World Wide Web; computer applications in school; record keeping; communications; computer applications in the home; entertainment; computer applications in business and commerce; Internet uses; word processing; spreadsheets; databases; multimedia presentations; desktop publishing; computer graphics; manufacturing applications; global positioning; personal organizers

Health and Safety

8: Good health; eat well-balanced meals; get enough sleep; exercise regularly; good grooming

9: What causes accidents?; lack of knowledge and skills; environmental hazards; poor safety attitudes; unsafe behavior; costs of accidents; preventing accidents; use machines and tools properly; wear protective clothing and use protective equipment; follow safety precautions; what to do when an accident occurs; the role of government in protecting your health

Government and Consumer Economics

8: Care labels

9: The role of government in protecting your health; OSHA, EPA

Career Exploration and Planning

4: Changing nature of the workplace; teams in the workplace

7: Careers and computers

10: Vocational student organizations

Part 3: Career Planning

SCANS Foundation Skills

Thinking Skills   12: Making a self-assessment; what are your interests?; what are your aptitudes?; what are your abilities?

14: Evaluating careers

15: The decision-making process; making a career plan; using the decision-making process

Personal Qualities   12: Your self-concept; self-esteem; making a self-assessment; your personal characteristics; personality traits; your values; ethics; your goals; standards

15: Making personal decisions

SCANS Workplace Competencies

Resources   12: Resources

14: Career research sources; libraries; career information guides; the Internet; school counselors; career conferences

15: Using the decision-making process

Information   13: Job market trends; future occupations

14: Career research sources; libraries; career information guides; the Internet; school counselors; career conferences

Systems   15: The decision-making process; using the decision-making process

Government and Consumer Economics

14: Armed Forces

15: Making consumer decisions

Career Exploration and Planning

13: Traditional and nontraditional careers; agriculture; business and office; communications and media; construction; family and consumer sciences; fine arts and humanities; health; hospitality and recreation; manufacturing; marine science; marketing and distribution; natural resources and environmental control; personal services; public service; transportation; job market trends; future occupations

14: Career research sources; evaluating careers; educational requirements; occupational training; apprenticeships; a college education; Armed Forces; work hours; work conditions; the pay: starting and potential; personal lifestyles and goals

15: Career decisions; making a career plan; making work decisions

Part 4: The Job Hunt

SCANS Foundation Skills

Basic Skills 16: Preparing a resume; preparing a portfolio; contacting an employer by telephone; letter of application; job application forms

17: Skill tests

18: After the interview

Thinking Skills 17: Skill tests; psychological tests; situational tests

Personal Qualities 17: Psychological tests; written honesty tests

SCANS Workplace Competencies

Resources 16: Finding job openings; friends and relatives; networking; school placement services; direct employer contact; want ads; trade and professional journals; government employment services; private employment agencies; searching the Internet

Interpersonal Skills 16: Contacting an employer by telephone

18: The interview

Information 16: Finding job openings; friends and relatives; networking; school placement services; direct employer contact; want ads; trade and professional journals; government employment services; private employment agencies; searching the Internet; job resume information; developing a home page; contacting an employer by telephone; letter of application

Systems 16: Networking

17: Situational tests

Technology 16: Developing a home page

Health and Safety

17: Medical examinations; physical disabilities and the interview process; drug testing

Government and Consumer Economics

16: Illegal questions on job applications

17: Government tests; civil service test; Armed Services Vocational Aptitude Battery

Career Exploration and Planning

16: Finding job openings; preparing a personal fact sheet; job resumes; preparing a portfolio; developing a home page; contacting an employer by telephone; letter of application; job application forms; illegal questions on job applications

17: Skill tests; psychological tests; situational tests; government tests; polygraph test; written honesty tests; medical examinations; how to take pre-employment tests

18: Preparing for an interview; the interview; after the interview; accepting a job offer; rejecting a job offer

Part 5: Job Satisfaction

SCANS Foundation Skills

Basic Skills   22: Pricing your product or service; financial record keeping

Thinking Skills   19: Evaluating job performance; training opportunities

21: Business management

Personal Qualities   19: Your conduct and job success

20: Diversity trends in the United States; cultural heritage; language; religion; gender; age; disability

22: What does it take to succeed?

SCANS Workplace Competencies

Resources   19: Unions

21: Private ownership and control of productive resources

22: Choosing a location; working from your home; setting up a home office; obtaining financing

Interpersonal Skills   19: Relating to others at work; working with your supervisor; working with coworkers; collective bargaining

20: Promoting diversity in the workplace; facing sexual harassment or discrimination

Information   19: Performance rating

20: Promoting diversity in the workplace; sexual harassment in the workplace

22: Financial record keeping

Systems   19: Organization of unions; collective bargaining

20: Diversity trends in the United States; the law and discrimination

21: The free enterprise system; how businesses are organized; proprietorship; partnership; corporation; how businesses are structured

22: Choosing your business structure

Health and Safety

19: Handling job stress

Government and Consumer Economics

19: Unions

20: The law and discrimination; sexual harassment in the workplace; facing sexual harassment or discrimination

21: The free enterprise system; private ownership and control of productive resources; profit motive; supply and demand; competition; limited government involvement; how businesses are organized

22: The importance of small business; opportunities for entrepreneurs; types of business ventures; pricing your product or service; legal and financial issues; zoning, licensing, and permits; obtaining financing; financial record keeping

Career Exploration and Planning

19: Your first day on the job; relating to others at work; your conduct and job success; handling job stress; evaluating job performance; job probation; changes in job status; making a job change; unions

20: The benefits of diversity in the workplace; promoting diversity in the workplace; diversity, rights, and discrimination; facing sexual harassment or discrimination

22: Opportunities for entrepreneurs; planning your own business; choosing a business; choosing a location; pricing your product or service; legal and financial issues; professional assistance

Part 6: Work-Based Learning

SCANS Foundation Skills

Basic Skills
23: Preparing tax returns

24: Budgeting your money; balance your budget; writing a complaint letter

26: Writing checks; recording changes to your account; balancing your checkbook

Thinking Skills
24: Budgeting your money; estimate your monthly income and expenses; evaluate the budget; managing your consumer spending; decide where to shop

25: Understanding credit; using credit wisely

26: Making investments

SCANS Workplace Competencies

Resources
23: Forms of income; social security; unemployment insurance

24: Budgeting your income; be an informed consumer; use available resources; decide where to shop

25: Understanding credit; dealing with credit problems

26: Choosing a financial institution; checking accounts; making deposits; using debit cards; cashing checks; safe-deposit boxes; savings accounts at financial institutions; regular savings accounts; money market deposit accounts; certificates of deposit; investing your money

27: Insurance; automobile insurance; health insurance; home insurance; life insurance; employer-sponsored insurance programs; choosing an insurance company, agent, and policy; filing an insurance claim

28: Maintaining the home; using leisure time effectively; managing your time; using community resources; working from home; consulting a lawyer

Interpersonal Skills
28: Family roles; building relationships; balancing family and work roles; citizenship responsibilities; community involvement

Information   23: Understanding your paycheck; taxes

24: Understand advertising and other promotional methods; writing a complaint letter

25: Understanding credit; what's in a credit record?; credit agreements

27: Filing an insurance claim

Systems   23: Social security

27: Health insurance

28: The court system

Technology   26: Electronic banking; automated teller machines; automatic transfer of funds; online banking; using debit cards; computerized personal financial management

Health and Safety

23: Social security benefits; disability benefits; Medicare benefits; Medicaid benefits

27: Health insurance; health maintenance organizations (HMOs); preferred provider organizations (PPOs); point-of-service plans (POS)

Government and Consumer Economics

23: Understanding your paycheck; taxes; social security; Medicare benefits; Medicaid benefits; workers' compensation; unemployment insurance

24: Budgeting your money; establish financial goals; estimate your monthly income and expenses; balance your budget; managing your consumer spending; be an informed consumer; understand advertising and other promotional methods; decide where to shop; develop shopping skills; exercising your consumer rights and responsibilities; know the right way to complain; use consumer protection services; use government protection agencies

25: Understanding credit; types of credit; establishing credit; credit agreements; the cost of credit; federal credit laws; using credit wisely; shopping for credit

26: Types of financial institutions; electronic banking; checking accounts; using debit cards; special types of checks; safe-deposit boxes; savings accounts at financial institutions; investing your money; making investments

28: The Family and Medical Leave Act; citizenship responsibilities; voting; obeying the law; criminal law; civil law; consulting a lawyer; the court system

Career Exploration and Planning

23: Forms of income; workers' compensation; unemployment insurance

28: Balancing family and work roles; the family-friendly workplace; family-friendly benefits and policies

SCANS Correlation Chart

The following chart is designed to identify activities in the *From School to Work* text, the *Student Activity Guide,* the *Teacher's Resource Guide,* and the *Teacher's Resource Binder* that specifically encourage the development of the SCANS competencies and foundation skills. The following abbreviations used in the chart indicate where the activities are located:

- **Text**—End of chapter activities in the "Applying Your Skills" section of the text.
- **SAG**—Activities in the *Student Activity Guide,* designated by letter.
- **TRG/B**—Student learning experiences described in the *Teacher's Resource Guide* and the *Teacher's Resource Binder,* referred to by number.

Activities are grouped by chapter and separated into six columns under two main headings. "SCANS Competencies" identify the abilities that students can develop through the complex activities titled "Developing SCANS Workplace Competencies" at the end of each chapter in the text. The section titled "SCANS Foundation Skills" uses the above abbreviations and divides activities into five categories, identified as follows:

- **Reading** activities include assignments designed to improve comprehension of information in prose as well as documents such as graphs and tables.
- **Writing** activities allow students to practice the written communication of ideas and thoughts by creating documents such as letters, reports, schedules, forms, and flow charts.
- **Arithmetic/Math/Science** activities require students to use basic principles of math and/or science as well as computation skills in solving typical problems.
- **Speaking/Listening** activities encourage students to organize ideas, develop interpersonal and group speaking skills, and respond appropriately to verbal messages. Activities include oral reports, debates, interviews, role-playing, and accurate note-taking.
- **Thinking Skills** include activities that involve the higher-order skills needed for thinking creatively, making decisions, solving problems, visualizing information, reasoning, and knowing how to learn.

SCANS Competencies		SCANS Foundation Skills				
		Reading	**Writing**	**Arithmetic/ Math/Science**	**Speaking/ Listening**	**Thinking Skills**
Chapter 1	Interpersonal skills Information	SAG: B, D TRG/B: 1, 12, 13	Text: 1, 2, 4 SAG: A, B, D TRG/B: 6, 7, 13, 15, 17, 21, 23, 25, 26, 27		Text: 1, 4, 5 SAG: A TRG/B: 3, 6, 8, 9, 11, 13, 14, 17, 25, 26, 27, 28, 29	Text: 1, 2, 3, 4, 5 SAG: B, C, D, E TRG/B: 4, 7, 15, 17, 18, 19, 20, 21, 23, 25, 26, 27
Chapter 2	Resources Interpersonal skills Information Systems	Text: 3 SAG: B, D TRG/B: 6, 20, 31	Text: 3 SAG: A, C, D, F TRG/B: 4, 17, 20, 32, 35, 39	Text: 4	Text: 1 SAG: F TRG/B: 8, 11, 13, 15, 19, 22, 23, 24, 29, 30, 31, 35, 36, 37, 38	Text: 1, 2 SAG: A, C, D, E TRG/B: 3, 15, 16, 19, 24, 25, 28, 29, 30, 32, 33, 34

SCANS Competencies		SCANS Foundation Skills				
		Reading	**Writing**	**Arithmetic/ Math/Science**	**Speaking/ Listening**	**Thinking Skills**
Chapter 3	Resources Interpersonal skills Information	SAG: E TRG/B: 11, 23, 27, 34, 38, 47, 50	Text: 1 SAG: B, E TRG/B: 14, 20, 22, 31, 34, 45, 49, 50	TRG/B: 36, 37, 38, 39	Text: 1, 2, 3 SAG: B TRG/B: 4, 5, 6, 8, 11, 12, 15, 18, 21, 25, 26, 28, 29, 32, 33, 35, 36, 37, 40, 41, 42, 44, 46, 50, 51, 52, 53	Text: 2, 3 SAG: A, C, D TRG/B: 4, 7, 9, 10, 12, 13, 16, 17, 19, 24, 27, 28, 30, 32, 36, 37, 39, 42, 43, 49
Chapter 4	Resources Interpersonal skills Information Systems	Text: 5 SAG: C, D TRG/B: 5, 19, 26, 30, 39, 44	Text: 5 SAG: C, D TRG/B: 5, 10, 16, 19, 20, 39, 43, 44, 46	Text: 5 TRG/B: 34	Text: 1, 2, 3, 4 SAG: B, C TRG/B: 3, 5, 7, 9, 11, 12, 15, 17, 21, 22, 25, 27, 29, 31, 32, 35, 41, 42, 43, 45	Text: 3, 4 SAG: A, B, C, E TRG/B: 6, 8, 9, 13, 20, 23, 33, 36, 37, 45, 46
Chapter 5	Interpersonal skills Information Technology	TRG/B: 16, 17, 18, 52, 53	Text: 2, 5, 6 SAG: A, C, D, E, F, G TRG/B: 8, 9, 25, 39, 55, 56		Text: 1, 2, 3, 4 SAG: H TRG/B: 1, 2, 3, 4, 6, 8, 9, 10, 11, 13, 14, 15, 16, 17, 18, 19, 20, 22, 26, 28, 30, 32, 33, 34, 35, 36, 37, 41, 42, 43, 44, 45, 46, 48, 49, 51, 52, 53, 54, 55, 56, 57, 58, 59, 60, 61	SAG: A, B, G, H TRG/B: 12, 27, 31, 38, 43, 50, 54
Chapter 6	Interpersonal skills Information Systems	TRG/B: 14, 22, 30, 34	TRG/B: 7, 9, 12, 22, 34	Text: 1, 2, 3, 4 SAG: A, B, C, D, E, F TRG/B: 3, 6, 14, 16, 17, 24, 30, 32	TRG/B: 1, 2, 3, 5, 11, 15, 18, 19, 21, 25, 26, 28, 33, 35, 36, 37	Text: 3 SAG: F TRG/B: 9, 10, 23, 25, 29

SCANS Competencies		SCANS Foundation Skills				
		Reading	**Writing**	**Arithmetic/ Math/Science**	**Speaking/ Listening**	**Thinking Skills**
Chapter 7	Resources Interpersonal skills Information Technology	Text: 3 SAG: C, E TRG/B: 5, 7, 9, 13, 18, 22, 28, 30, 32, 40, 41	Text: 3 TRG/B: 9, 12, 13, 20, 28, 29, 41, 45	Text: 1 SAG: B TRG/B: 1, 7, 8, 13, 22	Text: 4 TRG/B: 1, 2, 3, 10, 11, 14, 15, 16, 17, 18, 19, 21, 22, 23, 24, 25, 26, 27, 31, 32, 35, 36, 38, 39, 40, 43, 44, 46, 48, 50	Text: 2 SAG: A, B, D, E TRG/B: 12, 13, 15, 16, 23, 24, 36, 37, 44, 47, 49
Chapter 8	Interpersonal skills Information Systems	SAG: C TRG/B: 4, 7, 14, 18, 19, 22, 31, 37	TRG/B: 4, 8, 15, 18, 34, 37	Text: 1 TRG/B: 4, 14, 31, 33, 35, 41	Text: 3, 5 TRG/B: 1, 2, 5, 6, 7, 10, 11, 13, 14, 16, 20, 22, 24, 25, 26, 28, 31, 32, 35, 38, 39, 40, 41, 42, 43	Text: 1, 4 SAG: A, B, D, E TRG/B: 2, 6, 9, 14, 17, 36
Chapter 9	Resources Interpersonal skills Information Technology	Text: 2 SAG: A, D, E TRG/B: 19, 27, 29, 30, 33, 34, 37, 39	Text: 1, 2, 4, 6, 7 TRG/B: 5, 6, 8, 10, 22, 30, 33, 36, 43		Text: 3, 5 SAG: A, E TRG/B: 1, 2, 3, 4, 7, 8, 9, 10, 11, 12, 16, 17, 19, 23, 24, 27, 28, 29, 31, 34, 36, 37, 38, 39, 40, 41, 42, 44, 45	Text: 1 SAG: A, B, C, F TRG/B: 5, 10, 15, 20, 25, 31
Chapter 10	Resources Interpersonal skills Information Systems	Text: 1 SAG: C, D TRG/B: 1, 20, 25, 28	Text: 6 TRG/B: 20, 21, 27, 28, 29		Text: 2, 3 SAG: D TRG/B: 1, 2, 3, 5, 8, 9, 10, 11, 12, 13, 14, 15, 18, 19, 20, 22, 23, 35, 36, 30, 31, 32	Text: 5 SAG: A, B, C, E TRG/B: 7
Chapter 11	Resources Information Systems	Text: 1 SAG: A, C TRG/B: 1, 10, 19	TRG/B: 1, 12, 13, 19, 27		Text: 2 SAG: C, D TRG/B: 2, 3, 4, 5, 6, 7, 8, 12, 14, 15, 16, 17, 18, 20, 21, 24, 25, 26, 27	Text: 1 SAG: B, D TRG/B: 7, 8, 10, 19, 21, 24, 27

SCANS Competencies		SCANS Foundation Skills				
		Reading	**Writing**	**Arithmetic/ Math/Science**	**Speaking/ Listening**	**Thinking Skills**
Chapter 12	Interpersonal skills Information	SAG: D, F TRG/B: 12, 19	TRG/B: 2, 9, 10, 13, 17, 23, 26, 36		SAG: C, D TRG/B: 1, 3, 4, 6, 7, 13, 14, 16, 18, 19, 21, 25, 27, 28, 29, 30, 31, 32, 33, 36, 37, 38, 39, 40	Text: 1, 2, 3, 4 SAG: A, B, C, D, E TRG/B: 2, 6, 10, 11, 12, 15, 22, 31, 32, 33, 36
Chapter 13	Resources Information Systems Technology	TRG/B: 10, 11, 18, 19	Text: 3 TRG/B: 21, 22	TRG/B: 19	Text: 1 SAG: B TRG/B: 1, 2, 3, 4, 5, 6, 7, 9, 11, 12, 13, 14, 15, 16, 18, 19, 23, 24, 25	Text: 1, 2 SAG: A, C TRG/B: 10, 12, 15, 21
Chapter 14	Interpersonal skills Information	Text: 1, 2 SAG: A, B, E TRG/B: 4, 5, 6, 7, 14, 16, 17, 22, 24, 25, 30	Text: 1 TRG/B: 4, 5, 21, 22, 29	TRG/B: 24	Text: 3 SAG: C, D TRG/B: 1, 2, 6, 7, 12, 13, 14, 15, 17, 18, 19, 22, 23, 24, 26, 27, 30, 31, 32, 33, 34	Text: 2 SAG: A, B, C, D, F TRG/B: 12, 18, 19, 20, 23, 27
Chapter 15	Interpersonal skills Information Systems	SAG: A, D TRG/B: 18	TRG/B: 9, 16, 21, 22, 23		Text: 1, 2 TRG/B: 1, 2, 3, 4, 5, 6, 7, 13, 14, 15, 16, 20, 24, 26, 27, 28	Text: 1, 2 SAG: A, B, C, D, E TRG/B: 2, 5, 6, 13, 15, 16, 17, 18, 20, 21, 25
Chapter 16	Interpersonal skills Information Technology	Text: 1 SAG: A TRG/B: 4, 6, 8, 17, 27	Text: 3, 4, 5 SAG: B, E, G TRG/B: 5, 9, 12, 21, 27, 30, 32		TRG/B: 1, 2, 3, 4, 9, 11, 13, 17, 18, 22, 23, 24, 28, 29, 31, 33, 34, 35, 36	Text: 2, 6 SAG: C, D, F TRG/B: 3, 8, 10, 13, 14, 21, 22, 28

SCANS Competencies		SCANS Foundation Skills				
		Reading	**Writing**	**Arithmetic/ Math/Science**	**Speaking/ Listening**	**Thinking Skills**
Chapter 17	Interpersonal skills Information Systems	SAG: A, D TRG/B: 5, 18, 21, 28, 37	TRG/B: 6, 10, 12, 16, 21, 37	SAG: B TRG/B: 30, 39, 41	TRG/B: 1, 2, 3, 4, 5, 9, 11, 13, 14, 15, 17, 18, 19, 20, 22, 23, 24, 25, 26, 28, 29, 30, 32, 34, 35, 38, 39, 40, 41	Text: 2, 3 SAG: C TRG/B: 4, 10, 19, 20, 22, 23, 26, 27, 32, 36
Chapter 18	Information Social systems Technology	SAG: A	Text: 3 SAG: H TRG/B: 13, 22, 23, 30		Text: 2, 4 SAG: F, G, I TRG/B: 1, 2, 3, 4, 5, 6, 12, 16, 18, 19, 20, 21, 26, 27, 29, 30, 31, 32, 33, 34, 35, 36	Text: 1, 2 SAG: B, C, D, E, F TRG/B: 5, 6, 7, 8, 18, 22, 26, 27, 29, 33
Chapter 19	Resources Interpersonal skills Information	SAG: A TRG/B: 1, 13, 19, 38, 39	TRG/B: 2, 4, 8, 13, 20, 38, 42, 45		Text: 1, 2, 3 SAG: G, H TRG/B: 1, 2, 6, 7, 8, 9, 10, 13, 15, 16, 18, 19, 25, 26, 27, 28, 29, 30, 31, 32, 33, 34, 36, 37, 39, 41, 43, 44, 45, 46, 47, 48, 49	Text: 1, 3 SAG: B, C, D, E, F TRG/B: 6, 9, 10, 11, 14, 18, 22, 24, 26, 31, 32, 33, 37, 41, 44
Chapter 20	Resources Interpersonal skills Information	Text: 2 SAG: C, D, E TRG/B: 1, 6, 10, 14, 17, 27, 31, 32, 37	TRG/B: 10, 13, 19, 22, 36	TRG/B: 36	Text: 1, 4 SAG: A, C TRG/B: 1, 2, 3, 6, 7, 8, 9, 12, 13, 18, 20, 21, 23, 24, 25, 26, 27, 28, 29, 33, 34, 36, 38, 39	Text: 3 SAG: B, C, D TRG/B: 7, 13, 16, 26, 29, 30
Chapter 21	Interpersonal skills Information Systems	SAG: C, D TRG/B: 2, 3, 5, 8, 19, 22, 26, 27	TRG/B: 3, 5, 13, 14, 15, 27	TRG/B: 28	Text: 1, 3 SAG: A, B, C TRG/B: 1, 2, 4, 5, 7, 10, 13, 14, 18, 19, 21, 24, 28, 29, 30	Text: 2 SAG: E, F TRG/B: 1, 7, 10, 11, 12, 21, 23, 28

SCANS Competencies		Reading	Writing	Arithmetic/ Math/Science	Speaking/ Listening	Thinking Skills
Chapter 22	Resources Interpersonal skills Information Systems	Text: 1 SAG: E TRG/B: 3, 10, 11, 12, 18, 24, 26, 33	Text: 1, 2 TRG/B: 4, 13, 16, 19, 27, 28, 32, 33, 34	TRG/B: 22, 23, 29	Text: 3, 4, 5 SAG: B, D TRG/B: 1, 2, 6, 7, 9, 10, 11, 12, 13, 15, 16, 18, 21, 23, 25, 29, 32, 34, 35, 36	Text: 2, 3 SAG: A, C, D TRG/B: 7, 9, 13, 15, 19, 20, 21, 22, 23, 27, 30
Chapter 23	Resources Interpersonal skills Information Systems	Text: 3, 4 SAG: A, C, F TRG/B: 4, 5, 7, 13, 28, 36, 37, 38, 39, 46, 50	Text: 4 TRG/B: 5, 9, 17, 21, 24, 28, 31, 32, 35, 37, 38, 40, 43, 49, 50	TRG/B: 3, 23, 25, 48	Text: 1, 2, 3, 4, 5 TRG/B: 1, 2, 3, 4, 6, 7, 8, 10, 11, 12, 13, 14, 16, 19, 20, 22, 23, 25, 29, 30, 34, 36, 39, 42, 44, 45, 47, 48, 51, 52, 53, 54	SAG: B, C, D, E TRG/B: 2, 6, 8, 11, 12, 24, 30, 43
Chapter 24	Resources Interpersonal skills Technology	Text: 2 SAG: D TRG/B: 13, 14, 15, 16, 17, 21, 26, 41, 42, 45	Text: 5 SAG: H, I TRG/B: 3, 10, 12, 16, 24, 26, 27, 31, 34, 38, 43, 45	Text: 1 SAG: C, F TRG/B: 10, 11, 31, 44, 46	Text: 3 TRG/B: 1, 2, 3, 6, 7, 8, 10, 11, 14, 15, 17, 19, 21, 22, 25, 28, 29, 31, 32, 35, 37, 38, 40, 41, 42, 44, 45, 46, 47, 48	Text: 1, 2, 3, 4 SAG: A, B, C, D, E, F, G TRG/B: 6, 7, 11, 13, 18, 19, 22
Chapter 25	Information Systems	Text: 3 SAG: C, D TRG/B: 10, 19, 21, 30, 33	SAG: B TRG/B: 4, 15, 16, 31, 33	Text: 1 TRG/B: 21, 28, 34	Text: 2, 4 SAG: E TRG/B: 1, 2, 3, 4, 5, 6, 8, 10, 11, 12, 13, 14, 17, 28, 29, 30, 32, 35, 36, 37	Text: 1, 3 SAG: A, B, C, D, E TRG/B: 5, 9, 15, 16, 18, 21, 23, 26, 27, 28, 31, 32
Chapter 26	Resources Interpersonal skills Information Systems	SAG: E, F TRG/B: 3, 5, 15, 20, 23, 27, 29, 30, 32, 34, 35, 43, 44, 45, 46, 47	Text: 3, 6 TRG/B: 4, 5, 7, 12, 13, 20, 30, 34, 36, 47	Text: 4, 5, 6 SAG: C TRG/B: 22, 28, 32, 33, 44, 48	Text: 1, 2 SAG: A TRG/B: 1, 2, 8, 9, 10, 11, 14, 15, 18, 21, 23, 26, 27, 35, 37, 39, 40, 41, 42, 43, 46, 47, 48, 49, 50, 51	Text: 6 SAG: A, B, D TRG/B: 3, 10, 11, 15, 16, 18, 24, 28, 33, 35, 39, 40, 42, 44

SCANS Competencies		SCANS Foundation Skills				
		Reading	**Writing**	**Arithmetic/ Math/Science**	**Speaking/ Listening**	**Thinking Skills**
Chapter 27	Resources Interpersonal skills Information	Text: 4 SAG: A, E TRG/B: 4, 6, 13, 24, 34, 35, 39, 41, 44	Text: 3 SAG: B TRG/B: 8, 11, 12, 14, 29, 33, 36, 37, 38, 39, 44	SAG: D TRG/B: 17	Text: 1 TRG/B: 1, 2, 3, 4, 5, 6, 7, 9, 12, 13, 16, 19, 20, 25, 26, 27, 28, 32, 34, 35, 37, 39, 40, 41, 43, 45, 46, 47	Text: 1, 2, 4 SAG: A, B, C, D, F TRG/B: 22, 23, 25, 28, 32, 35, 38, 42
Chapter 28	Resources Interpersonal skills Information Systems	Text: 6, 7 SAG: D TRG/B: 25, 29, 30, 31, 33, 42, 45, 46, 49, 50, 53	Text: 1 TRG/B: 13, 26, 41, 46, 49, 50		Text: 1, 2, 3, 4, 5, 7 SAG: A, C TRG/B: 1, 2, 3, 5, 6, 7, 8, 9, 13, 15, 17, 18, 19, 20, 21, 23, 24, 27, 28, 31, 32, 33, 34, 35, 36, 37, 38, 42, 44, 47, 48, 51, 52, 54, 55, 56, 57, 58	Text: 2, 7 SAG: B, E, F TRG/B: 3, 11, 12, 14, 20, 22, 27, 30, 36, 37, 51

Bulletin Boards or Displays

The following section provides bulletin board or display ideas for your use. Three ideas are described for each of the six parts of the text, with one idea illustrated per part. Use these ideas to help introduce your students to major concepts presented throughout the chapters.

Part One   Work-Based Learning

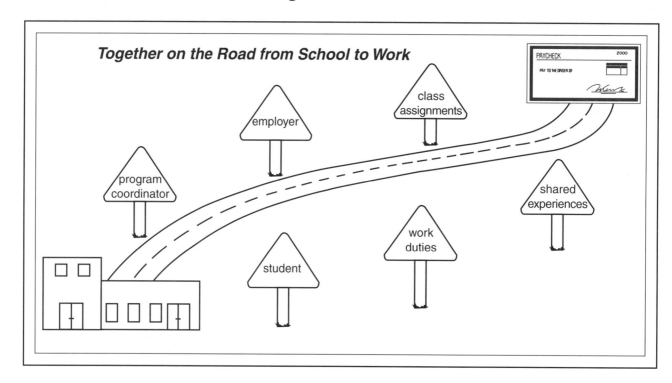

Title: *Together on the Road from School to Work*

Use the following items to illustrate the transition from school to work: a magazine picture or drawing to illustrate a school building, and a check stub or time card to represent work. Draw a curving road to connect the two elements. Along the road place triangular signs labeled *program coordinator, employer, class assignments, student, work duties,* and *shared experiences.* Discuss the roles and responsibilities of everyone involved in a work-based learning experience.

Title: *Reach for the Stars*

Take an instant-print photograph of each student for use in this display. Ask students to each make a construction paper cutout of a large star, paste his or her photograph on the star, and write a career goal. Have students place their stars on the bulletin board to create a "career galaxy." Discuss how work-based learning can help students reach their career goals.

Title: *The Work-Based Learning Team*

Using drawings or pictures of football helmets or players, portray the three-person, work-based learning team as a football team. Label the first helmet/player *program coordinator;* the second, *you;* and the last, *workplace supervisor.* Complete the display by placing a football labeled *work-based learning experience* with a goal post labeled *rewarding career.* Discuss the benefits of teamwork in a work-based learning experience.

Part Two   Skills for Success

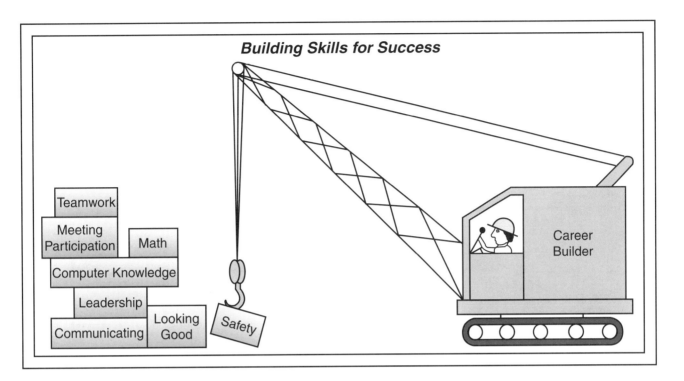

Title: *Building Skills for Success*

Use a picture or drawing of a crane lifting blocks to show the skills needed for success at school and work. Label and illustrate each block as follows:
- *Teamwork*—show a picture of a sports team.
- *Communicating*—show a picture of a telephone.
- *Math*—show math problems, a ruler, or a calculator.
- *Computer Knowledge*—show a picture of a computer.
- *Looking Good*—show a picture of well-groomed people.
- *Safety*—show pictures of protective devices.
- *Leadership*—show a picture of a hand pointing in a forward motion.
- *Meeting Participation*—show a group of people seated around a table.

Title: *Rise Up to Success*

Post seven colorful drawings of hot air balloons. Use each chapter title from part two as a caption beneath each balloon. Discuss the importance of each skill in school and in career success.

Title: *They All Add Up to Success!*

Link each of the following visual images with a + sign, as in a math problem:
- A sports team to show teamwork.
- A telephone and message pad to show communication skills.
- A calculator and invoice with prices to show math skills.
- A computer terminal to show computer skills.
- Two well-groomed people to show looking good on the job.
- A hand with the index finger pointing forward to show leadership.
- A group of people sitting around a table to show meeting participation.

At the end of the series, place an = sign and the words *Success on the Job*. Discuss how each skill contributes to job success.

Part Three Career Planning

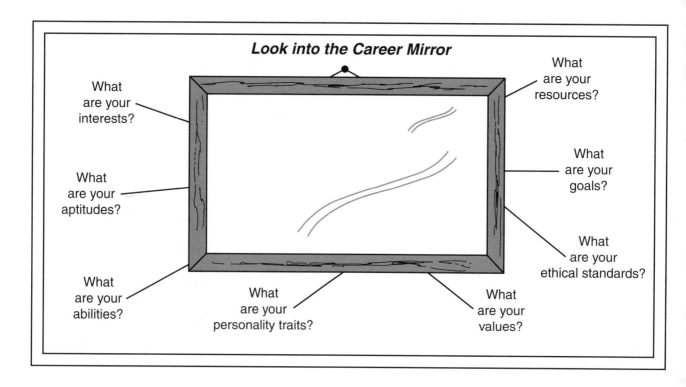

Title: *Look into the Career Mirror*

Post a mirror or reflective foil on the bulletin board. Place callouts around the mirror as shown to show what people need to know about themselves in order to choose careers that will lead to success and happiness. Use as a basis for class discussion. Discuss how students see themselves in the mirror.

Title: *Career Information Resources*

Make a display of various sources of career information and label each one. Include photocopies of pages from each of the U.S. Department of Labor publications. Make printouts of the home pages of various Web sites on the Internet. Include brochures on counseling that are available and ads for career conferences. Display sample career information brochures. Ask the school librarian to make additional suggestions.

Title: *The World of Careers*

Using a large visual of a world globe as a backdrop, post career photos that illustrate one or two careers within each career cluster discussed in the text. Have students decide which career cluster they think corresponds to each photo.

Part Four   The Job Hunt

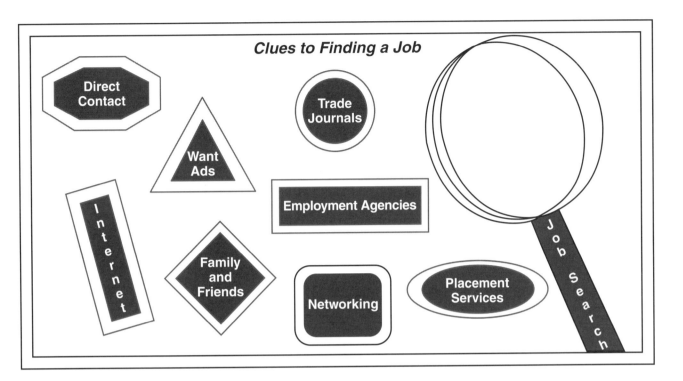

Title: *Clues to Finding a Job*

Post a drawing on the bulletin board of a large magnifying glass with *Job Search* written on the handle. For the clues, use cutouts of different geometric shapes. Write the words on the shapes as shown. Arrange the shapes randomly around the magnifying glass.

Title: *The Way to Find a Job*

Post a local street map in the center of the bulletin board. Highlight a course leading from the bottom of the map to the top. Label the destination at the top *My Job*.

Place different shaped road signs at different points along the road. Write the words shown in the illustrated bulletin board above on the signs. Discuss how each of these sources can be used in the job hunt.

Title: *Help Wanted*

Have students collect and then post want ads on the bulletin board for jobs for which they would be interested in applying. Use both newspaper ads and printouts of job openings listed on the Internet. Discuss the various job requirements, the types of interview questions that may be asked, and job resume requirements.

Part Five   Job Satisfaction

Title: *Keys to Job Satisfaction*

Cut seven large keys from construction paper. Write the phrases linked to job satisfaction on the keys and arrange on the bulletin board as shown.

Title: *Job Satisfaction: Then and Now*

Using materials from a library or local museum archive, post photos or illustrations showing the working conditions during the Industrial Revolution on one side of the bulletin board. On the other side, post photos or illustrations of today's safe, modern working conditions.

Have students use the bulletin board to compare past and present working conditions in this country. Discuss how working conditions affect job satisfaction. What role have unions had in these changes?

Title: *Be Your Own Boss*

Have students collect a variety of ads and notices from newspapers and magazines that advertise entrepreneurial opportunities. These items can range from franchises to "get rich quick" opportunities. Post these items on the bulletin board and discuss the pros and cons of each opportunity with students.

Part Six   Managing Your Income

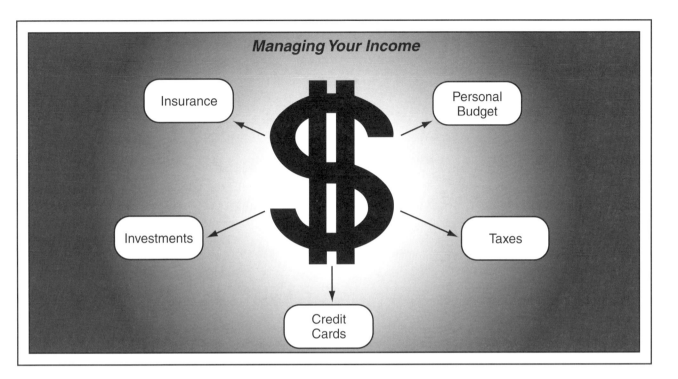

Title: *Managing Your Money*

Cut a large dollar sign and five arrows from construction paper. Place the dollar sign in the center of the bulletin board. Then arrange the arrows pointing away from the dollar sign. Write the words or phrases relating to managing income on separate sheets of construction paper, as shown in the illustration. Post them around the dollar sign. Discuss the responsibilities involved in managing income.

Title: *V.I.P.—Very Important Papers*

Collect samples of forms and papers that students must understand to manage their money, including a tax form, paycheck stub, personal check, credit card statement, bank statement, personal budget form, and an insurance claim form and policy. Arrange these items in a collage format on the bulletin board. Discuss how each item is used in money management.

Title: *Make Your Money Grow*

Cut several different tree shapes from construction paper. Write the following words or phrases on the shapes: savings, investments, insurance, limit credit card spending, and budgeting. Post the trees in a pattern on the bulletin board. Discuss how managing money wisely can make money grow.

Title: *Balancing Family and Work Roles*

Create a balance scale using black construction paper and marking pens on a white background. Cut out figures from a magazine representing family members, and place on one side of the scale. Cut out pictures of people in demanding career roles, and place them on the other side of the scale. Discuss the difficulties in balancing these roles.

Part 1
Work-Based Learning

Making the Transition from School to Work

Objectives

After studying this chapter, students will be able to
- explain how a work-based learning program is organized.
- list the purpose and types of work-based learning programs available.
- describe the benefits of work-based learning programs for students and employers.
- explain the importance of SCANS competencies.
- build SCANS competencies in using interpersonal skills and information.

Teaching Materials

Text, pages 19–29
  Terms to Know
  Facts in Review
  Applying Your Skills
  Developing SCANS Workplace Competencies
Student Activity Guide
  A. *Getting to Know Your Classmates*
  B. *Candidates for Work-Based Education*
  C. *The School-to-Work Experience*
  D. *The Benefits of School-to-Work Programs*
  E. *What Are Your Workplace Skills?*
Teacher's Resource Guide/Binder
  The Benefits of a Work-Based Learning Experience, transparency master 1-1
  Developing Workplace Know-How, reproducible master 1-2
  Review and Study Guide for Chapter 1, reproducible master 1-3
  Chapter 1 Test, reproducible master
Teacher's Resource Guide/Binder
  Work-Based Learning: How It Works, color transparency CT-1

Introductory Activities

1. Have students find the meaning of the term *transition* in the dictionary. Then, ask for examples of transitions students have already made in their lives at home and in school. What further transitions in life do they anticipate making?
2. Ask students to give examples of careers that interest them. Discuss the skills and knowledge required for each career. Have students list different ways individuals can acquire such skills and knowledge.

Instructional Concepts and Student Learning Experiences

Opportunities to Learn on the Job

3. *Work-Based Learning: How It Works,* color transparency CT-1, TRB. Use the transparency to introduce the key parties in work-based learning programs, emphasizing the role of the student.
4. Divide the class into small groups. Instruct each group to create either a poster, poem, or song titled "The Work-Based Learning Experience." Students should depict the relationship involving the student, employer, and program coordinator.
5. *Getting to Know Your Classmates,* Activity A, SAG. Each student is directed to interview a work-based learning program classmate and introduces that person to the class. (Note: You may want students to form pairs to interview each other.)
6. Invite students to interview a former work-based learning student about his or her advice to students beginning similar programs. Students should summarize the advice and their reaction to it in a brief written report.
7. Ask students to write you a letter explaining their understanding of the work-based learning program and the specific skills, knowledge, and experience they expect to gain.
8. Ask students to select a student, teacher, or parent who is not acquainted with work-based education and explain the program to that person. Students should be prepared to discuss their experiences in class.
9. Have students describe their ideal training station in brief oral descriptions.

10. *Candidates for Work-Based Education,* Activity B, SAG. Students are directed to read case histories about work-based learning programs and explain how the students described in each could benefit from the program.
11. Assign students to work in small groups to develop a list of possible additional training stations in the area.
12. Have students locate on a community map the training stations currently being used for work-based learning programs.

The Benefits of Learning on the Job

13. Have students write articles about the benefits of work-based learning for a class newsletter. For testimonials, have students interview each other as well as former students of work-based education programs. Have students read each other's articles to check them for proper spelling, grammar, and punctuation. Then, share the articles with other classes or submit them to the school newspaper.
14. Have students share with the class at least five benefits they hope to gain from the work-based learning experience. Encourage class discussion and questions.
15. Ask students to write a report or design a poster on the topic of *earning while you learn.* Instruct them to focus on the benefits of combining academic study with work experience.
16. *The School-to-Work Experience,* Activity C, SAG. Have students complete the crossword puzzle of work-based learning terms.
17. Have students prepare (but not send) letters that try to persuade an employer who does not hire students in work-based learning programs to consider doing so. Compare and discuss the letters in class and identify the qualities desired in such a letter.
18. *The Benefits of a Work-Based Learning Experience,* transparency master 1-1, TRG/B. Have students explain the value and importance of each of the benefits listed. What does *marketable skills* mean? Ask students to name skills that are no longer marketable, such as building a steam locomotive or driving a stagecoach.

Learning How to Learn

19. Have students discuss why a worker must have command of the foundation skills and qualities before he or she can acquire workplace competencies.
20. *Developing Workplace Know-How,* reproducible master 1-2, TRG/B. The worksheet directs students to identify activities that have helped them acquire and gain some proficiency in the SCANS workplace competencies and foundation elements.
21. Have students explain in a one-page paper why it is important to be prepared for the world of work before actually joining it.
22. *The Benefits of School-to-Work Programs,* Activity D, SAG. Students are asked to analyze a letter written by a former student in a work-based learning program to his program coordinator.
23. Have students describe workers who possess workplace know-how by listing examples of effective job performance. For each SCANS competency, students should list at least two examples that demonstrate workplace know-how.
24. *What Are Your Workplace Skills?* Activity E, SAG. The worksheet directs students to evaluate their workplace readiness and determine how their skills and qualities may influence career choice.

Activities to Enrich Learning

25. Ask students to write personal case histories, explaining why they chose a work-based learning program. Students may do a written report as well as present an oral report in class. Have students accompany the oral report with a poster, photos, a video, or some other visual illustrating their paths to the program. Their presentations should also explain how they plan to use the program to reach their career goals.
26. Divide the class into groups of three to role-play a student, program coordinator, and employer working together in a work-based learning program. Have each group develop a skit depicting how the three individuals work together to achieve a common goal. Students may choose to use props that enhance the skit.

Activities to Extend Learning

27. Invite an employer who hires work-based education students to explain how the company benefits by participating in the program. Have students write a brief paper about the speaker's comment that most impressed them.
28. Invite a panel of students formerly in work-based learning programs, who are now in successful careers, to speak about the benefits of work-based education.
29. Take the class to visit a student in a work-based learning program on the job. Arrange to tour the facility. Organize a question and answer session with the employer and the student afterwards.

Answer Key

Text

Facts in Review, page 28

1. (List two:) field trips, job shadowing, volunteering
2. A school-to-work coordinator matches the student's occupational goals to available work-based learning experiences. An employer hires the student part-time for on-the-job training. The student goes to school part-time to meet graduation requirements.
3. the student
4. the job supervisor
5. internship and youth apprenticeship
6. youth apprenticeship
7. (List four:) gaining on-the-job experience, acquiring marketable skills, recognizing career goals, learning to work with others, earning money
8. Secretary's Commission on Acquiring Necessary Skills
9. resources, interpersonal skills, information, systems, technology
10. basic skills, thinking skills, personal qualities

Student Activity Guide

The School-to-Work Experience, Activity C

1	2	3	4	5	6	7	8	9	10	11	12	13	14	15
			A							C				
G			P			E	M	P	L	O	Y	E	R	
R			P		B					O				
A			R		E					R			M	
D			E		N					D			E	
U		I	N	T	E	R	N	S	H	I	P		N	
A			T		F					N			T	
T	R	A	I	N	I	N	G	S	T	A	T	I	O	N
I			C		T					T			R	
O			E		S			S		O				
N			S					C	A	R	E	E	R	
			H					A						
			I					N						
	S	U	P	E	R	V	I	S	O	R				

The Benefits of School-to-Work Programs, Activity D

1. to tell him about his new job and how the work-based learning program benefited him
2. industrial cooperative education
3. to get work experience while in school and to find out if he would enjoy working in electronics
4. yes
5. because he was treated like a worker, not a student
6. (List five:) gained work experience before graduating from high school, learned that he enjoyed working in electronics, learned to work with supervisors and other employees, earned a paycheck, gained the job experience to obtain a full-time job, learned skills that were useful in the new job
7. (Student response.)

Teacher's Resource Guide/Binder

Review and Study Guide for Chapter 1, reproducible master 1-3

1. work-based learning (also school-to-work)
2. program coordinator
3. training station
4. job shadowing
5. mentor
6. cooperative education
7. internship
8. youth apprenticeship
9. student, employer
10. SCANS competencies
11. F
12. T
13. F
14. T
15. T
16. gaining on-the-job experience, acquiring marketable skills, recognizing career goals, learning to work with others, earning money

Chapter 1 Test

1. T		10. F	
2. T		11. B	
3. F		12. C	
4. T		13. D	
5. T		14. B	
6. T		15. D	
7. T		16. C	
8. F		17. D	
9. T			

18. They gain on-the-job experience, acquire marketable skills, recognize career goals, learn to work with others, and earn money.
19. The student, the program coordinator, and the employer work together as a team to ensure that the student gains the skills and experience needed for a meaningful career in the workplace.
20. competence with resources, interpersonal skills, information, systems, and technology. (Description is student response.)

Transparency Master 1-1

The Benefits of Work-Based Learning

Students who participate in work-based learning

- acquire marketable skills

- become aware of career goals

- learn to work with others

- gain on-the-job experience

- earn money

Reproducible Master 1-2

Developing Workplace Know-How

Name_____   **Date** _____   **Period** _____

Listed below are the five SCANS competencies plus the foundation skills and qualities that workers need to be effective in the workplace. These skills and qualities develop gradually and are strengthened through everything you do. For each item listed below, report at least one example of a related activity or accomplishment of yours.

Activities Report

Workplace Abilities	Recent Examples
• **Competence with resources**—allocating time, money, materials, space, and help from others	
• **Competence with interpersonal skills**—working on teams, teaching others, serving customers, leading, negotiating, and working well with people from culturally diverse backgrounds	
• **Competence with information**—acquiring and evaluating data, organizing and maintaining files, interpreting and communicating, and using computers to process information	
• **Competence with systems**—understanding social, organizational, and technological systems; monitoring and correcting performance; and designing or improving systems	
• **Competence with technology**—selecting equipment and tools, applying technology to specific tasks, maintaining equipment, and troubleshooting equipment problems	
Workplace Skills and Qualities	**Recent Examples**
• **Basic skills**—reading, writing, arithmetic and mathematics, speaking, and listening	
• **Thinking skills**—learning, reasoning, thinking creatively, making decisions, and solving problems	
• **Personal qualities**—displaying individual responsibility, self-esteem, sociability, self-management, and integrity	

Reproducible Master 1-3

Review and Study Guide for Chapter 1

Name_____ **Date** _____ **Period** _____

Completion: Fill in the blanks with the correct terms.

1. Acquiring job skills by taking a program that combines school and on-the-job learning is called _____-_____ _____.

2. School programs that combine classroom study with on-the-job learning are under the leadership of a special teacher called a(n) _____ _____.

3. A(n) _____ _____ is a school-approved job site where cooperative education students learn skills while they earn income.

4. Following a worker on the job and observing what that job involves is called _____ _____.

5. An assistant on the job that helps a student with day-to-day questions is a work-based _____.

6. _____ _____ is a school program that prepares students for an occupation through a paid job experience.

7. A(n) _____ is a school program providing paid or unpaid work experience for a specified period to learn about a job or an industry.

8. A(n) _____ _____ is a specialized program of job training to master a craft or trade.

9. Work-based learning is a three-way relationship between the _____, the program coordinator, and the _____.

10. _____ _____ consist of the five basic abilities that are needed to perform well in the workplace.

True/False: Circle *T* if the statement is true or *F* if the statement is false.

T   F   11. Work-based learning programs do *not* contribute to a person's employability.

T   F   12. Participating in a cooperative education, internship, or apprenticeship program is also a good opportunity for college-bound students.

T   F   13. Quitting school to work full-time is a good alternative to enrolling in a work-based learning program.

T   F   14. The training stations available to you will depend on the type of work-based learning program you follow and the participating employers in your area.

T   F   15. Work-based learning can change a student's outlook on life.

Essay Question: Provide a complete response to the following statement.

16. List the five benefits of learning on the job.

Making the Transition from School to Work

Name_____

Date _____ Period _____ Score _____

Chapter 1 Test

True/False: Circle *T* if the statement is true or *F* if the statement is false.

T   F   1. Cooperative education can help students acquire marketable skills and gain on-the-job experience.

T   F   2. Work-based learning gives students the opportunity to learn at two places—at school and at work.

T   F   3. Students in school-to-work programs work full-time at their jobs.

T   F   4. A program coordinator helps students make decisions, solve problems, and expand their knowledge.

T   F   5. A youth apprenticeship is job training to master a craft or trade.

T   F   6. An internship gives students a chance to test some of their career interests.

T   F   7. Students in school-to-work programs gain skills by working in a real job under real working conditions.

T   F   8. Employers do *not* benefit from a work-based learning program.

T   F   9. A satisfied employer may offer a student in a school-to-work program full-time employment after high school graduation.

T   F   10. Students involved in work-based learning programs cannot go to college after graduating.

Multiple Choice: Choose the best response. Write the letter in the space provided.

_____11. A school program combining classroom study with on-the-job learning is designed to prepare students for _____.
A. college
B. meaningful careers
C. unemployment
D. None of the above.

_____12. Before being assigned to a training station, a student's qualifications for work experience are carefully considered by _____.
A. the program coordinator
B. the employer
C. Both of the above.
D. None of the above.

_____13. A student's training station might be _____.
A. a manufacturing company
B. a hair salon
C. an insurance company
D. All of the above.

(Continued)

Name_____

_____14. Which of the following does *not* apply to students participating in work-based learning programs?
    A. They usually earn money while they work.
    B. They work full-time.
    C. They gain on-the-job experience.
    D. They become aware of career goals.

_____15. While participating in a work-based learning program, students can gain _____.
    A. skills
    B. knowledge
    C. work experience
    D. All of the above.

_____16. SCANS competencies are *not* _____.
    A. required in today's workplace
    B. the skills employers want in their employees
    C. developed one at a time
    D. developed through school, extracurricular, work, community, and volunteer activities

_____17. *Workplace know-how,* as defined by the Secretary's Commission on Achieving Necessary Skills, involves _____.
    A. mastery of five SCANS competencies
    B. possession of basic skills and thinking skills
    C. possession of important personal qualities
    D. All of the above.

Essay Questions: Provide complete responses to the following questions or statements.

18. List the benefits students can gain from a work-based learning experience.
19. Describe the three-way relationship between the student, the program coordinator, and the workplace supervisor.
20. List the five SCANS competencies and describe them.

Understanding Work-Based Learning

Objectives

After studying this chapter, students will be able to
- explain what their school expects of them as students in work-based learning programs.
- summarize the effects of the Fair Labor Standards Act on workers.
- identify ways in which they can improve their learning skills.
- build SCANS competencies in using resources, interpersonal skills, information, and systems.

Teaching Materials

Text, pages 31–43
> *Terms to Know*
> *Facts in Review*
> *Applying Your Skills*
> *Developing SCANS Workplace Competencies*

Student Activity Guide
> A. *Training Agreement Responsibilities*
> B. *Getting a Social Security Card*
> C. *The Training Plan*
> D. *Know the Law*
> E. *Your Study Habits*
> F. *Organizing Your Schedule*

Teacher's Resource Guide/Binder
> *Step-by-Step Training Plan,* reproducible master 2-1
> *Reorganizing Your Weekday Schedule,* reproducible master 2-2
> *Review and Study Guide for Chapter 2,* reproducible master 2-3
> *Chapter 2 Test,* reproducible master

Teacher's Resource Binder
> *The Training Agreement Benefits All,* color transparency CT-2A
> *Your Training Plan—An Important Component,* color transparency CT-2B

Introductory Activities

1. Examine expectations in different areas of life. For example, what expectations do students have of parents, friends, teachers, or teammates? What expectations do parents have of their children (the students)? What happens when people meet their expectations? What happens when they do not meet them?
2. Ask students to list at least five responsibilities they have now, including those at home and at school. Then ask them to list at least five freedoms they have, such as being allowed to borrow the family car, enjoy a later curfew, or go out on dates. Discuss with students the challenges of handling freedom and responsibilities wisely.

Instructional Concepts and Student Learning Experiences

Your Training Station

3. Ask students to research the types of workstations in their community that would apply to their chosen careers. Have them develop a chart listing each workstation and the advantages and disadvantages, if any, of each type.

Get a Social Security Number and a Work Permit

4. Have students list all the forms they must complete in order to participate in the work-based training program. Ask them to complete the forms neatly and accurately in class.
5. Instruct students to set up a personal file folder in which they can place important papers, forms, and reports related to their work-based learning experience.
6. Have students look up the address and phone number of the nearest social security office and bring the information to class. Locate the office on a map and make sure all students know how to get there.
7. *Getting a Social Security Card,* Activity B, SAG. Students are provided with a blank social security card application form to fill out.
8. Ask students to list at least three ways work permits protect the interests of teenage workers. Have students share their responses with the class and explain which reason they regard as most important.

Abide by the Training Agreement

9. *Training Agreement Responsibilities,* Activity A, SAG. The worksheet instructs students to summarize the responsibilities required of each person who signs the training agreement. (Give students a copy of the training agreement issued by the school to read carefully for this exercise.)
10. *The Training Agreement Benefits All,* color transparency CT-2A, TRB. Use the transparency to emphasize that the parties who sign a training agreement all benefit.
11. Ask each student to give a reason why the training agreement is important. List the reasons on the board and discuss them in class.

Following the Training Plan

12. *Your Training Plan—An Important Component,* color transparency CT-2B, TRB. Use the transparency to explain the importance of a training plan.
13. Have each student give one reason why a training plan is important to a work-based learning program. List reasons on the board and discuss.
14. *The Training Plan,* Activity C, SAG. Students are asked to complete the cover page of a training plan and describe their respective jobs in their own words.
15. Ask students to find, then write down, the definitions of *skill, attitude,* and *knowledge.* Discuss the definitions in class. Ask students to list the general skills, attitudes, and knowledge they already possess as well as those they plan to develop through the work-based learning program. Students may share their lists in class for discussion.
16. *Step-by-Step Training Plan,* reproducible master 2-1, TRG/B. Have students use the worksheet to check the behaviors they plan to develop at their workstations.
17. Have students explain in a written report the steps they would follow during their work-based learning experience to achieve their career goals.
18. Have students prepare calendars on which to write reminders to make regular training station reports.

Know the Law

19. Divide the class into two groups. Have one group present the advantages of the Fair Labor Standards Act from the employee's viewpoint. Have the other group present the advantages from the employer's viewpoint.
20. Provide students with copies of your state's labor laws. Have each student prepare a written report on one of the following topics: child labor, minimum wage, overtime, or equal pay.
21. *Know the Law,* Activity D, SAG. Students are asked to read case studies and determine how FLSA applies to each. Have students report their answers in class. (Students may work individually or in groups.)

Study and Learn

22. Read the following statements related to studying and learning in class. To respond to each statement, ask students to write *agree* or *disagree* on paper. (Pause for a few moments after each statement to allow students time to respond.) Discuss opinions in class.
    "Having a career goal helps a individual's study habits."
    "It's impossible to study a subject that isn't interesting."
    "A person with good study habits is organized for learning."
    "Improving reading skills means improving career possibilities."
    "Participating in class can help a student learn more and enjoy the time spent in the classroom."
23. Have students orally report on situations when they had to make extra efforts to achieve a goal. Ask them what problems they faced, how they overcame them, and how they felt when they achieved their goals. How can students use their past experiences as motivation to achieve future goals?
24. Have students work in small groups and brainstorm ways to develop study skills that would help them in the future. Compile the ideas into a master list, and distribute it to the class for future reference.
25. Ask students to design a poster or bulletin board that illustrates the following: "Developing Good Study Skills." Have them focus on how study skills can help students succeed in school, at their workstations, and in their future careers.
26. *Your Study Habits,* Activity E, SAG. The worksheet directs students to analyze their study habits. In class, have students share ideas for improving study habits.
27. *Organizing Your Schedule,* Activity F, SAG. The worksheet presents a blank time chart for students to prepare a weekday schedule, followed by questions that force students to evaluate their schedules. In class, have students discuss how this activity helped them.
28. *Reorganizing Your Weekday Schedule,* reproducible master 2-2, TRG/B. The handout directs students to relook at the schedules they prepared in Item 27, reconsider their evaluations, and develop better schedules. What improvements must they make to better organize their daily schedule?

29. Ask students to list the tasks they must do that day in a prioritized list. Have students explain in class how they determine priorities.
30. Have each student write a list of five ways to improve an individual's class participation. List suggestions on the board and discuss in class.
31. Instruct students to bring to class a newspaper or magazine article that interests them. Students should identify the main ideas and explain in class how they used the article's title, subheads, and illustrations to determine its content.
32. Read an article on a current event or other relevant topic aloud in class, instructing students to take notes according to the guidelines on page 41 of the text. On the following day, quiz students with several questions from the article. Allow students to use their notes to provide written answers. Have students evaluate their note-taking abilities in a brief written report.

Activities to Enrich Learning

33. Group students into teams of four to create skits depicting the responsibilities of all persons to abide by the training agreement. Each student should role-play one of the following: the student, parent, employer, or coordinator.
34. Have students work in small groups to develop a commercial or advertising campaign to promote good study skills. Have each group present its campaign to "sell" the importance of good study skills.
35. Ask students to take notes during a speech, lecture, or address given at school or on television. Ask them to write a summary based on their notes, then compare their summaries with those of other class members.

Activities to Extend Learning

36. Invite a reading teacher to speak to the class about tips to improve reading skills.
37. Invite the director of a community illiteracy program to speak to the class about the lifelong benefits of good reading skills.
38. Invite a former work-based learning program student to speak to the class about the importance of good study habits in relation to the work experience.
39. Show a videotape or play an audio cassette on time management. Ask students to take notes and write a brief summary.

Answer Key

Text

Facts in Review, page 42

1. by visiting it at the job interview

2. false
3. to assure the employer that the student is committed to the work experience, to assure the student that the employer is committed to training the student to do the job, to assure the parents/guardian that the student is involved in a well-planned educational experience, to assure the program coordinator that all parties understand their responsibilities and are committed to the student having a successful work experience
4. to help the student progress toward his or her career goals through the work-based experience
5. by reviewing the training station report and evaluation checks
6. 1½ times the person's regular pay rate
7. jobs performed under similar working conditions that require the same level of skill, effort, and responsibility
8. 18 years
9. (List five:) keeping a separate notebook for each class, clearly understanding the assignments, completing assignments daily, setting aside a time and place to study, beginning to study immediately when time to, studying in small segments, doing the difficult work first
10. briefly restating the main idea of each page, section, or paragraph

Student Activity Guide

Know the Law, Activity D

1. no, because employers may pay employees less during a training period
2. yes, because the Equal Pay Act requires equal pay to employees of both sexes for doing equal jobs; file a complaint with the U.S. Department of Labor or the Equal Employment Opportunity Commission
3. yes, $416
4. no, because pay exceptions may occur for differences in seniority
5. yes, because minimum wage is the lowest hourly pay rate that most employees must receive and Wu's job does not qualify for an exemption; file a complaint with the Wage and Hour Division of the U.S. Department of Labor
6. no, because she is too young to lawfully operate a meat-cutting machine, which is considered a hazardous job
7. no, because food service workers earn tips so they may lawfully be paid less than minimum wage
8. no, employees may be paid less during a training period
9. no, this is not considered a hazardous occupation for people 18 and older.

Teacher's Resource Guide/Binder

Reorganizing Your Weekday Schedule, reproducible master 2-2

1. (Student response. See page 40 in the text.)

Review and Study Guide for Chapter 2,
reproducible master 2-3

1. social security
2. work permit
3. training agreement
4. training plan
5. interview
6. training station report
7. summarizing
8. OSHA
9. priority
10. minimum wage
11. B
12. D
13. A
14. A
15. D
16. State facts; ask questions; give full attention to the teacher or speaker; get involved in class discussion.

Chapter 2 Test

1. E	12. T
2. B	13. F
3. D	14. T
4. F	15. F
5. C	16. T
6. A	17. D
7. T	18. B
8. T	19. D
9. F	20. B
10. T	21. C
11. T	

22. Keep a separate notebook for each class; be sure to clearly understand assignments; complete class assignments on time; set aside a time and place to study; begin studying immediately; study in small time segments; do more difficult assignments first.
23. State facts; ask questions; give full attention to the teacher or speaker; get involved in class discussions.

Reproducible Master 2-1

Step-by-Step Training Plan

Name_____ Date _____ Period _____

This example of a training plan consists of a list of attitudes, skills, and knowledge that a student in a work-based learning program is expected to acquire on the job and/or through school instruction. Review the following training plan and check the column titled "Training Station" for each item you plan to develop at your workstation.

Attitudes, Skills, and Knowledge to Develop	Training Station	School Instruction	
		Group	Individual
Demonstrating Appropriate Work Behavior			
The student will:			
1. Exhibit dependability.			
2. Demonstrate punctuality.			
3. Notify the employer and the teacher as soon as it is known that a shift will be missed or arrival will be delayed.			
4. Follow rules and regulations.			
5. Fill out time cards accurately.			
6. Recognize the consequences of dishonesty.			
7. Complete assignments in accurate and timely manner.			
8. Do other jobs when time permits.			
9. Control emotions.			
10. Accept responsibility on the job.			
11. Assume responsibility for own decisions and actions.			
12. Perform assigned duties without continuous supervision and directions.			
13. Exhibit pride and loyalty.			
14. Exhibit ability to handle pressures and tensions.			
15. Demonstrate ability to solve problems.			
16. Demonstrate ability to set priorities.			
Maintaining a Businesslike Image and Working Relationships			
The student will:			
1. Work productively with others.			
2. Show respect and support for fellow employees and customers.			
3. Demonstrate procedures and assist others when necessary.			
4. Recognize, analyze, and solve or report problems.			
5. Minimize occurrence of problems.			
6. Channel emotional reactions constructively.			
7. Participate in employer's orientation.			
8. Demonstrate knowledge of employer's products and services.			
9. Exhibit positive behavior.			
10. Read current job-related publications.			
11. Exhibit good grooming and appropriate dress for the job.			

(Continued)

Name_____

Attitudes, Skills, and Knowledge to Develop	Training Station	School Instruction	
		Group	**Individual**
Communicating on the Job			
The student will:			
1. Read and comprehend written communications and information.			
2. Use correct grammar.			
3. Speak effectively with others.			
4. Use job-related terminology.			
5. Listen attentively.			
6. Write legibly.			
7. Answer the telephone, take messages, and call other employees to the phone.			
8. Follow written and oral directions.			
9. Ask questions so assigned tasks can be completed.			
10. Locate information in order to accomplish task.			
11. Prepare written communication.			
12. Utilize computer skills.			
13. Utilize keyboard skills.			
14. Assist in training new employees.			
Understanding How a Business Works			
The student will:			
1. Recognize the role of business in a free enterprise system.			
2. Identify general responsibilities of employees.			
3. Identify general responsibilities of management/employers.			
4. Investigate opportunities and options for business ownership.			
5. Identify planning processes needed to open a business.			
6. Participate in meetings.			
Maintaining a Safe and Healthy Environment			
The student will:			
1. Comply with safety and health rules.			
2. Select correct tools and equipment.			
3. Utilize equipment correctly.			
4. Use appropriate action during emergencies.			
5. Maintain clean and orderly work area.			
6. Demonstrate personal hygiene and cleanliness.			
7. Recognize employer and employee responsibilities as related to OSHA guidelines.			

Reproducible Master 2-2

Reorganizing Your Weekday Schedule

Name _____   Date _____   Period _____

As a student in a work-based learning program, your weekday schedule differs from that of other students. After analyzing the schedule you prepared for Activity F of the *Student Activity Guide,* use this chart to make a revised schedule. (Remember to include the changes you recommended in Activity F.) Include the time you devote to class, work, homework, and relaxation. Then answer the question below.

Time	Monday	Tuesday	Wednesday	Thursday	Friday

1. Explain the importance of organizing your daily schedule. _____

_____

_____

Review and Study Guide for Chapter 2

Name_____ **Date** _____ **Period** _____

Completion: Fill in the blanks with the correct terms.

1. An employer needs to know a worker's _____ _____ number before the worker can be paid.

2. A(n) _____ _____ makes it legal for an underage student to work for an employer.

3. A(n) _____ _____ outlines the purposes of the work-based learning program and defines the responsibilities of everyone involved.

4. A(n) _____ _____ consists of a list of attitudes, skills, and knowledge that a student plans to learn during the work experience.

5. A planned meeting between a job applicant and an employer is a(n) _____.

6. A weekly or monthly job record is called a(n) _____ _____ _____.

7. _____ means writing down the main ideas in a study notebook.

8. The government agency that sets and enforces safety and health standards for workers is called _____.

9. _____ means ranking first in a "to do" list.

10. _____ _____ is the lowest hourly rate of pay that most employees must receive.

Multiple Choice: Choose the best response. Write the letter in the space provided.

_____ 11. What is *not* a purpose of the training plan?
    A. To help the student progress on the job toward career goals.
    B. To assure the employer that the student is committed to the work experience.
    C. To formally identify the student's training supervisor on the job.
    D. To give general statements or detailed plans about what the student will learn.

_____ 12. The _____ is a law that requires equal pay to employees of both sexes for doing equal jobs.
    A. Fair Labor Standards Act
    B. minimum wage amendment
    C. Equal Employment Opportunity Commission
    D. Equal Pay Act

_____ 13. Which of the following is a function of the FLSA child labor provision?
    A. It protects the educational opportunities of children.
    B. It allows 16-year-olds to learn how to operate motor vehicles and power-driven machinery.
    C. It stops children from taking jobs away from adults.
    D. All of the above.

_____ 14. Which of the following is *not* an example of a good study habit?
    A. Save the difficult assignments for last.
    B. Keep a separate notebook for each class.
    C. Complete class assignments every day.
    D. Set aside a time and place to study.

(Continued)

Name_____

_____15. Which of the following is a way to improve reading skills?
- A. Set aside more time for studying and reading.
- B. Join a reading improvement program at school.
- C. Try to grasp the main ideas expressed by the writer.
- D. All of the above.

Essay Question: Provide a complete response to the following statement.

16. List four ways you can participate in class.

Understanding Work-Based Learning

Name_____

Date _____ **Period** _____ **Score** _____

Chapter 2 Test

Matching: Match the following terms and identifying phrases.

_____ 1. Putting important tasks to be done first on a person's list.

_____ 2. A document that makes it legal for a student under age to work.

_____ 3. A list of attitudes, skills, and knowledge a student plans to learn during the work experience.

_____ 4. Writing down the main ideas in a study notebook.

_____ 5. A student's weekly or monthly job record.

_____ 6. A planned meeting between a job applicant and an employer.

A. interview
B. work permit
C. training station report
D. training plan
E. priority
F. summarizing

True/False: Circle *T* if the statement is true or *F* if the statement is false.

T   F   7. A student in a work-based learning program has a schedule that is different from that of other students.

T   F   8. Child labor standards protect the educational opportunities of children and prohibit jobs that may be hazardous to their health or well-being.

T   F   9. The primary goal of the FLSA is preventing accidents and injuries in the workplace.

T   F   10. An employer may interview several cooperative education students for the same job.

T   F   11. The employer needs to know a student's social security number before the student can be paid.

T   F   12. A training agreement is similar to a contract.

T   F   13. The training agreement is the same as the training plan.

T   F   14. The study skills students use in the classroom can be just as important as the job skills they will learn.

T   F   15. Learning to organize a schedule is *not* an important skill for work-based learning students.

T   F   16. Reading is a basic skill for studying and for schoolwork.

Multiple Choice: Choose the best response. Write the letter in the space provided.

_____ 17. An amendment to the Fair Labor Standards Act established _____.
A. the minimum wage
B. guidelines for overtime pay
C. Equal Pay Act of 1963
D. All of the above.

(Continued)

Name_____

_____18. Which of the following actions does *not* promote good study habits?
     A. Complete class assignments every day.
     B. Think about other things that need to be done.
     C. Study in small segments of time.
     D. Keep a separate notebook for each class.

_____19. Students can improve their reading skills by _____.
     A. reading more often
     B. setting aside more time for reading
     C. getting involved in a reading improvement program
     D. All of the above.

_____20. When taking notes, a student should *not* _____.
     A. organize them by chapter or date
     B. copy the entire paragraph from the book
     C. write the notes in his or her own words
     D. be brief

_____21. To get a social security card, a person must have _____.
     A. a work permit
     B. a job
     C. proof of age, identity, U.S. citizenship, or immigrant status
     D. a high school diploma

Essay Questions: Provide complete responses to the following questions or statements.

22. List the steps for developing good study habits.
23. Describe how a student can participate in class.

What Your Employer Expects

Objectives

After studying this chapter, students will be able to
- explain what employers expect of them as workers.
- identify things they can do to promote good working relationships with their supervisor and coworkers.
- build SCANS competencies in using resources, interpersonal skills, and information.

Teaching Materials

Text, pages 45–59
  Terms to Know
  Facts in Review
  Applying Your Skills
  Developing SCANS Workplace Competencies
Student Activity Guide
  A. *Personal Qualities on the Job*
  B. *An Employer's View*
  C. *Employer Job Evaluation*
  D. *Personal Traits*
  E. *Dependability and Work Ethic*
Teacher's Resource Guide/Binder
  Case Study: A Worker's Attitude on the Job,
    reproducible master 3-1
  Review and Study Guide for Chapter 3,
    reproducible master 3-2
  Chapter 3 Test, reproducible master
Teacher's Resource Binder
  Follow These Signs to On-the-Job Success, color
    transparency CT-3

Introductory Activities

1. Ask students to describe people they know who have a positive attitude about school, work, and life. Ask them to also describe people who have a negative attitude. Discuss which type of individual they prefer as a friend and why. Which type of person is more likely to succeed in a career?

2. *An Employer's View,* Activity B, SAG. Students are asked to interview an employer to learn what he or she expects from employees. Have students share their findings with the class.

Instructional Concepts and Student Learning Experiences

Personal Qualities Needed on the Job.

3. *Personal Qualities on the Job,* Activity A, SAG. Students are asked to imagine they are employers as they rank the employee work traits they consider most important. Have students work in groups and report their top five choices to the class.

Positive Attitude

4. Divide the class into pairs of students. After assigning each pair a career or job situation, assign one student the role of a worker with a positive attitude and the other student an opposite role. Ask students to show the contrast between the two attitudes either through written or oral presentations. Have them conclude which worker will be more successful on the job.

5. Ask students to observe the attitudes of workers in local businesses, such as a grocery store, during busy periods. In a class discussion, have students describe the workers they observed and their ability (or inability) to interact in a positive way with coworkers and customers.

6. In a class discussion, ask each student to offer a suggestion for maintaining a positive attitude at work.

7. Instruct students to design a bulletin board on the importance of a positive attitude on the job. Ask them to focus on how positive attitudes can help students in work-based learning programs succeed in their present job and future career.

Good Attendance

8. Ask students to describe the absenteeism policy at your school. How can good attendance at school help them succeed?
9. Have students provide examples of how an absent employee can cause extra work for others.
10. Divide the class in half. Ask one group of students to develop a list of acceptable reasons for being absent from work while the other group lists unacceptable reasons. List all reasons on the board and discuss.

Punctuality

11. Ask students to bring to class a copy of the attendance policies that affect their training stations. Have students read the policies in class and explain the reasons for each rule.
12. Have students discuss the problems caused by an employee coming to work late or leaving work early. Also discuss what employees should do if they must leave work in case of illness or emergency.
13. Ask students to create posters depicting the importance of punctuality at work.
14. Have students describe in writing the mode of transportation they will use to travel to their workstations and arrive punctually. Also, ask them to explain what other modes are available and why they ruled them out.

Performance

15. Have students demonstrate to the class how their employers trained them for their respective jobs.
16. Ask students to list the specific tasks they are expected to do on the job. Have them list ways they can learn how to do each skill faster and more efficiently. Discuss with the class.
17. Ask students to make a list of skills they lack for the job they have now. Discuss sources of help, such as a personal discussion with the program coordinator, employer, or a more experienced coworker. Help students develop a personal plan for gaining these skills.
18. Discuss with students how job performance is necessary for job success. Ask students to share examples from their training stations.

Initiative

19. Ask students to list at least five ways they can show initiative at their specific training stations. Discuss each in class.
20. Ask students to write an essay entitled "Why Initiative Leads to Success on the Job."

Cooperation

21. Ask students to recall their first opportunity to cooperate with coworkers. Have them describe that experience. Did coworkers react cooperatively in return?
22. Instruct students to write an essay on the importance of following directions carefully on the job and asking questions when more information is needed. Students should focus on specific situations at their present workstations.
23. *Case Study: A Worker's Attitude on the Job,* reproducible master 3-1, TRG/B. Students are asked to examine an employee's actions on the job and find ways to help him improve.
24. Have students create a list of tips to help workers get along with supervisors on the job. As a class, prepare a master list of the most important points. Copy the list and distribute it to students.
25. Ask each student to explain how his or her supervisor manages employees. Have students explain how they have adapted to their supervisors' styles.

Accepting Criticism

26. Ask students to give examples of constructive criticism directed at their coworkers which they have seen or heard. Have them explain the advantages of this type of criticism.
27. *Employer Job Evaluation,* Activity C, SAG. Students are directed to fill out a job evaluation chart regarding their individual performances and answer questions that evaluate personal strengths and weaknesses.
28. Divide the class into groups of three students. Have one student role-play an employee who tries to do the assigned job quickly but fails. Have the second student role-play a supervisor who gives constructive criticism, and the third student, a supervisor who gives nonconstructive criticism. After all groups finish, have "employees" describe their reactions to the two evaluations. Discuss why keeping a positive attitude in all situations is important.

Courtesy

29. Ask students to observe the courtesy of workers in their training stations and other local businesses for a week. How did workers show courtesy and how did coworkers or customers react?
30. Ask students to list at least five ways they can be courteous on the job. Have them link their recommendations to their workstations.
31. Ask students to imagine they are advice columnists for a student newspaper. Have them create a letter from a student in a work-based learning

program who has a problem showing courtesy at work. Ask them to write a response that would appear in the newspaper.

Personal Appearance

32. Ask students to clip magazine photos of people who represent the principles of good grooming on the job. Have students explain their choices to the class.
33. Have students present oral reports on the following: "Your appearance reflects the real you." Students should relate the report to their training station or chosen career.
34. Have students research the importance of personal appearance in the workplace and report their findings in a brief paper. Ask students to cite their references.
35. Ask students to express their feelings when, as customers, they encounter an employee without a neat, clean appearance. Have them discuss the importance of well-groomed employees to a company's image.

Good Health and Fitness

36. Ask students to create posters or develop skits illustrating the three basic guidelines to staying healthy and physically fit, as outlined in the text.
37. Divide students into groups to brainstorm ways they can stay healthy and fit. Make a master list of all responses from the class.
38. Ask students to look up information on the term *mental health* and identify its current meaning. Have students cite their references. Discuss the relationship between mental and physical health.
39. Ask students to list at least five ways poor health can interfere with job performance. Have them give specific examples from their training stations, if possible.

Ethics in the Workplace

40. Ask students if they would consider hiring a person with a reputation for dishonesty. Discuss responses in class.
41. Have students discuss how workers can show trustworthiness at their jobs.
42. Divide the class into two teams to debate whether employees should be fired if caught stealing.
43. *Personal Traits,* Activity D, SAG. Students are asked to complete a word puzzle on personality traits from the clues provided.
44. Ask students to express the feelings of loyalty they have to their respective work supervisors and

training stations. Have students explain how loyalty contributes to a positive attitude.
45. Ask students to explain in a brief paper what employees should do when they disagree with company policies or a supervisor's decisions.
46. Demonstrate how easily spoken messages are distorted by having students whisper a sentence, from one student to the next, until all have individually heard it. Write down a lengthy sentence of gossip about an imaginary employee and whisper it to the first student. Written notes are prohibited as each student whispers the sentence to the next person. The last student receiving the message should say it aloud to the class, then read the original message. Discuss how gossip and rumors in the workplace often result in inaccurate and harmful information.
47. *Dependability and Work Ethic,* Activity E, SAG. Students are asked to analyze a case study on workplace dependability.
48. *Follow These Signs to On-the-Job Success,* color transparency CT-3, TRB. Use the transparency to summarize the personal qualities needed by students in work-based learning programs for a successful work experience.

Activities to Enrich Learning

49. Ask students to write a case study about an imaginary employee with below-average job performance who is discourteous. (Case studies may also address other personal qualities discussed in the chapter.) After each case study is read to the class, ask students to provide constructive criticism so the imaginary employees can improve.
50. Ask students to research and write a report on the effects of employee theft on businesses. Refer them to library sources, and to local business leaders for firsthand reports.

Activities to Extend Learning

51. Show a videotape or play an audio cassette focusing on ways to develop a positive attitude. Discuss with students how these principles apply to their work experiences.
52. Ask a student to invite his or her employer to class. Have both the student and the employer speak on the importance of cooperation at work.
53. Ask a local employer to speak to the class about problems young workers often have in taking initiative on the job. Suggest ways to solve those problems and encourage student questions.

Answer Key

Text

Facts in Review, page 58

1. self-esteem, individual responsibility, self-management, sociability, integrity
2. basic skills, thinking skills
3. self-esteem
4. A worker's absence causes extra work for others and reduces the effectiveness of the work experience.
5. Contact the employer and the school mentor to explain the absence.
6. standards
7. by looking for work and doing it without being told, by looking for new skills to learn on the job
8. accept his or her share of the job and do the best work possible
9. It helps a worker get along with coworkers, supervisors, customers, and others.
10. by having clean, combed hair; clean hands; trimmed nails; and clean, neat, appropriate work clothes
11. Eat well-balanced, nutritious meals. Get adequate sleep and rest. Exercise regularly.
12. because the employee is stealing time from the employer
13. confidentiality
14. Talk to the program coordinator about it.
15. The person likes his or her job and puts great effort into it.

Student Activity Guide

Personal Traits, Activity D

1. responsible
2. appearance
3. cooperation
4. honesty
5. performance
6. dependable
7. loyalty
8. health
9. punctual
10. courtesy
11. attitude
12. initiative
13. work ethic
14. self-esteem

Teacher's Resource Guide/Binder

Case Study: A Worker's Attitude on the Job, reproducible master 3-1

1. (Student responses may include:) good attendance, punctuality, initiative, self-management, courtesy to customers, good performance and knowledge of job, individual responsibility, good personal appearance
2. (Student responses may include:) lack of cooperation, lack of courtesy to coworkers, lack of sociability, bad attitude toward constructive criticism, lack of self-esteem
3. (Student response.)

4. (Student response.)
5. (Student response.)
6. (Student response.)
7. (Student response.)
8. (Student responses may include:) integrity, honesty, confidentiality, loyalty, good health and fitness, good work ethic

Instructor's Guide/Teacher's Resource Binder

Review and Study Guide for Chapter 3, reproducible master 3-2

1. courtesy
2. positive attitudes
3. attendance
4. honest
5. initiative
6. job evaluation
7. punctuality
8. integrity
9. loyalty
10. self-esteem
11. cooperation
12. criticism
13. work ethic
14. confidential
15. appearance
16. self-management
17. nutritious
18. individual responsibility
19. exercise
20. mental

Chapter 3 Test

1. D	13. T
2. E	14. F
3. H	15. F
4. F	16. T
5. G	17. T
6. C	18. T
7. B	19. A
8. A	20. D
9. T	21. B
10. F	22. D
11. T	23. C
12. F	

24. Eat well-balanced, nutritious meals; get adequate sleep; get regular exercise.
25. gets along well with the supervisor and coworkers, asks questions, and is enthusiastic
26. (Identify three:) Accept one's share of the work; perform the job to the best of one's ability; follow directions carefully; ask questions on the job; be friendly, respectful, and considerate of other's feelings; be enthusiastic.

Reproducible Master 3-1

Case Study: A Worker's Attitude on the Job

Name_____ **Date** _____ **Period** _____

Three weeks ago, Greg started working as a retail salesperson at a popular clothing store. He always arrives early for work and starts straightening racks of clothes before his supervisor tells him to do so. When customers enter the store, Greg greets them with a big smile and a friendly, "Good evening!" Greg's sales have been up because he knows the merchandise and suggests additional purchases for customers. Greg also wears clothes that look good on him. He is always well groomed and well dressed.

Greg usually works with three other people on his shift. Angela, Dale, and James have worked at the store for several years. They are experienced salespersons, and they have tried to share sales tips with Greg. Greg doesn't want to listen to them. Yesterday, Angela suggested that Greg should not follow the customers so closely when they enter the store. "Some customers want time to look first and don't need help right away," she told him. Instead of thanking Angela, Greg took her comment personally. "If you don't like the way I'm working, just stay away from me," he said. "You're not my supervisor, anyway."

Similar situations have occurred with Greg's other coworkers. Greg's supervisor overheard a few of Greg's comments. She is concerned that Greg may not be the star employee she first thought. Today, the supervisor took Greg aside and said, "You've got to change your attitude toward your coworkers. We want a team atmosphere in this store, and people who can't get along with the team members won't last long here."

Can you help Greg keep his job? As a group, discuss and then answer the following questions:

1. What positive traits does Greg show on the job?_____

_____

_____

2. What negative traits does he show? _____

_____

_____

3. How can Greg overcome his negative traits? _____

_____

_____

4. Is Greg a valuable employee? Explain. _____

_____

_____

5. Do you think Greg will be a success at his job? Explain. _____

_____

_____

Name_____

6. How should Greg respond if James says, "I want to remind you of an important store policy. You need to ask for two forms of identification before you accept a personal check. You only took a driver's license when you rang up that last customer."

    Greg's response: _____

    _____

    _____

7. Role-play a conversation between Greg and his supervisor a few weeks later. Greg's supervisor says, "Greg, I've noticed that you're getting along better with your coworkers. How do you feel about that?"

    Greg's response: _____

    _____

    _____

8. What other positive traits not yet mentioned do you think Greg should have on the job? _____

    _____

    _____

    _____

Reproducible Master 3-2

Review and Study Guide for Chapter 3

Name_____ **Date** _____ **Period** _____

Completion: Fill in the blanks with the correct terms.

1. _____ is showing concern for other people.

2. Workers with _____ _____ get along with others.

3. Students with good _____ records avoid asking for time off from work to do personal errands.

4. A(n) _____ employee does the job he or she is assigned and does *not* waste time.

5. Showing _____ means looking for new skills to learn on the job without being told.

6. A(n) _____ _____ is a written review of an employee's job performance.

7. _____ means being on time for work, for school, and for appointments.

8. People who firmly follow moral values have _____.

9. _____ means being faithful to coworkers and the employer.

10. Having confidence and satisfaction in yourself is _____-_____.

11. _____ is the ability to get along with others.

12. A good employee has a good attitude toward constructive _____.

13. How you feel about your job and how much effort you put into it is called a _____ _____.

14. Company matters that should not be shared with those who do not need to know are private, or _____.

15. Your personal _____ is a reflection of you.

16. Workers with the SCANS foundation skill of _____-_____, or initiative, are independent thinkers who recognize what needs to be done next.

17. Healthy people eat well-balanced, _____ meals.

18. A willingness to answer for your conduct and decisions is _____ _____.

19. To maintain good health, workers need to stay physically active and _____ regularly.

20. Good _____ health is just as important as good physical health for job performance.

What Your Employer Expects

Name_____

Date _____   **Period** _____   **Score** _____

Chapter 3 Test

Matching: Match the following terms and identifying phrases.

_____ 1. Stresses the importance of regular attendance.

_____ 2. Being on time.

_____ 3. Being told or shown a better way to do a task.

_____ 4. Working well with others.

_____ 5. Doing the assigned job and *not* wasting time.

_____ 6. Looking for new skills to learn on the job.

_____ 7. Showing good manners and concern for other people.

_____ 8. A person's outlook on life.

A. attitudes
B. courtesy
C. initiative
D. absenteeism policy
E. punctuality
F. cooperation
G. honesty
H. constructive criticism

True/False: Circle *T* if the statement is true or *F* if the statement is false.

T   F   9. Employers expect workers to be courteous and well groomed.

T   F   10. People with positive attitudes do *not* get along well with other people.

T   F   11. When a person is absent from work it causes extra work for other people.

T   F   12. If an employee is three minutes late once in a while, it will make little difference to the employer.

T   F   13. Working fast and efficiently should be one of the performance goals of an employee.

T   F   14. To be effective on the job, an employee does *not* have to get along with the supervisor or coworkers.

T   F   15. A job evaluation is an oral review of an employee's job performance.

T   F   16. An employee who loafs on the job is actually stealing time from the employer.

T   F   17. A worker's personal appearance has much to do with his or her success.

T   F   18. Loyalty means being faithful to coworkers and the employer.

Multiple Choice: Choose the best response. Write the letter in the space provided.

_____ 19. An employer expects employees to _____.
   A. have a positive attitude
   B. be late for work
   C. blame others for their mistakes
   D. None of the above.

(Continued)

Name_____

_____20. Employers expect students in work-based learning programs to _____.
A. have some basic knowledge and skills in the area of employment
B. learn new skills on the job
C. increase their speed as they gain more experience
D. All of the above.

_____21. A dependable worker will most likely be _____.
A. taken for granted
B. given more responsibility, advancement, and pay raises
C. fired or given a cut in pay
D. reprimanded by the supervisor

_____22. A cooperative employee _____.
A. follows directions carefully
B. gets along well with coworkers
C. is enthusiastic about the job
D. All of the above.

_____23. If employees are assigned tasks they would rather *not* do, they should _____.
A. leave them for someone else to do
B. complain to the supervisor
C. accept them pleasantly and perform them as well as they would any other tasks
D. accept them but let everyone know they dislike doing them

Essay Questions: Provide complete responses to the following questions or statements.

24. Describe three ways to stay healthy and physically fit.
25. Describe an employee who has a positive attitude.
26. Identify three ways an employee can promote a good working relationship with coworkers.

Part 2
Skills for Success

4

Teamwork and Problem-Solving Skills

Objectives

After studying this chapter, students will be able to
- describe the importance of teamwork in the workplace.
- know how teams develop and work effectively.
- explain the problem-solving process.
- know how to manage conflict.
- build SCANS competencies in using resources, interpersonal skills, information, and systems.

Teaching Materials

Text, pages 63–79
Terms to Know
Facts in Review
Applying Your Skills
Developing SCANS Workplace Competencies
Student Activity Guide
A. *Handling Problems in Teams*
B. *Using a Chart as a Scheduling Tool*
C. *Let's Work as a Team*
D. *Team Problem-Solving Case Study*
E. *Teamwork and Problem-Solving Terms*
Teacher's Resource Guide/Binder
Qualities of an Effective Team, transparency master 4-1
Examining Team Roles, reproducible master 4-2
Problem Solving in Action, reproducible master 4-3
Review and Study Guide for Chapter 4, reproducible master 4-4
Chapter 4 Test, reproducible master
Teacher's Resource Binder
Be a Team Player at Work, color transparency CT-4

Introductory Activities

1. Ask students to recall a past experience in which they, working with others, accomplished something that would have been difficult or impossible to achieve on their own. Have students share recollections.
2. Ask students what they think is meant by the following saying: "Many hands make light work."

Instructional Concepts and Student Learning Experiences

Changing Nature of the Workplace

3. Ask students to interview a relative or neighbor nearing retirement age to learn what types of jobs he or she held throughout life and what importance teamwork played. Have students share their findings in an oral report.
4. *Be a Team Player at Work,* color transparency CT-4, TRB. Use the transparency to introduce the concepts of team and teamwork.
5. Have students survey three or more companies to learn their definitions of *quality.* Ask students to write a brief paper, comparing and contrasting the definitions. How do they compare to the definition found on page 64 of the text?

Teams in the Workplace

6. Have students recount the team efforts that made it possible for them to participate in a work-based learning program. Who were the team members and what did each contribute?
7. Ask students to report an example of teamwork that occurred at their respective training stations. Is teamwork encouraged by their employers?
8. Select a winning professional sports team and have students identify the features that it shares in common with a successful team of employees in the workplace.
9. Divide the class into small groups to identify types of work that are best accomplished by teamwork rather than individual effort. Ask the groups to list five jobs for each category and report their lists to the class. Have the class decide whether the jobs fit a single category or fall somewhere between the two.
10. Have students write a brief paper explaining how teamwork relates to the following saying: "Two heads are better than one."
11. Ask students to recall a past assignment in which they worked on a team whose members sharply

disagreed with one another. Was the assignment accomplished satisfactorily? What lessons did students learn from the experience?

12. Have students brainstorm the many reasons for silence during team meetings and ways to encourage members to participate.

13. Divide the class into small groups to develop a list of recommendations for preventing personality clashes from interfering with teamwork. Have the groups report their recommendations to the class.

14. *Handling Problems in Teams,* Activity A, SAG. Students are asked to review cases of mis-behaving team members and indicate how they would handle each case.

15. Ask students to write their names on a piece of paper and vote for the stage of team development that best describes the class. Collect the papers and tally the votes on the board. Call on several students to justify their votes.

16. Have students imagine they are assigned the job of leading a team to plan all school functions and events for this year's graduation ceremonies. Ask them to write a brief report explaining which type of team—functional, cross-functional, or multifunc-tional—they would assemble to help with the task.

Characteristics of an Effective Team

17. Ask students to recall the teamwork experience that gave them the greatest feeling of pride and share their recollections with the class.

18. *Qualities of an Effective Team,* transparency master 4-1, TRG/B. Use the transparency to introduce students to the behaviors associated with effective teamwork.

19. *Examining Team Roles,* reproducible master 4-2, TRG/B. Students are asked to examine a case study and identify the team roles of each individual discussed.

20. In a brief written report, have students identify the team roles they have held within various school and community group(s). Ask them to respond to the following questions: Do you tend to assume the same role(s) with each group? By assuming another role, how might you have improved team results?

21. Have students explain how effective teamwork relates to the following saying: "Humor is the best medicine."

22. Ask students to report several tips they use for staying focused on an assignment, such as doing homework or completing tasks at home. Discuss which of these tips can be used in team settings.

23. Divide the class into pairs of students to develop one example of a goal that is poorly stated versus one that is well defined. Have students report the possible results of following poorly stated goals.

24. *Using a Chart as a Scheduling Tool,* Activity B, SAG. Students are asked to work in small groups to develop a Gantt chart for a school fundraising project.

25. Have students discuss what a team should do when key steps of a task are mistakenly omitted from its Gantt chart. What should a team do when the deadline date is changed?

Problem Solving

26. Have students look up the definition of the term *problem.* Which definition most closely resembles the definition found on page 70 of the text.

27. Ask students to imagine a workplace consisting of two teams—one that possesses problem-solving skills and one that does not. Have students explain which team they would prefer to lead.

28. *Let's Work as a Team,* Activity C, SAG. The work-sheet directs students to work in small groups to accomplish an assignment as a team, then individually make a written assessment of how well the members worked together. The assign-ment involves creating a chart to help new car buyers decide what to buy.

29. Have students discuss the possible consequences of spending too little time or effort with the first problem-solving step—analyzing and identifying the problem.

30. Ask students to find the singular form of the plural term *criteria* in at least two dictionaries. What singular form of the word is recommended for common usage?

31. During brainstorming sessions, some leaders encourage ideas that many may consider extreme or crazy. Have students explain possible reasons for this approach.

32. Ask students why seating a group in a circle is the best arrangement for a brainstorming session.

33. *Problem Solving in Action,* reproducible master 4-3, TRG/B. Working in small groups, students are asked to examine and solve a problem using the problem-solving steps outlined in the text on pages 70-74.

34. Have students examine the six problem-solving steps for usefulness in figuring math word problems. Can all the steps, as outlined in the text, work well in solving math?

Managing Conflict

35. Have students explain the difference between work-place disagreements and conflict. Which has the greatest potential for destroying effective teamwork?

36. Ask the class to identify scenarios involving work-place conflict that are unwise for individuals to intervene. List the recommendations on the board.

37. To the following typical comments heard in the workplace, have the class brainstorm possible ways to restate the conflict-causing "you" messages into "I" messages:

    "You shouldn't hand in a report that sloppy."

    "It doesn't look like you spent much effort on this."

    "You shouldn't promise something that is beyond your control."

    "This is the second time this week that you've been told how this works."

    "You're not carrying your share of the workload."

    "Do you have any idea what you are doing?"

    "You ought to pay more attention to your work."

    "You did this all wrong."

38. *Team Problem-Solving Case Study,* Activity D, SAG. The worksheet directs students to use the problem-solving steps to analyze a case study involving possible workplace conflict.

39. Ask students to research and write a report on the effects—on individual employees and company morale—of workplace conflict that is not kept under control. Have students cite their reference(s).

40. *Teamwork and Problem-Solving Terms,* Activity E, SAG. The worksheet directs students to match definitions and descriptions with correct terms from the chapter.

Activities to Enrich Learning

41. Invite a local employer to discuss the common difficulties young workers often have in demonstrating teamwork and problem-solving skills in the workplace. Ask him or her to provide tips for developing such skills.

42. Show a videotape or play an audio cassette focusing on ways to control workplace conflict. Discuss with students how these principles apply to their work experiences.

43. Invite a conflict management instructor to speak to the class about the close link between poor communication and workplace conflict. Have students write a written report based on the notes they take during the presentation.

Activities to Extend Learning

44. Have students research the origin of the Gantt chart and report their findings in a brief paper.

45. Working in small groups, have students create a skit that incorporates the problem-solving steps. Ask a group representative to read it to the class for constructive criticism.

46. Ask students to write a case study about using teamwork effectively to avoid conflict in the workplace.

Answer Key

Text

Facts in Review, page 78

1. when quality became the number one goal and workers were expected to solve problems and make decisions
2. (List three:) better decisions, more creative decisions, faster gathering of information, good quantity and quality of work, enhanced feelings about self and work
3. (List three:) longer delays, greater frustrations, personality clashes, an unpleasant working environment, poor production
4. functional team, cross-functional team, multi-functional team
5. Members come together in the *forming* stage. Members clash and disagree in the *storming* stage. Members work cooperatively and leaders emerge in the *norming* stage. The team works as a unit at maximum efficiency in the *performing* stage.
6. shares leadership, rotates team roles, stays focused, works for the common good
7. by using humor, taking a break, and listing goals
8. Identify and analyze the problem; collect and analyze data; consider possible solutions; choose the best plan; implement the plan; observe; evaluate, and adjust the plan.
9. a problem, which is stated accurately; the criteria, or standards used to find the best solution; the constraints, or factors that hinder finding a solution
10. If the plan does not solve the problem, it may mean the problem was defined incorrectly.
11. false
12. false
13. Know when to intervene; address the conflict; identify the source and importance of the conflict; identify possible solutions; develop an acceptable solution; implement and evaluate.
14. "You" messages tend to put people on the defensive.

Student Activity Guide

Teamwork and Problem-Solving Terms, Activity E

1. F	10. G
2. I	11. R
3. B	12. H
4. E	13. J
5. Q	14. C
6. K	15. P
7. D	16. N
8. M	17. A
9. O	18. L

19. working toward a goal that is considered the best overall

20. when it relaxes team members and helps them focus on issues
21. Use humor effectively; takes breaks; list goals.
22. (Student response.)
23. (Student response.)
24. (Student response.)

Teacher's Resource Guide/Binder

Examining Team Roles, reproducible master 4-2

1. Bill—wrote the sales report, asked for ideas to increase sales
2. Kim—said she liked Craig's ideas; Andrew—said both Craig's and Kim's ideas were excellent
3. Jarrod—reminded the group to start the meeting, recommended ending the meeting and scheduling a brainstorming session
4. Mark—said Jim's and Mary's ideas were not enough; Andrew—said more facts and ideas were needed to convince him of Mark's idea
5. Craig—wrote the meeting summary and asked Mark to repeat his ideas
   (Students may justify other answers.)

Problem Solving in Action, reproducible master 4-3

1. deciding whether to take the trip, which could result in being fired
   A. to be an advertising account manager within three years
   B. She just started a new full-time job, is not entitled to paid vacation time, and has expensive car payments.
2. Can she get permission to take time off without pay because of the special opportunity? Can she get a loan to help pay the car payments? If she loses her job, how available are good jobs in her field? If circumstances force her to sell her car, will her credit record be tarnished?
3. She could pass up the travel opportunity now, stay employed, and plan for a trip later. She could quit her job, sell her car, take the trip, and look for a new job when she returns. She could try to persuade her employer to allow her a four-week unpaid leave because of the special opportunity. She might be able to find some way to have the bulk of her work covered during an absence which would allow her to more easily take time off. If the trip relates to her employer's needs or her work assignments in any way, she could try to argue that it will make her a more valuable employee. She could try asking for one unpaid week off, pay her own travel expenses, and meet up with her cruising friends at a specific city to spend part of the vacation with them.
4. (Student response.)

5. No matter which course of action she chooses, will she reach her goal of becoming an advertising account manager within three years?

Review and Study Guide for Chapter 4, reproducible master 4-4

1. team
2. multifunctional team
3. functional team
4. self-directed team
5. cross-functional team
6. Gantt chart
7. problem solving
8. criteria
9,. constraints
10. conflict

11. T	16. T
12. F	17. F
13. F	18. T
14. T	19. F
15. T	

20. (Describe three:) brainstorming—a group technique in which as many ideas as possible are identified in a short amount of time; compromise—when each side gives up something of value to help solve a problem; consensus—when all members of a group fully accept and support a decision

Chapter 4 Test

1. C	9. T	17. T
2. A	10. F	18. T
3. G	11. F	19. C
4. F	12. F	20. C
5. H	13. T	21. A
6. E	14. T	22. D
7. B	15. F	23. D
8. D	16. F	

24. (List two each:) pros—Teams reach better and more creative decisions than individuals; one member's comments will often inspire ideas from others; several people can gather information more quickly than one person can; effective teams make individuals feel better about themselves and the quality of their work.
    cons—Teams usually take more time to reach a decision than individuals; working with a group can be frustrating; personality clashes can create an unpleasant working environment; some people aren't good team members; some teams take a long time to develop or never become an effective team.
25. stage 1—forming; stage 2—storming; stage 3—norming; stage 4—performing (Descriptions are student response. See pages 67-68 in the text.)
26. (List three:) Use humor effectively; take breaks; list goals.

Qualities of an Effective Team

Members of an effective team

- share leadership

- rotate team roles

- stay focused

- work for the common good

Reproducible Master 4-2

Examining Team Roles

Name_____ **Date** _____ **Period** _____

Read the case study carefully and indicate which members of the meeting held a team role. (Individuals may have more than one role.) Explain your decisions in the space provided.

Case Study: At 2:05 p.m., Jarrod reminded everyone that the Friday two o'clock meetings were developing a pattern of starting late. Group members immediately turned their attention to Andrew's sales report, the focus of the meeting. The report contained bad news—the small candy company was losing sales. Andrew asked for ideas on how to improve sales. After discussion of the sales report, Craig complained about the candy wrappers and recommended design and color changes. Kim said she liked Craig's idea and asked him to make a rough sketch of some designs. Also, she recommended selling the candy through mail order catalogs since going through grocery stores put the business in competition with the nation's biggest candy makers. Andrew said the ideas offered by Craig and Kim were excellent. Mark, however, said more needed to be done. He recommended new flavor combinations to make the candy special and different. Mark was asked to repeat his flavor ideas so the meeting summary written by Craig would include them. Jarrod noticed the next group of employees scheduled to use the conference room were waiting outside the door. He recommended ending the Friday meeting early and scheduling a brainstorming session for Monday morning at 9:00. Andrew agreed, but warned that he'll need to hear more facts and ideas before he would change the traditional candy flavors linked to his family's 50-year-old business.

1. Team leader:_____

   Explanation: _____

   _____

2. Team encourager: _____

   Explanation: _____

   _____

3. Team taskmaster:_____

   Explanation: _____

   _____

4. Team critic: _____

   Explanation: _____

   _____

5. Team recorder: _____

   Explanation: _____

   _____

Reproducible Master 4-3

Problem Solving in Action

Name_____   **Date** _____   **Period** _____

Work with two or three classmates to solve the problem outlined in the case study. Then answer the questions below and report your team's recommendation to the class.

Case Study: Janice must decide whether to take the dream trip of a lifetime. Her best friend entered a radio contest and won the grand prize—an all-expenses-paid, four-week cruise around the world for four. Janice has been invited to join the group. The trip is scheduled for August, a busy period for her employer, Acme Advertising. In fact, no employee vacations will be allowed that month, but Janice is not even entitled to paid vacation time until next year. She worked for the company part-time while attending college and accepted a full-time position after graduation in June one month ago. Her friends have not yet found jobs and so are free to take the trip. Janice loves her job and sees a bright future there. In fact, she just bought a new car even though the payments take much of her salary. If she takes the four-week trip, her employer might fire her, leaving her jobless and without money for car payments. That could complicate her career goals and possibly ruin her credit rating. On the other hand, she would need to work for several years to afford a trip like this. Furthermore, she is not eligible for a four-week vacation until her 20th anniversary with the company. Janice doesn't know what to do. She doesn't want to mess up her long-range goal of being an advertising account manager within three years.

1. What is Janice's problem? _____

   _____

   _____

   A. Are there any criteria? _____

   _____

   B. Are there any constraints? _____

   _____

2. What data should Janice collect before she makes a choice? _____

   _____

3. What are some possible solutions? _____

   _____

4. What plan does your team recommend for Janice?_____

   _____

   _____

5. After Janice implements the plan, what factors should she observe and evaluate to determine if she made the

   best choice? _____

   _____

   _____

Reproducible Master 4-4

Review and Study Guide for Chapter 4

Name_____ **Date** _____ **Period** _____

Completion: Fill in the blanks with the correct terms.

1. A(n) _____ is a small group of people working together for a common purpose.

2. Members of a(n) _____ _____ have been cross-trained so each person is able to perform the duties of all the other team members.

3. All members of a(n) _____ _____ have similar skills and expertise although they would *not* be able to perform each other's jobs.

4. A(n) _____-_____ _____ has been given full responsibility for carrying out its assignment.

5. A(n) _____-_____ _____ consists of workers from different areas within a company who are assigned to work on a specific project.

6. A graph that shows the steps of a task divided across a timetable is a(n) _____ _____.

7. The process of making an expectation a reality is _____ _____.

8. _____ are standards you use to find the best solution.

9. _____ are factors that may restrict or hinder your ability to solve the problem.

10. _____ is a hostile situation resulting from opposing views.

True/False: Circle *T* if the statement is true or *F* if the statement is false.

T   F   11. One team member's comments will often inspire ideas from others.

T   F   12. A team approach is always the best way to solve problems.

T   F   13. If a team doesn't work well together right away, it probably never will.

T   F   14. When leadership is shared, everyone feels responsible for the success or failure of the team.

T   F   15. Concentrating on achieving goals can help keep a team focused.

T   F   16. Effective team members work for the common good.

T   F   17. A problem exists when the team's expectations and reality are the same.

T   F   18. Employers are finding that many benefits occur when workers are given more responsibility for solving work problems.

T   F   19. The first step in the problem-solving process is to consider possible solutions.

Essay Question: Provide a complete response to the following statement.

20. Describe three aids to problem solving.

Teamwork and Problem-Solving Skills

Name_____

Date _____   **Period** _____   **Score** _____

Chapter 4 Test

Matching: Match the following terms and identifying phrases.

_____ 1. A hostile situation resulting from opposing views.

_____ 2. A group technique used to develop many ideas in a relatively short time.

_____ 3. A pattern that is typical in the development of a social group.

_____ 4. That which a person wants to attain.

_____ 5. The process of making an expectation a reality.

_____ 6. Standards used to determine the best solution.

_____ 7. Each side gives up something of value to help solve a problem.

_____ 8. All members of a group fully accept and support a decision.

A. brainstorming
B. compromise
C. conflict
D. consensus
E. criteria
F. goal
G. norm
H. problem solving

True/False: Circle *T* if the statement is true or *F* if the statement is false.

T   F   9. After losing the leading role in the world's economy, U.S. industry was forced to focus on quality instead of quantity.

T   F   10. More companies are now using individual managers instead of teams to increase productivity in the workplace.

T   F   11. A functional team might include representatives from a company's design, marketing, and financial departments.

T   F   12. People who like to control others are the most effective team leaders.

T   F   13. Rotating team roles is a good way to keep all members involved.

T   F   14. A problem exists when there is a difference between reality and expectation.

T   F   15. Successful problem solvers immediately look for solutions at the first sign of a problem.

T   F   16. The quality of the ideas is the major concern during brainstorming.

T   F   17. A major problem with achieving consensus is that it is very time-consuming.

T   F   18. Some disagreements lead to improvements in the workplace.

(Continued)

Name_____

Multiple Choice: Choose the best response. Write the letter in the space provided.

_____19. Members of a(n) _____ team have been cross-trained so each person is able to perform the duties of all the other team members.
A. functional
B. cross-functional
C. multifunctional
D. self-directed

_____20. Which is the first step in problem solving?
A. Collect and analyze data.
B. Consider possible solutions.
C. Identify and analyze the problem.
D. Observe, evaluate, and adjust.

_____21. Which of the following is an example of a constraint to solving the problem of arriving late to work?
A. Not having a car.
B. Having dependable public transportation.
C. Having enough time to get to work from class.
D. All the above.

_____22. When addressing someone involved in a conflict, _____.
A. talk to him or her in front of other people
B. try to embarrass them
C. use "you" messages
D. treat the person as you would want to be treated

_____23. Why is it important to know when to intervene in a conflict?
A. What seems important at the moment may seem unimportant later.
B. Sometimes intervening may make a situation worse.
C. Avoiding a serious disagreement only postpones the time when action will be required.
D. All the above.

Essay Questions: Provide complete responses to the following questions or statements.

24. List two pros and two cons of solving problems with a team approach.
25. List and describe the four stages of team development.
26. Describe three ways to help keep a team focused.

Communicating on the Job

Objectives

After studying this chapter, students will be able to

- determine how well they listen and how to perfect this skill.
- identify ways they can improve their reading and comprehension skills.
- write business letters, memorandums, and reports.
- identify ways they can improve their speaking skills when interacting with others.
- describe technological tools in the workplace that aid communications with others.
- build SCANS competencies in using interpersonal skills, information, and technology.

Teaching Materials

Text, pages 81–107
   Terms to Know
   Facts in Review
   Applying Your Skills
   Developing SCANS Workplace Competencies
Student Activity Guide
   A. *Effective Communication*
   B. *How Well Do You Listen?*
   C. *Parts of Business Letters*
   D. *Writing a Business Letter*
   E. *Combining Good and Bad News*
   F. *Writing Memos*
   G. *Telephone Skills*
   H. *Your Speaking Skills*
Teacher's Resource Guide/Binder
   Using Good Listening Skills, transparency master 5-1
   Listening Skills, reproducible master 5-2
   Body Language Charades, reproducible master 5-3
   Speaking Skills, reproducible master 5-4
   Review and Study Guide for Chapter 5,
      reproducible master 5-5
   Chapter 5 Test, reproducible master
Teacher's Resource Binder
   Telephone Etiquette, color transparency CT-5

Introductory Activities

1. Ask students to use three different methods of communicating the following expressions: "Hello!" "I like you" "I'm sad." "I'm happy." "I'm angry." Discuss how the same message can be sent in different ways and still be understood.
2. Ask students to identify the communication skills with which they feel most competent. How do they use those skills to accomplish tasks at school and at their workstations? Ask students to list the communication skills they feel they need to improve. Discuss how the material in this chapter will help them improve those skills.
3. Ask students to list five ways to communicate while working at their training station. Students may share their lists in class and compare experiences.

Instructional Concepts and Student Learning Experiences

Effective Communication

4. Ask each student to give one reason why people often fail to "get the message" as intended. List their reasons for communication failures on the board and discuss.
5. *Effective Communication,* Activity A, SAG. Students are instructed to write a message on a computer, exchange it with a partner, then evaluate their own communication skills. Possible topics for the message include: a paragraph expressing opinions on a recent sporting event, movie, or class activity.
6. Ask students to track the different ways they use listening skills from the time they arise in the morning through class time. On the next day, have students discuss what they gained from each experience.
7. *How Well Do You Listen?* Activity B, SAG. Students are asked to recall recent conversations and evaluate their listening skills.

8. Read a paragraph from a book or newspaper article to the class. Have them practice listening by blocking out everything but the voice of the speaker. Immediately after listening, students should write a brief summary of what they heard. Check summaries to see how well students listened.

9. A day later, do a similar exercise in which you read aloud or give a lecture to the class. Arrange for another teacher or student to come into the classroom to interrupt you with a message or question, after which you then complete your reading or lecture. Ask students to write a brief summary of what you said, or ask them detailed questions. How did the interruption affect their listening?

10. *Using Good Listening Skills,* transparency master 5-1, TRG/B. Test students' listening skills by asking them to remain silent as you list the type of information they should quickly write on the first eight lines of the handout. Pause briefly between each as you list the following categories: *(1) your age, (2) your favorite food, (3) your chosen career, (4) your favorite subject, (5) your name, (6) today's date, (7) your birthday, (8) my name.* Have students exchange papers and grade them as you repeat the categories. Ask students to return the papers to their owners and finish the exercise independently.

11. Divide students into small groups. Have one student play the role of employer and the other students play employees. Drawing upon his or her work experience, the employer gives a list of assignments to the employees. The employees must repeat the instructions and ask questions if they don't understand them. After the exercise, have the class discuss the importance of listening and understanding instructions on the job.

12. *Listening Skills,* reproducible master 5-2, TRG/B. The worksheet focuses on listening do's and don'ts and directs students to write one *don't* for each *do* listed.

13. Ask students to list the ways they use reading skills on the job. Have students discuss how these reading skills can benefit them and their employer and ensure their safety in certain situations.

14. Instruct students to discuss how reading skills lay the groundwork for learning other skills, both personal and job related. For example, people must be able to read an instruction manual in order to learn how to use a computer. Ask students to think of examples from their life.

15. Have students suggest one way in which they could become better readers.

16. Ask students to bring in several pieces of written communication from their training stations. Have students read them out loud and explain the purpose or meaning of each written piece. Ask students to imagine what would happen on the job if they were not able to read the pieces.

17. Ask students to bring in newspaper or magazine articles about careers that interest them. Students may read parts of them out loud in class and answer questions students may have.

18. Ask students to list new words they have learned and now use at their workstations. Ask students to explain how they learned the meanings of the words. Before giving the definitions, students can quiz each other.

Business Letters

19. Discuss with students how writing good business letters can give a favorable impression of a company and its employees.

20. Ask students to list the differences between a personal letter and a business letter. Students should define the types of messages each letter communicates.

21. *Parts of Business Letters,* Activity C, SAG. Students identify the eight standard parts of a business letter.

22. Ask students to provide examples of different types of business letters. Suggest they obtain these from their training station or ask parents for samples from employers. Read several letters to the class. For each example, have students identify the type of business letter. Discuss the message and the purpose of each and critique them according to the guidelines in the chapter.

23. *Writing a Business Letter,* Activity D, SAG. Students are instructed to write a request letter. Make sure all details are provided so the order can be filled.

24. Using the letters in the exercise above, have students identify whether the letters are arranged in block form or modified-block form.

25. *Combining Good and Bad News,* Activity E, SAG. Students are instructed to write a modified-block business letter responding to a complaint letter whose demand—getting money back for a discolored, shrunken sweater—cannot be fulfilled as requested. The reply letter should state that money cannot be returned "because of company policy" and add the following good news: "the sweater may be exchanged for another of the same price." Also, students are asked to prepare the envelope for the reply letter.

26. Discuss with the class the importance of using sincere, courteous language when writing business letters to customers. Locate an example and share it with the class.

Memos

27. Ask students to list the differences between business letters and memos.

28. Have students discuss how memos are effective ways to communicate information and ideas to other employees.
29. *Writing Memos,* Activity F, SAG. Students write a memo to inform employees about an upcoming meeting.
30. Ask students to give examples from their experiences at their training stations on how mistakes in memos could lead to lost sales, failure in manufacturing, or a lost shipment.

Business Reports

31. Have students list the differences between memos and business reports.
32. Ask students to list the differences between formal reports and informal reports.
33. Discuss the importance of writing as a way of communicating information for permanent record. For example, discuss the importance of written instructions or business transactions.

Nonverbal Communication

34. Discuss the importance of nonverbal communication. Ask students why interpreting a coworker's nonverbal messages can be more difficult than interpreting those of a family member.
35. *Body Language Charades,* reproducible master 5-3, TRG/B. Use this activity to illustrate body language as a form of nonverbal communication. Have students work in small groups as they portray various emotional states for the rest of the class to identify.
36. Ask students to list feelings, such as anger, interest, and fear, and to portray them nonverbally by role-playing a job interview.

Speaking Skills

37. Ask each student to give one reason why speaking clearly is a vital skill at home and at work.
38. *Speaking Skills,* reproducible master 5-4, TRG/B. The worksheet focuses on speaking do's and don'ts and directs students to write one *don't* for each *do* listed.
39. Ask students to design a poster illustrating good telephone manners for the workplace.
40. *Telephone Skills,* Activity G, SAG. Students are instructed to work in pairs as they role-play giving and taking telephone messages and filling a telephone message form.
41. Divide the class into pairs and have them role-play a situation in which an employee gets an angry call from a customer who received only part of an order. Discuss how the situation can be handled and the importance of clear communication.

42. *Telephone Etiquette,* color transparency CT-5, TRB. Use this transparency to review basic telephone answering procedures. Discuss why these guidelines are important to an employer.
43. Ask students to call a business to request information. Have students evaluate the employee's telephone manners in regard to clarity of speech, good grammar, pleasant manner, and courtesy. Ask students to prepare a brief report on that experience to share with the class.
44. Ask each student to give a reason why practicing a speech before presenting it is important.
45. Show videos that portray famous public speakers, such as presidents, politicians, business leaders, or actors. Discuss the characteristics that make these people good speakers.
46. Ask students to pretend a tour group is visiting their training station and their supervisor has asked them to explain their job responsibilities to the group. Have students prepare a short speech explaining their job responsibilities.
47. *Your Speaking Skills,* Activity H, SAG. Students are directed to imagine they are news reporters who must prepare a 90-second news report entitled "Work-Based Learning at (name of your school)."
48. Host "expert day," an event in which students prepare speeches about a topic on which they are experts. If possible, videotape the speeches, play them back, and evaluate the presentations with constructive criticism.

Communication Technology

49. Have students describe their first impressions of new communications equipment that they learned to use at their workstations. (Note: Equipment considered "new" to some students may be regarded as "old" by others.)
50. Instruct students to listen to a radio or television announcer, such as a new anchor, and evaluate that person's speaking skills according to the characteristics discussed in the chapter. What lessons can be applied to using technology that carries voice messages?
51. Ask students to play the roles of salespeople and customers based on situations they encounter. (Examples may include greeting customers, answering questions, dealing with a dissatisfied customer.) Have students explain the importance of using good speaking skills in conjunction with appropriate communication technology.
52. Discuss telemarketing as an entry-level job in sales or marketing that requires good telephone skills. Ask students who are interested to research this field and share their findings with the class.

Activities to Enrich Learning

53. Host a speech contest in class. Select a topic that everyone can talk about after doing some research. Allow a set time for each speech. Have judges (other teachers or members of the school's debate team, for example) rate the speeches using criteria such as organization, content, delivery, and effectiveness.
54. Discuss the problem of adult illiteracy. Break the class into groups to discuss the issue, programs that fight illiteracy, and ways people can develop reading skills.
55. Have students write a detailed report describing a typical day at their training station.
56. Ask students to listen to a television newscast, televised speech, or live speech. Have them write a brief summary of what they heard and give an oral report to the class.

Activities to Extend Learning

57. Invite people from different career areas to speak to the class about the importance of good communication on the job. Choose people in varied positions, such as the president of a company, a bank clerk, or a city worker.
58. Take students to hear a speech by the mayor or another local community leader.
59. Invite the president of your school's debate team to speak to the class and give students practical public speaking tips.
60. Invite the local director of your community's reading development program to speak to the class about the advantages of having good reading skills.
61. Invite an administrative assistant to speak to the class and answer questions about formatting business letters and memos.

Answer Key

Text

Facts in Review, page 106

1. to know how to communicate well and where communication breakdowns may occur
2. (List four:) when interrupted, when they think they know what will be said, when they don't agree with what they hear, when they can't hear well, when distracted by the speaker, when they don't understand the words, when their thoughts wander
3. Reading is sounding out the words, while comprehension is understanding them.
4. because they are used to operate computers, which are used in practically all types of jobs

5. return address; date; inside address; salutation; body; complimentary close; signature, printed name, and business title; reference initials
6. request information; send good news or a neutral message; deliver bad news
7. letters that answer requests, grant favors, express appreciation, or make announcements
8. There is an additional step in writing a bad-news letter—to offer a constructive suggestion or alternative.
9. to prevent the reader from forming a bad impression of your company
10. by facial expressions and body movement
11. Speak clearly and distinctly; speak to the listener; use a friendly and courteous tone; use standard English; talk "with" the listener, not "to" the listener.
12. Answer the phone immediately; be pleasant; use the appropriate greeting; speak clearly; do not speak with anything in your mouth.
13. the date, time of call, name of the caller, name of the person who should get the message, the message itself
14. Tell them what you plan to tell them; tell them; then tell them what you told them.
15. to help you know what to say when and how
16. (List four:) computer—to process data; voice mail—to leave messages; cellular phone—to let you call anywhere and anytime; walkie-talkie—to communicate across short distances; headset—to hear related tasks being done by coworkers; teleconferencing—to allow the voice link-up of people in different locations; video conferencing—to allow the voice and video link-up of people in different locations
17. commuting, shift changes, work breaks
18. gossiping, not keeping confidential the comments expressed, misunderstandings with coworkers

Student Activity Guide

Parts of Business Letters, Activity C

A. return address
B. date
C. inside address
D. salutation
E. body
F. complimentary close
G. signature and typed name
H. reference initials

Teacher's Resource Guide/Binder

Using Good Listening Skills, reproducible master 5-1

1. (Students list their age.)
2. (Students list their favorite food.)
3. (Students list their chosen career.)
4. (Students list their favorite subject.)

5. (Students write their name.)
6. (Students write today's date.)
7. (Students write their birthday.)
8. (Students write your name.)
(The remaining answers are student response.)

Review and Study Guide for Chapter 5,
reproducible master 5-5

(Crossword puzzle solution)

Across and down entries:

- 1. C
- 2. BLOCK
- COOSE
- 4. MEMO / 5. T
- EP / O
- 6. READING
- E / E / 7. M
- 8. EIGHT / 9. N / U
- E / 10. DATE / L
- 11. RETURN / U / T
- S / 12. LISTENING
- I / R / T
- O / 13. F / A / A
- 14. NONVERBAL / S
- 16. B O / E A / K
- 17. MODIFIED / D / I
- D S / B / N
- Y E / A / 18. M 19. ESSAGE
- C / M
- K / A
- I
- L

Chapter 5 Test

1. B	12. F
2. D	13. T
3. C	14. F
4. A	15. F
5. H	16. T
6. G	17. T
7. F	18. C
8. E	19. A
9. T	20. B
10. T	21. C
11. F	22. B

23. sender = person who starts the communication process; encoder = sender's mind, which forms a mental image of message being sent; message = something understood by the senses; channel(s) = how the message is delivered; receiver = person who gets the message; decoder = receiver's mind, which forms a mental image of the received message; feedback = a clue about what message was received; noise = anything that interrupts the message

24. Tell them what you plan to tell them; tell them; then tell them what you told them. (*or* identify main points; discuss them; summarize them)

23. Write down the date, time of the call, caller's name, receiver's name, and message. Read the information back to the caller to confirm it.

Reproducible Master 5-1

Using Good Listening Skills

Name_____   **Date** _____   **Period** _____

Your teacher will give you directions on what to write on this paper. Listen carefully so you provide accurate information. Then exchange your paper with a classmate. Use the scale below to score the activity.

1. _____
2. _____
3. _____
4. _____
5. _____
6. _____
7. _____
8. _____

Consider the following rating scale and describe your listening ability:

   All correct = excellent listening skills
   6-7 correct = good listening skills
   4-5 correct = fair listening skills
   1-3 correct = poor listening skills
   0 correct = needs immediate improvement

Score: _____

(Description of your listening ability) _____

_____

_____

List the steps you can take to improve your listening skills. _____

_____

_____

_____

_____

_____

_____

Reproducible Master 5-2

Listening Skills

Name_____ **Date** _____ **Period** _____

Developing good listening skills involves taking steps to listen better. Good listening also involves avoiding certain steps that result in misunderstanding or not hearing a spoken message. The chart below lists several ways to improve listening skills. Follow the example in the first line and write a listening "don't" that relates to each listening "do."

Listening Do's and Don'ts	
Do	**Don't**
Avoid judging the message until you understand it.	**Example:** Tune the message out because you think you know better.
Give full attention to the speaker.	
Concentrate on the message.	
Let the speaker express the thought before responding.	
Listen for main and supporting ideas.	
Summarize what you heard to make sure you got the point.	
Ask questions if the message is unclear.	

Reproducible Master 5-3

Body Language Charades

Cut the groups of words below into strips of three words, fold the strips, and place them in a container. Then have a representative of each team draw a strip from the container and act out the words through nonverbal communication only. Ask the other students to guess the words each team demonstrates and write them down. After each group has finished, discuss how students used body language to communicate messages.

Happy	Bored	Friendly
Sleepy	Tired	Worried
Sad	Suspicious	Surprised
Panicky	Stressed	Interested
Distracted	Upset	Stubborn
Frightened	Disgusted	Nervous
Angry	Joyful	Frustrated

Reproducible Master 5-4

Speaking Skills

Name_____ **Date** _____ **Period** _____

Developing good speaking skills involves taking steps to speak more effectively and deliver better presentations. Good speaking skills also involves avoiding certain steps that result in poor presentations or confusing speeches. The chart below lists several ways to improve speaking skills. Follow the example in the first line and write a speaking "don't" that relates to each speaking "do."

Speaking Do's and Don'ts	
Do	**Don't**
Establish and maintain eye contact.	**Example:** Keep your eyes focused on your notes.
Speak clearly and distinctly.	
Speak with confidence and authority.	
Use a friendly and courteous tone.	
Keep most sentences short.	
Use the active voice.	
Use correct grammar and vocabulary.	

Reproducible Master 5-5

Review and Study Guide for Chapter 5

Name_____   Date _____   Period _____

Fill in the crossword puzzle with the correct terms.

Across

2. A letter in which all parts begin at the left margin is called a _____-form letter.
4. A _____ is an informal written message.
6. Increasing your vocabulary is one way to improve your _____ skills on the job.
8. Most business letters have _____ standard parts.
10. The _____ tells a reader when a letter was written.
11. The _____ address tells a reader where a letter is from.
12. _____ means understanding what is heard.
14. _____ communication is any message that does *not* use written or spoken words.
17. In a _____-block form letter, the paragraphs of the body are indented.
18. Something that is understood by the senses.

Down

1. In a business letter, the complimentary _____ is typed after the main message.
3. The ability to understand.
5. Speak to a listener with a friendly and courteous _____.
7. Doing more than one job at a time.
9. The type of business letter used to answer requests, grant favors, or make announcements is called a _____-message letter.
13. A clue that reveals what message was received.
14. Anything that interrupts a message.
15. The main purpose of a _____-news letter is to tell unfavorable news in a positive way.
16. The _____ of a letter contains the message.
19. A message delivered from one computer to another.

Communicating on the Job

Name_____

Date _____ Period _____ Score _____

Chapter 5 Test

Matching: Match the following terms and identifying phrases.

_____ 1. A letter in which all parts begin at the left margin.

_____ 2. An informal message written in the workplace.

_____ 3. A letter in which some parts begin at the left margin.

_____ 4. The process of conveying a message, thought, or idea.

_____ 5. The ability to understand what is read.

_____ 6. Any message that does *not* use written or spoken words.

_____ 7. Doing more than one job at a time.

_____ 8. Understanding what is heard.

A. communication
B. block form
C. modified block form
D. memo
E. listening
F. multitasking
G. nonverbal communication
H. comprehension

True/False: Circle *T* if the statement is true or *F* if the statement is false.

T F 9. In the world of work, poor communication can cause employers to lose business and money.

T F 10. If a person is *not* listening when a message is sent, communication does *not* take place.

T F 11. To be understood, a speaker should talk *to* the listener rather than *with* the listener.

T F 12. When delivering a speech, it is best to keep one's eyes on the speech instead of the audience.

T F 13. E-mail tends to resemble a memo and is usually very brief.

T F 14. The communications equipment most closely associated with multitasking is a walkie-talkie.

T F 15. Messages left on voice mail systems should be long and detailed.

T F 16. Video conferencing involves two or more people communicating through a video and voice link-up.

T F 17. Many businesses have their own vocabulary terms to describe their products or operations.

Multiple Choice: Choose the best response. Write the letter in the space provided.

_____ 18. When an employee writes a business letter, _____.
A. the style should be informal
B. no copies need to be kept
C. it should be a formal letter written in a style determined by the employee's company
D. it should be written in the style of a personal letter to a friend or relative

(Continued)

© Goodheart-Willcox

Name _____

_____ 19. In a business letter, the salutation is followed by a _____.
     A. colon (:)
     B. period (.)
     C. comma (,)
     D. semicolon (;)

_____ 20. When talking on the phone at work, it is acceptable to _____.
     A. chew gum quietly
     B. speak clearly and say each word distinctly
     C. eat or drink
     D. hang up immediately if it is a wrong number

_____ 21. Which of the following is *not* part of a formal business report?
     A. Cover.
     B. Table of contents.
     C. Complimentary close.
     D. Bibliography.

_____ 22. The words *to, from, date,* and *subject* refer to a _____.
     A. business letter
     B. memo
     C. informal business report
     D. good-news letter

Essay Questions: Provide complete responses to the following questions or statements.

23. Identify and describe the parts of the complete communication process.
24. Describe the three main steps to follow when delivering a speech to an audience.
25. Describe the correct way to take a telephone message.

Math in the Workplace

Objectives

After studying this chapter, students will be able to
- explain how to count change correctly.
- use a calculator properly.
- perform basic mathematical computations.
- read linear measurements and determine area measurements.
- explain how to measure in metric and make conventional conversions.
- explain the value of mean, median, and mode.
- communicate math data accurately in charts and graphs.
- build SCANS competencies in using interpersonal skills, information, and systems.

Teaching Materials

Text, pages 109-123
Terms to Know
Facts in Review
Applying Your Skills
Developing SCANS Workplace Competencies
Student Activity Guide
  A. *Making Change*
  B. *Using a Calculator*
  C. *Fractions, Decimals, and Percentages*
  D. *Taking Measurements*
  E. *Working with Metrics*
  F. *Analyzing Data*
Teacher's Resource Guide/Binder
  Counting Change, reproducible master 6-1
  Math Skills Refresher, reproducible master 6-2
  Review and Study Guide for Chapter 6,
    reproducible master 6-3
  Chapter 6 Test, reproducible master
Teacher's Resource Binder
  How Do You Measure? color transparency CT-6

Introductory Activities

1. Ask students to list the ways they use math every day at home and at school.

2. Instruct students to explain how they presently use math at their workstations. In the future, how will they use math in their chosen careers?

Instructional Concepts and Student Learning Experiences

Making Change

3. Have students demonstrate the proper way to count change to a customer. Use play money and have students refer to the prices of items in a catalog or advertising brochure.
4. *Making Change,* Activity A, SAG. Students write what should be said when counting back change and practice counting change with a partner.
5. Ask students to discuss situations in which they have to count change at their training station. Students should describe the type of cash register they use. If the register tells them how much change to return, have the students demonstrate how they count it back.
6. *Counting Change,* reproducible master 6-1, TRG/B. The worksheet directs students to write the correct way to count change for customers.

Using a Calculator

7. Have students write a brief report of the history of the calculator.
8. *Using A Calculator,* Activity B, SAG. Students use a calculator to solve basic math problems.
9. Ask students to prepare a report in which they compare five different types of calculators. Students should consider cost, size, features, and ease of use. Which kind would best meet their needs?
10. Ask students to list business problems that could result if workers do not check a calculator's display area after making an entry. Ask them to list similar problems that could result in their personal life (for example, making a mistake on balancing their checkbooks).

Using Fractions, Decimals, and Percentages

11. Ask students to list common math mistakes people make in everyday life and at work. Discuss why people make these mistakes and describe their possible consequences.
12. Instruct students to design a poster illustrating the use of basic math skills in the workplace.
13. *Fractions, Decimals, and Percentages,* Activity C, SAG. Students practice how to read fractions and solve math problems involving basic math skills.
14. Ask students to bring an advertising brochure to class that lists prices. Students should figure the sales tax for 10 items.
15. Discuss the relationship of percentages to interest rates, taxes, and discount sales. Ask students to give one example of each instance (for example, bank accounts, credit cards, sales tax, and discount prices).
16. Instruct students to figure out how much they would earn per hour if they received a 2 percent raise, a 5.5 percent raise, or a 12 percent raise.
17. *Math Skills Refresher,* reproducible master 6-2, TRG/B. The worksheet directs students to solve math problems involving basic math skills.

Taking Measurements

18. Ask students to list 10 types of measuring instruments and name the units of measure for each.
19. Students should bring a measuring instrument to class and demonstrate its use.
20. *Taking Measurements,* Activity D, SAG. Students use a ruler to draw lines of specific lengths and practice taking measurements and finding the areas of geometric shapes.
21. Ask students to give a brief oral report on the topic "The Importance of Measuring in My Occupation."

Using the Metric System

22. Ask students to prepare a research report on the history of the metric system.
23. Ask students to list the advantages and disadvantages of the metric system.
24. *How Do You Measure?* color transparency CT-6, TRB. Use the transparency to compare common conventional measurements to metric measurements.
25. Have students form teams and debate the advantages and disadvantages of the United States switching to the metric system.
26. Have students who use the metric system at their training stations describe how they use it.
27. *Working with Metrics,* Activity E, SAG. Students use the conversion table in the text to solve questions involving metrics.

28. Ask students to give examples of how they use the metric system daily.
29. Have students brainstorm reasons why using the metric system is essential for competing in the world market.

Analyzing Data

30. Have students bring to class examples of various tables and charts used in magazines and newspapers. Are some types used more than others? Discuss the values of each type used.
31. *Analyzing Data,* Activity F, SAG. Students analyze figures for the mean, median, and mode and match descriptions of graphs with their chapter terms.

Activities to Enrich Learning

32. Ask students to bring to class products that feature metric measurements. Students may convert the metric measurements into conventional measurements.
33. Ask students to demonstrate how to use different kinds of calculators. Have one student teach another.
34. Ask students to write a research report on using computers and bar code technology when managing inventory.

Activities to Extend Learning

35. Have students interview their training station supervisors about the importance of basic math skills on the job. If possible, have the students tape the interview.
36. Arrange for people with various occupations, such as machinists, bakers, tailors, carpenters, or graphic artists, to demonstrate their special measuring tools and explain the importance of correct measurements in their work.
37. Arrange for a class tour of a manufacturing company that uses the metric system in its manufacturing process. Ask a company representative to speak to the class about the importance of staying competitive in the international marketplace.

Answer Key

Text

Facts in Review, page 122

1. addition, subtraction, multiplication, division
2. It is important for providing customer satisfaction and avoiding embarrassment.
3. by reading the numerator first then the denominator
4. Both are nine-sixteenths.
5. by dividing the denominator into the numerator

6. .08
7. a part of a whole expressed in hundredths; by multiplying 40 by .06
8. square, rectangle, parallelogram
9. Area = pi (3.14) × radius^2
10. distance = inch, feet, yard, miles; weight = ounce, pound; volume = pint, quart, gallon; temperature = Fahrenheit degrees
11. distance = meter; weight = gram; volume = liter; temperature = Celsius degrees
12. 10
13. mean
14. true
15. simple table, bar graph, line graph, circle graph, pictograph

Student Activity Guide

Making Change, Activity A

1. $14.53; "$5.47 and 3 cents (the pennies) equals $5.50...and 50 cents (two quarters) equals $6.00...and 4 dollars (four one-dollar bills) equals $10.00...and 10 dollars (a ten-dollar bill) equals $20."
2. $5.77
   $4.66
   $3.45
   $8.25
   $.84
   $42.55

Using a Calculator, Activity B

1. 178
2. 1,349
3. 1,127.03
4. 9,481
5. 168
6. 889
7. 417.17
8. 2,946
9. 51,858
10. 710,512
11. 223.01
12. 724,808
13. 43
14. 275
15. 42.96
16. 135.11

Fractions, Decimals, and Percentages, Activity C

1. four-tenths
2. five-sixteenths
3. eighteen twenty-sevenths
4. eleven twenty-seconds
5. three-fifths
6. one-hundred twenty-five three-hundredths

7. seventy-five thousandths
8. ninety-five hundredths
9. six-tenths
10. five-thousand six-hundred twenty-one ten-thousandths
11. fifty-five hundredths
12. nine-tenths
13. eighty-eight ten-thousandths
14. six-hundred thirty-four thousandths
15. 0.33
16. 0.8
17. 1.75
18. 1.25
19. 0.5
20. 0.25
21. $1.49
22. $1852.50
23. $375
24. 87,500

Taking Measurements, Activity D

1-5. (Student response.)
6. 3 3/8 inches in length and 2 1/8 inches in width
7. 11 inches in length, 8 1/2 inches in width, 1/2-inch thick
   (8-10 are student response.)
11. 6 1/8 inches in length, 1 5/8 inches in width, (too thin to measure)
12. 206.8 sq. in.
13. 256 sq. in.
14. 24 sq. ft.
15. 50.24 sq. in.

Working with Metrics, Activity E

1. 355 milliliters
2. 88.5 kilometers per hour
3. 91.44 meters
4. 49.94 kilograms
5. 10.6 gallons
6. 86 degrees Fahrenheit
7. 20 by 25 centimeters
8. 5 meters
9. 37.78 degrees Celsius
10. 186.42 miles
11. 157.6 inches
12. 12.04 ounces
13. 0.946 liters
14. 39.37 feet

Analyzing Data, Activity F

1. $55,333.33
2. $42,000 (occurs four times)
3. $60,000
4. $42,000 because it is the mean average of salaries for the newer employees

5. E
6. D
7. B
8. C
9. A

Teacher's Resource Guide/Binder

Counting Change, reproducible master 6-1

1. "Your change is $8.45."
   "$5.00" (Hand back a $5.00 bill.)
   "$6.00, $7.00, $8.00" (Hand back three $1.00 bills.)
   "25 cents" (Hand back a quarter.)
   "35, 45 cents" (Hand back two dimes.)
2. "Your change is $14.02."
   "$10.00" (Hand back a $10.00 bill.)
   "$11.00, $12.00, $13.00, $14.00" (Hand back four
      $1.00 bills.)
   "and 2 cents" (Hand back two pennies.)
3. "Your change is $50.00."
   "$20.00" (Hand back a $20.00 bill.)
   "$30.00, $40.00, $50.00" (Hand back three
      $10.00 bills.)
4. "Your change is $39.75."
   "$10.00, $20.00, $30.00" (Hand back three
      $10.00 bills.)
   "$35.00" (Hand back a $5.00 bill.)
   "$39.00" (Hand back four $1.00 bills.)
   "25, 50, 75 cents" (Hand back three quarters.)
5. "Your change is $75.90."
   "$20.00, $40.00, $60.00" (Hand back three
      $20.00 bills.)
   "$70.00" (Hand back a $10.00 bill.)
   "$75.00" (Hand back a $5.00 bill.)
   "25, 50, 75 cents" (Hand back three quarters.)
   "85, 90 cents" (Hand back a dime and a nickel.)

Math Skills Refresher, reproducible master 6-2

1. 710	8. 63.01
2. 866.5	9. 5/8
3. 505.9	10. 13.50
4. 35,987	11. 67.20
5. 53,298	12. 5
6. 1,123,734	13. $7.12
7. 42	14. A.

Review and Study Guide for Chapter 6,
reproducible master 6-3

1. math
2. multiplication
3. decimals
4. percentages
5. change
6. remainder
7. units
8. parallelogram
9. calculator
10. ruler
11. C
12. G
13. H
14. J
15. A
16. F
17. E
18. I
19. B
20. D

Chapter 6 Test

1. H		13. T
2. F		14. T
3. A		15. F
4. D		16. T
5. C		17. F
6. B		18. T
7. G		19. A
8. E		20. C
9. T		21. B
10. T		22. B
11. T		23. A
12. F		

24. A. Area = base × height
    B. Area = ½ base × height
    C. Area = pi (3.14) × radius^2
25. (List four:) A table arranges data in rows and
    columns. A line graph shows the relationship of
    variables or trends. A bar graph shows com-
    parisons between categories. A circle graph
    shows the relationship of parts to the whole. A
    pictograph shows information with eye-catching
    images.

Reproducible Master 6-1

Counting Change

Name_____   **Date** _____   **Period** _____

In the workplace, counting change accurately is an important math skill. Usually cash registers automatically figure the change for the cashier. For each situation listed below, write down exactly what you would say as you count back the change to a customer. Then practice counting back change with another student.

1. $8.45 _____

_____

_____

_____

2. $14.02 _____

_____

_____

_____

3. $50.00 _____

_____

_____

_____

4. $39. 75 _____

_____

_____

_____

5. $75.90 _____

_____

_____

_____

Reproducible Master 6-2

Math Skills Refresher

Name_____ **Date** _____ **Period** _____

Sharpen your math skills by completing the following math problems in the space provided.

Addition:

1.   298
       + 412

2.   486.8
       + 379.7

Subtraction:

3.   855.5
       − 349.6

4.   40,886
       − 4,889

Multiplication:

5.   987
       × 54

6.   2,874
       × 391

Division:

7.   1470 ÷ 35 = _____

8.   11720.00 ÷ 186 = _____

Fractions:

9.   ¼ + ⅜ = _____

10.   1½ × 9 = _____

Percentages:

11.   21% of 320 = _____

12.   48 is _____ % of 960.

13. What would you have to pay for an $8.90 item with a 20% discount?

Metrics:

14. Lea mailed a package to a friend. The package weighed seven pounds. How many kilograms did the package weigh?
    A. 3.18 kg
    B. 7.5 kg
    C. 2.00 kg
    D. 1.34 kg

Reproducible Master 6-3

Review and Study Guide for Chapter 6

Name_____   Date _____   Period _____

Completion: Fill in the blanks with the correct terms.

1. People use the principles of _____ at work, at home, and at school.

2. _____ is a shortcut to add the same number over and over again.

3. _____ are used in the U.S. money system to separate dollars from cents.

4. Sales taxes are expressed as _____.

5. Workers who take money from customers need to know how to count and make _____ accurately.

6. The amount left over in a division problem is called the _____.

7. In the metric system, _____ increase and decrease in size by tens.

8. The areas of squares, rectangles, and _____ are figured by multiplying length by width.

9. To operate a _____ properly, information and instructions must be entered correctly.

10. A _____ is a basic measuring tool dividing inches into halves, fourths, eighths, and sixteenths.

Matching: Match the following terms and identifying phrases.

_____ 11. The mathematical average of the data.

_____ 12. A system used to measure distance, weight, volume, and temperature.

_____ 13. The number exactly in the middle when the data is listed in ascending or descending order.

_____ 14. A unit used to measure distance in many foreign countries.

_____ 15. The number below or after the line in a fraction.

_____ 16. A unit used to measure volume.

_____ 17. The number above the line in a fraction.

_____ 18. A fraction with a denominator of 10 or multiple of 10.

_____ 19. An instrument used to solve math problems quickly.

_____ 20. A unit used to measure weight or mass.

A. denominator
B. calculator
C. mean
D. gram
E. numerator
F. liter
G. metric
H. median
I. decimal fraction
J. meter

Math in the Workplace

Name_____

Date _____ Period _____ Score _____

Chapter 6 Test

Matching: Match the following terms and identifying phrases.

_____ 1. The answer to a subtraction problem.

_____ 2. The math operation used to find how many times a number is contained in another number.

_____ 3. The process of combining two or more numbers to find a total number.

_____ 4. A shortcut method of adding the same number over and over.

_____ 5. The amount left over in a division problem.

_____ 6. The process of taking away one number from another.

_____ 7. The answer to a division problem.

_____ 8. The answer to a multiplication problem.

A. addition

B. subtraction

C. remainder

D. multiplication

E. product

F. division

G. quotient

H. difference

True/False: Circle *T* if the statement is true or *F* if the statement is false.

T   F   9. The principles of math are used by people at work, at home, and at school every day.

T   F   10. To be successful on and off the job, an employee needs to master basic math skills.

T   F   11. Decimals are used in our money system to separate dollars from cents.

T   F   12. Sales taxes, interest on bank accounts and loans, and discount sales are all expressed as fractions.

T   F   13. The calculator is an instrument that can help students solve math problems quickly.

T   F   14. Workers who handle money on their jobs need to know how to count change accurately.

T   F   15. When the term *average* is used, it generally refers to the median.

T   F   16. On most rulers, inches are divided into halves, fourths, eighths, and sixteenths.

T   F   17. Fractional measurements are never reduced to lowest terms.

T   F   18. Metric units increase and decrease in size by tens.

Multiple Choice: Choose the best response. Write the letter in the space provided.

_____ 19. Tonya mailed a four-pound package to a friend. How many kilograms did the package weigh?
  A. 1.82 kg
  B. 3.5 kg
  C. 18.20 kg
  D. 2.34 kg

(Continued)

Name_____

_____20. Darren bought eight liters of milk. How many gallons of milk did he buy?
    A. 8 gallons
    B. .56 gallons
    C. 2.11 gallons
    D. 4 gallons

_____21. Pete lives five miles from school. How far is that in kilometers?
    A. 100 km
    B. 8.05 km
    C. 15.95 km
    D. 3.55 km

_____22. What is 21 percent of 320?
    A. 60.72
    B. 67.20
    C. 64.20
    D. 6.72

_____23. What is 19 percent of 870?
    A. 165.30
    B. 155.30
    C. 16.53
    D. 130.65

Essay Questions: Provide complete responses to the following questions or statements.

24. Give the formulas for finding the areas of the following geometric shapes:
    A. rectangle
    B. triangle
    C. circle
25. List and describe four basic types of charts.

Computer and Internet Skills

Objectives

After studying this chapter, students will be able to
- describe the role of computers in the home and in the workplace.
- identify the components of a computer system.
- explain various computer applications being used today.
- describe careers related to the computer field.
- build SCANS competencies in using resources, interpersonal skills, information, and technology.

Teaching Materials

Text, pages 125-147
Terms to Know
Facts in Review
Applying Your Skills
Developing SCANS Workplace Competencies
Student Activity Guide
A. *Role of Computers*
B. *Parts of a Computer*
C. *Computer Applications*
D. *Computer Uses*
E. *Computer-Related Careers*
Teacher's Resource Guide/Binder
Using Computers in the World of Work,
reproducible master 7-1
Parts of a Personal Computer, reproducible
master 7-2
The Fun and Games Toy Company, reproducible
master 7-3
Review and Study Guide for Chapter 7,
reproducible master 7-4
Chapter 7 Test, reproducible master
Teacher's Resource Binder
Need to Send a Message? color transparency CT-7

Introductory Activities

1. Ask students to describe daily situations they encounter in which computers are used. Discuss how these computerized operations (such as scanners in grocery stores) have changed the way we live and do business.
2. Poll the class to see how many students have personal computers at home. Students may share how various family members use the computer.
3. Ask students to explain how they learned to use computers. Discuss both the positive and negative aspects of their learning experiences.
4. *Role of Computers,* Activity A, SAG. Students are to list ways computers are used and answer questions about their own use and knowledge of computers.

Instructional Concepts and Student Learning Experiences

Computer Systems

5. Ask students to bring advertisements or catalogs for personal computer equipment to class. Have them read the descriptions of different computer components and explain the functions of each.
6. *Parts of a Computer,* Activity B, SAG. Students are to identify various computer components and answer related questions.
7. Using computer advertisements or catalogs, have students determine the total cost of a basic personal computer system for home use.
8. *Parts of a Personal Computer,* reproducible master 7-2. Students are to identify the parts of a computer shown in the diagram.
9. Instruct students to research different personal computers. In a written report, students should compare the advantages and disadvantages of each system.
10. Have students find out how to properly use and care for disks and hard drives. Suggest talking to a technician at a computer store.
11. Ask students to call or visit a local computer store to inquire about the advantages of computer add-ons, such as scanners and zip drives.
12. Instruct students to write a report comparing and contrasting Microsoft Windows® with Macintosh operating system software.

13. Instruct students to research and compare at least three software programs for each of the following: word processing, desktop publishing, and tele-communications. Students should also compare the prices and features of each program within each category.

Connecting to the Internet

14. Ask students how many of them have access to the Internet at home. Ask how much time they spend online on a daily or weekly basis. Have them describe the Web sites they visit. For example, are the sites related mostly to school, work, or leisure?
15. Poll students on the different online providers to which they subscribe. Have students list the advantages and disadvantages for each provider. Then have a class discussion on what features students think are most important when choosing a provider.
16. Hold a class debate on the pros and cons of online censorship. How effective are parental controls available through providers?
17. *Need to Send a Message?* color transparency CT-7. Use this transparency to discuss the methods of sending messages over computers, such as e-mail, instant messages, and chat rooms. Ask students to give examples of the types of messages that would be most appropriate for each method, as well as pros and cons of each method.

Computer Applications in School

18. Have students list ways to get experience on computers at home, school, and work. Also ask students to research course catalogs from community colleges, technical schools, and colleges at the library. Discuss the content and cost of offered courses.
19. Explain or demonstrate in class different ways computers are used in your school.
20. Instruct students to design a poster illustrating how computers make learning easier.

Computer Applications in the Home

21. Ask students to list all the items in their homes that operate with microprocessors. Students may bring the list to class and briefly explain how each item makes their lives easier.
22. Have students research different home security systems and explain how the computerized operation of such systems can save lives and protect property.
23. Divide the class into two groups to debate the pros and cons of video games on home computers.

24. Ask students to list the kinds of jobs that could be done from a person's home by telecommuting. Discuss the advantages and disadvantages of working from home.

Computer Applications in Business and Commerce

25. Ask students to give oral reports on how they use computers or computerized items at their training stations.
26. Discuss how computers make personal banking easier. Ask students who have checking accounts to give specific examples. If students have ATM cards, have them discuss the advantages and disadvantages of using them.
27. Have students bring in examples of product bar codes. Students may explain how this kind of product labeling benefits the customer and the retail store owner.
28. Have students research and write a brief report on how a fax machine works. Discuss findings in class.
29. Have students write a report on one of the following topics: computers in the IRS, computers in police work, or computers in libraries.
30. *Using Computers in the World of Work,* reproducible master 7-1. Students are to research and list three ways computers are used in given occupations.
31. Have students list how computers are used in the health field. Suggest students interview a family doctor for examples and give a brief oral report to the class.
32. Ask students to find articles in newspapers and magazines about computers in science and technology. Have them share the information with the class in brief oral reports.
33. *Computer Applications,* Activity C, SAG. Students are to complete statements using computer-related terms from the chapter.
34. *Computer Uses,* Activity D, SAG. Students are to answer questions relating to the most common applications of computers used in the workplace today.
35. Have students list at least three occupations in which a worker would use computer-aided drafting or design. Discuss how these computerized functions are changing the worker requirements for these jobs.
36. Divide the class into two groups. One group should prepare a panel report on computer-aided manufacturing and robotics. The second group should prepare a panel report on computer-integrated manufacturing. Each group should discuss advantages and disadvantages as they pertain to the manufacturing process.

37. *The Fun and Games Toy Company,* reproducible master 7-3. Students are to imagine they are the president of a company that is using computers for the first time. Students are to first give hardware and software suggestions for each department. Then students should answer questions employees might have about learning to use computers in their work.

Careers and Computers

38. Have students state their career objectives, then describe how computers are used in their chosen career fields and what programs they will be expected to know.
39. Poll students to see how many are interested in computer-related careers. Students who are interested may prepare oral reports on their specific interests. Have other members of the class participate by preparing a list of questions to ask after each presentation.
40. Using library references or personal interviews, have students report about a typical workday for a computer programmer.
41. Instruct students to write a research report on the topic "Information Technology." Students should focus on the types of careers in this field and the necessary computer skills.
42. *Computer-Related Careers,* Activity E, SAG. Students match computer-related occupations to appropriate job descriptions and answer related questions.

Computers in the Future

43. Have students name some of the most significant recent advances in technology. Ask if the technology is widely available and at what cost. Have the students discuss what effect these advances will have on everyday living.
44. Ask students to consider recent advances in computer technology, such as expanded memory, DVD-ROMS, and rewritable CDs. Then ask students to predict what computer capabilities may be common in five, 10, and 25 years.

Activities to Enrich Learning

45. Have students write an essay describing their first encounter with learning how to use a computer.
46. If a computer is available in class, have students demonstrate how to use a specific software program.
47. Ask students to create their dream computer system, determine its cost, and explain how they would use the system for career advancement or personal use.

Activities to Extend Learning

48. Invite a technical representative from a computer store or company to speak to the class about the care, maintenance, and proper use of computer hardware and software.
49. If your library has a computer lab, arrange for students to take a class in either the Microsoft Windows® or Macintosh operating system software.
50. Invite people from the following professions to speak to the class on how computers and software enhance their jobs: writer or secretary (word processing software); graphic designer (desktop publishing software); health care professional; manager in a manufacturing facility (CAD, CAM, CIM); a television weather reporter; a bank employee; a retail manager or clerk.

Answer Key

Text

Facts in Review, page 146

1. scanner
2. plotter
3. true
4. false
5. (List two:) record keeping, communications, educational uses, entertainment
6. the Internet sites visited, type and quantity of data downloaded, content of e-mail sent and received, amount of time spent on the Internet
7. word-processing software
8. They organize large amounts of numbers and data into special formats and make mathematical computations.
9. (List three:) to create architectural drawings, to create landscape drawings, to design the layout of wiring and circuits in electronic products, to create fashion designs, to grade fashion patterns; to arrange pattern pieces for the least waste in cutting fabric
10. Solid modeling by showing three dimensions can be done on the screen. Objects can be turned and viewed at different angles. The effects of outside influences on a design can be tested.
11. The management function is added so the entire process can be monitored through one computer system.
12. A computer programmer writes instructions for computer software, while a systems analyst plans methods for computerizing business and scientific tasks.

Student Activity Guide

Role of Computers, Activity A

(List three for each:)

Computer applications in school: Students use computers for instructional purposes, accessing library resources, and linking with distant classrooms and worldwide databases through the Internet; teachers use computers for testing and grading; school administrators use computers for record keeping, contacting parents, school maintenance, managing transportation systems, and food services.

Computer applications in the home: Microprocessors are used in entertainment electronics and home appliances; home security systems are used to protect health, safety and security; personal computers are used for entertainment, information, or telecommuting.

Computer applications in business and commerce: Business managers use computers to track profits and losses; office personnel use computers to process data; bank personnel use computers to handle customer accounts; travel agents use computers to make and track reservations; retail business personnel use computers to scan codes, track inventories, and read credit cards; newspapers use computers for all phases of production; writers use computers to prepare and edit articles or manuscripts; telephone communication utilizes computers to connect calls, keep track of calls for billing, find a telephone number, or fax documents. (Answers to remaining questions are student response.)

Parts of a Computer, Activity B

1. A. output device
   B. central processing unit
   C. memory
   D. input device
   E. mouse
2. (Student response.)
3. The two kinds of memory in a computer are Read Only Memory (ROM) and Random Access Memory (RAM). ROM is built into the computer.
4. from 16 to 64 MB of RAM
5. (Student response.)
6. (Student response.)

Computer Applications, Activity C

1. modem
2. hardware
3. cursor
4. Random Access Memory (RAM)
5. spreadsheets
6. computer graphics
7. fax
8. mouse
9. CAD
10. word processing
11. software
12. electronic mail (e-mail)
13. laptop
14. Internet
15. databases

Computer Uses, Activity D

1. They make all word processing functions easier.
2. keyboard, monitor, CPU, disk, CD or tape (storage device), scanner, printer
3. It allows maximum coordination and centralized control of industrial operations.
4. (List three:) access to Web sites, e-mail, online research, network systems
5. (Student response may include automobile manufacturing, welding, painting, and circuit wiring.)
6. (Student response may include weather forecasting, surveying, tracking people and objects, agricultural uses.)
7. (Student response.)
8. personal voice organizer, digital diary
9. (Student response may include multimedia presentations, desktop publishing, and computer graphics.)

Computer-Related Careers, Activity E

1. C
2. F
3. D
4. B
5. G
6. A
7. E
8. (Student response.)
9. (Student response.)
10. (Student response may include meter readers, bank tellers, and travel agents.)

Teacher's Resource Guide/Binder

Parts of a Personal Computer, reproducible master 7-2

1. monitor
2. disk drive
3. keyboard
4. mouse
5. disk
6. printer
7. CPU

Review and Study Guide for Chapter 7,
reproducible master 7-4

```
 I
 N           C
 T       S O F T W A R E
 E           M       O
 R           P       R     R     D
 N           U       D     O     R           L
 D E S K T O P P U B L I S H I N G
 T           E       R     O     V     T     R               C
 C               F   C                 E     R               I
 H A R D W A R E         X   S   O U T P U T   I N P U T  (program at row 9: P R O G R A M)
 D               X   S         O U T P U T   I N P U T
 D               M   S               U   E   C
                 O N L I N E               S
                 D         N
                 D E S I G N
                 M
```

Chapter 7 Test

#	Ans	#	Ans
1.	B	13.	F
2.	G	14.	T
3.	H	15.	T
4.	E	16.	F
5.	A	17.	T
6.	F	18.	F
7.	D	19.	D
8.	C	20.	A
9.	T	21.	C
10.	T	22.	B
11.	F	23.	D
12.	T		

24. (List three. Student response. See pages 143-145 in the text.)
25. (List three. Student response. See pages 134-142.)
26. (List three:) the Internet sites visited, type and quantity of data downloaded, content of e-mail sent and received, amount of time spent on the Internet

Reproducible Master 7-1

Using Computers in the World of Work

Name_____ **Date** _____ **Period** _____

No matter which occupation you choose, you will probably use computers for different functions. For each of the following occupations, research and list three ways computers are used.

Teacher

1. _____

2. _____

3. _____

Police officer

1. _____

2. _____

3. _____

Writer in an advertising agency

1. _____

2. _____

3. _____

Inventory control manager in a warehouse

1. _____

2. _____

3. _____

Nurse

1. _____

2. _____

3. _____

Construction company manager

1. _____

2. _____

3. _____

Restaurant manager

1. _____

2. _____

3. _____

Reproducible Master 7-2

Parts of a Personal Computer

Name_____ **Date** _____ **Period** _____

Identify the computer parts and common accessories shown below, and write the names of the items in the appropriate blank.

1. _____

2. _____

3. _____

4. _____

5. _____

6. _____

7. _____

Reproducible Master 7-3

The Fun and Games Toy Company

Name_____ Date _____ Period _____

Imagine you are the president of the Fun and Games Toy Company. After 20 years in business, you have decided to introduce computers to the employees. Unfortunately, helping employees adjust to using computers won't be fun and games. How will you ever convince Renata in the warehouse that computers can store data better than the tattered notebook she's used for 20 years? How will you deal with your secretary, Dylan, who swears he will never give up his typewriter? How will Don, the graphic designer, react? Will he be willing to design the company's brochures on the computer instead of by hand on his drafting board?

Good communication between you and your employees is the answer to this problem. Begin now by reviewing the operations of each department. Ask your employees to brainstorm ideas about which computer hardware and software will best suit their needs and the company's needs. Also, respond to those employees who have doubts about using computers on the job.

1. **Warehouse operations**—shipping, receiving, tracking inventory

    Hardware and software suggestions:_____

    _____

    _____

    _____

    Renata, the warehouse manager, says, "No computer can replace the notebook method I've used successfully for 20 years."

    Your response is: _____

    _____

    _____

    _____

2. **Production department operations**—manufacturing, assembly of parts, packaging

    Hardware and software suggestions:_____

    _____

    _____

    _____

    Jim, the production engineer, says, "I don't see how a machine can do a person's job."

    Your response is: _____

    _____

    _____

    _____

(Continued)

Name_____

3. **Advertising/catalog department operations**—copywriting, editing, proofreading, graphic design, preparing artwork for printing

Hardware and software suggestions:_____

_____

_____

_____

Don, the graphic designer, says: "Those software programs are too difficult to learn, and I don't have the time."

Your response is: _____

_____

_____

_____

4. **Research and development department operations**—designing new products, making prototypes, testing products for quality

Hardware and software suggestions:_____

_____

_____

_____

Joyce, a game designer, asks, "How can a computer substitute for my creativity?"

Your response is: _____

_____

_____

_____

5. **Accounting department operations**—keeping track of expenditures, receipts, profits, tax information; paying bills; issuing purchase orders; sending invoices

Hardware and software suggestions:_____

_____

_____

_____

Maria, an accountant, says, "Nothing can replace my ledger book. I won't use the computer."

Your response is: _____

_____

_____

_____

(Continued)

Name_____

6. **Secretarial department operations**—typing correspondence, doing mass mailings to customers, responding to customer requests for information, filing, taking and delivering messages

   Hardware and software suggestions:_____

   _____

   _____

   _____

   Dylan, your secretary, says, "I'm never giving up my typewriter. Computers are too difficult to learn."

   Your response is: _____

   _____

   _____

   _____

7. **Security operations**—preventing and detecting internal employee theft, protecting employees from intruders during work hours, giving security clearance to trucks entering and leaving the warehouse, guarding the property from theft at night.

   Hardware and software suggestions:_____

   _____

   _____

   _____

   Ed, the security guard, says: "I'm just not a technical person. Those computers will give me just one more thing to worry about."

   Your response is: _____

   _____

   _____

   _____

Reproducible Master 7-4

Review and Study Guide for Chapter 7

Name_____ **Date** _____ **Period** _____

Across

3. _____ provides instructions for the computer.
8. The use of personal computers to create, edit, and produce documents ready for printing is called _____ _____.
13. A software _____ is a set of instructions designed to guide a computer in performing a specific task.
14. The physical equipment used in computer systems is called _____.
16. A(n) _____ device is part of a computer system that takes information from the computer and provides a workable format for the user.
17. The _____ device is used to enter data into a computer system.
19. When you access the Internet, you are _____.
20. Computer-aided _____ is the use of computers and graphics software to assist a designer in preparing a drawing.

Down

1. The _____ consists of thousands of computer networks around the world joined together.
2. A(n) _____ is an electronic device that processes information according to specific directions.

4. The entering, editing, storing, and printing of words using a computer is called _____ _____.
5. A(n) _____ is a reprogrammable manipulator that moves by computer commands.
6. The hard disk _____ stores the data to operate the computer as well as information entered by the operator.
7. A person who is computer _____ knows how to operate a computer and the basic software programs.
9. The use of computers to create drawings is called computer _____.
10. The letters _____ stand for a system in which all of the computer systems used to produce a product communicate with one another.
11. The use of computers and graphics software in preparing three-dimensional drawings is known by the letters _____.
12. A reproduction of a document or image sent electronically via phone lines.
15. The part of a computer system that controls what is done with the data received is known by the letters _____.
18. A device that sends computer data over telephone lines using sequences of tones is called a(n) _____.

Computer and Internet Skills

Name_____

Date _____   **Period** _____   **Score** _____

Chapter 7 Test

Matching: Match the following terms and identifying phrases.

_____ 1. The computer part that controls what is done with the data received.

_____ 2. Events occurring now that are accessed through the Internet.

_____ 3. A program that tells the computer what to do.

_____ 4. The use of personal computers to create, edit, and produce documents at a quality ready for printing.

_____ 5. The use of computers and graphics software to assist a drafter or designer in preparing a drawing.

_____ 6. Being linked to the Internet.

_____ 7. A device that sends computer data over telephone lines using sequences of tones.

_____ 8. The entering, editing, storing, and printing of words, using a computer.

A. CAD
B. CPU
C. word processing
D. modem
E. desktop publishing.
F. online
G. real-time
H. software

True/False: Circle *T* if the statement is true or *F* if the statement is false.

T   F   9. Students preparing for tomorrow's jobs need to know where computers are being used, how they work, and what functions they serve in the workplace.

T   F   10. Televisions, stereos, and video game systems contain small computers called microprocessors.

T   F   11. Personal computers serve as a source of entertainment only.

T   F   12. Knowing how to use a computer and basic software programs is called computer literacy.

T   F   13. Computers cannot follow programmed instructions without an operator on site.

T   F   14. The keyboard is the most widely used input device for entering data into a computer.

T   F   15. The memory of a computer stores data to be processed.

T   F   16. Computer hardware tells the computer what to do.

T   F   17. Computer technology has made it easier for people to create and electronically send graphic images.

T   F   18. Computer technology offers few career opportunities.

Name_____

Multiple Choice: Choose the best response. Write the letter in the space provided.

_____19. A computer can _____.
   A. perform mathematical calculations
   B. store data for later use
   C. compare and summarize data
   D. All of the above.

_____20. The primary job of a computer systems analyst is _____.
   A. linking computers and planning methods for computerizing tasks
   B. writing applications for computer software
   C. setting controls, loading the equipment, and monitoring the computer operations
   D. repairing computer equipment

_____21. An industrial robot is _____.
   A. a simplified CAD system
   B. a large-scale microprocessor
   C. a reprogrammable manipulator that moves on command from a computer
   D. None of the above.

_____22. A computer user can send e-mail anywhere in the world with _____.
   A. a cursor, mouse, and RAM
   B. a modem and access to the Internet
   C. a rewritable CD
   D. CADD and CIM

_____23. Special computer software that organizes data and/or numbers into rows and columns produces _____.
   A. multimedia programs
   B. desktop publishing
   C. databases
   D. spreadsheets

Essay Questions: Provide complete responses to the following questions or statements.

24. List and describe three careers in the computer field.
25. List and describe three workplace uses of computers.
26. List three aspects of Internet use by employees that may be monitored in the workplace.

8

Looking Good on the Job

Objectives

After studying this chapter, students will be able to

- explain how their health habits, grooming habits, and clothes influence their appearance and the way other people see them.
- explain the guidelines they need to follow to stay physically healthy.
- describe the grooming habits they need to practice to stay neat and clean.
- evaluate their wardrobes and make wise clothing selections for school, work, and other occasions.
- care for clothes properly and follow the clothing care labels.
- build SCANS competencies in using interpersonal skills, information, and systems.

Teaching Materials

Text, pages 149-161
  Terms to Know
  Facts in Review
  Applying Your Skills
  Developing SCANS Workplace Competencies
Student Activity Guide
  A. *Good Health*
  B. *Exercise Regularly*
  C. *Looking Good*
  D. *Appropriate Clothes for the Job*
  E. *Your Wardrobe*
Teacher's Resource Guide/Binder
  Good Grooming and Clothing Care Checklist,
    reproducible master 8-1
  Review and Study Guide for Chapter 8,
    reproducible master 8-2
  Chapter 8 Test, reproducible master
Teacher's Resource Binder
  The Food Guide Pyramid, color transparency CT-8

Introductory Activities

1. Ask students to explain what is meant by the statement "Make a good first impression." Ask them to name situations in which making a good first impression is important.
2. Ask students to list factors that influence their appearance, especially on the job. Have them list favorable and unfavorable factors. Ask volunteers to share their list in class. Discuss with students how health habits, grooming habits, and clothing influence appearance and the way others see them.

Instructional Concepts and Student Learning Experiences

Good Health

3. *Good Health,* Activity A, SAG. Students use a chart to record their food intake for one day. Then they evaluate their eating habits and answer related questions.
4. Ask students to write research reports on the six groups of nutrients and how they function in the body.
5. *The Food Guide Pyramid,* color transparency CT-8, TRB. Use the transparency to illustrate how the food groups in the Pyramid work together to form a balanced diet. Point out the symbols for fat (circle) and sugars (triangle), and note which foods contain the largest concentrations.
6. Have students plan menus for one day (including snacks) for a typical co-op student's school and work schedule using the Food Guide Pyramid. For each menu item, have students name the food group to which it belongs. Ask students to share their menus with the class. Discuss whether or not the menus are well balanced.
7. Ask students to bring to class magazine articles or newspaper ads about weight loss clinics. Discuss the difference between a fad diet and a nutritious eating plan with controlled portions.
8. Have students design a bulletin board illustrating the Dietary Guidelines for Americans. Use the bulletin board to discuss how students can follow these guidelines as they make food choices.
9. Have students make a list of junk food snacks. For each item on their list, have them suggest a

healthful alternative. Make a master copy of the list and distribute it in class.

10. Discuss how students can make healthier food choices at fast food restaurants.

11. Have students describe incidents in which lack of sleep affected their school or work performance. What steps can they take to improve poor sleeping habits?

12. *Exercise Regularly,* Activity B, SAG. Students review an example of a student's exercise plan and answer questions relating to the plan.

13. Ask students to give brief speeches about the benefits of the exercise or sport they enjoy most. Have them demonstrate the exercise or sport, if possible, or show the class the needed equipment.

14. Ask students to research and evaluate the cost, advantages, and disadvantages of joining a health club. Have students present their findings in a class discussion.

Good Grooming

15. Have students imagine they are reporters for a teen magazine. Ask them to write articles about good grooming techniques for young women and men. Suggest they highlight the articles with magazine pictures of well-groomed people. Collect all articles, put them in a binder, and add them to the classroom library.

16. Ask students to list ways to develop good grooming habits. Share the ideas in a class discussion.

17. *Good Grooming and Clothing Care Checklist,* reproducible master 8-1, TRG/B. Students rate their grooming and clothing care habits, then tally their scores. Have students assign 5 points for each check mark under *Always,* 3 points for each check mark under *Sometimes,* and 0 point for each check mark under *Never.*

18. Ask students to write a research report on different skin types and how to care for them. Have them determine their own skin type and prepare a cleansing routine.

19. Ask students to bring in magazine pictures of persons with different hairstyles. Discuss with the class whether or not the styles are acceptable for work.

20. Ask students to describe how they use their hands on the job. Then, have them prepare a care routine, including nail care.

21. Ask students to research the cost of regular manicures. Also, have them locate three places where they could receive a manicure.

22. Ask students to bring in ads for toothpaste and mouthwash or report on television commercials for these products. Discuss with students the social and professional disadvantages of having bad breath and bad teeth.

23. *Looking Good,* Activity C, SAG. Students read a case history and complete a list of grooming tips.

Dressing for the Job

24. Ask students to give brief speeches describing what they wear to work and why. Have them wear or bring their work clothes to class. Discuss how the work clothing differs from school clothing or casual clothing.

25. Discuss clothing fads, fashions, and trends with students. Before the discussion, have students ask their parents or older siblings about fashion trends from earlier years and compare them to the present.

26. Discuss how well-fitted clothes help a person feel more confident and create a good impression.

27. *Appropriate Clothes for the Job,* Activity D, SAG. Students answer questions about what clothes would be appropriate for various types of jobs. Discuss answers in class.

28. Ask students to give reasons why having a clothing budget is important before shopping for clothes.

29. *Your Wardrobe,* Activity E, SAG. Students prepare a wardrobe inventory of all of their school and work clothes, shoes, and accessories. Then, they evaluate their inventory and estimate the cost of needed future purchases.

30. After completing SAG Activity E, ask students to bring their discarded (clean) clothes to class. Donate them to a homeless shelter or charity.

31. Ask students to bring in clothing catalogs or sale flyers. Divide the class into small groups and have them compare the costs of similar clothing items from different companies. Have each group report their findings to the class.

32. Ask students to list the important factors they must evaluate before buying clothes. Have them relate these factors to their specific job and lifestyle.

Caring for Clothes

33. Ask students to investigate the cost of dry cleaning different items of clothing, such as men's suits, women's dresses, etc. How does that cost compare to regular laundry costs?

34. Ask students to design a poster illustrating tips on caring for clothes.

Activities to Enrich Learning

35. Host a class food fair to emphasize healthy foods. Ask students to bring in healthful beverage and snack samples to share. Discuss the nutritional value of each food.

36. Show some popular exercise video in class. Ask students to make notes on the length and intensity

of the workout and determine how realistic the program is for young people.

37. Ask students to write research reports on sleep disorders and how they can affect a person's job performance.

38. Have students develop skits in which one student convinces a drunk friend not to drive.

Activities to Extend Learning

39. Invite a registered dietitian to speak to the class about making healthy food choices and scheduling meals.

40. Take the class on a tour of the local YMCA. Ask an aerobics instructor to discuss the benefits of aerobic exercise.

41. Invite a sports medicine physician to class to discuss guidelines for developing and maintaining an exercise plan.

42. Invite a retail clothing store manager or wardrobe planner to speak to students about choosing and caring for a work-related wardrobe.

43. Invite a manicurist to class to discuss proper hand and nail care.

Answer Key

Text

Facts in Review, page 160

1. your health, grooming habits, and clothes
2. a desire to succeed at the job
3. Eat well-balanced meals, get adequate sleep; exercise regularly.
4. They supply the nutrients needed to stay healthy and grow.
5. The two guidelines are the Food Guide Pyramid and the Dietary Guidelines for Americans. The Food Guide Pyramid organizes food into basic groups to help a person choose various foods to meet daily nutrient needs. The Dietary Guidelines for Americans list recommendations that promote good health.
6. (List three:) to look rested and alert, to feel refreshed, to stay healthier, to be more productive, to give the body time to heal and repair itself
7. (List five:) better heart and blood circulation, greater lung capacity, improved digestion, stronger muscles, muscle flexibility, better coordination, improved posture, weight control, resistance to infectious diseases
8. relieve anger, stress, and depression
9. (List six:) Bathe or shower; use deodorant or antiperspirant; shave cleanly, use proper skin care for your complexion type; shampoo and condition hair; style hair; keep hands and fingernails clean; brush teeth; freshen breath; dress in clean, neat clothes.
10. to learn how to properly clean the garment

Student Activity Guide

Looking Good, Activity C

1. grooming
2. hygiene
3. deodorant, antiperspirant
4. shave
5. shaped
6. cleansing
7. astringent
8. dermatologist
9. moisturizer
10. shampooing, conditioning, styling
11. manicured
12. brush
13. appropriate

Teacher's Resource Guide/Binder

Review and Study Guide for Chapter 8, reproducible master 8-2

1. healthy
2. Nutrients
3. Food Guide Pyramid
4. physical
5. deodorant
6. appropriate
7. grooming
8. label
9. dermatologist
10. cuticle
11. hygiene
12. Dietary Guidelines
13. shampooing
14. impression (or image)
15. stains

Chapter 8 Test

1.	B	9.	T	16.	T
2.	D	10.	F	17.	T
3.	G	11.	T	18.	B
4.	A	12.	F	19.	A
5.	E	13.	T	20.	D
6.	C	14.	F	21.	C
7.	F	15.	F	22.	D
8.	T				

23. Eat a variety of foods; maintain a healthy weight; choose a diet with plenty of vegetables, fruits, and grain products; avoid too much fat, saturated fat, cholesterol, sugar, and sodium; avoid alcohol. The guidelines work together to help people choose healthful foods and to promote good health.

24. (List five:) to do the job well, to withstand wear and tear from the job, to withstand adverse weather conditions, to promote job safety, to promote good health, to make a good impression on customers and the general public, to avoid sending the wrong message to coworkers

25. cleaning the body, shaving, caring for the complexion, caring for hair, keeping hands attractive, caring for teeth and breath, dressing neatly and appropriately

Reproducible Master 8-1

Good Grooming and Clothing Care Checklist

Name_____   **Date** _____   **Period** _____

Read the statements below. Place a check mark in the column that applies to your grooming and clothing care habits. Your teacher will tell you how to add up your score.

Always	**Sometimes**	**Never**	
_____	_____	_____	1. I bathe or shower every day.
_____	_____	_____	2. I use a deodorant or antiperspirant every day.
_____	_____	_____	3. I cleanse my skin regularly with warm soapy water or a cleanser.
_____	_____	_____	4. I shampoo and condition my hair regularly.
_____	_____	_____	5. I have my hair styled regularly.
_____	_____	_____	6. I keep my hands clean and my fingernails clean and manicured.
_____	_____	_____	7. I brush and floss my teeth every day.
_____	_____	_____	8. I wear clothing appropriate for the occasion.
_____	_____	_____	9. I hang up my clothes carefully after wearing them.
_____	_____	_____	10. I open all fastenings before putting on or taking off a garment.
_____	_____	_____	11. I remove spots and stains as soon as they appear.
_____	_____	_____	12. I repair and mend my clothes as needed.
_____	_____	_____	13. I keep my clothes clean and pressed.
_____	_____	_____	14. I keep my shoes brushed and polished.
_____	_____	_____	15. I follow the care and cleaning directions on clothing labels.
_____	_____	_____	16. I fold knitted tops and sweaters and store them in a drawer or on shelves.

Total score: _____

- 60-80 points = good grooming and clothing care habits. Keep up the good work!
- 45-60 points = fair grooming and clothing care habits. Work on improving them.
- less than 45 points = poor grooming and clothing care habits. Start making improvements now.

Reproducible Master 8-2

Review and Study Guide for Chapter 8

Name_____ **Date** _____ **Period** _____

Completion: Fill in the blanks with the correct terms.

1. A person needs to eat balanced meals, exercise, and get adequate sleep in order to stay _____.

2. _____ are chemical substances found in food that help your body function properly.

3. The _____ _____ _____ is a plan that divides foods into basic groups.

4. Walking, participating in team sports, or doing household chores are examples of good _____ activities.

5. Both _____ and antiperspirants help control body odor by interfering with the growth of bacteria.

6. An employee's clothes should be _____ for the job he or she performs.

7. Cleanliness and neatness are the two components of good _____.

8. When shopping for clothes, evaluate the garment's clothing care _____ to determine how the garment should be cleaned.

9. A doctor who specializes in treating skin problems is a(n) _____.

10. For well-groomed hands, the _____ around each fingernail should be pushed back and nails should be filed and shaped.

11. Keeping one's body clean is called _____.

12. The _____ _____ for Americans recommends eating a variety of foods and maintaining a desirable weight.

13. Hair care involves three steps, _____, conditioning, and styling.

14. The clothing worn to work should be appropriate for the job and should present a good _____ of the company to customers and the general public.

15. To care for clothes properly, they should be checked after each wearing for _____, tears, and missing buttons.

Looking Good on the Job

Name_____

Date _____   **Period** _____   **Score** _____

Chapter 8 Test

Matching: Match the following terms and identifying phrases.

_____ 1. A plan that divides foods into basic groups.

_____ 2. Keeping one's body clean.

_____ 3. Rules for obtaining good health.

_____ 4. Chemical substances in foods that nourish your body.

_____ 5. A doctor who specializes in treating skin.

_____ 6. Taking care of yourself and looking your best.

_____ 7. The skin around fingernails.

A. nutrients
B. Food Guide Pyramid
C. grooming
D. hygiene
E. dermatologist
F. cuticle
G. Dietary Guidelines for Americans

True/False: Circle *T* if the statement is true and *F* if the statement is false.

T   F   8. To stay physically healthy, a person needs to eat well-balanced meals, get adequate sleep, and exercise regularly.

T   F   9. No one food contains all the nutrients a person needs to stay healthy.

T   F   10. Skipping meals or eating only one big meal a day promotes good health.

T   F   11. A person's work performance can be affected by *not* getting enough sleep.

T   F   12. Watching television, talking on the phone, and going to a movie are examples of good physical activities.

T   F   13. An employee needs to be clean and neat from head to toe every day on the job.

T   F   14. Employers do *not* have the right to expect employees to dress appropriately for work.

T   F   15. The impressions people form about a company have no relationship to the clothing worn by employees.

T   F   16. Before buying clothes, a person should check the care labels to find out how the garments should be cleaned.

T   F   17. Caring for clothes on a routine basis will keep clothes in good condition and ready to wear.

(Continued)

Name_____

Multiple Choice: Choose the best response. Write the letter in the space provided.

_____18. Employees are dressed right for the job if they wear _____.
     A. their very best clothes
     B. clean clothes that are properly fitted and appropriate of the work that they do
     C. whatever they want to wear
     D. the latest style in clothes

_____19. To decide what is best to wear for work _____.
     A. observe what other people in the department wear to work
     B. look in fashion magazines
     C. learn about the current fads
     D. None of the above.

_____20. Taking care of clothes will help them _____.
     A. look better
     B. last longer
     C. give the wearer an attractive appearance
     D. All of the above.

_____21. Which of the following from the Food Guide Pyramid supplies the fewest nutrients to the diet?
     A. Bread, cereal, rice, and pasta.
     B. Milk, yogurt, and cheese.
     C. Fats, oils, and sweets.
     D. Fruit.

_____22. To have fresh breath, a person should _____.
     A. brush and floss daily
     B. see a dentist regularly
     C. gargle with a mouthwash
     D. All of the above.

Essay Questions: Provide complete responses to the following questions or statements.

23. List and explain the Dietary Guidelines for Americans.
24. List five reasons for wearing appropriate clothes to work.
25. Describe the grooming habits a person should practice to stay neat and clean every day.

Safety on the Job

Objectives

After studying this chapter, students will be able to
- describe the causes of accidents on the job.
- describe how the costs of accidents can affect you, the employer, and the economy.
- identify safety procedures workers can follow to avoid and prevent accidents.
- explain what the Occupational Safety and Health Administration and Environmental Protection Agency do to protect people's health and safety.
- build SCANS competencies in using resources, interpersonal skills, information, and technology.

Teaching Materials

Text, pages 163-181
Terms to Know
Facts in Review
Applying Your Skills
Developing SCANS Workplace Competencies
Student Activity Guide
    A. *Job Safety Procedures*
    B. *Protection from Environmental Hazards*
    C. *Accident Prevention*
    D. *Safety on the Job*
    E. *Safety Committee Presentation*
    F. *Protective Devices and Procedures*
Teacher's Resource Guide/Binder
Job Safety Checklist, reproducible master 9-1
Job Safety: Personal Protection Equipment,
    reproducible master 9-2
Review and Study Guide for Chapter 9,
    reproducible master 9-3
Chapter 9 Test, reproducible master
Teacher's Resource Binder
Safety on the Job, color transparency CT-9

Introductory Activities

1. Ask students if they have ever been the victim of an accident or have seen an accident happen. Have them describe the incident.

2. Ask students to argue or support the statement "Safety is everyone's responsibility on the job." Ask students if this concept is enforced where they work.

Instructional Concepts and Student Learning Experiences

What Causes Accidents?

3. Ask students to list types of accidents that can happen at home or at work. In class, discuss each type of accident and determine the probable cause of each.
4. Ask students to interview a parent about safety conditions on the job. Have students give oral reports to the class.
5. Ask each student to write a case study in which a worker causes an accident. Have students exchange case studies. After each student reads his or her case study aloud, have the class identify the accident cause and describe ways to prevent it.
6. Instruct students to make posters that illustrate office safety guidelines. Display the posters in school offices and work-based learning program classrooms.
7. Ask students to list any environmental hazards they encounter on the job, such as machinery or chemicals. Then have students describe how to work safely with those hazards. Have them give a brief oral report on their findings.
8. Divide the class into small groups. Ask each group to create a poster, song, or skit portraying the effect of an employee's poor safety attitude on the employer and other employees.
9. Ask students to list 15 unsafe practices that may occur at their training stations. Have them also list at least one way to correct each unsafe practice.
10. Have students write three accounts of accidents that have happened at home, at school, or at work. Have students explain the cause of each accident and how each could have been prevented. Share stories in class.

11. Ask students to describe how their emotional states affect them while on the job. Why is it best not to bring personal feelings to work?
12. Ask students to describe how an employee who uses drugs or alcohol on the job affects coworkers and customers.
13. *Job Safety Procedures,* Activity A, SAG. Students are to interview a supervisor who is responsible for job safety procedures and then answer questions about safety.
14. *Protection from Environmental Hazards,* Activity B, SAG. Students complete a matching exercise and answer questions on environmental hazards and proper safety procedures. Have them reanswer the questions at the end of the chapter.
15. *Job Safety Checklist,* reproducible master 9-1, TRG/B. Have students use the checklist to evaluate working conditions at their job sites. Students who are not employed may use the checklist to interview a parent and evaluate conditions at his or her workplace.

Costs of Accidents

16. Ask students to interview their employers to find out why accidents are costly to a company and employees.
17. Have students contact the state labor department to find out about workers' compensation laws. Discuss their findings in class.

Preventing Accidents

18. *Accident Prevention,* Activity C, SAG. Students are to analyze accident prevention practices where they work.
19. Ask students to bring in or show catalog pictures of protective clothing they wear on the job. Students may discuss how the clothing protects them.
20. Have students brainstorm a list of jobs requiring the use of a ladder. For each job listed, ask students to write a safety policy for workers using the ladder.
21. Demonstrate for students how to properly lift heavy objects.
22. Instruct students to create posters illustrating fire prevention.
23. Discuss with students their biggest housekeeping shortcomings at home, school, and work. How can good housekeeping prevent accidents?
24. *Safety on the Job,* color transparency CT-9, TRB. Use the transparency to show different types of safety equipment used on different jobs. Ask students to give other examples.
25. *Job Safety: Personal Protection Equipment,* reproducible master 9-2, TRG/B. Students identify protection equipment required at their jobs and

respond to a question about job safety responsibility. Emphasize that every worker shares this responsibility regardless of whether they are required to wear protective equipment.
26. *Safety on the Job,* Activity D, SAG. Students complete a crossword puzzle using terms related to job safety.
27. Students may research universal precautions and present an oral report on proper procedures.

What to Do When an Accident Occurs

28. Have students role-play calling the fire station or 911 to report a fire.
29. Have students bring in newspaper or magazine articles in which lives were saved because someone was able to administer first aid quickly. Ask students to share any personal experiences.

The Role of Government in Protecting Your Health

30. Instruct students to write a research paper about the history of OSHA.
31. Discuss with students the pros and cons of OSHA.
32. *Safety Committee Presentation,* Activity E, SAG. Students are to work in groups to research a given safety topic and make a presentation to the class on their findings.
33. Ask students to write a research report on the role of the EPA in protecting their health.
34. Ask students to bring in newspaper articles about the EPA and its work with environmental hazards. Discuss in class how these actions affect workers' safety.
35. *Protective Devices and Procedures,* Activity F, SAG. Students are to check appropriate protective devices and procedures they would recommend for each given occupation.

Activities to Enrich Learning

36. Ask students to prepare oral reports on one of the following industrial safety topics: safety training, first aid, personal protective devices, fire prevention, protection from nuclear radiation, protection from hazardous chemicals. Encourage students to enhance reports with posters, diagrams, photos, or demonstrations.
37. Instruct students to research the hours lost each year at their training station because of accidents. Have them share the findings in class.
38. Show a film or videotape about job safety programs or preventing workplace accidents.
39. Instruct students to research the topic of office automation safety and share their findings in class.

Activities to Extend Learning

40. Invite a community safety officer to speak to the class about safety responsibility.
41. Organize a trip to a local fire station. Arrange for the fire chief to speak about fire prevention.
42. Invite an OSHA representative to speak to students about OSHA standards.
43. Involve students in a community cleanup day or establish a cleanup event at your school. Students may make posters to promote the event. Contact the EPA for proper disposal of everyday items considered hazardous waste.
44. Invite a panel of training station employers to discuss job safety, the costs of accidents, and accident prevention.
45. Invite a representative from the National Safety Council to speak to students about safety programs available to employers.

Answer Key

Text

Facts in Review, Page 180

1. lack of knowledge and skills, environmental hazards, poor safety attitudes, unsafe behavior
2. none
3. Seek information on how to perform the job; make sure you have the knowledge and skills to perform the task correctly and safely before you begin.
4. Watch a skilled worker perform the task; have the worker give you a step-by-step lesson; perform the task slowly yourself while the skilled worker watches; practice the task until you do it safely and accurately.
5. (List three. Student response.)
6. (List five:) recklessness, bad temper, lack of consideration, disobedience, carelessness, laziness, fatigue, impatience, emotional state, use of drugs or alcohol
7. time, money
8. Stay healthy; use machines and tools properly; use protective clothing and equipment; follow safety precautions.
9. Use ladders safely; lift properly; prevent fires; and keep work areas neat.
10. oxygen, fuel, heat
11. OSHA, the law, sets job safety and health standards for the workplace. OSHA, the government agency, enforces the law.
12. Read the OSHA poster; follow employer and OSHA safety standards; report any workplace injury; wear the required protective equipment; use safety devices properly; participate in fire drills and other safety practices; report unsafe working conditions and practices.

13. by punishing polluters, researching the effects of pollution, and providing pollution-prevention assistance to states and cities

Student Activity Guide

Protection from Environmental Hazards, Activity B

1. G
2. H
3. F
4. B
5. A
6. C
7. E
8. D

Safety on the Job, Activity D

	¹C		²D		³E								
	O		I		R		⁴C	I	⁵T	A	T	I	⁶O	N
	M		S		G				O				S	
	P		A		O				U		⁷T		H	
	E		B		N				R		R		A	
⁸E	N	V	I	R	O	N	⁹M	E	N	T	A	L	
	S		L		M		S		I		I		
	A		I		I		D		Q		N		
	T		T		C		S		U		I		
	I		Y		S				E		N		
	O								T		G		
¹⁰U	N	I	V		¹¹E	R	S	A	L				
					P								
			¹²F	L	A	M	M	A	B	L	E		

Teacher's Resource Guide/Binder

Review and Study Guide for Chapter 9,
reproducible master 9-3

1. safety
2. environmental hazards
3. ergonomics
4. flammable
5. disability
6. first aid
7. EPA
8. workers' compensation
9. F
10. T
11. T
12. F
13. T
14. F
15. F
16. T
17. T
18. F
19. Stay healthy; use machines and tools properly; wear protective clothing and use protective equipment; follow safety precautions.
20. (Student response. See pages 176-177 of the text.)

Chapter 9 Test

1. B	12. T
2. C	13. F
3. E	14. F
4. G	15. T
5. A	16. T
6. D	17. F
7. F	18. B
8. T	19. A
9. F	20. D
10. T	21. B
11. T	22. C

23. (List four:) environmental hazards, lack of knowledge or skills, poor safety attitudes, and unsafe behavior. (Examples are student response.)
24. sets and enforces job safety standards for workers, makes it mandatory for an employer to provide a safe place to work, inspects workplaces, has training and education programs, issues citations and fines
25. (List three:) Stay healthy; use machines and tools properly; wear protective clothing; use protective equipment; follow safety precautions.

Reproducible Master 9-1

Job Safety Checklist

Name_____   **Date** _____   **Period** _____

How safe are the working conditions at your job site? Use this checklist to evaluate each of the following unsafe acts or conditions where you work. Then place a check mark in the appropriate column. Share the results in class. Discuss ways to correct any safety hazards you found.

Unsafe Acts	Yes	No	Not Applicable
1. Untrained workers using hazardous machinery or tools without supervision			
2. Careless smokers using wastebaskets as ashtrays			
3. Coworkers wiping or cleaning moving machinery			
4. Improper use of ladders			
5. Use of boxes or tables as makeshift ladders			
6. Reckless "playing around" in work area			
7. Lazy, moody, or fatigued coworkers			
8. Coworkers who use drugs or alcohol on the job			
9. Workers failing to wear protective clothing or equipment			
10. Failure to follow proper lifting procedures			
11. Workers lifting too-heavy loads			
12. Workers failing to follow safety rules or safety signs			
13. Warning signs not posted for hazardous materials or conditions			
14. Faulty electrical wiring and/or heating equipment			
15. Careless use of flammable liquids			

(Continued)

Name_____

Unsafe Acts	Yes	No	Not Applicable
16. Unattended open flames in labs or kitchens			
17. Grease buildup under kitchen hoods			
18. Workers not knowing location of fire alarm and fire extinguishers			
19. Spilled liquids not cleaned up immediately			
20. No first aid kit available			
21. Phone numbers for fire department and police not clearly posted			
22. Oily rags stored in paper boxes			
23. Tools stored incorrectly			
24. File or desk drawers left open			
25. Walkways or doorways blocked by boxes or other items			
26. Poor lighting in work areas			
27. Paper cutter blades left exposed.			

(Check one.)

Safety Evaluation: ❏ Excellent ❏ Good ❏ Fair ❏ Poor

List suggestions for making your job site safer.

1. _____
_____

2. _____
_____

3. _____
_____

4. _____
_____

5. _____
_____

Reproducible Master 9-2

Job Safety: Personal Protection Equipment

Name_____   **Date**_____   **Period**_____

If you are required to wear protective equipment on the job, describe it in the space provided. Also, circle any illustration that resembles the item(s) you must wear. Then, review the chart and answer the question below.

(Protective equipment required for the job:)   _____

_____

_____

Equipment	Protects Against
Leather gloves and apron shields	Welding burns
Gloves	Cuts and abrasions
Safety goggles and face shields	Eye injuries
Hard hats and safety shoes	Injuries from falling objects
Rubber gloves, aprons, and face shields	Burns from acids, caustics, and alkalis
Asbestos gloves and leggings	Burns from flames and hot metal
Earplugs and earmuffs	High-frequency sounds
Masks and respirators	Harmful gases

Should workers who are required to wear personal protection equipment assume a greater share of responsibility

for safety in the workplace? _____

_____

Reproducible Master 9-3

Review and Study Guide for Chapter 9

Name_____ **Date** _____ **Period** _____

Completion: Fill in the blanks with the correct terms.

1. Job _____ is the responsibility of every employer and employee.

2. Possible dangers or unsafe conditions in the workplace are known as _____ _____.

3. The science of examining motions and how to perform them properly is _____.

4. _____ materials ignite easily and burn rapidly.

5. A permanent, job-related injury is called a(n) _____.

6. Until proper medical help arrives, a person injured on the job should be given _____ _____.

7. The _____ is a government agency that works to eliminate environmental hazards, such as air and water pollution.

8. _____ _____ is insurance against the loss of income from work-related accidents.

True/False: Circle *T* if the statement is true or *F* if the statement is false.

T   F   9. People who practice safety on the job have poor safety attitudes.

T   F   10. The way people feel on the job influences their attitudes about safety.

T   F   11. Being alert and healthy is the best way for workers to do their job well and safely.

T   F   12. Workers in logging, mining, agriculture, and meat processing are *not* involved in dangerous work.

T   F   13. Most accidents that occur are caused by careless people and unsafe conditions.

T   F   14. Employers are *not* affected when workers are injured on the job because other employees can take the injured workers' places.

T   F   15. If careful, workers can operate any type of machinery without receiving operating instructions or supervision.

T   F   16. A fire needs oxygen, fuel, and heat to start.

T   F   17. Office workers come in contact with unsafe conditions in the workplace.

T   F   18. Employees have no responsibilities under the Occupational Safety and Health Act.

Essay Question: Provide complete responses to the following statements.

19. List three safety procedures workers can follow to help prevent on-the-job accidents.
20. List the six steps of universal precautions.

Safety on the Job

Name_____

Date _____   **Period** _____   **Score** _____

Chapter 9 Test

Matching: Match the following terms and identifying phrases.

_____ 1. Insurance against loss of income from work-related accidents.

_____ 2. Giving an ill or injured person immediate, temporary treatment until proper medical help arrives.

_____ 3. A government agency that works to eliminate environmental hazards, such as air and water pollution.

_____ 4. Materials that ignite easily and burn rapidly.

_____ 5. Possible dangers or unsafe conditions in the workplace.

_____ 6. The science of examining motions and how to perform them properly.

_____ 7. A permanent job-related injury.

A. environmental hazards
B. workers' compensation
C. first aid
D. ergonomics
E. EPA
F. disability
G. flammable

True/False: Circle *T* if the statement is true or *F* if the statement is false.

T   F   8. Many accidents can be prevented when workers are alert, careful, and knowledgeable about their jobs.

T   F   9. Work injuries from job-related accidents do *not* cost employers time and money.

T   F   10. People who don't think and act safely while on the job have poor safety attitudes.

T   F   11. Most accidents that occur are caused by careless people and unsafe conditions.

T   F   12. Knowledge and skill are especially important when working with machinery, equipment, chemicals, and materials.

T   F   13. Office workers do *not* come in contact with unsafe conditions in the workplace.

T   F   14. The way people feel on the job does *not* influence their attitudes about safety.

T   F   15. Being alert and healthy is the best way for workers to do their jobs well and safely.

T   F   16. A person should never operate any type of machinery without receiving proper operating instructions and supervision.

T   F   17. Only employers have certain responsibilities under the Occupational Safety and Health Act.

(Continued)

Name_____

Multiple Choice: Choose the best response. Write the letter in the space provided.

_____18. If employees do *not* know how to operate a machine, they should _____.
  A. pretend they know how
  B. learn as much as possible about the machine before operating it
  C. try to operate it and then ask questions
  D. None of the above.

_____19. Safety rules are developed to _____.
  A. protect employees and others
  B. cause problems for employees
  C. please employers
  D. create more work for employees

_____20. Using ladders safely means _____.
  A. choosing the right ladder for the job
  B. being sure the ladder is in good condition
  C. making sure the ladder is strong enough to support the person using it
  D. All of the above.

_____21. Which of the following statements does *not* apply to the costs of job-related accidents?
  A. A job-related accident could lead to lost time on the job or possible wage loss for an injured worker.
  B. The nation's economy would *not* be affected by a smaller workforce.
  C. Employers are responsible for providing workers' compensation to employees injured on the job.
  D. Consumers may pay higher prices for goods and services because of the high costs of accidents.

_____22. Lack of knowledge and skill on the job can cause _____.
  A. no problems for workers
  B. workers to get promoted
  C. workers to have accidents
  D. None of the above.

Essay Questions: Provide complete responses to the following questions or statements.

23. List the four major causes of accidents on the job. Give an example for each cause.
24. Explain what the Occupational Safety and Health Administration does to protect employees' health and safety.
25. List three safety procedures workers can follow to prevent accidents on the job.

Leadership and Group Dynamics

Objectives

After studying this chapter, students will be able to
- explain the different types of authority leaders possess.
- identify the qualities and abilities of a good leader.
- explain group dynamics and the effect of good leadership.
- describe the school groups and vocational student organizations in which they can participate and develop good leadership skills.
- explain the value of good leadership and group dynamics in the workplace.
- build SCANS competencies in using resources, interpersonal skills, information, and systems.

Teaching Materials

Text, pages 183-193
 Terms to Know
 Facts in Review
 Applying Your Skills
 Developing SCANS Workplace Competencies
Student Activity Guide
 A. *What Makes a Leader?*
 B. *Evaluating Leaders*
 C. *Leadership and Group Dynamics*
 D. *Vocational Student Organizations*
 E. *Leadership and Self-Evaluation*
Teacher's Resource Guide/Binder
 Follow the Leader, reproducible master 10-1
 Review and Study Guide for Chapter 10,
  reproducible master 10-2
 Chapter 10 Test, reproducible master
Teacher's Resource Binder
 What Does It Take to Lead? color transparency
  CT-10A
 Vocational Student Organizations, color
  transparency CT-10B

Introductory Activities

1. Ask each student to define *leadership.* Compare student responses to the definition in the text and discuss in class.

2. Ask students to give examples of people they consider to be leaders. Discuss in class the qualities or abilities that make these people leaders.
3. Discuss with students their own leadership experiences. How did they feel about holding a leadership role?

Instructional Concepts and Student Learning Experiences

Leadership and Authority

4. *What Makes a Leader?* Activity A, SAG. Working independently, students rank 15 leadership qualities. Then, working with three or four classmates, each group rates its top five leadership qualities and reports them to the class.
5. *What Does It Take to Lead?* color transparency CT-10A, TRB. Use the transparency to emphasize the skills and qualities of a good leader.
6. *Evaluating Leaders,* Activity B, SAG. Students distinguish positive leadership qualities from negative qualities, then name impressive leaders and the qualities that make them so.
7. *Follow the Leader,* reproducible master 10-1, TRG/B. Students examine five well-known leaders in terms of their skills and effects on others.
8. Have students role-play each leadership type and rate the effectiveness of each. Students may indicate both positive and negative leadership qualities.
9. Divide the class into two groups to discuss the responsibilities of a good leader and a good follower. Have each group handle one topic and elect a leader to introduce the discussion. Why did group members choose the student as a leader?
10. Make a list of local leaders in your school and community. Have students describe their leadership qualities.
11. Divide the class into several small groups. Have each group list all the qualities that make a leader effective. One person from each group should write the list on the board. Discuss the lists with students and look for similarities.

12. Ask students to role-play the type of leader they would like to be in the workplace.

Dynamics and Groups

13. Have students give examples of environmental factors that fostered positive group dynamics. Also, ask for examples of such factors that fostered negative group dynamics.
14. Hold a class discussion on the responsibilities of a group leader to foster positive group dynamics. What are the responsibilities of the group members?
15. Ask students to speak about the type of group dynamics evident in the student clubs or organizations to which they belong. If students are active members, have them describe their participation and duties.

Leadership and Group Dynamics in School

16. *Leadership and Group Dynamics,* Activity C, SAG. Students evaluate the type of leadership and group dynamics evident in two case studies.
17. *Vocational Student Organizations,* Activity D, SAG. Students give the full names of various student organizations represented by their acronym. They also write a brief description of each organization.
18. *Vocational Student Organizations,* color transparency CT-10B, TRB. Use the transparency to ask students to identify each student organization's logo and purpose.
19. Have any students ever held an office in a student club or organization? Ask them to describe their experiences in class.
20. Have students obtain and read copies of school policies that govern student organizations. Discuss these in class. Ask students to prepare files for future reference as their organizations plan activities.
21. Ask students to design a poster illustrating the leadership skills students can gain from participating in student organizations.
22. Review the vocational organizations at your school. Then, have students create a new mock vocational organization. Students may determine members' responsibilities and leadership qualities.

Leadership and Group Dynamics in the Workplace

23. Ask each student to identify one skill he or she has learned or developed through participation in a school group that can be applied in the workplace. Write responses on the board.

24. *Leadership and Self-Evaluation,* Activity E, SAG. Students rate their leadership skills and answer questions about their past leadership roles.

Activities to Enrich Learning

25. Assign the students to read the biography of a well-known leader and give an oral report to the class.
26. Show films or videos portraying famous world leaders. Ask students to list the leadership qualities they recognize in each.
27. Ask students to prepare a news report about a vocational organization at school that interests them. Have them submit the reports to the student newspaper or local newspaper for publication.
28. Ask students to write a research report on a business or professional organization that relates to their present job or future career.
29. Ask students to write an article for the school newspaper on leadership skills students can gain from participating in student organizations.

Activities to Extend Learning

30. Invite student leaders from various vocational organizations to conduct a panel discussion on the purposes of each organization.
31. Invite a community leader to speak to students about the role of leadership qualities like confidence, enthusiasm, and a positive attitude, and reasons these qualities are important to attain.
32. Invite a business owner or manager to speak to the class about the responsibilities of leadership on the job.

Answer Key

Text

Facts in Review, page 192

1. A team is a small group of people working together for a common purpose. (Examples are student response.)
2. granted by higher authority, may not be deserved, is never questioned by those with less authority, is generally short-lived, is usually less effective than earned authority
3. granted by subordinates, is deserved, may be questioned by subordinates, tends to be long-lasting, is usually more effective than position authority
4. (List five. See Chart 10-3 on page 185.)
5. (List two:) seating arrangement, room temperature, lighting, room size, room location (Students may justify other answers.)
6. (List four:) more self-esteem, better understanding of others and respect for their differences,

improved communication and relationship skills, more able to work easily with people of diverse backgrounds, greater job satisfaction, pride in a job well done
7. (List three:) attends meetings, learns parliamentary procedure, serves on a committee, supports/participates in organization activities, holds an office
8. to reinforce and expand what is learned in the classroom and on the job
9. (List five:) Business Professionals of America; DECA–An Association of Marketing Students; Future Business Leaders of America; National FFA Organization; Family, Career, and Community Leaders of America; Health Occupations Students of America; Technology Student Association; Skills USA-VICA
10. Employers seek employees with the strong leadership and teamwork skills that VSOs help to develop.

Student Activity Guide

Evaluating Leaders, Activity B

1. P	9. P
2. P	10. P
3. N	11. P
4. N	12. P
5. P	13. N
6. P	14. P
7. P	15. N
8. N	

(Answers to remaining questions are student response.)

Leadership and Group Dynamics, Activity C

Case 1: earned authority; Robin is viewed as a knowledgeable and respected member of the department, and others value her opinion. The group dynamics evident include: a spirit of cooperation, positive interaction, and understanding and respect for diversity in the workplace.

Case 2: position authority; Tyrone was officially appointed team leader by the store manager, but has not gained the respect of team members so does not possess earned authority. The group dynamics likely to occur include: group conflict and arguing over unfair schedules and task assignments leading to low morale, resistance to follow orders, possible resignations, and/or complaints to the store manager. (Customers may also receive less than satisfactory treatment as a result of disgruntled or too few store employees.)

Vocational Student Organizations, Activity D

BPA = Business Professionals of America
DECA = DECA–An Association of Marketing Students

FBLA = Future Business Leaders of America
FFA = National FFA Organization
FCCLA = Family, Career, and Community Leaders of America
HOSA = Health Occupations Students of America
TSA = Technology Student Association
VICA = SkillsUSA–VICA
(Remaining chart information is student response.)

Teacher's Resource Guide/Binder

Review and Study Guide for Chapter 10, reproducible master 10-2

A. group
B. earned
C. organization
D. vision
E. position
F. delegate
G. leadership
H. dynamics
1. G
2. F
3. A
4. E
5. H
6. B
7. C
8. D

Chapter 10 Test

1. G	14. F
2. B	15. T
3. I	16. F
4. F	17. T
5. E	18. F
6. C	19. T
7. H	20. T
8. J	21. B
9. A	22. D
10. D	23. C
11. T	24. D
12. T	25. A
13. T	

26. A leader directs the group and motivates individuals to act.
27. (List six. Student response. See pages 184-185 of the text.)
28. The purpose of student organizations is to help members gain leadership experience as they participate in activities and projects. (Examples are student response.) Five types of activities/projects include professional, civic, service, social, and fund-raising.

Reproducible Master 10-1

Follow the Leader

Name_____ **Date** _____ **Period** _____

Listed below are five well-known leaders, past and present. Identify the type of leadership they represent, then evaluate their leadership skills. Also, explain what effect their leadership had on the people who followed them.

1. George Washington, first U.S. president

   A. Type of leadership: _____

   B. Leadership skills: _____

   _____

   C. Effect on followers: _____

   _____

2. Martin Luther King, civil rights leader

   A. Type of leadership: _____

   B. Leadership skills: _____

   _____

   C. Effect on followers: _____

   _____

3. Adolf Hitler, German chancellor and Nazi leader

   A. Type of leadership: _____

   B. Leadership skills: _____

   _____

   C. Effect on followers: _____

   _____

4. Abraham Lincoln, sixteenth U.S. president

   A. Type of leadership: _____

   B. Leadership skills: _____

   _____

   C. Effect on followers: _____

   _____

5. Michael Jordan, basketball all-star

   A. Type of leadership: _____

   B. Leadership skills: _____

   _____

   C. Effect on followers: _____

   _____

Reproducible Master 10-2

Review and Study Guide for Chapter 10

Name_____ **Date** _____ **Period** _____

Completion: Fill in the missing letters of these chapter terms.

A. __ __ o __ __ dynamics

B. __ a __ __ __ __ authority

C. vocational student o __ __ __ n __ z __ __ __ __ n

D. __ __ s __ __ n

E. __ __ s __ __ __ o __ authority

F. d __ __ __ __ a __ __

G. __ __ a __ __ __ s __ __ __

H. __ y __ __ m __ __ __

Matching: Match the chapter terms above with the definitions below.

_____ 1. The capacity to direct a group.

_____ 2. Assigning responsibility or authority to another person.

_____ 3. The interacting forces within a human group.

_____ 4. Gives a person certain powers as defined by the source of the title.

_____ 5. Underlying causes of change or growth.

_____ 6. Power granted by other members of a group.

_____ 7. Organizations that have leadership and teamwork skills as major objectives.

_____ 8. Knowing what's most important to the organization and how to achieve it.

Leadership and Group Dynamics

Name_____

Date _____   **Period** _____   **Score** _____

Chapter 10 Test

Matching: Match the following terms and identifying phrases.

_____ 1. An organization that helps students "preparing for leadership in the world of work."

_____ 2. Power granted by the other members of a group.

_____ 3. An organization for students enrolled in technology education courses.

_____ 4. An organization that prepares students for leadership and careers in the science, business, and technology of agriculture.

_____ 5. The only student organization with the family as its central focus.

_____ 6. Knowing what's important to an organization and how to achieve it.

_____ 7. An organization that helps students succeed as members of the business workforce.

_____ 8. An organization that helps members develop into competent leaders and health care workers.

_____ 9. Something that gives a person certain powers as defined by the source of the title.

_____ 10. The interacting forces within a human group.

A. position authority
B. earned authority
C. vision
D. group dynamics
E. FCCLA
F. National FFA Organization
G. SkillsUSA-VICA
H. BPA
I. TSA
J. HOSA

True/False: Circle *T* if the statement is true or *F* if the statement is false.

T   F   11. People who are leaders in some situations become followers in others.

T   F   12. The best harmony occurs when leaders and followers work together for a common goal.

T   F   13. Position authority tends to be short-lived and may *not* be deserved.

T   F   14. Setting a good example for other group members is *not* the responsibility of the leader.

T   F   15. Leaders are needed in every occupation and at all job levels.

T   F   16. Social activities are *not* an important part of student organizations.

T   F   17. Taking an active role in a student organization can help a person develop as a leader.

T   F   18. DECA is an organization for students enrolled in family and consumer sciences classes.

T   F   19. Future Business Leaders of America (FBLA) helps students explore business careers.

T   F   20. The temperature and seating arrangement in a room are examples of environmental forces that may contribute to group dynamics.

                                      (Continued)

Name_____

Multiple Choice: Choose the best response. Write the letter in the space provided.

_____21. When voting for a club officer, a person should vote for _____.
    A. a friend
    B. the person best qualified for the position
    C. the most popular person
    D. None of the above.

_____22. An active member of an organization can participate by _____.
    A. attending meetings
    B. serving on committees
    C. supporting and/or participating in club activities
    D. All of the above.

_____23. As followers, it is important to _____.
    A. blindly follow the leader
    B. have separate goals from the leader
    C. help the leader plan a course of action and support the course that is set
    D. ignore the leader

_____24. Good leaders are _____.
    A. self-confident and personable
    B. capable of handling responsibility
    C. enthusiastic and knowledgeable
    D. All of the above.

_____25. An example of a service activity is _____.
    A. raising money for a charity
    B. organizing a picnic
    C. taking a field trip
    D. sponsoring an employer-employee banquet

Essay Questions: Provide complete responses to the following questions or statements.

26. Explain the role of a leader in a group situation.
27. List six qualities of a good leader.
28. Explain the purpose of student organizations. Then give examples of the types of student club activities and projects in which students participate.

Participating in Meetings

Objectives

After studying this chapter, students will be able to
- identify reasons for meetings.
- explain the order of business most organizations follow.
- describe the difference between a main motion and a secondary motion.
- explain how to make, amend, and table a motion.
- describe the two methods most groups use to nominate and elect officers.
- build SCANS competencies in using resources, information, and systems.

Teaching Materials

Text, pages 195-205
> *Terms to Know*
> *Facts in Review*
> *Applying Your Skills*
> *Developing SCANS Workplace Competencies*

Student Activity Guide
> A. *Terms Used at Meetings*
> B. *Order of Business*
> C. *Organization Constitutions and Bylaws*
> D. *Conducting a Meeting*

Teacher's Resource Guide/Binder
> *Understanding Parliamentary Procedure,*
> reproducible master 11-1
> *Case Study: The Drama Club Meeting,*
> reproducible master 11-2
> *Review and Study Guide for Chapter 11,*
> reproducible master 11-3
> *Chapter 11 Test,* reproducible master

Teacher's Resource Binder
> *Why Use Parliamentary Procedure?* color
> transparency CT-11A
> *The Order of Business,* color transparency CT-11B

Introductory Activities

1. Bring a copy of *Robert's Rules of Order* to class and pass it around to students. Instruct students to write a brief report on the book's origin.

2. Discuss with students the value of having order and rules for other group activities, such as games and sports.

Instructional Concepts and Student Learning Experiences

Why Have Meetings?

3. Ask students if they have ever been to a meeting where parliamentary procedure was not used. Ask if any of the group's goals were accomplished at the meeting.

4. *Why Use Parliamentary Procedure?* color transparency CT-11A, TRB. Use the transparency to discuss with students reasons to use parliamentary procedure during meetings.

Order of Business

5. Ask students to list reasons it is important to have an order of business for every meeting of an organization.

6. *The Order of Business,* color transparency CT-11B, TRB. Use the transparency to discuss with students the order of business in parliamentary procedure.

7. Divide the class into small groups. Have students examine and discuss the order of business suggested in the text. Students may suggest additions, deletions, or rearrangement of items.

8. Have students role-play in small groups. Each student should assume a part in a simulated business meeting. Students may demonstrate how to properly conduct the order of business.

9. *Terms Used at Meetings,* Activity A, SAG. Students are to match terms used at meetings with their description.

10. *Understanding Parliamentary Procedure,* reproducible master 11-1, TRG/B. Students are to use *Robert's Rules of Order* to find the correct parliamentary procedure terms for given expressions and answer questions on parliamentary procedure.

11. *Order of Business,* Activity B, SAG. Students are to complete an exercise about using parliamentary procedure in meetings.

Motions

12. Divide the class into small groups. Instruct students to make posters depicting a diagram of the correct procedures for making and amending a motion.
13. Ask students to write a report on the importance of parliamentary procedure in relation to making and discussing motions.
14. Have students role-play situations in which a motion is (a) made, (b) amended, and (c) tabled.

Committees

15. Divide the class into three groups. Have Group 1 discuss how committee members are selected. Ask Group 2 to discuss who appoints the members. Have Group 3 discuss the role committees play in an organization. Students may share discussion topics in class.
16. Instruct students to list the responsibilities of a committee chairperson. What qualities should a good committee chairperson have?
17. Have students list the responsibilities of committee members. What qualities should good committee members have?
18. Divide the class into small groups. Assign each group an organization to work with and have students prepare a list of committees for the organization.
19. *Case Study: The Drama Club Meeting,* reproducible master 11-2, TRG/B. Students are to read a case study on a meeting conducted without the use of parliamentary procedure. Students are then to write a description of the meeting in which the club members used parliamentary procedure.

Electing Officers

20. Ask students who belong to clubs or organizations to describe the procedures for nominating and electing officers.
21. Conduct a mock class election to introduce students to the correct way to nominate and elect officers. Discuss the pros and cons of the process.
22. *Organization Constitutions and Bylaws,* Activity C, SAG. Students are to obtain and read a copy of the constitution and bylaws of a school organization to which they belong or might like to join. They are to then find the answers to a list of related questions.
23. *Conducting a Meeting,* Activity D, SAG. Students are to work in groups to participate in a classwide mock meeting using the rules of parliamentary procedure. After the meeting, students will answer given questions.

Activities to Enrich Learning

24. Establish a mock club in your classroom. Students must write a constitution and bylaws, nominate and elect officers, and hold one meeting according to parliamentary procedure.

Activities to Extend Learning

25. Invite a parliamentarian or presiding officer of a local organization, such as the Jaycees or the Rotary, to speak to the class about parliamentary procedure.
26. Take the class to observe a meeting of a club that employs parliamentary procedure.
27. Ask students to attend a group meeting. Have them note how the order of business was conducted and then write a critique of the meeting. Students should critique how much members accomplished during the meeting, members' level of participation, and what students learned from the meeting.

Answer Key

Text

Facts in Review, page 204

1. to develop socialization skills, to conduct the business of the organization
2. to conduct meetings and discuss group business in an orderly way
3. to have the number of members necessary to legally conduct group business
4. (List one of each:) standing committee—membership or program committee; special committee—parade float or spring picnic committee (Student may justify other answers.)
5. Unfinished business includes motions that have been tabled, but new business is an issue discussed for the first time.
6. must be made when no other business is under discussion in the proper order of business and by the member who has the floor; must be seconded by another member; must be stated by the chair; may be discussed; must be handled in a manner acceptable to the group
7. A main motion is an item of business for the group to consider. A secondary motion is made while considering a main motion for the purpose of changing the main motion.
8. secondary motion
9. to postpone a vote until a time when the motion has a better chance of passing; to postpone discussion due to lack of time
10. by accepting nominations from the floor or appointing a committee to nominate a slate of officers

Student Activity Guide

Terms Used at Meetings, Activity A

1. F		9. A	
2. N		10. O	
3. I		11. E	
4. G		12. K	
5. H		13. J	
6. M		14. L	
7. C		15. D	
8. B			

Order of Business, Activity B

(The parts of the meeting are listed in the following order:) 5, 6, 9, 1, 8, 10, 2, 7, 3, 4.

Parliamentary procedure helps groups conduct meetings in an efficient and fair manner.

(Student response.)

Teacher's Resource Guide/Binder

Understanding Parliamentary Procedure, reproducible master 11-1

1. adjourn the meeting
2. announcement
3. majority
4. table the motion
5. minutes
6. motion
7. new business
8. second the motion
9. special committee
10. present the program
11. unfinished business
12. standing committee
13. call to order
14. amend a motion
15. (Student response.)
16. (Student response.)

Review and Study Guide for Chapter 11, reproducible master 11-3

¹T	²A	B	L	E									³P		
	G			⁴A		⁵S	E	C	O	N	D	A	R	Y	
⁶S	E	C	O	N	D		T					R			
N				J		A			⁷F	L	O	O	R		
D		⁸M	O	T	I	O	N		I						
A		U				D			A						
		R				I			M	⁹N	¹⁰E	W			
	¹¹A	M	E	N	¹²D	N			E		L				
	E				E	G	¹³N	O	M	I	N	A	T	E	
¹⁴C					B		T			C					
H	¹⁵M	A	J	O	R	I	T	Y		A		T			
A	¹⁶Q		T				A			R					
¹⁷M	I	N	U	T	E	S	R		¹⁸B	Y	L	A	W	¹⁹S	
R	O													P	
R														E	
U														C	
²⁰M	E	E	T	I	N	G								I	
														A	
														L	

Chapter 11 Test

1. E		13. T	
2. H		14. F	
3. D		15. F	
4. A		16. T	
5. F		17. F	
6. C		18. T	
7. G		19. C	
8. B		20. A	
9. T		21. D	
10. T		22. B	
11. T		23. D	
12. F			

24. (Student response. See 11-2 on page 196 in the text.)
25. (Student response. See pages 199-201 in the text.)
26. Most groups nominate officers from the floor or appoint a committee to nominate a slate (list) of officers.

Reproducible Master 11-1

Understanding Parliamentary Procedure

Name_____   **Date** _____   **Period** _____

Use *Robert's Rules of Order* or the *From School to Work* text to find the correct parliamentary procedure terms for the following expressions. Then answer the questions that follow.

Expression	Parliamentary Procedure Term
1. Let's end the meeting.	
2. Our next meeting will be on Tuesday, March 4, in this room.	
3. Over half the members agree on this matter.	
4. I don't think we should make a decision on that issue at this meeting.	
5. Write down what happened at the meeting.	
6. I want to suggest something.	
7. Let's talk about something new.	
8. I agree with what was just suggested.	
9. These members will be in charge of the holiday party.	
10. I want to introduce the speaker for our meeting.	
11. Let's talk about the same thing we discussed at the last meeting.	
12. These members will be in charge of the finances.	
13. Let's begin the meeting.	
14. I don't think we should have a candy sale for our fund-raising project as Jim suggested. I feel we should have a car wash instead.	

15. Why do you think so many groups use parliamentary procedure? _____

_____

_____

16. What do you think would happen if parliamentary procedure was not followed at a group meeting?_____

_____

Reproducible Master 11-2

Case Study: The Drama Club Meeting

Name_____ **Date** _____ **Period** _____

Read the case study and describe a similar meeting below that uses parliamentary procedure. Then answer the question on the next page.

   It's 7:05 p.m. The monthly meeting of the drama club should have begun five minutes ago. Lee, the president, is becoming upset. The other members are so busy chatting they don't notice him sitting alone at the head of the table. Finally the members sit on opposite sides of the table. They are still chatting and laughing when Lee speaks. "So what are we going to do first tonight?" he asks. "We're supposed to talk about our float for the homecoming parade," says Diane. "Didn't we talk about the float at our last meeting?" Angela asks. Everyone shrugs their shoulders and looks at Lee. "I don't remember," he responds, "but let's talk about it anyway. Anyone have suggestions for a theme?" Juan starts to speak, but Diane interrupts him and says, "I think the theme should be the same as our fall musical, *West Side Story.*" Lee replies, "That's fine with me." Juan starts to speak again, but is drowned out by the cries of the rest of the group as they agree or disagree with Diane's suggestion. Lee finally lets out a shrill whistle to get the group's attention. "Because we can't agree on a float theme, let's go on to our monthly program," he says. The group gives him a blank stare. "What program?" asks Angela. "Were we supposed to do the program this month?" Lee is so exasperated he doesn't notice Juan raise his hand to get his attention. "Hey, I think Juan wants to say something," Diane shouts. Now the group is silent and all eyes are on Juan. He stands up and holds a poster in front of him. "I have an idea for the float and I sketched it out here. Could we talk about it now?" he asks. Lee looks at his watch. "Sorry, Juan, there's no time left," he says. "Let's just go with Diane's idea. Well, I've got to go. See you at next month's meeting." Angela asks, "When is it?" "Oh, I don't know when this room is available again," Lee says. "I'll call all of you and let you know."

(Description of meeting with parliamentary procedure) _____

_____

_____

_____

_____

_____

_____

_____

_____

_____

_____

_____

_____

(Continued)

Name_____

You probably won't be surprised to learn that the drama club was the only club without a float in the homecoming parade. Also, the group disbanded shortly after this meeting. Why was the drama club meeting more productive when members used parliamentary procedure? _____

_____

_____

_____

_____

_____

_____

_____

_____

_____

_____

_____

_____

_____

_____

_____

_____

_____

_____

_____

_____

_____

_____

Reproducible Master 11-3

Review and Study Guide for Chapter 11

Name_____   Date _____   Period _____

Across

1. To _____ a motion means to delay making a decision on it.
5. A(n) _____ motion is one that can be made while a main motion is being considered.
6. To _____ the motion means to get the approval of a motion by another member.
7. The _____ is the right to speak in a meeting without interruption from others.
8. A(n) _____ is a suggestion by a member that a certain action be taken by the group.
9. _____ business includes discussing future group activities or setting dates for activities.
11. To _____ a motion means to change the wording of a motion that has just been made.
13. Most organizations _____ and elect officers once a year.
15. A(n) _____ is at least one more than half of the members present at the meeting.
17. _____ are a written record of the business covered at the meeting.
18. An organization's rules are also known as _____.

20. School organizations hold _____ to conduct the business of the organization and to develop socialization skills.

Down

2. A list of things to be done and discussed at a meeting is called a(n) _____.
3. *Robert's Rules of Order is* a famous book on _____ procedure.
4. To _____ a meeting means to end a meeting.
5. _____ committees, such as membership committees, are the permanent structures of the group.
10. A majority vote is taken by a group to _____ a candidate to office.
12. To _____ a motion is to speak for or against it.
14. The presiding officer at a meeting is the _____.
16. A(n) _____ is the number of members who must be present to legally conduct business at a meeting.
19. A(n) _____ committee is set up for a special purpose or for a short time.

Participating in Meetings

Name_____

Date _____ **Period** _____ **Score** _____

Chapter 11 Test

Matching: Match the following terms and identifying phrases.

_____ 1. A suggestion for group members to consider.

_____ 2. To speak *for* or *against* a motion.

_____ 3. A committee set up for a special purpose or a short time.

_____ 4. To end a meeting.

_____ 5. A suggestion relating to a motion just made.

_____ 6. The permanent committees of a group.

_____ 7. A written record of the business covered at a meeting.

_____ 8. An orderly way of conducting a meeting and discussing group business.

A. adjourn

B. parliamentary procedure

C. standing committees

D. special committee

E. main motion

F. secondary motion

G. minutes

H. debate

True/False: Circle *T* if the statement is true or *F* if the statement is false.

T F 9. When group members know parliamentary procedure, meetings can proceed much more smoothly and productively.

T F 10. The chair is the presiding officer at a meeting.

T F 11. The purpose of the treasurer's report is to inform the officers and members of the group's financial status.

T F 12. Examples of standing committees are a parade float committee, a spring picnic committee, and a banquet committee.

T F 13. Some clubs have their programs first and then their business meetings.

T F 14. Most groups nominate and elect new officers twice a year.

T F 15. Nominations, like motions, must be seconded.

T F 16. Members may still nominate from the floor after the nominating committee has prepared and presented a slate of candidates.

T F 17. After a club member makes a motion, another member can discuss a change to the motion by seconding it.

T F 18. Committees play an important part in every club.

(Continued)

Name_____

Multiple Choice: Choose the best response. Write the letter in the space provided.

_____19. The purpose of parliamentary procedure is to _____.
   A. give the president more power
   B. give the group members more power
   C. help groups conduct meetings in an efficient and fair manner
   D. confuse members with unfamiliar terms

_____20. The number of members who must be present to legally conduct business at a meeting is called a _____.
   A. quorum
   B. majority
   C. motion
   D. debate

_____21. Which of the following are examples of announcements?
   A. "We would like to thank the committee for doing a great job."
   B. "We will serve refreshments in Room A."
   C. "Reba won the regional debate."
   D. All of the above.

_____22. To *second the motion* means _____.
   A. to delay making a decision on a motion
   B. to approve the motion just made
   C. to change the wording of a motion previously made
   D. to speak *for* or *against* a motion

_____23. Part of the job of a committee chairperson is to _____.
   A. explain what the committee is supposed to do
   B. guide the discussion at the committee meeting
   C. prepare a written report and present it at the next chapter meeting
   D. All of the above.

Essay Questions: Provide complete responses to the following questions or statements.

24. List and define four terms used in parliamentary procedure.
25. Explain how to make a motion, amend a motion, and table a motion.
26. Describe the two methods most groups use to nominate and elect officers.

Part 3
Career Planning

12

Learning About Yourself

Objectives

After studying this chapter, students will be able to
- explain how their self-concepts and self-assessments help them understand themselves better.
- describe how personalities may influence life choices.
- list several personality traits and explain how they may influence life choices.
- explain how identifying their values, goals, standards, ethics, and resources can help them understand themselves better.
- build SCANS competencies in using interpersonal skills and information.

Teaching Materials

Text, pages 209-221
Terms to Know
Facts in Review
Applying Your Skills
Developing SCANS Workplace Competencies
Student Activity Guide
   A. *How I See Myself*
   B. *Identifying Personal Interests*
   C. *Identifying Your Personality Traits*
   D. *Matching Traits and Abilities to Jobs*
   E. *Values, Goals, Standards, and Resources*
   F. *A Learning Review*
Teacher's Resource Guide/Binder
Case Study: A Writer's Career Choice,
   reproducible master 12-1
Your Personality and Career Choices,
   reproducible master 12-2
Review and Study Guide for Chapter 12,
   reproducible master 12-3
Chapter 12 Test, reproducible master
Teacher's Resource Binder
Choosing a Career? These Pieces Need to Fit,
   color transparency CT-12

Introductory Activities

1. Explain to students how you decided to become a teacher.

2. Ask students the question, "Who are you?" Ask them to write a one-sentence answer and save it in a notebook.

Instructional Concepts and Student Learning Experiences

Your Self-Concept

3. *Choosing a Career? These Pieces Need to Fit,* color transparency CT-12, TRB. Use the transparency to make students aware of the many aspects that should be considered before they make a career decision.
4. Discuss with students some factors that may cause a person's self-concept to change. Ask for examples.
5. *How I See Myself*, Activity A, SAG. Students make informal self-assessments by providing information about themselves for a chart and answering questions.
6. Ask students to review the sentence in their notebooks written for Item 2. Can students identify any aspects of their self-concept in the answers? (Limit class responses to only those students who wish to volunteer them.)

Making a Self-Assessment

7. Discuss with students the importance of interests in their lives.
8. *Identifying Personal Interests*, Activity B, SAG. Students assess various interests, determine their top five, and answer questions about related careers.
9. Ask students to write an essay on the topic "Interests Are Learned." Students should give examples of how they developed their career or personal interests.
10. Ask students to create a time line on which they trace their interests over the years. How have their experiences affected their interests?
11. Ask students to make a list of what they consider to be their strongest aptitudes. Have them relate each aptitude to a suitable occupation.

12. *Case Study: A Writer's Career Choice,* reproducible master 12-1, TRG/B. Students review a case study to recognize how personal interests and abilities influence career choice.
13. Ask students to create posters or collages depicting their interests. Each student may explain his or her work to the class.
14. Divide the class into two groups. Have one group discuss physical aptitudes that are factors for career success, while the other group discusses mental aptitudes. Ask each group to share their findings with the class.
15. Have students make an appointment with a guidance counselor to take an aptitude test. Compare each student's test results with his or her career choice. Discuss how the tests gives them a better idea of the careers in which they have the best chance for success.
16. Have the class discuss the relationship between interests and aptitudes to a person's abilities. Ask what students can do to improve their abilities.
17. Ask students to select a career that interests them. Have them write a report on the abilities a person needs to be successful in that career.
18. Ask students to list the abilities they have as well as the abilities they would like to have. How might the abilities on both lists help them in a career?

Your Personality Characteristics

19. Ask students to write a definition for the term *personality.* Students may share their definitions in class.
20. *Identifying Your Personality Traits,* Activity C, SAG. Students work with three or four classmates to identify general personality traits. Then students work independently to identify the traits they individually possess plus those they need to develop.
21. Divide the class into groups. Have them list as many undesirable personality traits as they can. Then, have them list ways to improve those traits. Share findings in class.
22. *Your Personality and Career Choices,* reproducible master 12-2, TRG/B. Students examine their personality traits and identify suitable career choices.
23. Have students pretend they are employers. Ask them to write a want ad describing the type of person they want to hire for an office job. Have them do the same for a construction job.
24. *Matching Traits and Abilities to Jobs,* Activity D, SAG. Students work in small groups to determine the personality traits, abilities, and skills needed for various jobs.
25. Have students role-play a worker in a chosen occupation who has desirable personality traits. Students can give monologues or work as teams to present skits.

26. Refer students to the personality traits discussed in the text. Have students write an essay on how each of these personality traits is important for success, especially in their chosen occupation.
27. Discuss the difficulty of establishing new and breaking old habits. How do habits begin? How can a person correct bad habits?

Your Values

28. Discuss with the class the importance of values in relation to the decisions they make, both personal and career oriented.
29. Have the class list examples of good behavior, examples of bad behavior, and the values associated with each. Write answers on the board.
30. Ask students to discuss the influence of aging and maturing on personal values. What values do they possess today that they did not possess 10 years ago?

Your Goals

31. Have students list their long-term goals and short-term goals as they relate to their chosen occupation. Discuss the reasons for having both kinds of goals.
32. Ask students to explain the standards they must meet at their workstation. Have them compare the job's standards to their standards of living.
33. Have students list the human resources they possess that could help them reach goals. Students then may list nonhuman resources that could help them reach their goals. How can identifying these resources help them identify their strengths and weaknesses? How can knowing their strengths and weaknesses help them set realistic personal and career goals?
34. *Values, Goals, Standards, and Resources,* Activity E, SAG. Students list five values and rank them in order of importance. Students also list their career goals and explain how their values, standards, and resources are related.
35. *A Learning Review,* Activity F, SAG. Students match chapter terms with correct definitions and answer questions about concepts presented in the chapter.

Activities to Enrich Learning

36. Once again, ask students the question, "Who are you?" Students may write a one-sentence answer and discuss the answers in class. Then instruct them to read the answer they wrote in their notebooks for Item 2. Discuss with students how their answers have changed.
37. Show an employee training film or video in which personality traits and values are discussed as attributes of good employees.

38. Ask students to interview a parent, teacher, or family friend to find out how that person's interests, aptitudes, and abilities relate to his or her career choice. Have students include the question, "Why did you choose your present occupation?" Have students record their findings in class.

Activities to Extend Learning

39. Invite a school guidance counselor to speak to the class about using an aptitude test to determine career goals.
40. Invite a college placement service representative to speak to the class about personality traits and values that employers look for in different occupations. Ask the speaker to share relevant case histories.

Answer Key

Text

Facts in Review, Page 220

1. (List four:) Believe in your capabilities; believe you can control your life; exercise self-discipline and self-control; use effective communication skills; demonstrate flexibility and integrity.
2. The more a person understands himself or herself, the better prepared he or she is to make decisions about a career and the future.
3. when the person matures
4. Talk to others; take an activities preference inventory.
5. a text designed to help a person determine a preference for working with people, objects, or ideas
6. Aptitudes are natural talents, while abilities are performance skills which may have been learned. (Student response for example.)
7. through hard work and genuine interest
8. because different careers require different personalities
9. Values determine what a person considers important, which guides one's actions.
10. the ethics of the individuals in the group
11. The things you consider important and set goals to achieve are the things for which you will have high standards.
12. time

Student Activity Guide

A Learning Review, Activity F

1. K		8. N	
2. H		9. L	
3. G		10. F	
4. M		11. D	
5. B		12. A	
6. I		13. C	
7. J		14. E	

15. (Student response.)
16. An aptitude is a natural physical and mental talent for learning. An ability is how you perform the task or skill. Abilities are learned through training and practice.
17. (List two:) skills, knowledge, experience, determination, motivation, imagination (Other positive traits are acceptable answers.)
18. GATB, testing, personal work experience

Teacher's Resource Guide/Binder

Case Study: A Writer's Career Choice, reproducible master 12-1

1. first, to be a high school teacher; later, to write
2. Her interest in writing persuaded her to become a writer, a field with more opportunities.
3. good aptitude for communicating ideas clearly in writing, verbal ability, general learning ability, spatial aptitude, form perception, clerical perception, finger dexterity
4. the abilities to edit and proofread; handle direct marketing; write promotion copy; know sales, advertising, and marketing principles; write and design newsletters; increase computer skills and learn graphic design; write feature articles; meet deadlines; working independently and as a team member
5. positive attitude
6. to grow professionally as a writer and change her career path to feature writing
7. (Student response.)
8. (Student response.)

Review and Study Guide for Chapter 12, reproducible master 12-3

1				S	E	L	F				
2				R	E	S	O	U	R	C	E	S
3				H	A	B	I	T			
4			S	H	O	R	T	T	E	R	M
5		L	I	V	I	N	G				
6			A	P	T	I	T	U	D	E	S
7			C	O	N	C	E	P	T		
8			L	O	N	G	T	E	R	M	
9			G	O	A	L	S				
10			A	B	I	L	I	T	I	E	S
11		P	E	R	S	O	N	A	L		
12			H	U	M	A	N				
13			S	T	A	N	D	A	R	D	S
14	B	A	T	T	E	R	Y				
15			N	O	N	H	U	M	A	N	
16		V	A	L	U	E	S				

Chapter 12 Test

1. H	13. T
2. A	14. T
3. B	15. F
4. D	16. T
5. F	17. T
6. G	18. T
7. C	19. C
8. E	20. B
9. T	21. A
10. T	22. C
11. F	23. D
12. F	

24. Self-concept is shaped by self-esteem because a person's own mental image is dependent on his or her feeling of self-worth, or the lack of it.
25. (Student response. Responses may include:) It can help a person make better choices, set better goals, and choose a satisfying career.
26. Short-term goals are goals a person wants to achieve in a short period of time, such as in a day, week, or month. Long-term goals are those that may take several months or years to achieve. (Examples are student response.)

Reproducible Master 12-1

Case Study: A Writer's Career Choice

Name_____   Date _____   Period _____

Read the following interview about Pauline Everett, who chose writing as a career. Then answer the questions that follow.

Why did you decide to become a writer?

"I didn't! I started my career as a high school teacher, but my interests changed. I found that my aptitude for clearly communicating ideas in writing would open up more career opportunities for me. After one year of teaching, I moved to Chicago where I pursued a job in a publishing company. At the publishing company, I learned professional editing and proofreading skills. I also learned about the direct marketing field because the company marketed its books that way. I researched that field and found it offered many opportunities, especially for a writer.

"My first writing job was for a company that marketed collectible items by direct mail. Then, I moved on to work for a small advertising agency. Now I am employed as a promotion writer for a trade show company. Promotion copywriting is a field that offers many opportunities for writers. However, you also need to understand sales, advertising, and marketing principles.

"My other experience as a writer has come from the editorial side. I have had a few feature articles published in national consumer magazines. I also write a community column twice weekly for a suburban Chicago newspaper. To make myself more marketable, I learned how to design newsletters with computer desktop publishing software. For that, you do need to know the basics of graphic design. As a writer, you will probably work with graphic designers who can tell you what you need to know. In addition, I have done a few projects for an educational publisher."

What is your present job?

"Currently, I work as a promotion writer for a trade show company. I work as a team member with a promotion manager and a graphic designer. I also interact with trade show managers and advertising account executives. Deadlines are crucial. Meeting them is an absolute must in order to be a success in this field. You also have to be willing to accept constructive criticism gracefully and not take it personally. A writer's copy is always reviewed by several other people and often changed. Some of these people have no professional writing experience, but they may try to rewrite your work.

"Overall, my job is fast-paced. I have many deadlines to meet. I deal with many people to get information needed to write the brochures, ads, and press releases. I also have to be creative in my writing as well as believe in the products."

What do you like most about your job?

"I like the creative process of developing an idea. First, I work with my team coworkers to come up with a creative theme for a promotion campaign. Second, we each do our part to create it. Eventually, we see the final printed work. Getting good results from the campaign gives us satisfaction, too.

"I also like working with language. I like the challenge of creating concise, clear copy that meets the goals of the promotion campaign.

"My freelance projects, which I do at home, give me even more satisfaction. It's a great feeling to see your article and name in a national magazine. Also, you are your own boss with these projects. That can be a pleasant change of pace after answering to managers all day."

(Continued)

Name_____

What are your present career goals?

"I have been working on the same trade shows for over five years, and my writing assignments haven't changed much during that time. My career goal is to find a full-time writing position as a feature writer for a magazine. I find I get more personal satisfaction from writing features. Also, I plan to continue my freelance writing projects. Although they take up much of my free time, these projects help me grow as a professional writer. They also expand my opportunities for employment."

1. What were Pauline's career interests? _____

_____

_____

_____

2. How did her interests influence her career choice? _____

_____

_____

_____

3. What are her aptitudes as a writer? _____

_____

_____

_____

4. What abilities has she developed in her writing career? _____

_____

_____

_____

5. What attitude does she express about her present job? _____

_____

_____

_____

6. What future career goals does she have? _____

_____

_____

_____

7. What other career choices are available to writers? Use library resource to find alternatives and list them below.

_____

_____

_____

8. Would you enjoy a career as a writer? Explain. _____

_____

_____

_____

Reproducible Master 12-2

Your Personality and Career Choices

Name_____   **Date** _____   **Period** _____

Use the following list of personality traits to answer the questions below.

cooperative	talkative	tolerant
agreeable	loyal	critical
stubborn	honest	jealous
self-disciplined	dishonest	capable
friendly	irritable	lazy
shy	pleasant	moody
intelligent	enthusiastic	nervous
thoughtful	outgoing	patient
impulsive	quiet	cruel
energetic	confident	kind
ambitious	happy	religious
generous	sad	polite
greedy	funny	respectful
aggressive	witty	sarcastic
assertive	boring	helpful
independent	dependable	selfish
dependent	unreliable	dedicated

1. Which personality traits best describe you?_____

_____

_____

2. Which personality traits would you like to possess? _____

_____

_____

3. List ways to develop your desired personality traits. _____

_____

_____

_____

4. Explain how your personality traits may influence your career choices. _____

_____

_____

_____

5. Considering your personality traits, what careers do you think would suit you best? _____

_____

_____

6. Based on your personality traits, what careers do you think you should avoid? _____

_____

_____

Reproducible Master 12-3

Review and Study Guide for Chapter 12

Name＿＿＿＿＿＿＿＿＿＿＿＿＿＿＿＿＿＿＿＿＿＿＿＿＿ **Date** ＿＿＿＿＿＿＿＿＿＿ **Period** ＿＿＿＿＿＿

Completion: Fill in the word puzzle using the terms from the chapter.

1	L
2	E
3	A
4	R
5	N
6	I
7	N
8	G
9	A
10	B
11	O
12	U
13	T
14	Y
15	O
16	U

1. ＿＿＿＿-assessment is the process of taking stock of your interests, aptitudes, and abilities.

2. All the things people have or can use to help them reach their goals.

3. Something done the same way every time.

4. The goals you want to reach tomorrow, next week, or within a few months. (two words)

5. A person's standard of ＿＿＿＿ refers to the goods and services considered essential for living.

6. A person's natural physical and mental talents for learning.

7. Your self-＿＿＿＿ is your mental image of yourself.

8. The goals that may take several months or years to achieve. (two words)

9. That which people want to obtain or achieve.

10. A person's physical and mental powers to perform a task or skill well.

11. Type of characteristics that makes a person distinct and separate from everyone else.

12. The resources you have within yourself, such as skills, knowledge, and experience.

13. Accepted levels of achievement.

14. The General Aptitude Test ＿＿＿＿ is a series of tests to measure nine aptitudes.

15. The material resources you have or can use to achieve goals, such as money, tools, or clothes.

16. The principles and beliefs people consider important.

Learning About Yourself

Name_____

Date _____   Period _____   Score _____

Chapter 12 Test

Matching: Match the following terms and identifying phrases.

_____ 1. All the things people have or can use to help reach their goals.

_____ 2. The mental image a person has of himself or herself.

_____ 3. A person's natural physical and mental talents for learning.

_____ 4. The principles and beliefs a person considers important.

_____ 5. Whatever a person wants to obtain or achieve in a lifetime.

_____ 6. Accepted levels of achievement.

_____ 7. A person's physical and mental powers to perform a task or skill well.

_____ 8. Doing something the same way every time.

A. self-concept
B. aptitude
C. ability
D. values
E. habit
F. goals
G. standards
H. resources

True/False: Circle *T* if the statement is true or *F* if the statement is false.

T   F   9. Interests tend to change as people mature, meet new people, and participate in new activities.

T   F   10. Having a work experience or observing others on the job can help students understand what a job involves.

T   F   11. Skills, experience, and knowledge are examples of nonhuman resources.

T   F   12. A person is born with certain abilities but must develop aptitudes.

T   F   13. Different careers require different personality traits.

T   F   14. Self-assessment is the process of taking stock of one's interests, aptitudes, and abilities.

T   F   15. A person cannot change or improve his or her personality.

T   F   16. Like values, goals influence and shape decisions that a person makes.

T   F   17. Every individual has a personal standard of living.

T   F   18. Identifying resources helps a person recognize his or her strengths and weaknesses.

Multiple Choice: Choose the best response. Write the letter in the space provided.

_____ 19. It is best to choose a career by _____.
   A. following the family interests
   B. taking tests
   C. matching your interests and abilities
   D. taking suggestions from friends

(Continued)

Name_____

_____20. The GATB series of tests measures _____.
    A. abilities
    B. aptitudes
    C. attitudes
    D. None of the above.

_____21. To develop a sense of direction in life, it is most important to know your _____.
    A. values
    B. resources
    C. abilities
    D. personality

_____22. A high school student says, "I want to become a teacher." This is an example of a _____.
    A. short-term goal
    B. standard
    C. long-term goal
    D. value

_____23. An example of a human resource is _____.
    A. money
    B. clothes
    C. tools
    D. experience

Essay Questions: Provide complete responses to the following questions or statements.

24. What is the relationship between self-concept and self-esteem?
25. Explain how identifying your values, goals, standards, and resources can help a person understand himself or herself more fully.
26. Define and give one example of a short-term goal and a long-term goal.

Learning About Careers

Objectives

After studying this chapter, students will be able to
- identify myths regarding employment in nontraditional jobs.
- discuss the many different types of career clusters.
- describe the wide range of jobs within career clusters.
- identify careers and occupations that interest them.
- list occupations with the greatest number of job openings and their educational requirements.
- build SCANS competencies in using resources, information, systems, and technology.

Teaching Materials

Text, pages 223-261
Terms to Know
Facts in Review
Applying Your Skills
Developing SCANS Workplace Competencies
Student Activity Guide
    A. *Career Clues and Clusters*
    B. *Occupation Interview*
    C. *Occupational Interests*
Teacher's Resource Guide/Binder
    Fifteen Career Clusters, transparency master 13-1
    Retail Sales Workers, reproducible master 13-2
    Review and Study Guide for Chapter 13,
       reproducible master 13-3
    Chapter 13 Test, reproducible master
Teacher's Resource Binder
    Check Out Career Clusters, color transparency
       CT-13

Introductory Activities

1. Ask students to list all the workers with whom they have contact on a typical day. Have them also list the workers with whom they have contact when they need special services. Discuss how these workers represent only a handful of the 20,000 different job titles that exist. Also discuss why being aware of the many careers available is important.

2. Introduce career clusters by saying the name of each cluster aloud and asking students to list at least three words that immediately come to mind. The words can be job titles, educational or training requirements, or places of employment within the cluster. Discuss responses with students.

Instructional Concepts and Student Learning Experiences

Traditional and Nontraditional Careers

3. *Fifteen Career Clusters,* transparency master 13-1, TRG/B. Use the transparency to acquaint students with the basic categories into which all jobs can be classified.
4. Have students list and discuss all the career clusters represented by student workers in the class.
5. Expand the discussion for Item 4 to include the career clusters represented by students' parents.
6. *Check Out Career Clusters,* color transparency CT-13, TRB. Use the transparency to illustrate an important fact: many different types of jobs exist within each of the career clusters. The transparency shows some of the many jobs available in the *construction* career cluster.
7. Discuss with students the reasons jobs and careers are classified into clusters.
8. *Career Clues and Clusters,* Activity A, SAG. Students identify various career clusters by reading identifying clues.
9. Have students list occupations that fall within a single cluster and, for each, indicate the typical places of employment.
10. *Retail Sales Workers,* reproducible master 13-2, TRG/B. Students read *Occupational Outlook Handbook* information on retail sales workers, then answer questions about the occupation.
11. Ask students to bring the want-ad section of a local newspaper to class. Students may circle or cut out two or three jobs for each cluster discussed in the chapter. Have each student read one ad to the class, name the cluster to which it belongs, and discuss the qualifications listed.

12. Instruct students to list as many examples of occupations as possible within a single career cluster for 10 minutes. (Textbooks should be closed.) Afterwards, compare the students' lists to the text.
13. Divide the class into four groups and instruct each group to choose five jobs that involve working with the following: people (Group 1), things (Group 2), words (Group 3), and numbers (Group 4). Have each group give an oral report, perform a skit, or create posters to describe each of their job choices.

Job Market Trends

14. Ask students to review Charts 13-2, 13-3, and 13-4 on pages 256-258 in the text. Have each student identify the one job on each chart that interests him or her most and report those selections to the class.
15. Working in small groups, students may select an occupation and list its job characteristics. Each group prepares a presentation on each job and gives a brief quiz after the presentation.
16. Have students list several ways that career selection relates to a person's goals. Have students share their responses and discuss them in class.
17. *Occupation Interview*, Activity B, SAG. Students choose a nontraditional occupation and select someone employed in that occupation to interview. Students record the worker's responses in their worksheets and discuss their interview experiences in class. (If workers in nontraditional careers are unavailable, have students interview workers in any occupation.)

Future Occupations

18. Have students investigate how it is possible for people to transfer their job skills from one occupation to another. Discuss their findings in class.
19. Ask students to bring in newspaper or magazine articles that report advancements in technology. Discuss in class how these advancements cause occupational opportunities to constantly change.
20. *Occupational Interests*, Activity C, SAG. Students name and describe two occupations for each of the career clusters, then choose their top five to research. Students are asked to explain why the five chosen careers appeal to them.

Activities to Enrich Learning

21. Instruct students to write a case history of an imaginary person who is pursuing a specific occupation (chosen by the students). Have students describe the job cluster into which this occupation falls and other job characteristics the fictional person must consider.

22. Have students write letters to the human resources director of an employer in an occupation that interests them. In the letters, they should ask for general information about the job functions of the employees, job requirements, and other characteristics of the occupation.

Activities to Extend Learning

23. Invite a career counselor to talk to the class about opportunities in new or emerging occupations. Have students prepare interview questions in advance.
24. Have students vote on what they think are the three most interesting career clusters. Arrange for students to tour local businesses and observe people working within those clusters.
25. Show a videotape presenting information on career exploration or occupational trends.

Answer Key

Text

Facts in Review, page 260

1. (List two. See Chart 13-1 on page 225.)
2. by common skills and interests
3. (List six. See page 236.)
4. skill in communicating
5. operate, maintain, and repair communications equipment; print publications; transmit telephone, computer and satellite signals
6. two to three years generally, but four years if a bachelor's degree is obtained
7. improving the quality of individual and family life
8. may need to work hours when other people are off
9. They must work together as a team for the organization to succeed.
10. work with bodies of water and their resources
11. the buying, selling, promoting, and delivering of goods and services
12. He or she must perform the services well and deal effectively with customers.
13. (List six. See page 252.)
14. (List six. See Charts 13-2, 13-3, and 13-4 on pages 256-258.)

Student Activity Guide

Career Clues and Clusters, Activity A

1. business and office
2. agriculture
3. construction
4. health
5. family and consumer sciences
6. fine arts and humanities
7. construction

8. personal services
9. hospitality and recreation
10. agriculture
11. communications and media
12. transportation
13. manufacturing
14. fine arts and humanities
15. family and consumer sciences
16. marine science
17. marketing and distribution
18. transportation
19. natural resources and environmental control
20. public services
21. natural resources and environmental control
22. family and consumer sciences
23. agriculture
24. business and office
25. communications and media

Teacher's Resource Guide/Binder

Retail Sales Workers, reproducible master 13-2

1. to help customers find what they're looking for and interest them into buying it
2. (List three:) making out sales checks; receiving cash, check, and charge payments; bagging/packaging purchases; giving change and receipts; handling returns and merchandise exchanges; opening or closing the register
3. because the retail industry is very competitive and customers form their first impression of a store by its sales force
4. clean, comfortable surroundings; the need to stand for long periods and stay confined to a particular area; evening and weekend hours; sometimes door-to-door work
5. true
6. repetitive work, demanding customers
7. no formal education but a high school diploma is preferred, a desire to help customers, the tact and patience to deal with difficult customers
8. Experienced workers can move to positions offering greater responsibility and earnings, either with their employer or another.
9. Growth in jobs is expected to increase as fast as the average for all occupations through the year 2006.
10. minimum wage
11. an employee discount in practically all establishments; vacation, sick leave, health and life insurance, and pension plans in large establishments
12. (List five:) manufacturers' and wholesale trade sales representatives, service sales representatives, securities and financial services sales representatives, counter and rental clerks, real estate sales agents, purchasers and buyers, insurance agents and brokers, cashiers

13. personnel offices of retail stores, state merchants' associations, National Retail Federation, International Mass Retail Association, United Food and Commercial Workers International Union, National Automobile Dealers Association
14. marketing and distribution

Review and Study Guide for Chapter 13, reproducible master 13-3

Chapter 13 Test

1. H
2. A
3. C
4. D
5. E
6. B
7. F
8. G
9. I
10. T
11. T
12. T
13. F
14. T
15. T
16. T
17. T
18. T
19. F
20. C
21. D
22. A
23. B
24. B

25. Myths place artificial limitations on career choices and sometimes prevent workers from obtaining jobs ideal for them, but which are considered nontraditional.
26. Studying each one can help you think about a career choice. You can explore the wide range of jobs within a career area and identify those that interest you.
27. (Student response. Answers may include:) Occupational trends help predict future job opportunities. Knowing what jobs will be needed may help you select and prepare now for a future career. Getting the training, skills, and education needed for a growing field means more opportunities in the future.

Transparency Master 13-1

Fifteen Career Clusters

Job categories grouped by common skills and interests include

- Agriculture

- Business and Office

- Communications and Media

- Construction

- Family and Consumer Sciences

- Fine Arts and Humanities

- Health

- Hospitality and Recreation

- Manufacturing

- Marine Science

- Marketing and Distribution

- Natural Resources and Environmental Control

- Personal Services

- Public Services

- Transportation

Reproducible Master 13-2

Retail Sales Workers

Name_____ Date _____ Period _____

A retail sales worker is just one example of the many careers in the marketing and distribution career cluster. Read the following article from the *Occupational Outlook Handbook* about this career. Then, on a separate sheet of paper, answer the questions that follow.

Significant Points
- Good employment opportunities are expected due to the need to replace the large number who leave the occupation each year.
- Most salespersons can expect to work some evening and weekend hours, and longer than normal hours may be scheduled during Christmas and other peak retail periods. Plentiful opportunities for part-time work exist.

Nature of the Work

Whether selling shoes, computer equipment, or automobiles, retail sales workers assist customers in finding what they are looking for and try to interest them in the merchandise. This may be done by describing the product's construction, demonstrating its use, or showing various models and colors. For some jobs, particularly those selling expensive and complex items, special knowledge or skills are needed. Personal computer sales workers, for example, must have sufficient knowledge of electronics to explain to customers the features of various brands and models, the meaning of manufacturers' specifications, and the types of software that are available.

Consumers often form their impressions of a store by its sales force. The retail industry is very competitive and, increasingly, employers are stressing the importance of customer service and satisfaction. As a result, providing courteous and efficient service is becoming a very important component of this position. When a customer wants an item that is not on the sales floor, for example, the sales worker may check the stockroom and, if there are none there, may call another store to locate the item. Depending on the type of store, the sales clerk may offer to special order the item.

In addition to selling, most retail sales workers make out sales checks; receive cash, check, and charge payments; bag or package purchases; and give change and receipts. Depending on the hours they work, they may have to open or close the cash register. This may include counting the money in the cash register; separating charge slips, coupons, and exchange vouchers; and making deposits at the cash office. Sales workers are often held responsible for the contents of their register, and repeated shortages are cause for dismissal in many organizations.

Sales workers also handle returns and exchanges of merchandise, perform gift wrapping services, and keep their work areas neat. In addition, they may help stock shelves or racks, arrange for mailing or delivery of a purchase, mark price tags, take inventory, and prepare displays.

Frequently sales workers must be aware of, not only the promotions their store is sponsoring, but also those that are being sponsored by competitors. Also, salespersons must often recognize possible security risks and know how to handle such situations.

Although most sales workers have many duties and responsibilities in jobs selling standardized articles, such as hardware, linens, and housewares, they often do little more than take payments and wrap purchases.

Working Conditions

Most sales workers in retail trade work in clean, comfortable, well-lighted stores. However, they often stand for long periods and often need supervisory approval when they want to leave the sales floor.

The five-day, 40-hour week is the exception rather than the rule in retail trade. Most salespersons can expect to work some evening and weekend hours, and longer than normal hours may be scheduled during Christmas and peak retail periods. In addition, most retailers restrict the use of vacation time from Thanksgiving through early January.

This job can be rewarding for those who enjoy working with people. At times, however, the work may be repetitious and the customers demanding.

(Continued)

Name_____

Employment

Retail sales workers worked in stores ranging from small specialty shops employing several workers to the giant department store with hundreds of salespersons. In addition, some were self-employed representatives of direct sales companies and mail-order houses. The largest employers of retail sales workers, however, are department stores, apparel and accessories stores, furniture and home furnishing stores, and car dealers.

This occupation offers many opportunities for part-time work and is especially appealing to students, retirees, and others looking to supplement their income. However, most of those selling big-ticket items, such as cars, furniture, and electronic equipment, work full time and have substantial experience.

Because retail stores are found in every city and town, sales positions are distributed geographically in much the same way as the population.

Training, Other Qualifications, and Advancement

There generally are no formal education requirements for this type of work, although a high school diploma or equivalent is increasingly preferred. Employers prefer persons who enjoy working with people and have the tact to deal with difficult customers. Among other desirable characteristics are an interest in sales work, a pleasant personality, a neat appearance, and the ability to communicate clearly. The ability to speak more than one language may be helpful for employment in stores in communities where people from various cultures tend to live and shop. Before hiring a sales worker, some employers may conduct a background check, especially for selling high-priced items.

In most small stores, an experienced employee or the proprietor instructs newly hired sales personnel in making out sales checks and operating the cash register. In larger stores, training programs are more formal and usually are conducted over several days. Topics usually discussed are customer service, security, the store's policies and procedures, and how to work a cash register. Depending on the type of product they are selling, they may be given specialized training. For example, those working in cosmetics receive instruction on the types of products available and for whom the cosmetics would be most beneficial. Likewise, sales workers employed by motor vehicle dealers may be required to participate in training programs designed to provide information on technical details of standard and optional equipment available on new models. Because providing the best service to customers is a high priority for many employers, employees are often given periodic training to update and refine their skills.

As salespersons gain experience and seniority, they usually move to positions of greater responsibility and may be given their choice of departments. This often means moving to areas with potentially higher earnings and commissions. The highest earnings potential is usually found in selling big-ticket items. This type of position often requires the most knowledge of the product and the greatest talent for persuasion.

Traditionally, capable sales workers without a college degree could advance to management positions. However, a college education is becoming increasingly important for management jobs. Large retail businesses generally prefer to hire college graduates as management trainees. Despite this trend, capable employees without a college degree should still be able to advance to administrative or supervisory work in large stores. In addition, large stores often have several departments where employees are paid on a commission basis, that is, their earnings are a percentage of the sales they make. Earnings in these departments are usually higher than in salaried departments, and, as a result, transferring into these departments is usually considered a promotion.

Opportunities for advancement vary in small stores. In some establishments, advancement opportunities are limited because one person, often the owner, does most of the managerial work. In others, however, some sales workers are promoted to assistant managers.

Retail selling experience may be an asset when applying for sales positions with larger retailers or in other industries, such as financial services, wholesaling, or manufacturing.

Job Outlook

Employment of retail sales workers is expected to increase about <u>as fast as the average</u> for all occupations through the year 2006 due to anticipated growth in retail sales created by a growing population. Job openings will be created as sales workers transfer to other occupations or leave the labor force. As in the past, replacement needs will generate a large number of sales jobs because the occupation is large and turnover is higher than average. There will continue to be many opportunities for part-time workers, and demand will be strong for temporary workers during peak selling periods such as the Christmas season.

(Continued)

Name_____

During recessions, sales volume and the resulting demand for sales workers generally decline. Purchases of costly items such as cars, appliances, and furniture tend to be postponed during difficult economic times. In areas of high unemployment, sales of all types of goods may decline. Layoffs, however, are unlikely. Since sales worker turnover is usually very high, employers often can control employment levels simply by not replacing all those who leave.

Earnings

Weekly earnings of retail sales workers vary widely by type of goods sold, as the following tabulation shows.

Motor vehicles and boats	$539
Radio, television, hi-fi, and appliances	423
Parts	409
Furniture and home furnishings	403
Hardware and building supplies	372
Street and door-to-door sales workers	372
Shoes	328
Apparel	265

The starting wage for many part-time positions is usually the Federal minimum wage. In some areas where employers are having difficulty attracting and retaining workers, wages are much higher than the established minimum.

Compensation systems vary by type of establishment and merchandise sold. Some sales workers receive salary plus commissions. Others are paid only on a commission or salary basis. Those paid by commission may find their earnings greatly affected by ups and downs in the economy.

Benefits tend to be few in smaller stores, but in large establishments they are comparable to those offered by other employers and usually include vacation and sick leave, health and life insurance, and pension plans. In addition, nearly all sales workers are able to buy merchandise at a discount, often from 10 to 30 percent below regular prices.

Related Occupations

Sales workers use sales techniques with their knowledge of merchandise to assist customers and encourage purchases. These skills are used by people in a number of other occupations, including manufacturers' and wholesale trade sales representatives, service sales representatives, securities and financial services sales representatives, counter and rental clerks, real estate sales agents, purchasers and buyers, insurance agents and brokers, and cashiers.

Sources of Additional Information

- Personnel offices of local stores and merchants' associations in each state
- National Retail Federation, 325 7th St. NW., Suite 1000, Washington, DC 20004
- International Mass Retail Association, 1700 N. Moore St., Suite 2250, Arlington, VA 22209
- United Food and Commercial Workers International Union, Education Office, 1775 K St. NW., Washington, DC 20006
- National Automobile Dealers Association, Communication/Public Relations Dept., 8400 Westpark Dr., McLean, VA 22102

(Continued)

Name_____

Questions

1. What is the primary nature of retail sales work?

2. Besides selling, what are three duties of a salesperson?

3. Why is customer service so important in retail sales?

4. What are the usual working conditions in retail sales?

5. True or False: The five-day, 40-hour work week is the exception rather than the rule in retail trade.

6. What are two drawbacks to working in retail sales?

7. What qualifications or training are needed?

8. What are the opportunities for advancement?

9. What is the job outlook for retail sales?

10. What is the usual starting wage for persons in retail sales?

11. What fringe benefits are offered in retail sales jobs?

12. Name at least three related sales occupations.

13. Where can you get additional information about a career in retail sales?

14. Into which career cluster does this occupation fall?

Reproducible Master 13-3

Review and Study Guide for Chapter 13

Name_____ Date _____ Period _____

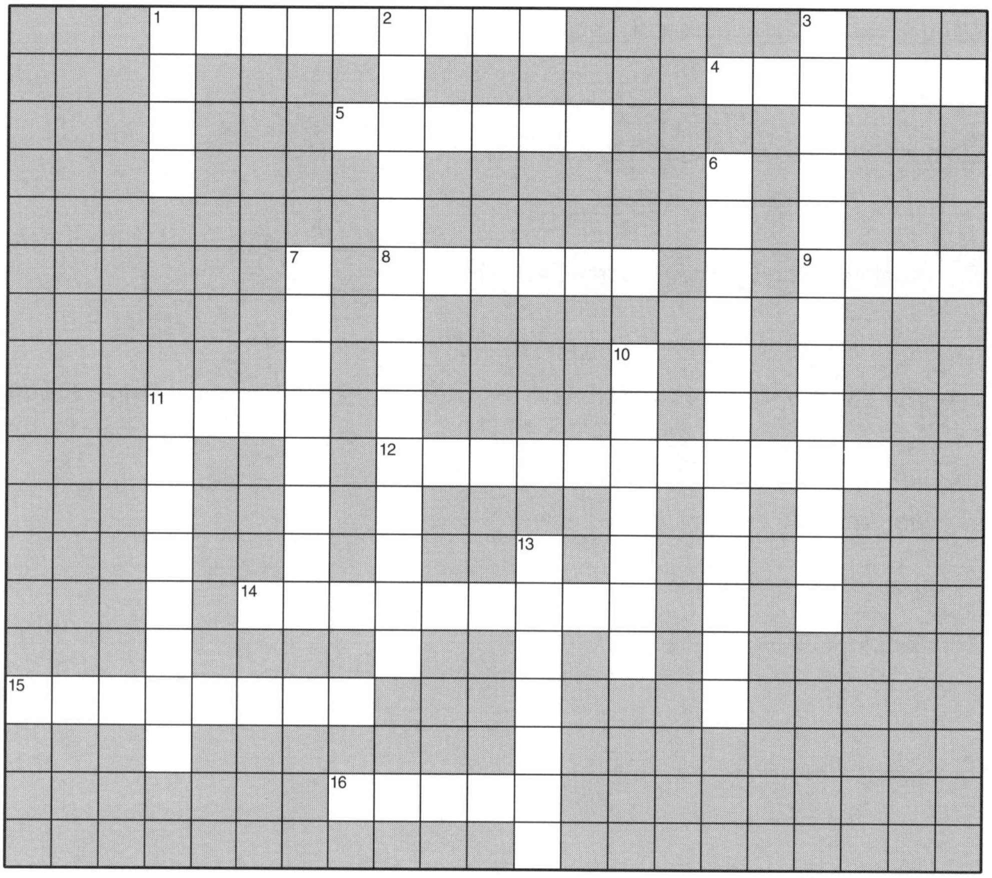

[crossword grid]

Across

1. _____ and distribution refers to the buying, selling, promotion, and delivery of goods and services.
4. Hospitals employ about half of all workers in the _____ field.
5. An oceanographer is classified in the _____ science career cluster.
8. A teacher is classified in the _____ service career cluster.
9. Musicians, sculptors, artists, and actors are occupations in the fine _____ and humanities field.
11. Manufacturing employees are called _____- collar workers because their duties usually require special work clothes or protective clothing.
12. A florist is classified in the _____ career cluster.
14. An _____ degree is a two-year college degree.
15. Barbers, cleaners, and child care workers are occupations in the _____ services field.
16. Newspaper reporters, writers, and commercial photographers are part of the communications and _____ field.

Down

1. An unfounded belief or notion.
2. _____ by land, water, and air offers many opportunities for employment.
3. Machining, production, and technical careers are in the _____ field.
6. _____ trends are predictions of what jobs will most likely be needed in the future.
7. Dietitians, clothing buyers, and home designers all work in the family and consumer _____ cluster.
10. A career _____ is a group of jobs that are similar to each other.
11. _____ and office workers include office managers, lawyers, and accountants.
13. Conservationists, environmentalists, and ecologists are careers related to _____ resources and environmental control.

Learning About Careers

Name_____

Date _____   **Period** _____   **Score** _____

Chapter 13 Test

Matching: Match the following terms and identifying phrases.

_____ 1. A job in the public service cluster.

_____ 2. A group of jobs that are similar to each other.

_____ 3. Workers in manufacturing occupations who operate, install, and maintain machinery.

_____ 4. Engineers, scientists, technicians, and production managers.

_____ 5. A job in the marine science cluster.

_____ 6. Predictions of what jobs will most likely be needed in the future.

_____ 7. A job in the natural resources and environmental control cluster.

_____ 8. A job in the personal services cluster.

_____ 9. A job in the transportation cluster.

A. career cluster

B. occupational trends

C. blue-collar workers

D. white-collar workers

E. oceanographer

F. hazardous waste engineer

G. building custodian

H. teacher

I. aircraft technician

True/False: Circle *T* if the statement is true or *F* if the statement is false.

T   F   10. A feed mill operator, a tree nursery worker, and a florist all belong to the agriculture career cluster.

T   F   11. Office workers need to be good communicators when writing, talking over the phone, or speaking to others in person.

T   F   12. High school courses in speech, drama, and creative writing can help students prepare for careers in communications and media.

T   F   13. A person does *not* need a college education to become an architect or engineer.

T   F   14. Careers in the arts and humanities require a great deal of self-discipline

T   F   15. A medical laboratory, drugstore, and optical shop are typical places of employment in the health field.

T   F   16. Family and consumer sciences workers may specialize in areas such as interior design, child development, and food and nutrition.

T   F   17. Many jobs in the hospitality and recreation cluster require no special education.

T   F   18. Production and technical careers are in the manufacturing cluster.

T   F   19. In marketing and distribution, wholesalers sell directly to consumers.

(Continued)

Name_____

Multiple Choice: Choose the best response. Write the letter in the space provided.

_____20. Which of the following jobs is in the personal services cluster?
    A. Police officer.
    B. Florist assistant.
    C. Child care worker.
    D. All of the above.

_____21. A radio dispatcher is a job in which cluster?
    A. Public services.
    B. Transportation.
    C. Personal services.
    D. Communications and media.

_____22. An art studio and a dance company are typical places of employment in which career cluster?
    A. Fine arts and humanities.
    B. Hospitality and recreation.
    C. Communications and media.
    D. Public service.

_____23. Housing and interior design is a major category in which cluster?
    A. Manufacturing.
    B. Family and consumer sciences.
    C. Business and office.
    D. None of the above.

_____24. A residential home builder is a typical place of employment for workers in which career cluster?
    A. Marketing and distribution.
    B. Construction.
    C. Marine science.
    D. Manufacturing.

Essay Questions: Provide complete responses to the following questions or statements.

25. How can myths affect an individual's career choice?
26. Explain the purpose of studying the 15 career clusters.
27. Explain the importance of knowing about occupational trends.

Researching Careers

Objectives

After studying this chapter, students will be able to
- explain how to research careers and occupations.
- evaluate careers based on educational require-ments, work hours, work conditions, pay, and personal lifestyles and goals.
- build SCANS competencies in using interpersonal skills and information.

Teaching Materials

Text, pages 263-277
  Terms to Know
  Facts in Review
  Applying Your Skills
  Developing SCANS Workplace Competencies
Student Activity Guide
  A. *Library Research*
  B. *Using the Internet*
  C. *Your School Counselor*
  D. *Talking with Workers*
  E. *Sources for Career Research*
  F. *Evaluating Careers*
Teacher's Resource Guide/Binder
  Job Education Benefits, reproducible master 14-1
  Review and Study Guide for Chapter 14,
    reproducible master 14-2
  Chapter 14 Test, reproducible master
Teacher's Resource Binder
  Which Path Will Take You to the Workplace? color transparency CT-14

Introductory Activities

1. Ask students to tell how they first learned about occupations that interest them. Discuss how they plan to research the occupations.
2. Before studying the text, have students list all the ways they know of to research careers.

Instructional Concepts and Student Learning Experiences

Career Research Sources

3. *Library Research,* Activity A, SAG. Students are to research two occupations of their choice using three library sources of information.
4. Have students visit the school or community library to find the following sources of career infor-mation for the occupation of their choice: one book, one brochure, one magazine article, and one audiovisual material. Students should compile a bibliography of the resource materials.
5. Ask students to read the career-related book they located in Item 4 and summarize it in a brief written report.
6. Obtain copies of the *Dictionary of Occupational Titles, Occupational Outlook Handbook,* and *Guide for Occupational Exploration* and bring them to class. Divide the class into three groups and give each group one of the reference books. Each group should examine the book and note its features. Have each group explain to the class how to use the book to research an occupation.
7. Have students visit a library with a computer search system. Students should research one career choice using the system. Instruct students to explain how to use the system and report their research results to the class.
8. *Using the Internet,* Activity B, SAG. Students are to continue researching the occupations they chose in Activity A using at least three Web sites.
9. *Your School Counselor,* Activity C, SAG. Students are to visit the school counselor and gather information on the occupations chosen in Activities A and B.
10. *Talking with Workers,* Activity D, SAG. Students are to consult workers in informal interviews to find out about two occupations chosen in Activities A, B, and C.

11. *Sources for Career Research,* Activity E, SAG. Students are to supply letters missing from terms related to career research and complete given statements.

Evaluating Careers

12. *Which Path Will Take You to the Workplace?* color transparency CT-14, TRB. Use this transparency to illustrate the various ways a student can obtain the job skills necessary to enter the world of work. Discuss the advantages and disadvantages of each pathway. Ask students to identify jobs that interest them in each type of educational option.
13. Survey the educational and career goals of students. Discuss the relationship between the two kinds of goals with the class.
14. Instruct students to investigate loans, scholarships, and grants available for further vocational training and education. Suggest the library or school as sources. Have students bring in related brochures and explain their findings in class.
15. Ask each student to explain the on-the-job training they will receive at their training station. Discuss why on-the-job training is considered an important company benefit.
16. Instruct students to research the postsecondary educational requirements for an occupation that interests them.
17. Instruct students to investigate and describe apprenticeships.
18. Ask students to list the pros and cons of enlisting in the armed forces as a source of job training. Obtain brochures about opportunities in the armed forces, pass them around the class, and discuss impressions with students.
19. Divide the class in half. Have one half brainstorm jobs for which a high school education is not required. Have the other half brainstorm jobs that require a minimum of a high school education. Have each group present their findings to the other for open discussion.
20. *Job Education Benefits,* reproducible master 14-1, TRG/B. Students are to list two benefits for each given type of job education program.
21. Ask students to describe in writing the ideal working conditions for their chosen occupations. Then have them describe the most unfavorable working conditions. Discuss how working conditions affect people's job selection and their feelings about a job.
22. Have students prepare research presentations on one aspect of working conditions in any time period they choose. Suggest they bring in reference materials with photos or use visual aids, such as posters, to illustrate their presentation.
23. Poll students to see who prefers daytime versus nighttime work hours. Discuss which jobs fit into each category, then have students debate the pros and cons of day or evening working hours.
24. Have students list how much they would like to earn for an occupation that interests them and how much they think they would earn if they worked full-time at that occupation. Then have them research average salary levels for that occupation, compare the figures to those listed, and share their findings in class.
25. Have students examine the newspaper want ads. Students should select three ads for the same occupation and note fringe benefits cited. Which job offers the best benefits?
26. Survey the class about occupations represented by students' work-based learning experiences. Compare occupations in terms of working conditions, hours, pay, and fringe benefits.
27. Have groups of three students role-play married couples with one child in dual-career families. Ask them to create the following situations: the husband and wife both need the family car to get to work; the parents can't find a babysitter and one must stay home from work; and one spouse gets transferred to a distant city.
28. *Evaluating Careers,* Activity F, SAG. Students are to analyze the occupational research they have done in Activities A, B, C, and D, then evaluate the occupations they have researched.
29. Have students design a poster illustrating the factors to consider in evaluating a career.

Activities to Enrich Learning

30. Have students deliver a five-minute presentation on their career research plans to the class. Suggest they use books, brochures, or audiovisual materials to supplement their presentation.
31. Have students tape an interview with a person who works in the students' chosen occupation. Students should focus on how the interviewee researched his or her job before finding it.
32. Have your class sponsor a career day and invite representatives from various occupations to speak to the class. Students should be prepared to introduce and interview the representatives they have invited.

Activities to Extend Learning

33. Take the class to visit the community library. Arrange for a librarian to explain the services and sources of occupational information the library offers.
34. Arrange for a school counselor to speak to students about using the school counseling service as a source of career information.

Answer Key

Text

Facts in Review, page 276

1. (List five:) libraries, career information guides, the Internet, school counselors, career conferences, consultations, personal observations
2. card file
3. *Dictionary of Occupational Titles, Occupational Outlook Handbook, Guide for Occupational Exploration*
4. by providing career exploration information, personality tests, tools to identify suitable careers, information on the training/education needed, and job listings
5. provides career information, compares job requirements to personal interests and abilities, answers questions about educational requirements and suitable educational institutions
6. (List two:) to gain insight into their careers, to practice interviewing skills, to develop future job contacts
7. (List four:) What educational requirements are needed? What are the work hours? What are the work conditions? What pay level can be expected? How will the career fit the person's lifestyle and goals?
8. (List four:) occupational schools, skill centers, community colleges, company training programs, correspondence courses
9. (List five. See Chart 14-6 on page 270.)
10. advantages—pay little or nothing for training, receive pay and benefits, have opportunities for travel and advancement; disadvantages—must adhere to strict discipline, must follow orders regarding what to do and wear, cannot leave or resign before one's term expires
11. because a job's work hours will greatly determine a person's lifestyle
12. because their dollar value can exceed that of a higher paying job with few or no benefits
13. because a career can affect where one lives as well as one's friends, income, and family
14. (Student response. See pages 274-275.)

Student Activity Guide

Sources for Career Research, Activity E

1. workers; insight into careers, future job contacts, and practice interviewing
2. libraries; they provide a wide variety of materials
3. *Dictionary of Occupational Titles;* it provides standard descriptions for over 20,000 jobs
4. *Occupational Outlook Handbook;* it describes occupations that account for nearly 80 percent of U.S. jobs

5. *Guide for Occupational Exploration;* realistically assess themselves and judge their ability to meet different job requirements
6. Internet; it provides a wealth of information at your fingertips
7. America's Career InfoNet; explore the outlook and trends for all types of careers
8. O*Net; identifies and describes the key components of modern occupations
9. America's Learning Exchange; it is supported by the public workforce development system and helps all learners, young and old
10. counselor; up-to-date information about specific careers and help with relating your abilities and goals to various career options
11. career days; various occupations, professions, and schools

Teacher's Resource Guide/Binder

Job Education Benefits, reproducible master 14-1

Work-based learning programs: (Student response.)

Apprenticeships: (Student response. Typical responses may include the following:) learn skills on the job under a skilled tradesperson; a wide range of apprenticeships from which to choose; opportunity to learn entire trade on the job and in the classroom

Vocational schools or community colleges: (Student response. Typical responses may include the following:) graduate with a technical or vocational degree in two years; more affordable education for many students; located close to many students' homes

Colleges and universities: (Student response. Typical responses may include the following:) more in-depth education that prepares students for a professional position; by learning more skills, a person may earn a higher income after graduation

Company training programs: (Student response. Typical responses may include the following:) the chance to develop new job skills; the chance to improve job skills; better job security because a person is trained in a skill needed within the company

Military training: (Student response. Typical responses may include the following:) educational training can be used in the military or in civilian careers; little or no cost to the student for training; students get a salary while being trained; students get fringe benefits like paid vacations, paid health care, and free housing

Review and Study Guide for Chapter 14,
reproducible master 14-2

A. work conditions
B. school counselor
C. consultation
D. fringe benefits
E. occupational training
F. registered apprenticeship
G. career information guides
H. dual-career family
I. educational requirements
J. transfer

1. C
2. B
3. I
4. D
5. J
6. E
7. F
8. H
9. G
10. A

Chapter 14 Test

1. B
2. E
3. A
4. C
5. D
6. T
7. T
8. T
9. F
10. T
11. T
12. F
13. F
14. T
15. T
16. C
17. D
18. A
19. D
20. B

21. (List four:) libraries, career information guides, Internet, school counselors, career conferences, consultations, personal observations (Descriptions are student response.)
22. educational requirements, work hours, work conditions, starting and potential pay, personal lifestyle and goals
23. (Student response. See pages 274-275 of the text.)

Reproducible Master 14-1

Job Education Benefits

Name_____ Date _____ Period _____

List two more benefits for each of the following types of programs that provide job education.

Work-based learning programs:

1. Allow students to learn about a career field that interests them.

2. _____

3. _____

Apprenticeships:

1. A way to learn a skilled craft or trade.

2. _____

3. _____

Vocational schools or community colleges:

1. Offer many fields of study.

2. _____

3. _____

Colleges and universities:

1. Give students a choice of hundreds of majors at thousands of schools.

2. _____

3. _____

Company training programs:

1. Prepare employees to do specific jobs.

2. _____

3. _____

Military training:

1. May allow people to begin career training while serving in the military.

2. _____

3. _____

Reproducible Master 14-2

Review and Study Guide for Chapter 14

Name_____ **Date** _____ **Period** _____

Completion: Fill in the missing letters of these chapter terms.

A. _ _ _ _   c _ _ d _ _ _ _ n _

B. _ c h _ _ _   c _ _ _ _ e _ _ _

C. _ o _ _ _ l t _ _ _ _ _ _

D. _ _ i _ _ e _ _ n _ _ i _ _

E. _ c c _ _ _ t _ _ _ _ _   _ r _ _ _ i _ _

F. _ _ _ i _ _ _ r _ _   _ p p _ _ _ _ _ _ _ s _ _ _ _

G. c _ _ e e _   i _ _ _ _ m _ _ _ _ _   _ u i _ _ _

H. d _ _ _ - _ _ r _ e r   _ _ m _ _ y

I. _ _ u _ t _ _ _ _ l   _ _ _ u _ _ m _ _ _ _

J. _ r _ _ s _ _ _

Matching: Match the chapter terms above with the definitions below.

_____ 1. A discussion for seeking advice.

_____ 2. This person can help students consider career possibilities in relation to their abilities and personal goals.

_____ 3. One of the most important factors to consider when evaluating careers.

_____ 4. Financial extras in addition to the regular paycheck.

_____ 5. If you plan to attend a school later but take correspondence courses now, make sure your credits do this.

_____ 6. This type of training prepares a person for a job in a specific field.

_____ 7. An advanced training program that operates under standards approved by the Bureau of Apprenticeship and Training.

_____ 8. When a husband and wife both have careers outside the home and raise a family.

_____ 9. Books that identify occupations and career options.

_____ 10. Every occupation has desirable and undesirable types of these.

Researching Careers

Name_____

Date _____   **Period** _____   **Score** _____

Chapter 14 Test

Matching: Match the following terms and identifying phrases.

_____ 1. Prepares a person for a job in a specific field.

_____ 2. Financial extras in addition to the regular paycheck.

_____ 3. A discussion for seeking advice.

_____ 4. An advanced training program for a skill or craft that operates according to Department of Labor standards.

_____ 5. The acceptance of course work completed at one school by another school.

A. consultation
B. occupational training
C. registered apprenticeship
D. transfer
E. fringe benefits

True/False: Circle *T* if the statement is true or *F* if the statement is false.

T   F   6. The more information you can learn about different occupations, the easier it will be for you to plan your career.

T   F   7. Schools and public libraries are both important sources of career information.

T   F   8. A school counselor can help students consider career possibilities in relation to their abilities and personal goals.

T   F   9. Informal interviews with people are *not* helpful in learning about specific occupations.

T   F   10. The educational requirement is often the most important consideration when evaluating careers.

T   F   11. Company training offers new employees the opportunity to develop new skills.

T   F   12. All of an apprentice's training is learned on the job.

T   F   13. People in the military can drop out or resign before the end of their terms if they don't like military life.

T   F   14. Every occupation has desirable and undesirable work conditions.

T   F   15. Your career can affect your future lifestyle, place of residence, income, friends, and family.

Multiple Choice: Choose the best response. Write the letter in the space provided.

_____ 16. When researching careers in the library, it is best to begin by going to the _____.
   A. librarian
   B. encyclopedia
   C. card file
   D. periodicals

(Continued)

Name_____

_____17. When evaluating a specific career, consider _____.
   A. hours of work
   B. work conditions
   C. educational requirements
   D. All of the above.

_____18. The *Dictionary of Occupational Titles* describes _____.
   A. jobs in terms of job duties and work characteristics
   B. the training and education needed for different occupations
   C. occupations by interests, by abilities, and by traits needed for successful job performance
   D. All of the above.

_____19. Types of job training include _____.
   A. college or university courses
   B. armed forces training
   C. occupational training
   D. All of the above.

_____20. People who like to work with their hands and want to learn a specific craft should _____.
   A. go to college
   B. get an apprenticeship
   C. take a correspondence course
   D. enlist in the Armed Forces

Essay Questions: Provide complete responses to the following questions or statements.

21. List four sources available to help you research careers and describe what type of information each source can provide.
22. What five basic factors should be considered when evaluating each career option?
23. Explain the importance of evaluating careers based on your lifestyle and goals.

Making Career Decisions

Objectives

After studying this chapter, students will be able to
- explain the decision-making process.
- use the decision-making process to developing a career plan.
- identify other applications for the decision-making process.
- build SCANS competencies in using interpersonal skills, information, and systems.

Teaching Materials

Text, pages 279-289
  Terms to Know
  Facts in Review
  Applying Your Skills
  Developing SCANS Workplace Competencies
Student Activity Guide
  A. *Examining Decisions*
  B. *The Decision-Making Process*
  C. *Preparing a Career Plan*
  D. *Preparing a Career Ladder*
  E. *It's Your Decision*
Teacher's Resource Guide/Binder
  Creating a Career Ladder, reproducible master 15-1
  Decisions, Decisions, reproducible master 15-2
  Decision-Making Case Studies, reproducible master 15-3
  Review and Study Guide for Chapter 15, reproducible master 15-4
  Chapter 15 Test, reproducible master
Teacher's Resource Binder
  The Steps in Making a Career Decision, color transparency CT-15

Introductory Activities

1. Have students describe the decisions they plan to make today. Discuss in class the types of decisions students face every day, including routine and major decisions.

2. Poll students to find out how many have already made a career decision and how many are still undecided. Ask decided students to share the decision-making process they followed. Discuss how the decision-making process can make important decisions easier to handle.

Instructional Concepts and Student Learning Experiences

The Decision-Making Process

3. *The Steps in Making a Career Decision,* color transparency CT-15, TRB. Use the transparency to introduce students to the seven steps of the decision-making process.
4. Discuss the importance of goal setting in the decision-making process. Have students name decisions they must make and list at least three examples of goal statements.
5. Divide the class into small groups. Instruct students to use the decision-making process to solve a classroom management problem, such as classroom material organization. Assign each group one or two steps of the decision-making process. Have each group share results in class.
6. Ask students to give examples of decisions they often make in haste, from habit, on impulse, and because of someone else's influence. Discuss the possible consequences of such decisions.
7. Instruct students to ask their training station employers about the importance of decision making in business. Suggest that students take notes or record an interview. Students may give brief oral reports on their findings.
8. *Examining Decisions*, Activity A, SAG. Students define major decisions and routine decisions and identify examples of each.
9. Ask students to write an essay on the topic "The Most Difficult Decisions I Ever Made." Would using the seven-step decision-making process have helped students make the decisions more easily?

10. *The Decision-Making Process,* Activity B, SAG. Students refer to the occupations they researched in Chapter 14. Using the decision-making steps, students decide which of those occupations (or another occupation) would be right for them.

Career Decisions

11. *Preparing a Career Plan,* Activity C, SAG. Students prepare a career plan for the career decision made in Activity B.
12. *Preparing a Career Ladder,* Activity D, SAG. Students prepare a career ladder for the career decision made in Activity B.
13. *Creating a Career Ladder,* reproducible master 15-1, TRG/B. Students work in small groups to create a career ladder for either a high school teacher or police officer.
14. Have students list the name of a job that interests them. Students should list all of the opportunities the job offers, such as salary, career advancement, and job location. Did students list opportunities they hadn't considered before doing this exercise? Discuss in class.
15. Discuss career decision-making as an ongoing process. To illustrate the process, students may role-play employers who offer employees a new position in the company. Students acting as employees may use the decision-making process to decide whether the new position is right for them.
16. Instruct students to make long-range career plans for themselves using the decision-making process. Students may write out these plans and share them in class.

Using the Decision-Making Process

17. *Decisions, Decisions,* reproducible master 15-2, TRG/B. Students analyze several topics needing decisions, then describe the type of decision each is and how to apply the decision-making process.
18. *Decision-Making Case Studies,* reproducible master 15-3, TRG/B. Students apply the decision-making process to two case studies.
19. *It's Your Decision,* Activity E, SAG. Students apply the decision-making process to a recent important decision they made that is unrelated to a career decision.
20. Divide the class into small groups. Assign each group a life decision to make. These decisions might include when to marry, whether to buy a home or rent an apartment, what car to buy, or whether to go to school or to work after graduation. Students should use the decision-making process, then illustrate how they made the decision with a poster, skit, or oral presentation.

21. Have students keep a "Decisions Diary" for two days. In it they should list every decision they had to make at home, at school, at work, and as a consumer. After each decision, students should list how they made the decision and what occurred as a result.
22. Ask students to write an essay on the topic "The Choices I Make Can Affect My Life."

Activities to Enrich Learning

23. Instruct students to write a report on how the work-based learning experience can affect career decisions.
24. Students should give oral presentations illustrating how the decision-making process can help people make career decisions.
25. Using the decision-making process, students should decide how they want to spend the next day's class period.

Activities to Extend Learning

26. Invite a panel of training station employers to discuss the types of business decisions they make at work and the process they use to make them.
27. Invite your school's guidance counselor to speak to students about the resources available to help them make career decisions. Have students prepare a list of career-related questions to ask the counselor.
28. Invite a city official to speak to the class on how decision making can affect other people besides the decision maker. Ask the official to give examples of difficult business decisions they've made, the factors they considered to make the decisions, and how the decisions have affected the community.

Answer Key

Text

Facts in Review, page 288

1. because the decisions tend to have long-lasting effects
2. Define the problem; establish goals; identify resources; consider alternatives; make a decision; implement it; evaluate results.
3. to identify resources so a person knows what is available to help reach a goal
4. Will the decision have a bad effect on me or anyone else? Will it help me reach my goals? Is it illegal? Will I be happy with it?
5. to evaluate results so decision-making skills are improved in the future
6. how you live, who you meet, what you earn, what satisfaction you get from life

7. (List two:) take any job and hope for the best, let parents decide, let friends decide
8. (List four:) interests, aptitudes, abilities, strengths, weaknesses, significant personality traits, values, short- and long-term goals, resources
9. false
10. personal decisions, work decisions, consumer decisions

Teacher's Resource Guide/Binder

Review and Study Guide for Chapter 15,
reproducible master 15-4

1. career plan
2. job
3. routine
4. major
5. decision-making process
6. career ladder
7. define
8. career
9. consumers
10. personal
11. D
12. A
13. D
14. C
15. B
16. A
17. C
18. A
19. B
20. D

Chapter 15 Test

1. E
2. A
3. B
4. D
5. C
6. T
7. F
8. T
9. F
10. T
11. T
12. T
13. T
14. T
15. T
16. C
17. B
18. D
19. A
20. C
21. Define the problem. Establish goals. Identify resources. Consider alternatives. Make a decision. Implement the decision. Evaluate the results. (Explanations are student response.)
22. (Student response. Answers may include:) to help make a more logical decision about a career, to choose a more satisfying career
23. (Student response. Answers may include:) to make personal decisions, to make decisions at work, to make decisions as a consumer

Reproducible Master 15-1

Creating a Career Ladder

Name_____   **Date** _____   **Period** _____

Working with three or four classmates, create a career ladder for either a high school teacher or a police officer. (A specialty area may be selected, such as a high school *math* teacher or a *crime scene investigations* officer.) You may use the *Occupational Outlook Handbook* as a reference for creating the ladder.

Career ladder for _____

Advanced degree

Bachelor's degree

Advanced training/
associates degree

High school diploma

Part-time jobs during
high school

Reproducible Master 15-2

Decisions, Decisions

Name_____ **Date** _____ **Period** _____

People make decisions every day. Many are routine decisions. Some may be major, life-changing decisions. For each of the following situations, write down the type of decision you would have to make. Then briefly describe how you would use the decision-making process to make the decision.

1. Choosing an occupation

    Type of decision: _____

    When using the decision-making process, you would (do what?): _____

    _____

    _____

    _____

    _____

2. Choosing a restaurant for lunch

    Type of decision: _____

    When using the decision-making process, you would (do what?): _____

    _____

    _____

    _____

    _____

3. Buying a new CD player

    Type of decision: _____

    When using the decision-making process, you would (do what?): _____

    _____

    _____

    _____

    _____

4. Making a date for the prom

    Type of decision: _____

    When using the decision-making process, you would (do what?): _____

    _____

    _____

    _____

    _____

(Continued)

Name_____

5. Proposing marriage

Type of decision: _____

When using the decision-making process, you would (do what?): _____

_____

_____

_____

_____

6. Renting an apartment

Type of decision: _____

When using the decision-making process, you would (do what?): _____

_____

_____

_____

_____

7. Choosing an investment plan for your savings

Type of decision: _____

When using the decision-making process, you would (do what?): _____

_____

_____

_____

_____

8. Changing jobs

Type of decision: _____

When using the decision-making process, you would (do what?): _____

_____

_____

_____

_____

Reproducible Master 15-3

Decision-Making Case Studies

Name_____   **Date** _____   **Period** _____

Using the decision-making process, explain what you believe should be done in each of the following cases. Then write your answers in the space provided.

Case 1. Jeff Wants to Buy a Car.

Jeff lives 10 miles away from his job, which is at a paper company warehouse. Because the location is not close to public transportation, Jeff's parents have been driving him to and from work. Jeff wants a car so he can drive himself. He also wants to be able to stop after work to socialize with his friends. Having a car will make Jeff feel more independent. Also, Jeff wants to apply for the paper salesperson position that has just been posted at work. Having dependable transportation is one of the requirements. Jeff wants to use $6,000 from his savings account to buy a car. When he goes shopping for cars, he finds that he has two choices. One choice is to buy a used car or use the money as a down payment on a new car.

1. Define Jeff's problem.

2. Establish and set Jeff's goals.

3. Identify Jeff's resources.

4. Consider the choices available to Jeff.

5. Make a decision for Jeff.

6. What can Jeff do to implement the decision?

7. Imagine you are Jeff and evaluate the results of the decision.

(Continued)

Name_____

Case 2. Martina Looks for an Apartment.

Martina has a good job at an advertising agency, but must commute by train one hour each way from her parents' home. Martina wants to rent an apartment closer to work and have more personal time in the mornings and evenings. Six blocks away from Martina's workplace is a high-rise apartment building. If Martina lived there she could walk to and from work. The building has a security guard in the front lobby. Other benefits, such as a heated swimming pool, a health club, and a garage for tenants' cars, are included in the rent. Martina does not have a car. She does have a cat, but pets are not allowed. The rent for a studio (one-room) apartment is $750 a month. Martina can afford it if she cuts back on her clothing budget. A deposit equal to the first and last month's rent is required.

Martina checked another apartment building where a coworker lives. This building is a 15-minute bus ride to her workplace and has a guard on duty during the evenings. Garage parking is also available for a monthly fee, but there is no swimming pool or health club. Pets are allowed, but the tenant has to put down an extra $100 security deposit. The rent for a one-bedroom (two-room) apartment is $650. Martina can afford this rent without much adjustment to her budget. A deposit equal to the first and last month's rent is required.

1. Define Martina's problem.

2. Establish and set Martina's goals.

3. Identify Martina's resources.

4. Consider the choices available to Martina.

5. Make a decision for Martina.

6. What can Martina do to implement the decision?

7. Imagine you are Martina and evaluate the results of the decision.

Reproducible Master 15-4

Review and Study Guide for Chapter 15

Name_____ Date _____ Period _____

Completion: Fill in the blanks with the correct terms.

1. A(n) _____ _____ is a list of steps to take to reach a career goal.

2. A(n) _____ is a task performed by a worker, usually to earn money.

3. Deciding what to wear and what to eat are examples of _____ decisions.

4. Decisions that guide a person's career and personal life are called _____ decisions.

5. Making career decisions and other important decisions can be easier when people use the _____-_____ _____.

6. A(n) _____ _____ shows job options for a career at different educational levels from entry-level to advanced.

7. The first step to follow when making an important decision is to _____ the problem.

8. A(n) _____ is a progression of related jobs that result in employment and personal growth.

9. When people decide whether to buy something, they are making decisions as _____.

10. Deciding whether to confront a friend who shoplifts is an example of a(n) _____ decision.

Multiple Choice: Choose the best response. Write the letter in the space provided.

_____11. The decision-making process can be used in _____.
   A. business
   B. your personal life
   C. shopping
   D. All of the above.

_____12. Rolando is trying to decide which career to choose. This is an example of a _____.
   A. major decision
   B. minor decision
   C. regular decision
   D. routine decision

_____13. The career you choose will largely determine the _____.
   A. way you live and the people you meet
   B. money you earn
   C. satisfaction you get out of life
   D. All of the above.

_____14. You can judge the success of a decision by asking yourself the following:
   A. "Did I follow all the steps in the process?"
   B. "Am I making any money?"
   C. "Did the decision meet my goals?"
   D. "Am I using all my skills and training?"

(Continued)

Name_____

_____15. When you have important decisions to make, _____.
    A. have someone else make them for you
    B. approach them carefully and logically
    C. wait to see what others do
    D. None of the above.

_____16. Which of the following is an example of an entry-level job?
    A. sales assistant
    B. divisional merchandising manager
    C. general merchandise manager
    D. vice president of merchandising

_____17. Which of the following is an example of an advanced-level job?
    A. baby-sitter
    B. child care attendant
    C. children's program director
    D. playground assistant

_____18. Implementing a decision means _____.
    A. carrying out the decision
    B. choosing an alternative
    C. looking back on the results
    D. None of the above.

_____19. The logical way to make decisions is to _____.
    A. ask your parents
    B. use the decision-making process
    C. wait to see what your friends do
    D. make them quickly, using little thought

_____20. Which of the following problems does *not* require the decision-making process?
    A. Choosing a bank.
    B. Getting married.
    C. Accepting a new job.
    D. None of the above.

Making Career Decisions

Name _____

Date _____   **Period** _____   **Score** _____

Chapter 15 Test

Matching: Match the following terms and identifying phrases.

_____ 1. Deciding whether or *not* to confront a friend who shoplifts.

_____ 2. Deciding what to wear, what to eat, and what time to leave for school.

_____ 3. Decisions that guide a person's career and personal life.

_____ 4. Approaching decisions carefully and logically.

_____ 5. A list of steps to take to reach a career goal.

A. routine decisions

B. major decisions

C. career plan

D. decision-making process

E. personal decisions

True/False: Circle T if the statement is true or F if the statement is false.

T   F   6. Making decisions is something that people do every day.

T   F   7. Some of the easiest decisions to make are career decisions.

T   F   8. Many people have no idea what they want to do for a living.

T   F   9. A career ladder only identifies advanced-level job options within a career area.

T   F   10. Researching careers at the school library can help people identify the jobs they want.

T   F   11. Along with career decisions, people have to make major decisions relating to other parts of their life.

T   F   12. Relationships with family, friends, and coworkers often involve decision making.

T   F   13. Solving business problems is easier when people use the decision-making process.

T   F   14. Making a major purchase, such as buying a car or a computer, requires careful thinking and planning.

T   F   15. Decision making is a skill a person can use throughout his or her life.

Multiple Choice: Choose the best response. Write the letter in the space provided.

_____ 16. The logical way to make decisions is to _____.
   A. ask your parents
   B. wait to see what your friends do
   C. use the decision-making process
   D. make them quickly, using little thought

_____ 17. Tonya is trying to decide which career to choose. This is an example of a _____.
   A. routine decision
   B. major decision
   C. regular decision
   D. minor decision

(Continued)

Name_____

_____ 18. The work you choose will largely determine the _____.
        A. way you live and the people you meet
        B. money you earn
        C. satisfaction you get out of life
        D. All of the above.

_____ 19. A series of increasingly challenging jobs during a lifetime describes a(n) _____.
        A. career
        B. assignment
        C. advanced-level job
        D. None of the above.

_____ 20. A career plan is sometimes called a career path because _____.
        A. it distinguishes career decisions from personal decisions
        B. it separates routine decisions from major decisions
        C. it shows the job-related steps that lead to a career goal
        D. None of the above.

Essay questions: Provide complete responses to the following questions or statements.

21. List and briefly explain each of the seven steps in the decision-making process.
22. Explain why it is important to use the decision-making process when making a career decision.
23. In your own words, explain how the decision-making process can be used throughout your life.

Part 4
The Job Hunt

16

Applying for Jobs

Objectives

After studying this chapter, students will be able to
- explain how to find job openings.
- prepare job resumes, letters of application, and portfolios.
- fill out job application forms correctly.
- build SCANS competencies in interpersonal skills, information, and technology.

Teaching Materials

Text, pages 293–315
> *Terms to Know*
> *Facts in Review*
> *Applying Your Skills*
> *Developing SCANS Workplace Competencies*

Student Activity Guide
> A. *Checking Want Ads*
> B. *Your Resume*
> C. *Preparing a Portfolio*
> D. *Telephoning an Employer*
> E. *Letter of Application*
> F. *Illegal Questions*
> G. *Filling Out a Job Application*

Teacher's Resource Guide/Binder
> *Finding Job Leads,* reproducible master 16-1
> *Preparing a Personal Fact Sheet,* reproducible master 16-2
> *Review and Study Guide for Chapter 16,* reproducible master 16-3
> *Chapter 16 Test,* reproducible master

Teacher's Resource Binder
> *Check Out These Job Leads,* color transparency CT-16

Introductory Activities

1. Ask students to list ways in which they found jobs in the past. Discuss the advantages and disadvantages of each.
2. *Check Out These Job Leads,* color transparency CT-16, TRB. Introduce students to the different types of job leads explored in the chapter.

3. Ask students to brainstorm reasons why gaining job-seeking skills now will help them stay employed in the future.

Instructional Concepts and Student Learning Experiences

Finding Job Openings

4. Ask students to choose a job that pertains to their chosen occupation and find at least one job lead from each of the following sources: friends, relatives, school placement services, direct employer contacts, want ads, trade journals, and the state employment service. Have students share their leads and how they obtained them. Discuss the most and least successful sources for job leads.
5. Ask the class to locate the office address and phone number of the nearest state employment agency. Have students collectively write a letter to the agency's director, asking for information on how the agency helps job seekers.
6. Instruct students to read want ads from the local newspaper for jobs that pertain to their career interests. Students should define ad abbreviations and keep a list of the qualifications specified.
7. *Checking Want Ads,* Activity A, SAG. Students are asked to mount at least two want ads related to their career interests on the worksheet and identify sources of helpful job leads. Students may use newspaper, magazine, or Internet ads.
8. Ask students to find at least two professional journals in the career area of their choice at the library. If they can check the journals out, students should bring them to class for a presentation. Have students evaluate the journals for the quantity and quality of job leads provided.
9. Students should contact three private employment agencies and inquire about each agency's specialization, fees, contracts, and success rate. Students may report findings in writing and discuss them in class.
10. *Finding Job Leads,* reproducible master 16-1, TRG/B. Students are asked to imagine helping

workers in various occupations find job leads. Students list the names and locations of potential employers and recommend sources of job leads.

Before You Apply

11. Ask students to list the sources of the information required to complete a personal fact sheet.
12. *Preparing a Personal Fact Sheet,* reproducible master 16-2, TRG/B. The worksheet directs students to prepare a personal fact sheet.

Job Resumes and Portfolios

13. Have students list the information that should and should not be included in a resume. Have them explain their choices.
14. Have students work individually to compile a personal list of three references for their resumes. The list should include names, business titles (if applicable), and addresses. Ask students to explain why they chose their references.
15. *Your Resume,* Activity B, SAG. Students are directed to write and design a resume, proofread it carefully, and submit it to you or a school counselor for review. Students should produce a final resume on a computer and make copies. They may submit the finished resume to potential employers and prepare a portfolio to accompany their resume.
16. *Preparing a Portfolio,* Activity C, SAG. Students are asked to explain the relevance of various items in a job seeker's portfolio.

Contacting an Employer by Telephone

17. Ask students to locate want ads in the local paper that require applicants to call the employer. Students should discuss in class how to respond to such ads. Students may refer to the guidelines on page 306 of the text.
18. Divide the class into groups of two to role-play contacting an employer by telephone. Have each pair choose a specific job for the role-play. Ask for volunteers to role-play their telephone conversation to the class.
19. *Telephoning an Employer,* Activity D, SAG. Students respond to statements about a teen telephoning a potential employer.

Letter of Application

20. *Letter of Application,* Activity E, SAG. Students are directed to write a letter of application for a job they want. They should refer to the sample letter on page 308 of the text.
21. Have students exchange letters of application and discuss their effectiveness. Do students feel their letter would earn them an interview? Discuss in class.

22. Have students list the similarities and differences between a resume and a letter of application. Discuss how the two work together to make a good first impression on an employer.

Job Application Forms

23. Have students list the guidelines to follow in filling out a job application. Stress the importance of neatness and correct spelling.
24. Have students ask their training station supervisor why it is important for applicants to fill out job applications. Students should also ask what employers look for in applications. Have students share findings in class.
25. *Illegal Questions,* Activity F, SAG. The worksheet asks students to determine which questions can or cannot legally be asked on job application forms.
26. *Filling Out a Job Application,* Activity G, SAG. Students fill out a sample job application form.
27. Have students research and write a report on the origins of the laws that protect job applicants from discrimination.
28. Divide the class into pairs. Have students exchange the job application forms they filled out in Item 26. Ask students to critique each other's application from an employer's perspective.
29. Have students role-play incidents in which they are asked illegal questions on a job application. Have students respond to each incident. Discuss the correctness of the responses in class.

Activities to Enrich Learning

30. Have students work independently to create their own "visual resume" by designing a poster or collage that depicts them as job applicants in their chosen career fields.
31. Instruct students to create their own "spoken resume" in which they tell the class their qualifications for jobs in their chosen career fields.
32. Ask students to write a report summarizing their experiences in applying for jobs. Share reports in class.

Activities to Extend Learning

33. Arrange a class tour of the closest state employment agency.
34. Arrange for a personnel or job placement officer from a local business to speak about preparing effective resumes.
35. Invite someone who is currently unemployed to speak about the challenges of finding a job. Have the guest speaker discuss the importance of maintaining an updated resume.
36. Organize a panel of former students in work-based learning programs to discuss their experiences in finding and applying for jobs.

Answer Key

Text

Facts in Review, page 314

1. Make a list of ideal employers; prepare a resume that summarizes your qualifications; contact the person with each employer who has hiring authority.
2. usually the director or manager of the personnel/human resource department, otherwise the manager of the department you want to join or the company president
3. After learning who to contact, write or call the person to express interest in a job.
4. the types of jobs most available, the skills needed for certain jobs, the salaries paid
5. Only 15 percent of job openings are advertised.
6. The employer pays the fee.
7. *job objective, education, work experience, honors and organizations* (or *activities* or *organizations*)
8. job title, employment dates, employer's name and location, brief job description
9. a collection of samples of your best work (Student response for contents of portfolio.)
10. (List five:) Be prepared; choose a quiet room; have a list of questions; have paper and pencil nearby; use good telephone manners; express interest in a job; summarize your background and qualifications; request an interview; note the details of any interview scheduled.
11. A letter of application is a job request written to an employer to obtain a personal job interview.
12. purpose of the letter, type of job you seek, your abilities and qualifications for the job, reference to a resume enclosed, request for an interview
13. Draw a dash through the space or write *does not apply.*
14. Write *open* or *negotiable.* This prevents the applicant from committing to a figure too high or low.

Student Activity Guide

Preparing a Portfolio, Activity C

1. demonstrates organizational and writing skills
2. demonstrates computer literacy
3. should always be included in a portfolio
4. demonstrates organizational and writing skills
5. should always be included in a portfolio
6. demonstrates computer literacy
7. demonstrates organizational and writing skills as well as the ability to work as a team member
8. demonstrates computer literacy

Telephoning an Employer, Activity D

1. true
2. false
3. true
4. false
5. true
6. true
7. false
8. true
9. false
10. false

Illegal Questions, Activity F

1. no
2. yes
3. no
4. no
5. yes
6. no
7. no
8. yes
9. no
10. no
11. yes
12. yes
13. no
14. no
15. no
16. no (However, an employer can ask if you have a disability that could prevent you from performing on the job.)
17. yes
18. no
19. no
20. yes
 (Answer to question is student response.)

Teacher's Resource Guide/Binder

Review and Study Guide for Chapter 16,
reproducible master 16-3

1. equal opportunity employer
2. networking
3. reference
4. resume
5. personal fact sheet
6. letter of application
7. work, volunteer
8. application
9. illegal
10. telephone
11. Part-time office assistant position available at medical clinic. Medical experience helpful. Must type 40 words per minute. Some evening hours. Good salary and pleasant working conditions. Some benefits. Call for appointment, 555-1234.
12. Manufacturing company seeks warehouse workers. Temporary positions, no experience necessary. Company will train. Afternoon and evening shifts available. Apply at office. Acme Manufacturing Company, 123 Front Street. Equal Opportunity Employer.

Chapter 16 Test

1.	G	13.	T
2.	A	14.	F
3.	E	15.	F
4.	F	16.	T
5.	C	17.	T
6.	H	18.	T
7.	B	19.	D
8.	D	20.	B
9.	T	21.	C
10.	T	22.	C
11.	F	23.	A
12.	T		

24. List the companies where you can apply for a job. Prepare a resume. Contact the person in each company who has hiring ability.
25. when answering a newspaper ad, when mailing a resume to a prospective employer, when an employer requests it
26. (List three. See page 312 of the text.) Explanation is student response.

Reproducible Master 16-1

Finding Job Leads

Name_____ **Date** _____ **Period** _____

Many sources of job leads exist besides newspaper want ads. Some of these include employment agencies, friends and relatives, directories of businesses and associations, trade and professional journals, community bulletin boards, and even the telephone book. Use job lead sources to help a job hunter in each of the occupations listed below. Then fill in the chart with the requested information. Do not use newspaper want ads as a job-lead source.

Occupation	Job Lead Source	Company Name and Location
1. Retail salesperson		
2. Computer data processor		
3. Teacher		
4. Cosmetologist		
5. Veterinarian		
6. Chef or cook		
7. Security guard		
8. Forklift driver		

Reproducible Master 16-2

Preparing a Personal Fact Sheet

Name_____ **Date** _____ **Period** _____

Fill in the form with information about yourself, following the directions on page 300 of your text.

Personal Fact Sheet

Name _____

Address _____

Telephone _____ Social security number _____

E-mail _____ Date of birth _____

Education	Name	Location	Date Attended	Date Graduated	Grade Average
Primary school	_____	_____	_____	_____	_____
Junior high school	_____	_____	_____	_____	_____
High school	_____	_____	_____	_____	_____
College	_____	_____	_____	_____	_____
Training school	_____	_____	_____	_____	_____
Other	_____	_____	_____	_____	_____

Work Experience

Name of employer _____

Address _____
            (street address)   (city)   (state)   (zip)

Telephone _____ Employed from _____ to _____
                                              (mo./yr.)   (mo./yr.)

Job title _____ Supervisor _____

Starting salary _____ Final salary _____

Job duties _____

_____

Name of employer _____

Address _____
            (street address)   (city)   (state)   (zip)

Telephone _____ Employed from _____ to _____
                                              (mo./yr.)   (mo./yr.)

Job title _____ Supervisor _____

Starting salary _____ Final salary _____

Job duties _____

_____

Skills _____

Honors and Activities _____

_____

Hobbies and Interests _____

_____

References

Name/Title _____

Address _____

Telephone (daytime) _____ E-mail _____

Name/Title _____

Address _____

Telephone (daytime) _____ E-mail _____

Name/Title _____

Address _____

Telephone (daytime) _____ E-mail _____

Reproducible Master 16-3

Review and Study Guide for Chapter 16

Name _____   **Date** _____   **Period** _____

Completion: Fill in the blanks with the correct terms.

1. EOE is an abbreviation in a want ad that means _____ _____
   _____.

2. Talking with people and establishing relationships that can lead to more information or business is
   _____.

3. A person who knows the job applicant well and can discuss personal and job qualifications with an
   employer is called a(n) _____.

4. A(n) _____ is a brief history of a person's education, work experience, and qualifications for employment.

5. A document containing all of the important facts about yourself is called your _____
   _____ _____.

6. When you answer a newspaper ad, you will need to send a(n) _____
   _____ _____ to the employer.

7. A person should list all _____ experience and _____ activities that
   directly relate to the job being sought.

8. Most employers will ask you to fill out a job _____ form when you apply for a job.

9. To avoid job discrimination and preserve your rights, avoid answering any _____ questions
   in interviews and on job forms.

10. When applying for some jobs, your first contact with an employer may be by _____.

Identification: Use chapter information to identify the abbreviations used in want ads. Then read the want ads
below. In the space provided, write out each ad without using the abbreviations.

11. P/t ofc ass't pos avail at med clinic. Med exp helpful. Must type 40 wpm. Some eve hrs. Good sal and pleasant
    work cond. Some ben. Call for appt., 555-1234.

12. Mfg co seeks warehouse workers. Temp pos, no exp nec. Co will train. Aft and eve shifts avail. Apply at off.
    Acme Mfg. Co., 123 Front St. EOE

Applying for Jobs

Name _____

Date _____   **Period** _____   **Score** _____

Chapter 16 Test

Matching: Match the following terms and identifying phrases.

_____ 1. A well-organized collection of materials that supports a job applicant's qualifications.

_____ 2. A document containing all the important facts about a job seeker.

_____ 3. Talking with people and establishing relationships that can lead to more information or business.

_____ 4. Employers use this to screen job applicants, so it must be filled out neatly and accurately.

_____ 5. A brief history of a person's education, work experience, and other qualifications for employment.

_____ 6. The first heading in a resume that gives employers an idea of the type of job for which a person is applying.

_____ 7. A person who knows the job applicant well and could discuss personal and job qualifications with an employer.

_____ 8. A letter written to an employer to apply for a job.

A. personal fact sheet
B. reference
C. resume
D. letter of application
E. networking
F. job application form
G. portfolio
H. job objective

True/False: Circle *T* if the statement is true or *F* if the statement is false.

T   F   9. Job offers won't come to job seekers; they have to go and find the jobs.

T   F   10. Competition is often stiff for good jobs.

T   F   11. One of the worst ways to find job openings is to contact employers directly.

T   F   12. The federal government has established public employment offices in every state.

T   F   13. The more sources a job seeker uses, the more job openings he or she is likely to find.

T   F   14. For most entry-level jobs, the job seeker is usually *not* expected to pay the fee at a private employment agency.

T   F   15. A person should *not* list part-time jobs or volunteer work on his or her personal fact sheet.

T   F   16. Reading a resume is a quick and easy way for an employer to learn about an applicant.

T   F   17. Resumes must look professional and be free of errors.

T   F   18. A job application that is incomplete, difficult to read, or smudged with dirt may *not* make it beyond the first screening.

(Continued)

Name_____

Multiple Choice: Choose the best response. Write the letter in the space provided.

_____ 19. A personal fact sheet can help a person _____.
   A. write letters of application
   B. prepare resumes
   C. fill out job application forms
   D. All of the above.

_____ 20. It is best to send a letter of application to _____.
   A. the president of the company
   B. the person who has the authority to hire
   C. the company's general office
   D. an employee with the company

_____ 21. The first thing to do when filling out an application form is _____.
   A. mark out items that do *not* apply
   B. print your name
   C. read the entire form carefully
   D. print your address

_____ 22. In the employment history section on a job application, do *not* write in _____.
   A. part-time jobs
   B. the present job
   C. negative comments about former employment
   D. a job that ended with firing

_____ 23. Before registering with a private employment agency, be sure to _____.
   A. ask for the opinions of the school counselor or program coordinator
   B. have enough money to pay the fee
   C. fill out a job application
   D. prepare a resume

Essay Questions: Provide complete responses to the following questions or statements.

24. List the three-step plan a job seeker can follow to be successful on a job hunt.
25. Describe the three situations in which you would be required to write a letter of application.
26. List three questions that an employer cannot legally ask you on a job interview. Explain why.

Taking Pre-Employment Tests

Objectives

After studying this chapter, students will be able to
- explain why employers give pre-employment tests.
- describe the types of pre-employment tests commonly given to prospective employees.
- prepare for pre-employment tests.
- build SCANS competencies in interpersonal skills, information, and systems.

Teaching Materials

Text, pages 317-327
Terms to Know
Facts in Review
Apply Your Skills
Developing SCANS Workplace Competencies
Student Activity Guide
  A. *Pre-Employment Perception Test*
  B. *Pre-Employment Math Skills Testing*
  C. *Pre-Employment Testing*
  D. *Types of Pre-Employment Tests*
Teacher's Resource Guide/Binder
  Controversial Pre-Employment Tests,
    reproducible master 17-1
  Review and Study Guide for Chapter 17,
    reproducible master 17-2
  Chapter 17 Test, reproducible master
Teacher's Resource Binder
  Employment Test-Taking Tips, color
    transparency CT-17

Introductory Activities

1. Ask students to express how they feel when they take school- or sports-related tests. Discuss how students can deal with feelings of anxiety taking a pre-employment test.
2. Ask if any students have taken a pre-employment test. Have students share their experiences in class.
3. *Employment Test-Taking Tips,* color transparency CT-17, TRB. Use the transparency to review the basic advice for taking tests well.

Instructional Concepts and Student Learning Experiences

Pre-Employment Tests

4. Divide the class into small groups. Instruct students to brainstorm a list of reasons why employers give pre-employment tests. Write these reasons on the board and discuss in class. Which reasons do students feel are most important?
5. Have students research what pre-employment tests employers in their chosen careers give. Ask each student to share his or her findings in a brief oral report.
6. Instruct students to write an essay on how employment tests in their chosen careers can help them as well as the employer.

Skill Tests

7. *Pre-Employment Perception Test,* Activity A, SAG. Students take a pencil-and-paper test to measure their ability to recognize details quickly.
8. *Pre-Employment Math Skills Testing,* Activity B, SAG. Students take a basic math test.
9. Ask students to list as many skill tests as they can, then identify the tests that apply to their chosen careers or current job. Have students explain in class why employers require such tests.

Psychological Tests

10. Have students write a response to a typical psychological test essay question, "Describe yourself in a paragraph."
11. Discuss with students the importance of psychological tests for measuring a prospective employee's cooperation, assertiveness, loyalty, and honesty. Ask students why employers value these traits.
12. Have students identify the personal qualities that psychological tests examine and write a descriptive sentence about each.
13. Have students tell the class about any psychological tests they may have taken to obtain their current jobs.

Situational Tests

14. Have students list the requirements of a firefighter that situational tests should examine in job applicants. One example is steadiness on a ladder at great heights.
15. Have the class discuss cases of occupational plans that clearly are unsuitable for the individual, such as planning to become a nurse but not being able to stand the sight of blood.

Government Tests

16. Instruct students to write a report on the purpose of the civil service test and jobs that require this test.
17. Students should investigate where the closest location is for taking a civil service test. Have students share this information with the class.
18. Have students investigate and list the federal and state job openings that require testing. Discuss the job openings in class.
19. Obtain a copy of the ASVAB test. Develop a brief sample test using questions from each of the individual tests. Have students take the exam. Discuss students' reactions to the test and how the ASVAB can be useful in their career planning.

Polygraph Tests

20. Divide the class into two groups for a debate. Have one group argue why polygraph tests are useful. Have the other group argue why they are not.
21. Instruct students to research and write a report on whether polygraph tests should be used in jobs related to national security.

Written Honesty Tests

22. Have students debate whether a person's honesty, or lack of it, can truly be determined with a paper-and-pencil test.
23. Obtain a copy of the Phase II Profile written honesty test and administer it to students. Discuss the advantages and disadvantages of the test in class.
24. Have students discuss why personality tests can sometimes be used to test an applicant's honesty.

Medical Examinations

25. List 10 different occupations. Have students give reasons why a medical or physical examination is important for each.
26. Divide the class into teams of three or four students. Have students imagine they are grocery store managers meeting to list the "essential functions" of a grocery bagger's job before they interview job applicants with physical disabilities.

Based on their list, which of the following candidates would be disqualified from consideration? Applicants include a person: in a wheelchair; without sight; without hearing ability; with AIDs; with infrequent seizures; with limited reach. Have each team report its decision, summarize the group's rationale, and read the list of duties it developed for the job position.

27. *Controversial Pre-Employment Tests,* reproducible master 17-1, TRG/B. Students express their opinions about tests used on job applicants.
28. Have students find newspaper or magazine articles about the physical effects of stress, especially job-related stress. Have each student share the information with the class in an oral report.
29. Have students develop skits in which a group of employers meet to discuss the effects of drug abuse on workers' safety.
30. Ask students to survey the personnel directors of three companies to ask if drug testing is required of job applicants? of current employees? Have students share their findings in class.
31. *Pre-Employment Testing,* Activity C, SAG. Students indicate what types of pre-employment tests may be required for selected occupations and answer related questions.
32. Divide the class into two groups. Have each group discuss the pros and cons of drug testing—one group, from the employer's viewpoint; and the other, from the employee's.
33. *Types of Pre-Employment Tests,* Activity D, SAG. Students complete a crossword puzzle on types of pre-employment tests.

How to Take Pre-Employment Tests

34. Have students role-play how to prepare for pre-employment tests.
35. Have students list tips to consider before and during pre-employment tests. Discuss the benefits of each tip in class.

Activities to Enrich Learning

36. Obtain several types of pre-employment tests and administer them to students.
37. Have students choose one specific pre-employment test, research its origins and characteristics, and prepare a written report.

Activities to Extend Learning

38. Invite a counselor to speak to the class about the advantages and disadvantages of psychological testing.
39. Invite a doctor to speak to students about the benefits of getting a physical before starting a new job.

40. Invite a representative of the Armed Forces to explain the ASVAB test for students.
41. Invite a panel of health professionals to discuss drug testing programs and the effects of drug abuse in the workplace.

Answer Key

Text

Facts in Review, page 326

1. (List two:) may reinforce interest in a chosen career, may show unsuitability for a career area, may reveal a need for more training, may indicate that skills and interests better match another career field
2. a test that checks one's ability to operate tools and machines (Example is student response.)
3. to determine how well an applicant will adjust to the job and get along with coworkers
4. The Civil Service Commission administers the tests for federal jobs, and the employment service within each state does so for state jobs.
5. to select the best qualified person for each job regardless of sex, race, religion, or political influence
6. to identify one's aptitudes for vocational careers outside the military
7. changes in the subject's blood pressure, perspiration, and pulse rate
8. a certified polygraph test examiner
9. overt honesty tests, personality tests
10. to identify health problems that may prevent a person from performing the job safely and successfully, to identify applicants with health problems that may become expensive insurance liabilities for the employer

Student Activity Guide

Pre-Employment Perception Test, Activity A

1. A	7. B
2. B	8. C
3. A	9. C
4. C	10. A
5. B	11. C
6. A	12. B

Pre-Employment Math Skills Testing, Activity B

1. 64	11. $44.30
2. 552	12. $115.89
3. 180	13. 23
4. 158	14. 25
5. 239	15. 48
6. 193	16. 94
7. 153	17. $280.00
8. 119	18. 17
9. $144.28	19. 17
10. $106.09	20. $2.00

Pre-Employment Testing, Activity C

1. A, B	9. B, G
2. B	10. H
3. A	11. A, B
4. B, C, G	12. D
5. D	13. A
6. E	14. B, H
7. C, D, F, G, H	15. C, H
8. H	

16-22. (Student response.)

Types of Pre-Employment Tests, Activity D

Teacher's Resource Guide/Binder

Review and Study Guide for Chapter 17, reproducible master 17-2

1. situational
2. polygraph
3. written honesty
4. psychological
5. skill
6. civil service test
7. drug
8. practice
9. sleep (or rest)
10. directions
11. relevant, control
12. Vocational Aptitude Battery
13. early
14. medical (or physical)
15. easiest
16. (List four. Student response. See page 325 of the text.)

Chapter 17 Test

1. F	12. T
2. E	13. T
3. C	14. F
4. A	15. T
5. D	16. T
6. B	17. D
7. T	18. D
8. T	19. A
9. F	20. C
10. T	21. C
11. F	

22. to screen prospective employees in order to hire the best people available
23. (Student response. See page 325 of the text.)
24. Try to find out in advance what type of tests will be taken. If one is a skill test, practice, but not to the point of getting tired.

Reproducible Master 17-1

Controversial Pre-Employment Tests

Name_____   **Date** _____   **Period** _____

Respond to the statements below to indicate your opinions about certain pre-employment tests. Then choose a numbered statement with which you strongly agree or disagree and explain your opinion. Discuss your opinions in class.

Agree	Disagree	Unsure	
_____	_____	_____	1. A polygraph test is a helpful tool to the employer when administered by a qualified, competent examiner.
_____	_____	_____	2. Polygraph tests are not accurate indicators of a person's honesty or dishonesty.
_____	_____	_____	3. I would refuse to take a polygraph test as part of a job application.
_____	_____	_____	4. Written honesty tests are less threatening than polygraph tests.
_____	_____	_____	5. I would take a written honesty test voluntarily.
_____	_____	_____	6. Medical exams should be required for all persons in all jobs.
_____	_____	_____	7. Job applicants should not be tested for drug use.
_____	_____	_____	8. Employees who test positive for drug use should be fired immediately.
_____	_____	_____	9. Drug testing infringes on a person's right to privacy.
_____	_____	_____	10. I would voluntarily submit to a drug test.

I strongly (agree/disagree) with statement _____ because_____

_____

_____

_____

_____

_____

Reproducible Master 17-2

Review and Study Guide for Chapter 17

Name_____ **Date** _____ **Period** _____

Completion: Fill in the blanks with the correct terms.

1. A _____ _____ is used to examine the ability of job applicants in a work setting similar to the job's.

2. A lie detector test is also called a _____ test.

3. A _____ _____ test is a paper-and-pencil test that helps employers identify applicants who are likely to be dishonest employees.

4. There are no right or wrong answers in _____ tests.

5. A(n) _____ test is used to test the physical or mental abilities of a job applicant.

6. The _____ _____ _____ is the exam given by the federal government to applicants applying for a federal or state government job.

7. The main purpose of _____ testing is to help employers provide a safer work environment for employees.

8. Sometimes you can _____ for a certain pre-employment test, such as a keyboarding test.

9. Get plenty of _____ the night before a pre-employment test.

10. When taking any type of pre-employment test, be sure to follow _____ exactly.

11. In a polygraph test, a _____ question is much more precise than a _____ question.

12. The military uses the Armed Services _____ _____ _____ test to help place people in military careers.

13. When taking a pre-employment test, arrive at the test site _____.

14. _____ exams are required by some employers to determine an applicant's physical condition.

15. When taking a written test, answer the _____ questions first.

Essay Question: Provide a complete response to the following statement.

16. List four ways you can prepare yourself for any pre-employment test.

Taking Pre-Employment Tests

Name_____

Date _____ **Period** _____ **Score** _____

Chapter 17 Test

Matching: Match the following terms and identifying phrases.

_____ 1. The government agency that hires employees for federal government jobs.

_____ 2. A test to screen applicants for general honesty.

_____ 3. An examination a person may be required to take before being considered for a federal government job.

_____ 4. A test used to evaluate the physical or mental skills of a job applicant.

_____ 5. A group of tests used by the military to help predict a person's success in military training schools.

_____ 6. A test given to find out more about an applicant's personality, character, and interests.

A. skill test
B. psychological test
C. civil service test
D. Armed Services Vocational Aptitude Battery
E. written honesty test
F. Civil Service Commission

True/False. Circle *T* if the statement is true and *F* if the statement is false.

T   F   7. Almost all government employees have to take one or more pre-employment tests.

T   F   8. A word processing test is a good example of a skills test.

T   F   9. A clerical skills test is a good example of a combined written and performance test.

T   F   10. There are no right or wrong answers in psychological tests.

T   F   11. Polygraph tests are *not* the same as lie detector tests.

T   F   12. A situational test examines the ability of a job applicant to perform well in a setting similar to the job's.

T   F   13. Drug abuse in the workplace is a major concern for employers.

T   F   14. The main purpose of employee drug testing is to catch people who are breaking the law.

T   F   15. Certain jobs, such as airline pilots and professional athletes, require employees to be in top physical condition.

T   F   16. There are few pre-employment tests for which you can study.

Multiple Choice: Choose the best response. Write the letter in the space provided.

_____17. A skill test might be required of _____.
A. a drafter
B. a welder
C. an instrument technician
D. All of the above.

(Continued)

Name_____

_____18. A person applying for a job as a bank teller, clerk, or computer operator might have to take _____.
    A. a written test
    B. an oral test
    C. a performance test
    D. All of the above.

_____19. Situational tests are given to _____.
    A. determine how well a person will actually perform on the job
    B. measure a person's knowledge or aptitudes
    C. test an applicant's physical or mental abilities
    D. screen dishonest job applicants

_____20. Polygraph tests are given to help judge a person's _____.
    A. math ability
    B. aptitudes
    C. honesty
    D. intelligence

_____21. One purpose for giving medical exams is to _____.
    A. measure a person's honesty in the workplace
    B. test the physical or mental abilities of an applicant
    C. identify health problems that might prevent a person from performing a job safely and successfully
    D. provide a safer work environment for employees

Essay Questions: Provide complete responses to the following questions or statements.

22. Explain why employers give pre-employment tests.
23. Give two reasons why employee drug testing is a controversial issue.
24. Describe what a person can do to prepare for a pre-employment test in his or her career area.

Interviewing for Jobs

Objectives

After studying this chapter, students will be able to
- prepare for an interview.
- explain how to make a good impression on the interviewer during the interview.
- write a follow-up letter after an interview.
- describe the factors they need to consider before accepting or rejecting a job offer.
- build SCANS competencies in using information, social systems, and technology.

Teaching Materials

Text, pages 329-341
Terms to Know
Facts in Review
Applying Your Skills
Developing SCANS Workplace Competencies
Student Activity Guide
    A. *Learning About an Employer*
    B. *Interview Preparation*
    C. *Deciding What to Wear*
    D. *Interview Questions*
    E. *Interviewing for a Job*
    F. *Interview Practice*
    G. *Informational Interview Practice*
    H. *The Follow-Up Letter*
    I. *Fringe Benefits*
Teacher's Resource Guide/Binder
    The Interview Process, reproducible master 18-1
    Review and Study Guide for Chapter 18,
       reproducible master 18-2
    Chapter 18 Test, reproducible master
Teacher's Resource Binder
    Do's and Don'ts for a Successful Job Interview,
       color transparency CT-18

Introductory Activities

1. Ask students to imagine they are employers and list questions they would ask a prospective employee. Discuss the response they expect from each question.

2. Ask students to imagine they are employers and describe the appearance and attitude of a person they would want to hire.
3. Ask students who have been on interviews to describe their experiences in class. How did students prepare for the interview?

Instructional Concepts and Student Learning Experiences

Preparing for an Interview

4. *Do's and Don'ts for a Successful Job Interview,* color transparency CT-18, TRB. Use the transparency to introduce the chapter by previewing the job-interview guidelines that the chapter covers.
5. Have students brainstorm a list of reasons why employers interview prospective employees. What could happen if an employer hired employees without interviewing them?
6. Divide the class into two groups. Have one group give a presentation on how the interview process benefits the employer. Have the other group give a presentation on how the interview process benefits prospective employees. Students can use posters, skits, or other visual aids for their presentations.
7. Quiz students' knowledge of company information sources. Review answers in class and discuss the advantages and disadvantages of each source.
8. *The Interview Process,* reproducible master 18-1. Students read tips on the interview process and answer questions.
9. *Learning About an Employer,* Activity A, SAG. Students choose a company for which they would like to work and research the company by consulting library sources, annual reports, the Internet, or others.
10. *Interview Preparation,* Activity B, SAG. Students prepare for a mock interview by listing four questions they would ask about the job, items they would bring to the interview, and questions they would ask about accepting or rejecting the job offer.

11. *Deciding What to Wear,* Activity C, SAG. Students describe appropriate interview clothing for given jobs. Discuss their choices in class.
12. Have students come to class prepared for a job interview in a chosen career. Referring to Activities B and C, ask students to wear appropriate clothing and bring the items they listed.
13. Have students write a case study entitled "The Night Before the Interview." Have students describe how the person in the case study would prepare for the interview.
14. *Interview Questions,* Activity D, SAG. Students read a list of interview questions and answer them as they would during an actual interview.
15. *Interview Practice,* Activity F, SAG. Students practice interviewing for jobs by role-playing. Students are to interview each other and offer feedback on the experience.
16. Discuss the importance of knowing the correct time and place for an interview. Have students role-play and practice noting directions, places, and times for interviews. Remind students to ask about available and public transportation options.

The Interview

17. *Interviewing for a Job,* Activity E, SAG. Students complete statements about interviewing for a job by selecting the best answer and give reasons for their choices. Discuss their choices in class.
18. Review the discriminatory questions an employer cannot ask on a job application or during an interview. Have students practice responding to such questions.
19. Have students demonstrate through skits, posters, or other creative expressions how people can express their positive traits during interviews.
20. Discuss the importance of verbal and nonverbal communication skills during an interview. How can these skills help a person make a good impression during an interview?
21. Discuss the option of a virtual interview. Ask students if they would be comfortable being interviewed this way and have them give reasons for their opinions.

After the Interview

22. Have students develop and write a follow-up plan for *after* an interview. As part of their plan, have students explain what to do if they don't hear from an employer, don't get a job, do get a job, or want to reject a job offer.
23. Have students prepare a note card file to track interviews and note ways to improve their interview techniques.

24. *Informational Interview Practice,* Activity G, SAG. Students interview a classmate employed in a job area of interest using the questions provided.
25. *The Follow-Up Letter,* Activity H, SAG. Students write a follow-up letter to a potential employer following an interview. Students may wish to refer to the sample letter in the text for an example.
26. Have students pretend they have been offered a job in their chosen field. What questions should they ask the employer before accepting the job? Students may role-play questions and responses.
27. Have students list all the fringe benefits they would expect in a job. Would students accept a job that offered some but not all these fringe benefits? How important do students consider fringe benefits to be?
28. *Fringe Benefits,* Activity I, SAG. Students interview an employer in their community about fringe benefits offered to employees of the company.
29. Have students brainstorm reasons a person might not want to accept a job offer. Which of these situations might students encounter in the future?
30. Have students role-play rejecting a job offer over the telephone, during a second interview, and by writing a letter to the employer.
31. Discuss with students why it is important to courteously reject a job offer if they aren't interested instead of simply ignoring the offer.

Activities to Enrich Learning

32. Have students practice responses to the following interview situations: The interviewer remains silent for a very long time after asking only a few questions. The interviewer makes inappropriate discriminatory and/or offensive remarks. The interviewer asks a question the prospective employee simply can't answer. The prospective employee realizes halfway through the interview that he or she is not interested in the job.
33. Divide the class into groups of three to develop and role-play interview situations. Have students take turns playing an interviewee while the other two students role-play interviewers. The three roles played by interviewees are: a perfect interviewee, a poor interviewee, an interviewee in a virtual interview. Their attitudes and actions should reflect the roles they are playing. Have each group present their role-play to the class. As a group, evaluate each role-play. Then compile a master list of do's and don'ts for students to follow during an interview.

Activities to Extend Learning

34. Invite a career counselor to discuss interview preparation tips with students. What can interviewees expect from employers in various career areas?

35. Invite a local employer to speak to the class on how employers prepare for interviews of prospective employees, what they look for, and how they evaluate interviewees.
36. Arrange for representatives of a local company's personnel department to conduct mock interviews with students for specific positions. Have students select positions that interest them ahead of time and prepare for the interview following text guidelines.

Answer Key

Text

Facts in Review, page 340

1. to evaluate a job seeker in person; to convince the employer of being the right person for the job
2. (List five:) Learn about the employer and the job. Make a list of questions to ask the employer. List the materials to take. Decide what to wear. Be prepared for questions. Practice for the interview. Know where to go for the interview.
3. the employer's products/services, size, reputation, and future plans
4. shows a serious interest in the company, helps with the interview discussion
5. helps with making a decision about working for the employer
6. pen, personal fact sheet, resume, list of questions to ask the interviewer, folder or large envelope for papers/portfolio
7. Dress one step above what is worn on the job.
8. interview date and time, employer's name, interview location, name of contact person, title of job, notes about questions asked and how well they were answered
9. It gives the impression that the applicant can handle matters alone.
10. Ask when a hiring decision will be made.
11. by requesting an informational interview for practice and asking the interviewer for recommendations
12. pay and benefits
13. (List four:) insurance, paid vacation, sick pay, retirement or profit sharing plans, bonuses

Student Activity Guide

Interviewing for a Job, Activity E

1. A	7. C
2. C	8. B
3. A	9. C
4. C	10. B
5. B	11. A
6. A	12. A

(Reasons are student response.)

Teacher's Resource Guide/Binder

Review and Study Guide for Chapter 18, reproducible master 18-2

1. interview
2. research
3. illegal
4. eye
5. informational
6. virtual
7. fringe benefits
8. follow-up letter
9. early
10. postmark
11. 401(k)

(Essay questions are student response.)

Chapter 18 Test

1. D	11. F
2. B	12. T
3. E	13. F
4. A	14. T
5. C	15. T
6. T	16. D
7. T	17. A
8. F	18. A
9. T	19. B
10. T	20. C

21. Learn about the employer and the job. Make a list of questions to ask. List the materials to take with you. Decide what to wear. Be prepared for questions. Practice for the interview. Know where to go for the interview.
22. (Student response. See pages 334-335 of the text.)
23. (Student response. See pages 337-339 of the text.)

Reproducible Master 18-1

The Interview Process

Name _____   **Date** _____   **Period** _____

Read the job interview tips listed below to learn more about the interview process. Then complete the activity as directed.

Before the Interview

1. **Learn about the employer**.
   List two sources of information about employers:

   A. _____

   B. _____

2. **Make a list of questions to ask the employer.**
   List two sample questions:

   A. _____

   B. _____

3. **List the materials to take with you.**
   List two examples:

   A. _____

   B. _____

4. **Think about the questions you might be asked.**
   List two examples:

   A. _____

   B. _____

5. **Practice for the interview.**
   List two ways to practice:

   A. _____

   B. _____

6. **Decide what to wear.**
   List two examples of what not to wear:

   A. _____

   B. _____

7. **Know where to go for the interview.**
   List two reasons why this is important:

   A. _____

   B. _____

During the Interview

8. **Arrive 5 to 10 minutes early.**
   List two reasons why this is important:

   A. _____

   B. _____

(Continued)

Name_____

9. **Go alone to the interview.**
   List two reasons why this is important:

   A. _____

   B. _____

10. **Greet the interviewer with a firm handshake and a friendly greeting.**
    List two ways you can prepare yourself for this:

    A. _____

    B. _____

11. **When you are offered a seat, sit in a comfortable position.**
    List two things you should not do when seated:

    A. _____

    B. _____

12. **Answer questions about yourself and your experiences in a positive and honest way.**
    List two other ways you may respond to the interviewer's questions:

    A. _____

    B. _____

13. **Show an interest in what the interviewer is saying. Be enthusiastic about the job and the company.**
    List two things you should not do during the interview:

    A. _____

    B. _____

After the Interview

14. **Send a follow-up letter.**
    Define a follow-up letter and explain its purpose.

    _____

    _____

    _____

15. **Make a follow-up call if the interviewer promised to contact you by a certain date and didn't.**
    Write down an example of what you would say to the employer.

    _____

    _____

16. **Don't be discouraged if you don't get a job right away.**
    List two questions you can ask yourself if you are applying for jobs and not getting job offers.

    A. _____

    B. _____

Reproducible Master 18-2

Review and Study Guide for Chapter 18

Name_____   **Date** _____   **Period** _____

1. The _____ is usually the most important step in getting a job.

2. To learn more about an employer, take time to _____ a company before going on an interview.

3. _____ questions are forbidden by law and should never be asked at a job interview or on a job application form.

4. During an interview, making _____ contact with the interviewer is important.

5. A(n) _____ interview can help a person learn more about an occupation.

6. The _____ interview is conducted between a job candidate and a potential employer who are miles apart using a computer and the Internet.

7. Health insurance, sick pay, and paid vacation are examples of _____.

8. A(n) _____ is written in business form to thank the employer for the interview.

9. A person should arrive 5 or 10 minutes _____ for the interview.

10. A(n) _____ is the official U.S. Postal Service stamp on delivered mail.

11. A type of retirement program that companies offer to employees is a(n) _____ program.

Essay Questions: Provide complete responses to the following questions or statements. Pretend you are interviewing for a job at a company in your career field. Write down what you feel are the best answers to the interview questions. Discuss your answers with your school coordinator.

12. Tell me about yourself. _____

_____

_____

_____

13. What do you want to know about our company? _____

_____

_____

_____

14. Why do you want to work for this company? _____

_____

_____

_____

(Continued)

Name_____

15. Why do you think you will like this kind of work? _____

_____

_____

_____

16. What were your best subjects in school?_____

_____

_____

_____

17. What were your poorest subjects in school? _____

_____

_____

_____

18. What is your major strength? _____

_____

_____

_____

19. What is your major weakness? _____

_____

_____

_____

20. What are your future plans?_____

_____

_____

_____

21. Why should I hire you for this job? _____

_____

_____

_____

Interviewing for Jobs

Name_____

Date _____ **Period** _____ **Score** _____

Chapter 18 Test

Matching: Match the following terms and identifying phrases.

_____ 1. The official U.S. Postal Service stamp on delivered mail.

_____ 2. A planned meeting in which a job applicant learns more about an occupation from a person employed in that job area.

_____ 3. A type of retirement program that companies offer employees.

_____ 4. A planned meeting between a job applicant and an employer.

_____ 5. A brief letter written in business form to thank the employer for the interview.

A. interview
B. informational interview
C. follow-up letter
D. postmark
E. 401(k) program

True/False: Circle *T* if the statement is true and *F* if the statement is false.

T   F   6. The interview is usually the most important step in getting a job.

T   F   7. Having some knowledge of the company will help a person talk intelligently with the interviewer.

T   F   8. A person's appearance does *not* influence an interviewer's impression of him or her.

T   F   9. Practicing for an interview will give a person more self-confidence during an interview.

T   F   10. A person should arrive five or ten minutes early for an interview.

T   F   11. It is *not* proper to make eye contact with the interviewer.

T   F   12. Usually jobs are *not* offered at the end of an interview.

T   F   13. A person does *not* have to explain to the interviewer why he or she is rejecting a job offer.

T   F   14. A person should ask questions about the pay and fringe benefits before accepting a job offer.

T   F   15. Before accepting or rejecting a job offer, a person should carefully evaluate the job and the company.

Multiple Choice: Choose the best response. Write the letter in the space provided.

_____16. Which items should a person take along on an interview?
A. Pen.
B. Personal fact sheet and resume.
C. List of questions to ask the interviewer.
D. All of the above.

(Continued)

Name_____

_____17. When deciding what to wear for an interview, _____.
    A. dress one step above what you would wear on the job
    B. dress one step below what you would wear on the job
    C. wear what you would normally wear on the job
    D. wear clothes you would wear to a formal party

_____18. During an interview, the interviewer will ask many questions to _____.
    A. find out if the applicant is the right person for the job
    B. make the applicant nervous
    C. find out the applicant's personal business
    D. None of the above.

_____19. If asked about your qualifications during the job interview, you should _____.
    A. brag about your accomplishments
    B. briefly describe them
    C. give a long description
    D. avoid responding

_____20. To avoid being nervous at an interview, you should _____.
    A. avoid eye contact with the interviewer
    B. chew gum
    C. practice ahead of time
    D. keep looking at your watch

Essay Questions: Provide complete responses to the following questions or statements.

21. Describe how to prepare for an interview.
22. Explain how to make a good impression on the interviewer during an interview.
23. What factors should be considered before accepting or rejecting a job offer?

Part 5
Job Satisfaction

19

Succeeding on the job

Objectives

After studying this chapter, students will be able to
- explain how getting along with others can help them succeed on the job.
- identify the rules of proper work conduct.
- describe ways to recognize and handle stress.
- evaluate their job performance and the job itself.
- explain the purpose of job performance reviews.
- describe the options for changing their job status.
- recognize the signs of a stalled career and the best way to change jobs.
- cite the pros and cons of union membership.
- build SCANS competencies in using resources, interpersonal skills, and information.

Teaching Materials

Text, pages 345-363
 Terms to Know
 Facts in Review
 Applying Your Skills
 Developing SCANS Workplace Competencies
Student Activity Guide
 A. *Terms for Success*
 B. *Starting a New Job*
 C. *Workplace Conduct and Job Success*
 D. *Handling Job Stress*
 E. *Job Satisfaction*
 F. *How Am I Doing?*
 G. *Changing Jobs*
 H. *Unions*
Teacher's Resource Guide/Binder
 People's Attitudes, reproducible master 19-1
 Successful Job Conduct, reproducible master 19-2
 Case Study: Linda's Negative Behavior,
  reproducible master 19-3
 Review and Study Guide for Chapter 19,
  reproducible master 19-4
 Chapter 19 Test, reproducible master
Teacher's Resource Binder
 Stress: The Good, The Bad, color
  transparency CT-19

Introductory Activities

1. Ask students to read the dictionary definition of the word *success*. Have students share examples of incidents in which they successfully accomplished a task or reached a goal. Discuss how long it took to attain success.
2. Ask students to write a brief paragraph to answer the question "What does it mean to succeed on the job?" Have students share their answers in class.

Instructional Concepts and Student Learning Experiences

Your First Day on the Job

3. *Terms for Success*, Activity A, SAG. Students complete statements about job success by doing a fill-in-the-blank exercise.
4. Ask students to write an essay on the topic "My First Day on the Job." Students should describe how they felt and what they did on the first day at their training station. Students who are not yet working may write an essay on the topic "My First Day in High School." This experience shares some similarities to the first day on a job.
5. *Starting a New Job*, Activity B, SAG. Students respond to questions about their first day on the job.
6. Have students prepare a checklist to help them prepare for the first day of a new job. Discuss how this preparation can help them overcome nervousness.
7. Have students role-play situations in which some students portray new employees and other students portray supervisors who must orient employees to the new workplace.

Relating to Others at Work

8. Ask students to write a want ad for the ideal supervisor. Then discuss how to adapt to the reality of having supervisors with varying personalities and managerial styles.

9. Have a class discussion of the topic "You Can't Succeed at Work Alone—Cooperate with Coworkers." Summarize the discussion with a brainstorming session on ways to get along with others on the job.
10. Have students role-play situations in which a new employee is introduced to a group of long-time employees. Have students portray one situation in which the new employee has a positive attitude and is cooperative, and another situation in which the new employee is a self-centered know-it-all.

Your Conduct and Job Success

11. *People's Attitudes,* reproducible master 19-1, TRG/B. Students read given situations and explain how each person's workplace conduct would improve if he or she had a more positive attitude.
12. *Workplace Conduct and Job Success,* Activity C, SAG. Students determine if given examples indicate good or bad conduct, then answer related questions.
13. Have students imagine they are news reporters for the school paper. Instruct them to write an article about how good conduct promotes job success. Students may interview other students in work-based learning programs, their employer, or teachers. Encourage them to use library resources for more information.
14. *Successful Job Conduct,* reproducible master 19-2, TRG/B. Students agree or disagree with given statements about their conduct in the workplace and answer related questions.

Handling Job Stress

15. *Stress: The Good, The Bad,* color transparency CT-19, TRB. Use this transparency to discuss how positive stress can help you rise to a challenge, while negative stress can cause you to become angry, frustrated, unproductive, and even ill. Ask students to give examples of positive and negative stress in the workplace. Discuss ways to avoid stress at work as well as how to handle workplace stress.
16. Have students evaluate their stress levels by listing recent positive and negative changes in their lives that have caused them stress. Ask for volunteers to discuss their experiences in class.
17. *Handling Job Stress,* Activity D, SAG. Students respond to a series of questions about recognizing and handling job stress. Discuss responses in class.
18. Present hypothetical stressful work situations in class and have students brainstorm ways to cope with stress.

Evaluating Job Performance

19. Have students investigate salary ranges for jobs in their chosen occupations and discuss qualifications for jobs that command higher salaries. Ask students to share findings in class.
20. Ask students to make a poster featuring a ladder labeled *Moving Up on the Job.* On each rung beginning at the bottom, students should list different levels of jobs in their chosen occupations from entry level to top management. Students should include the responsibilities and salary levels of each job.
21. *Job Satisfaction,* Activity E, SAG. Students react to statements related to job satisfaction and complete a personal job satisfaction statement.
22. Have students compare and contrast the process of being graded on school assignments with being evaluated on job performance.
23. *How Am I Doing?* Activity F, SAG. Students rate their job performances and explain how they can improve.
24. Have students ask training station supervisors to rate their performance on the job. Students should analyze the ratings and list their strengths, weaknesses, and ways to improve their work performance.
25. Discuss with students the advantages and disadvantages of job probation periods for both employers and employees.
26. Invite students to participate in a panel discussion on how work-based learning experiences will help students adjust to future jobs more easily.

Changes in Job Status

27. Ask students to describe the position above entry level in their chosen occupation. Have students list the greater responsibilities involved with the higher position and the steps they must take to prepare themselves for a promotion to that level.
28. Have students role-play the part of an employee interacting positively with coworkers after he or she has been promoted to supervisor.
29. Have students work in small groups to develop a skit on how to be an effective supervisor. Skits should illustrate positive leadership and communication skills.
30. Quiz students on reasons employees get fired from jobs. Ask students to research and report on their employer's termination policies. Do students know someone who was fired from a job? Discuss in class.
31. Discuss how a worker may be emotionally affected by losing a job, either by being fired or laid off. Have students discuss how this may influence other family members.

32. Have students brainstorm a list of ways a worker could deal with losing a job. After discussing the list, students should develop a plan of action for the worker to implement to find new employment.

Making a Job Change

33. Divide the class into two groups. Instruct students to debate the pros and cons of changing jobs.
34. Students may investigate the concept of job-hopping by asking employers and school guidance counselors their perceptions of employees who change jobs too often. How often is *too often?*
35. *Changing Jobs,* Activity G, SAG. Students interview a person who has changed jobs and discuss the interview in class.
36. Divide the class into groups of three to role-play job resignation situations. Have one student play the role of the employer. The other two students should play the role of employees resigning from their job. The first employee resigns in a professional manner, giving a two-week notice and offering to train another worker. The second employee resigns in an unprofessional manner without giving notice. Have the groups present their role-plays to the class. Discuss the importance of leaving a job on good terms.
37. *Case Study: Linda's Negative Behavior,* reproducible master 19-3. Students read the case study, then work in small groups to role-play situations displaying proper workplace conduct.

Unions

38. Instruct students to write a report on the origin of unions.
39. Have students scan current newspapers and magazines for articles about unions. Students should bring articles to class to discuss.
40. *Unions,* Activity H, SAG. Students use the questions provided to interview a union worker.
41. Have students role-play a collective bargaining session with labor and management representatives. Imagine labor representatives are demanding a salary increase while management representatives show proof that the business is losing money and customers. One student should serve as mediator.

Activities to Enrich Learning

42. Have students observe their supervisor at work for an entire shift, then write a case study describing the supervisor's typical day.
43. Have students listen to a motivational cassette tape program that focuses on job success. Have students obtain these tapes from a library and prepare a brief oral report on their effectiveness.

44. Have students create a video on dealing with job stress in which they portray stressful job situations and ways to cope with them.
45. Discuss the importance of giving an employer a letter of resignation when resigning from a job. Ask each student to imagine resigning from his or her current job as they write a suitable letter of resignation for the occasion.

Activities to Extend Learning

46. Invite the training director from a local company to speak about using company training. How does training prepare employees for advancement?
47. Invite a local businessperson known for his or her career success to speak to the class about career advancement.
48. Arrange for a panel to discuss the importance of job satisfaction with students. Include a former work-based learning program student, an employer, and an experienced worker.
49. Invite labor and management representatives from a local union to discuss the roles of unions in the workplace.

Answer Key

Text

Facts in Review, page 362

1. Have your clothes out the night before; allow enough time to get ready; arrive at work early; keep a positive attitude.
2. (List six:) Follow directions. Enjoy learning. Act responsibly. Be enthusiastic. Deal with mistakes. Handle gossip. Control anger. Assert yourself. Take responsibility.
3. change
4. motivation to get things done or face new challenges
5. Am I making progress in this job? Does this job give me personal satisfaction? Am I adequately paid for the work I do? Can I foresee opportunities for advancement?
6. to be hired for a trial period to see how well the worker can do the job
7. They help both recognize the weaknesses and strengths of employees.
8. promotion, lateral move, demotion, being fired
9. absenteeism, loafing, personality conflicts, violating company rules, incompetence
10. at least two weeks
11. no change in job responsibilities in three or four years, no important projects or committee work, no promotion, a demotion, reduced responsibilities, no interest in the job, poor relationship with boss or coworkers

12. to combat poor working conditions, low wages, child labor, and unfair treatment of employees
13. union's track record, size of the workplace, cost of union membership
14. Craft unions are formed by workers having the same craft or trade. Industrial unions are formed by workers belonging to the same industry.

Student Activity Guide

Terms for Success, Activity A

1. orientation
2. incentive
3. conviction
4. stress
5. probation
6. performance
7. fire
8. absenteeism
9. promotion
10. union
11. union shop
12. open shop
13. collective bargaining
14. labor contract

Workplace Conduct and Job Success, Activity C

1. good
2. bad
3. bad
4. good
5. bad
6. good
7. good
8. bad
9. good
10. good
11. good
12. good
13. bad
14. good
15. good
16. bad
17. good

(Descriptions are student response.)

Teacher's Resource Guide/Binder

Review and Study Guide for Chapter 19, reproducible master 19-4

1. conduct
2. promotion
3. stress
4. learn
5. demotion
6. union
7. evaluate
8. fired
9. probation
10. performance
11. E
12. D
13. I
14. G
15. J
16. H
17. B
18. F
19. C
20. A

Chapter 19 Test

1. E
2. D
3. C
4. G
5. A
6. H
7. B
8. F
9. T
10. T
11. T
12. T
13. T
14. F
15. T
16. F
17. T
18. T
19. D
20. B
21. B
22. C
23. A

24. to help supervisors identify the strengths and weaknesses of employees, and to help employees learn how they can improve their work and become more productive
25. absenteeism, loafing, personality conflicts, violating company rules, incompetence (Descriptions are student response.)
26. (List four:) no added job responsibilities in three or four years, reduction of responsibilities, no important projects or committee work, no promotion, a demotion, frequent boredom and difficulty staying focused, strained relationships with boss or coworkers

Reproducible Master 19-1

People's Attitudes

Name_____   **Date** _____   **Period** _____

The people in the following situations have typical negative attitudes. These attitudes influence their conduct at home, school, and work. Read each situation. Then explain how each person's work conduct would improve if he or she had a more positive attitude.

1. Todd always assumes other people won't like him. On his first day on a new job, his coworkers were polite, but no one asked him to have lunch with them. Todd thought, "I knew the others wouldn't like me. There must be something wrong with me." If Todd had a more positive attitude, he would _____

_____

_____

_____

2. Shawna always thinks situations will have negative outcomes. She wants to begin a nationally recognized weight loss program but says to herself, "Why bother? I always go back to my old eating habits. I'll never be able to control my weight." If Shawna had a more positive attitude, she would _____

_____

_____

_____

3. Dustin blows events out of proportion. At the fast-food restaurant where he works, he accidentally gave a customer an extra order of French fries. He didn't realize it until the customer left. Dustin is afraid the manager will find out and think Dustin is giving food away to his friends on a regular basis. If Dustin had a positive attitude, he would _____

_____

_____

_____

4. Chan jumps to conclusions and thinks other people are always critical of him. Twice he has applied for better positions at work, and twice he has not been promoted. "The managers here must think I'm not a good worker," he said. If Chan had a positive attitude, he would _____

_____

_____

_____

5. Angela is often controlled by negative emotions. While waiting for a job interview at a new company, she sees another candidate, professionally dressed and groomed, leaving the office. Suddenly she feels dejected. "I don't look half as good as that woman," she says to herself. "My resume probably isn't as good as hers either. I might as well just leave now and spare myself some embarrassment." If Angela had a positive attitude, she would _____

_____

_____

_____

(Continued)

Name_____

6. Cortez views a negative event as the beginning of an endless pattern of failure. When he was laid off from his first job because of budget cuts, Cortez said, "I'll always be the one to be laid off because the least experienced workers always get cut first. I'll never be able to get ahead." If Cortez had a positive attitude, he would

_____

_____

_____

7. Tracy takes personal blame for events for which she is not entirely responsible. When her softball team was practicing in a neighborhood park, one of her teammates hit the ball and broke a neighbor's window. The other girls ran away and left Tracy to be reprimanded by the home owner. Tracy left the park blaming herself and taking responsibility for replacing the window. If Tracy had a positive attitude, she would _____

_____

_____

_____

8. Mary Louise thinks she is worthless because she makes honest mistakes. When Brian came to pick her up for their date at 7 p.m., Mary Louise wasn't ready. She thought Brian had said 8 p.m. Mary Louise believes Brian will never ask her out again because he thinks she can't do anything right. If Mary Louise had a positive attitude, she would _____

_____

_____

_____

9. Cindy thinks people look down on her because of her job as a waitress. "My customers are so rude to me every day," she says. "They must think I'm not good enough because I don't have an executive job." If Cindy had a positive attitude, she would _____

_____

_____

_____

10. Louis is a complainer. At his new retail sales job he is always complaining about vacuuming the store every night before closing. He gets grouchy around closing time and his coworkers avoid him. He says, "They think I'm a nobody because I have to do the worst job in the store. I hate vacuuming." If Louis had a positive attitude he would _____

_____

_____

_____

Reproducible Master 19-2

Successful Job Conduct

Name _____ **Date** _____ **Period** _____

Behaving properly on the job is important for job success. Respond to the following statements by placing a check mark in the appropriate column. Think about your answers and be honest. Then answer the questions that follow.

Agree **Disagree**

_____ _____ 1. I am willing to work with my coworkers as a team.

_____ _____ 2. I get along with people at work.

_____ _____ 3. I am friendly at work.

_____ _____ 4. I accept criticism positively.

_____ _____ 5. I perform tasks I don't want to do as well as any others.

_____ _____ 6. I listen to my supervisor and follow through with the supervisor's suggestions.

_____ _____ 7. I do not act self-centered.

_____ _____ 8. I do not act like a know-it-all.

_____ _____ 9. I look for something else to do when I have completed my assignments.

_____ _____ 10. I have a good sense of humor at work.

_____ _____ 11. I avoid arguments with coworkers.

_____ _____ 12. I don't gossip or spread rumors.

_____ _____ 13. I have a positive attitude toward my work.

_____ _____ 14. I respect my coworkers' positive qualities as people.

_____ _____ 15. I practice ways of handling stress on the job.

16. Whose on-the-job conduct do you most admire? What personal qualities are reflected in his or her conduct?

_____

_____

_____

_____

_____

_____

_____

_____

_____

_____

_____

_____

Reproducible Master 19-3

Case Study: Linda's Negative Behavior

Name_____ **Date** _____ **Period** _____

Work in small groups to read the case study and role-play each of the situations in the team exercise described below.

Ever since Linda came to work in the supermarket as a bagger, her coworkers have wished she would quit. Linda never smiles or speaks to anyone, including the customers. When she does speak, it's usually to complain about something. "I hate bagging," she says. "I'm just doing this because my parents made me get a job. This job wouldn't be so bad if I could be a checker, but being a bagger is awful."

Because Linda hates her job, she doesn't do any more than what is required of her. She usually refuses to pitch in to help another bagger when her line isn't busy. She will never change schedules with another bagger if asked. In fact, she gets grouchy with her coworkers. "Don't ever ask me to change schedules with you again," she snaps.

One day Linda was having something to eat in the employee lunchroom when she noticed that she was the only one sitting alone. Everyone else was engaged in conversation at other tables. "No wonder I hate it here so much," thought Linda. "These people aren't friendly and they sure don't accept me." Everyone has made it clear to Linda that they don't like working with her. In fact, many of them have asked the manager not to schedule Linda for their checkout line.

Finally, Linda's negative behavior got her into trouble. A customer asked Linda to put certain items in certain bags. Linda ignored the customer and bagged the items however she pleased. When the customer noticed this, she asked Linda again to change the bags. "Look, I'm just doing my job," Linda snapped at the customer, who immediately called for the manager. After the manager calmed the customer, he took Linda aside and said, "Linda, you'll have to change your ways, or else I won't be able to keep you on here." Linda took off her employee badge and threw it to the floor. "I knew you'd fire me!" she shouted. "I hated this dumb job anyway."

Team Role-Playing Exercise

Show how a positive attitude can lead to proper workplace conduct and can help Linda do the following: enjoy her job, advance in it, and be a well-liked coworker.

Role-play the following:
1. Having a more positive attitude about working as a bagger
2. Helping coworkers and being willing to change schedules
3. Having lunch in the employee lunchroom
4. Responding to a customer request
5. Responding to a warning from the supervisor

Reproducible Master 19-4

Review and Study Guide for Chapter 19

Name_____ **Date** _____ **Period** _____

Completion: Fill in the blanks with the correct terms.

1. The rules of workplace _____ list the behavior expected of all employees on the job.

2. A(n) _____ is a job advancement that employees must earn by being productive and responsible on the job.

3. Recognizing the cause and then learning to handle it can help people manage _____ in their lives.

4. When an employee is fired from the job, he or she should try to _____ from the experience so the same mistake is not repeated.

5. A transfer to a classification in a lower grade is a(n) _____.

6. A(n) _____ is a group of workers who have formed together to voice their opinions to their employer or employer's representative.

7. Workers can _____ their own job performance to find out if they are having success with their jobs.

8. When a worker is *released* or *let go,* he or she is _____.

9. Job _____ means a worker is hired for a trial period of time to see how well he or she can do the job.

10. _____ ratings help employers judge how well employees are doing their jobs.

Matching: Match the following terms and identifying phrases.

_____11. A strong belief.

_____12. A feeling of pressure, strain, or tension that results from change.

_____13. Something that inspires a person to act.

_____14. A group formed by workers who belong to the same industry.

_____15. A program for new workers in which they learn the company's policies, history, and rules.

_____16. An agreement that spells out the conditions for wages, benefits, job security, work hours, working conditions, and grievance procedures.

_____17. A transfer to a different department or another classification in the same pay grade.

_____18. The process that labor and management use to discuss what they expect from each other in a workplace.

_____19. Employees may choose to join or not to join a union if their workplace has this type of agreement.

_____20. A group formed by workers who have the same trade.

A. craft union
B. lateral move
C. open shop
D. stress
E. conviction
F. collective bargaining
G. industrial union
H. labor contract
I. incentive
J. orientation

Succeeding on the Job

Name_____

Date _____   **Period** _____   **Score** _____

Chapter 19 Test

Matching: Match the following terms and identifying phrases.

_____ 1. Group of workers who have formed together to voice their opinions to their employer or employer's representative.

_____ 2. A feeling of pressure, strain, or tension that results from change.

_____ 3. A strong belief.

_____ 4. A group formed by workers who have the same trade.

_____ 5. A program for new workers in which they learn the company's policies, history, and rules.

_____ 6. An agreement that spells out the conditions for wages, benefits, job security, work hours, working conditions, and grievance procedures.

_____ 7. Something that inspires a person to act.

_____ 8. The process that labor and management use to discuss what they expect from each other in a workplace.

A. orientation
B. incentive
C. conviction
D. stress
E. union
F. collective bargaining
G. craft union
H. labor contract

True/False: Circle *T* if the statement is true or *F* if the statement is false.

T   F   9. As a beginner, an employee should *not* perform tasks he or she does *not* know how to do.

T   F   10. An employee's ability to get along with the supervisor and other coworkers will contribute to his or her success on the job.

T   F   11. The first step toward job success begins the first day on the job.

T   F   12. Every person reacts differently to stress.

T   F   13. If an employee is having trouble learning a task, he or she should ask the supervisor for assistance.

T   F   14. A person should expect to begin an entry-level job at a high salary.

T   F   15. At most companies, employees are reviewed every six months or once a year.

T   F   16. If a workplace has an open shop agreement, employees must join a union as a condition of employment.

T   F   17. A promotion is an advancement that employees must earn.

T   F   18. Quitting a job without giving notice is *not* fair to the employer.

(Continued)

Name_____

Multiple Choice: Choose the best response. Write the letter in the space provided.

_____ 19. To succeed on the job, new workers need to become aware of their _____.
A. strengths
B. weaknesses
C. successes
D. All of the above.

_____ 20. Workers who have problems learning how to do a task should _____.
A. ask someone else to do it
B. ask the supervisor for assistance
C. ask for something else to do
D. do nothing

_____ 21. When an employee is promoted, he or she should *not* _____.
A. develop new relationships with employees being supervised
B. brag about the promotion to other workers
C. delegate responsibility and helps workers accomplish tasks
D. earn respect by treating others fairly

_____ 22. When leaving a company, a general rule is to _____.
A. notify your supervisor the day you leave
B. notify your supervisor one week before you leave
C. notify your supervisor two weeks before you leave
D. give no notice and walk off the job

_____ 23. When changing jobs, try to _____.
A. leave on good terms
B. get back at a supervisor you dislike
C. tell off another coworker
D. write a letter about the company's problems

Essay Questions: Provide complete responses to the following questions or statements.

24. Explain the purpose of job performance ratings.
25. Describe the five most common reasons employers give for firing employees.
26. List four signs of a stalled career.

Diversity and Rights in the Workplace

20

Objectives

After studying this chapter, students will be able to
- explain how current population trends affect workplace diversity.
- list the benefits of diversity to an employer.
- describe ways that employers and employees can promote workplace diversity.
- provide examples of employment discrimination forbidden by law.
- explain how to take action against any sexual harassment or discrimination directed at them in the workplace.

Teaching Materials

Text, pages 365–385
   Terms to Know
   Facts in Review
   Applying Your Skills
   Developing SCANS Workplace Competencies
Student Activity Guide
   A. *My Heritage*
   B. *Diversity Awareness*
   C. *Promoting Diversity*
   D. *Know Your Rights*
   E. *Diversity Terms*
Teacher's Resource Guide/Binder
   Which Laws Apply? reproducible master 20-1
   Workplace Case Studies, reproducible master 20-2
   Review and Study Guide for Chapter 20,
      reproducible master 20-3
   Chapter 20 Test, reproducible master
Teacher's Resource Binder
   Workplace Improvements Due to Diversity, color
      transparency CT-20

Introductory Activities

1. Ask each student to write a definition of the word *diversity.* Ask several volunteers to read their definitions to the class. What similarities are there in the definitions? What differences? Then ask someone to read a definition from the dictionary and compare.
2. After students are clear on the definition of diversity, have them read the title of the chapter. What might be the relationship between *diversity* and *rights in the workplace*? Why would these two topics be studied together?
3. Ask students to react to this sentence on page 365 in the text: "Everyone in the United States has experienced some form of diversity." Do they agree or disagree with this statement? Have each of them experienced some form of diversity?

Instructional Concepts and Student Learning Experiences
Diversity Trends in the United States

4. *My Heritage*, Activity A, SAG. Students are asked to interview a grandparent or another older relative, asking them to recall being the student's age when responding to the statements.
5. *Diversity Awareness*, Activity B, SAG. Students are to answer a series of true/false questions regarding diversity. Use the activity as a basis for class discussion.
6. Review the definition of *assimilation.* Do students feel that assimilation is being practiced more today than in the early 1900's among new immigrants to this country?
7. Ask students why increasing numbers of women are choosing to work outside the home. What reasons can they site for this trend? Have them debate the pros and cons of this trend.
8. Have students interview their employers to find out their views on hiring older workers. Do their employers hire previously retired workers? How do they view these workers? Have students develop a series of questions to ask their employers. Then have them report back to the class to compare their responses.

243

The Benefits of Diversity in the Workplace

9. *Workplace Improvements Due to Diversity*, color transparency CT-20, TRB. Use this transparency as you discuss the benefits of diversity in the workplace.
10. Have students research the topic "Benefits of Diversity in the Workplace." Write a report on their findings. Ask them to find and report on specific companies that have established diversity programs. What benefits do these companies report?

Promoting Diversity in the Workplace

11. *Promoting Diversity*, Activity C, SAG. Working in groups of four or five, students design programs to promote diversity in the community or in one member's workplace.
12. Go over the list of employer strategies for promoting workplace diversity listed on page 370 of the text. Have students explain in their own words what each strategy means and give possible examples.
13. Review the list of employee actions that encourage workplace diversity given on page 371 of the text. Have students give examples to illustrate each point or, working in pairs, write scenarios that provide examples of each action. Share with the class.

Diversity, Rights, and Discrimination

14. Review the various definitions of the word *discrimination* given in the text.
15. *Know Your Rights*, Activity D, SAG. A variety of employment situations are described in this activity. Students read each situation, identify the federal law or guideline that covers each, and describe what they would advise the person to do first in each case.
16. *Which Laws Apply?* reproducible master 20-1, TRG/B. Students match several laws that affect the workplace with descriptions of the laws.
17. Ask students to read a daily newspaper each day for a week. Some students might be able to access newspapers online. Clip (or print out) any articles related to discrimination. Bring to class and be prepared to state the law at issue in each case. Post the articles on a bulletin board.
18. Ask students to interview their employers about reasonable accommodations they have made for disabled employees as well as customers. Report back to the class.
19. Have a group of students prepare a report on the steps workers should take if they feel their rights have been violated, and they need to report this to the EEOC.

20. Ask a student to interview a female executive about her career. What were her experiences, if any, regarding sexual discrimination? Report back to the class.
21. Ask students if there will be instances where men and women are paid differently for the same job. (Exceptions will be time with company, experience in the job, advanced training, and productivity.)
22. Ask each student to write a paper reflecting on how their behavior is affected by their own cultural background. Emphasize that these papers will be read only by the teacher and will not be graded.
23. Ask students to imagine being in a place where they are the minority, or to share past experiences where they were in the minority. What factors did they *not* share with the majority. (These could involve any factor listed in Chart 20-1 on page 366 of the text.)
24. Ask students if they have seen places of employment where provisions were made for the disabled. Where have they seen disabled people employed?
25. Ask if all age requirements or preferences are illegal. Have students give examples of age requirements that *are* and *are not* legal.
26. Discuss why sexual harassment is a topic we hear more often today than in years past. Does the lack of discussion in earlier times mean that sexual harassment did not occur?
27. List the two types of sexual harassment on the board. Ask students to define these two terms and give examples of each type of harassment.
28. Go over the list of questions to use in identifying sexual harassment given on page 380 of the text. If a person answers yes to most of these questions, it is likely that sexual harassment is occurring.
29. Discuss these topics: What one person considers sexual harassment might not be considered harassment by someone else. Is this true or false? Explain. Can a person's dress and behavior send the wrong message? What part does the setting play in sexual harassment?
30. *Workplace Case Studies*, reproducible master 20-2, TRG/B. Students review two case studies to determine if sexual harassment is occurring and what should be done in each case.

Facing Sexual Harassment or Discrimination

31. Have students obtain a copy of the school's policies and procedures for reporting harassment. Review it with the students. Find out who is responsible for handling cases of sexual harassment in your school.
32. Have students check with their employers to see if policies exist in writing for handling cases of sexual harassment. If so, ask for a copy of the policy to review.

33. Review what employees can do to try to prevent sexual harassment from occurring.
34. Go over the steps for taking action against discrimination or harassment as listed on page 382 of the text. Have students role-play telling an aggressor to stop.
35. *Diversity Terms*, Activity E, SAG. Students complete a word puzzle on diversity and answer questions related to it.

Activities to Enrich Learning

36. Have students do a survey of women workers to see if they feel gender bias still exists in the workplace. List the different types of discrimination that still occurs in the workplace. Also ask what employer policies exist where these women work to help women report instances of sexual discrimination. Tabulate the results and prepare a written summary.
37. Have students research reported claims of workplace discrimination brought against any local or state employers. For each case discovered, ask students to find answers to the following questions: What was the claim and who made it? Against which employer was it made and when? What is the status of the case? (If it has already gone to court, what was the outcome?)

Activities to Extend Learning

38. Ask someone who has recently immigrated to this country to speak to the class about their experiences. Have students prepare a list of questions they would like the speaker to discuss.
39. Have a human resources manager or personnel director of a company discuss laws that protect workers from discrimination. How have these laws affected personnel jobs and the policies of companies?

Answer Key

Text

Facts in Review, page 384

1. (List seven:) age, cultural heritage, disabilities/abilities, gender, language, national origin, race, religion, sexual orientation, traditions
2. (List eight:) fewer lawsuits, high morale, increased creativity, increased productivity, more quality workers, improved decision making, faster decision making, more customers reached, more positive ties with business and government groups
3. U.S. businesses selling globally
4. (List six. See Chart 20-8 on page 371.)

5. 1964 Civil Rights Act
6. Americans with Disabilities Act of 1990
7. Equal Employment Opportunity Commission
8. It is unlawful to link any work to a specific sex unless there is a legitimate reason for it, such as restricting the job of women's restroom attendant to a woman.
9. Racial discrimination involves one individual's actions toward a member of a different race. Color discrimination may involve actions toward a member of the same race.
10. all beliefs plus nonbelief
11. The job primarily involves the ability to hear, not see.
12. *Quid pro quo harassment* occurs when one person makes unwelcome sexual advances toward another while promising certain benefits if the person complies. *Hostile environment harassment* is behavior that makes an atmosphere uncomfortable enough to interfere with a person's performance.
13. (See Chart 20-17 on page 380.)
14. Tell the aggressor to stop; keep detailed records; report the offense.

Student Activity Guide

Diversity Awareness, Activity B

1. T		14. F
2. T		15. T
3. F		16. F
4. F		17. F
5. T		18. T
6. T		19. T
7. T		20. T
8. T		21. T
9. F		22. F
10. T		23. T
11. F		24. T
12. T		25. T
13. T		

Know Your Rights, Activity D

(For each, the answer to the second question is student response.)

1. Immigration Reform and Control Act of 1986
2. Equal Pay Act of 1963
3. Fair Labor Standards Act of 1938
4. Civil Rights Act of 1964
5. Americans with Disabilities Act of 1990
6. Equal Employment Opportunity Commission (EEOC) guidelines
7. Equal Employment Opportunity Commission (EEOC) guidelines
8. Age Discrimination in Employment Act of 1967

Diversity Terms, Activity E

1.   G E N D E R
2.   C R I M I N A L
3.   C I V A L
4.   A G E
5.   D I S C R I M I N A T I O N
6.   A S S I M I L A T I O N
7.   R A C I S M
8.   E T H N I C
9.   S T E R E O T Y P E
10. (Student response.)

Teacher's Resource Guide/Binder

Which Laws Apply? reproducible master 20-1

1. E		7. F
2. F		8. A
3. B		9. B
4. C		10. A
5. D		11. G
6. B		12. F

Workplace Case Studies, reproducible master 20-2

1. Yes. Anita is being touched and looked at in a sexual way by Mr. Marshall and it is unwelcome.
2. hostile environment
3. Probably not. Wanda and Joyce do not find Mr. Marshall's behavior offensive.
4. (Student response. Should include steps listed on page 382 of the text.)
5. Yes. The supervisor is making sexual advances and promising Roberto a promotion if he complies.
6. quid pro quo
7. (Student response. Should include steps listed on page 382 of the text.)

Review and Study Guide for Chapter 20, reproducible master 20-3

1. quid pro quo harassment
2. hostile environment harassment
3. sexual orientation
4. reprisal
5. sexual harassment
6. body language

7. A		14. F
8. C		15. T
9. B		16. F
10. C		17. T
11. D		18. T
12. B		19. F
13. T		20. F

Chapter 20 Test

1. H		13. F
2. G		14. T
3. E		15. T
4. B		16. T
5. A		17. F
6. F		18. T
7. D		19. B
8. C		20. D
9. T		21. B
10. T		22. C
11. F		23. A
12. T		

24. (Describe five:) There are fewer lawsuits; morale is high; creativity increases; productivity increases; quality workers are attracted to the organization; the decision-making process improves; decision-making speed improves; more customers are reached; goodwill and positive ties are formed with businesses and government groups.
25. (List five. See page 371 in the text.)
26. Ask yourself the following questions: Is the behavior sexual in nature? Do others consider it sexual in nature? Is it unwelcome? Is it offensive? Does it interfere with work or school performance? Does the harasser know I want it stopped?

Reproducible Master 20-1

Which Laws Apply?

Name_____ **Date** _____ **Period** _____

In the blank spaces below, write the letter of the law that applies. Answers can be used more than once.

    A. Americans with Disabilities Act of 1990

    B. Fair Labor Standards Act of 1938

    C. Age Discrimination in Employment Act of 1967

    D. The Equal Pay Act of 1963

    E. Immigration Reform and Control Act of 1986

    F. 1964 Civil Rights Act (and amendments)

    G. 1991 Civil Rights Act

_____ 1. Established criminal penalties for discriminating against U.S. citizens born outside this country.

_____ 2. Established criminal penalties for interfering with a person's employment rights.

_____ 3. Established minimum wages.

_____ 4. Bans unfair treatment of workers over 40.

_____ 5. Forbids different pay scales for men and women.

_____ 6. Includes many child labor standards.

_____ 7. Bans employment discrimination on the basis of race, color, religion, sex, or national origin.

_____ 8. Gives people with disabilities a chance to be hired for their skills.

_____ 9. Limits number of hours employees can work without receiving overtime pay.

_____ 10. Requires public transportation services be accessible to people with disabilities.

_____ 11. Allows victims of discrimination to take their cases to court and be awarded compensatory and punitive damages.

_____ 12. Created the Equal Employment Opportunity Commission to enforce all labor laws and regulations.

Reproducible Master 20-2

Workplace Case Studies

Name_____ **Date** _____ **Period** _____

Read each of the cases described below. Decide if the situation describes possible sexual harassment. Answer the questions that follow.

Case I

My name is Anita. I'm 17 years old and started working as a waitress at the Midtown Coffee House three months ago. I really liked my work at first. Everyone was nice, and I made friends with some of the other waitresses right away. At break one day, a couple of the older waitresses, Wanda and Joyce, were laughing about watching out for Mr. Marshall's hands. He's the assistant manager. They talked about how he likes to touch them when he talks to them. They seemed to be kidding around about it and didn't seem to mind.

Well, a couple of weeks ago, I noticed a change. Mr. Marshall used to put his arm across my shoulders sometimes when he was pointing out which section of tables was mine. I didn't think too much about it, but then he started placing his hand on my back, on my waist, and even lower. Just yesterday, I swear he tried to look down my blouse every chance he got. I'm really feeling uncomfortable with this, but I'm afraid to say anything. Obviously, the other waitresses think it's a big joke! But it's not to me. I'm scared, and I don't know what to do.

1. Is this sexual harassment? Explain. _____

_____

_____

2. If it is sexual harassment, which type is it? _____

3. Would the behavior toward Wanda and Joyce be considered sexual harassment? Explain your answer. ____

_____

_____

4. What would you advise Anita to do? _____

_____

_____

_____

_____

_____

_____

_____

(Continued)

Name_____

Case II

My name is Roberto. I work as a baggage handler at the airport. I've been working there for about two years now. It's good work and the pay is decent. I was hoping to get a promotion soon so I could save up enough money to get my own place.

A few months ago they put a new supervisor over my shift. At first I thought he was going to be a good guy to work for. He was friendly and well liked by all the crew. Last week, he called me into his office. He said he'd heard that I was interested in a promotion. I told him he'd heard right. Then he said he could make that happen for me real easily. All I had to do was go out with him after work some night. Then he showed me some pictures of guys together, and I figured out what he wanted real fast. When I said I wasn't interested, he said that I could forget about ever getting a promotion. Now I don't know what to do. I need the work, but this isn't right.

5. Is this sexual harassment? Explain. _____

_____

_____

6. If it is sexual harassment, which type is it? _____

7. What would you advise Roberto to do? _____

_____

_____

_____

_____

_____

_____

_____

Reproducible Master 20-3

Review and Study Guide for Chapter 20

Name_____ Date _____ Period _____

Completion: Fill in the blanks with the correct terms.

1. _____ _____ _____ _____
   occurs when one person makes unwelcome sexual advances toward another while promising certain benefits
   if the person complies.

2. _____ _____ _____ is a type of sexual harassment
   that makes an atmosphere uncomfortable enough to interfere with a person's performance.

3. _____ _____ refers to the gender preferred when choosing someone
   for an emotional/sexual relationship.

4. _____ is the revenge-motivated act of retaliating, or "getting back at" someone.

5. _____ _____ generally means unwelcome or unwanted advances,
   requests for favors, or other verbal or physical conduct of a sexual nature.

6. _____ _____ is a means of expressing a message through body
   movements, facial expressions, or hand gestures.

Multiple Choice: Choose the best response. Write the letter in the space provided.

_____ 7. Presently the majority of Americans have _____ ancestors.
   A. European
   B. Asian
   C. African
   D. Hispanic

_____ 8. Diverse languages are more common in the workplace because _____.
   A. less misunderstandings result when employees and customers speak different languages
   B. people prefer having private conversations that others cannot understand
   C. a growing segment of workers are first-generation immigrants who know little English
   D. All of the above.

_____ 9. Which of the following is *not* a benefit of diversity in the workplace?
   A. There are fewer lawsuits.
   B. Morale decreases.
   C. Productivity increases.
   D. Creativity increases.

_____ 10. Workplace discrimination refers to _____.
   A. treating people on a basis other than individual merit
   B. treating one or more workers negatively compared to the treatment of the larger group
   C. excluding some workers from a special treatment offered to others
   D. All of the above.

(Continued)

Name_____

_____11. The law that made it more difficult for noncitizens to obtain employment in the U.S. is the _____.
   A. 1964 Civil Rights Act
   B. Equal Pay Act of 1963
   C. Fair Labor Standards Act
   D. Immigration Act of 1990

_____12. The law that forbids the practice of using different pay scales for men and women doing the same work is the _____.
   A. 1964 Civil Rights Act
   B. Equal Pay Act of 1963
   C. Fair Labor Standards Act of 1938
   D. Immigration Act of 1990

True/False: Circle *T* if the statement is true or *F* if the statement is false.

T   F   13. The mission of the EEOC is to assure equal opportunity in employment for everyone.

T   F   14. Women no longer face sex discrimination in the workplace.

T   F   15. An example of a BFOQ is hiring a male attendant for a men's locker room.

T   F   16. There are federal laws that specifically prohibit discrimination based on sexual orientation.

T   F   17. Sexual harassment victims must prove they did *not* welcome or encourage the offensive behavior.

T   F   18. Workers are protected from retaliation when they file discrimination complaints.

T   F   19. An employer is *not* legally responsible for workplace discrimination when it occurs without his or her knowledge.

T   F   20. The laws prohibiting religious discrimination only cover the major religious denominations.

Diversity and Rights in the Workplace

Name_____

Date _____ Period _____ Score _____

Chapter 20 Test

Matching: Match the following terms and identifying phrases.

_____ 1. A label given to a person based on assumptions held about all members of that person's racial or cultural group.

_____ 2. The gender preferred when choosing someone for an emotional/sexual relationship.

_____ 3. The belief that one race is superior or inferior to all others.

_____ 4. Treating people on a basis other than individual merit.

_____ 5. Blending people into society by helping them become more like the majority.

_____ 6. Unwelcome or unwanted advances.

_____ 7. Occurs when one person makes unwelcome sexual advances toward another while promising certain benefits if the person complies.

_____ 8. A type of sexual behavior that makes an atmosphere uncomfortable enough to interfere with a person's performance.

A. assimilation
B. discrimination
C. hostile environment harassment
D. quid pro quo harassment
E. racism
F. sexual harassment
G. sexual orientation
H. stereotype

True/False: Circle *T* if the statement is true or *F* if the statement is false.

T   F   9. All Americans are part of some ethnic group.

T   F   10. A key component of sexual harassment is *not* considering the feelings of the person receiving the aggressive behavior.

T   F   11. Diverse languages are less common in the workplace because too many misunderstandings occur.

T   F   12. Religious conflicts often arise when employers have religious displays that express one group's beliefs but *not* others'.

T   F   13. In the future, women are expected to enter the labor force at a greater rate than men.

T   F   14. Everyone is a potential candidate for some form of disability in a lifetime.

T   F   15. Unskilled older workers who lose or leave their jobs may *not* be able to find replacement work.

T   F   16. Experts believe diversity in the workplace will help U.S. companies compete more effectively in worldwide markets.

T   F   17. To discriminate is never a positive trait.

T   F   18. Much of the discrimination directed at women is due to society's concepts of what types of work are appropriate for women.

(Continued)

Name_____

Multiple Choice: Choose the best response. Write the letter in the space provided.

_____19. The diversity of the U.S. population is most evident in _____.
  A. small towns
  B. large cities
  C. rural areas
  D. None of the above.

_____20. Which of the following is a form of workplace discrimination?
  A. Restricted entry to training programs.
  B. Difficulty in gaining promotions.
  C. No access to jobs offering higher pay or prestige.
  D. All the above.

_____21. The type of discrimination directed at a worker because of his or her birth outside of the U.S. is _____ discrimination.
  A. color
  B. national origin
  C. language
  D. religious

_____22. Which of the following is *not* an example of sexual harassment?
  A. Inappropriate sexual remarks.
  B. Posted pictures with a sexual message.
  C. Welcomed sexual advances.
  D. Unwanted touching.

_____23. Which is *not* a step a person should take if he or she is the victim of sexual harassment?
  A. Let time go by and hope the aggressor stops.
  B. Tell the aggressor to stop.
  C. Keep detailed records.
  D. Report the offense.

Essay Questions: Provide complete responses to the following questions or statements.

24. Describe five benefits of diversity in the workplace.
25. List five employee actions that promote workplace diversity.
26. What questions should a person ask to identify a case of sexual harassment?

21

Succeeding in Our Economic System

Objectives

After studying this chapter, students will be able to
- describe our economic system.
- compare the three forms of business ownership.
- describe the responsibilities involved in managing a business.
- build SCANS competencies in using interpersonal skills, information, and systems.

Teaching Materials

Text, pages 387-399
Terms to Know
Facts in Review
Applying Your Skills
Developing SCANS Workplace Competencies
Student Activity Guide
A. *Another Economic System*
B. *Business in a Free Enterprise System*
C. *The Competitive Business World*
D. *Free Enterprise System*
E. *Forms of Business Ownership*
F. *Business Structures*
Teacher's Resource Guide/Binder
The Free Enterprise System, transparency master 21-1
Supply and Demand in Our Economic System, reproducible master 21-2
Review and Study Guide for Chapter 21, reproducible master 21-3
Chapter 21 Test, reproducible master
Teacher's Resource Binder
Types of Business Organizations, color transparency CT-21

Introductory Activities

1. Ask students to brainstorm the names of well-known business leaders and inventors who lived during the Industrial Revolution and influenced the U.S.'s growth and development. Discuss the personality traits, attitudes, and aptitudes of these successful people.

2. Discuss the role of immigrants in the development of the U.S. economic system. Ask students to share stories of family members who immigrated to the U.S. and succeeded in businesses.
3. Have students research and write a brief report on the U.S. patent system, discussing its history and influence on the U.S. economic system.

Instructional Concepts and Student Learning Experiences

The Free Enterprise System

4. *The Free Enterprise System,* transparency master 21-1, TRG/B. Use the transparency to explain to students how the free enterprise system works.
5. Divide the class into several groups. Have each group research and prepare a panel report on the following economic and political systems: capitalism, socialism, democracy, and communism. Students should illustrate reports with visual aids. Have all students summarize findings in a report that compares each economic and political system.
6. *Another Economic System,* Activity A, SAG. Students interview someone who has lived under an economic system that is different from that of the United States. Students will then discuss the interview in class.
7. Students should list their personal resources and an accompanying list of wants and needs. Discuss how resources are limited while wants and needs are unlimited.
8. Have students choose a local business or corporation and research its role in the free enterprise system. Students should focus on profits, losses, and the actions businesses must take to stay profitable.
9. *Business in a Free Enterprise System,* Activity B, SAG. Students interview a business owner and describe the business.
10. Have the class debate the topic "Free enterprise is the only economic system suitable for a democracy."

11. Students should investigate the concept of supply and demand by brainstorming and listing popular consumer items from over the past decade. Discuss what happened to the prices of these items during high demand versus low demand.
12. *Supply and Demand in Our Economic System,* reproducible master 21-2, TRG/B. Students are to answer questions about how supply and demand affect product prices.
13. Have students work in groups and create posters or diagrams that illustrate the relationship of supply, demand, and prices in the economic system of the U.S. Discuss how each factor affects the other.
14. Create a case study illustrating a business operating in the free enterprise system. Imagine you own a local clothing store that sells coats. Describe your business to students in terms of pricing, quality of merchandise, and customer service. Have students develop a competitive strategy for their imaginary coat store by determining the quality of the coats they buy wholesale, the retail prices they set, the customer service they offer (such as free alterations or layaway), store hours, etc. Considering the students' responses, discuss whose store would get the most business and why.
15. Instruct students to write a short essay describing life in an economic system that allows monopolies.
16. *The Competitive Business World,* Activity C, SAG. Students work in groups to research the price of a compact disc from four different sources then answer questions and compare their findings in class.
17. *Free Enterprise System,* Activity D, SAG. Students fill in the blanks with words from the word bank.

How Businesses Are Organized

18. *Types of Business Organizations,* color transparency CT-21, TRB. Use the transparency to discuss the three different types of business organizations.
19. Have students bring advertisements from local businesses to class. Students should determine each business's form of ownership and discuss the characteristics of each.
20. *Forms of Business Ownership,* Activity E, SAG. Students match the form of business ownership with the appropriate description, then list two examples of each form of ownership in their community.
21. Divide the class into three groups. Students in group one are to pretend they own various proprietorships. Students in group two will form various regular or limited partnerships. Students in group three should act as corporate stockholders and members of the board of directors. Through monologues and role-plays, students describe the advantages and disadvantages of each form of business ownership.
22. Have students clip articles about local and national corporations from the business section of the newspaper and bring them to class. Considering the collected information, what are the advantages and disadvantages of becoming stockholders in these corporations?

Business Management

23. Have students compare the benefits of good management in their personal lives to good management in a business.
24. Have students role-play a typical business day from the perspective of various individuals linked to the organization. Ask students to select a type of business for the role-play, then portray the following individuals: an entry-level employee, a department supervisor, the company president, a member of the board of directors, and a stockholder. Students should role-play the responsibilities of the person at each level.
25. *Business Structures,* Activity F, SAG. Students make a chart showing the levels of management at their workplace or school.

Activities to Enrich Learning

26. Have students research the availability of documentaries or feature films at the library that describe the growth of the U.S. economic system. Show one or two of the films in class.
27. Instruct students to read the business section of the local newspaper for one week. Ask them to keep a daily log of what they learned regarding the present state of our economic system.
28. Have the class form its own business, selling goods and/or services. Donate profits to a local charity or school organization. Have students discuss what they learned.

Activities to Extend Learning

29. Invite people at various managerial levels to speak to students about their job responsibilities. How do their jobs affect the profit margins of the companies for which they work?
30. Arrange for students to observe a stockholder's meeting at a local corporation.

Answer Key

Text

Facts in Review, page 398

1. private ownership and control of productive resources, a free market, the profit motive, supply

and demand, competition, limited government involvement

2. to establish and enforce laws and policies to promote economic growth and stability, to protect consumers from unsafe or unfair practices
3. They could charge unfair prices and limit production and availability of goods and services.
4. A proprietorship has one owner. A proprietorship has two or more owners. A corporation is owned by many people.
5. availability of more money, more people to offer more skills and experiences
6. disagreements between/among partners, uneven workload between/among partners
7. an investor in the business who does not work for the business
8. debts equal to the amount invested
9. limited liability, ability to raise money for the business
10. board of directors and top-level managers

Student Activity Guide

Free Enterprise System, Activity D

1. profit
2. monopoly
3. capital
4. competition
5. supply
6. needs
7. demand
8. free market
9. government
10. productive
11. proprietorship
12. corporation

Forms of Business Ownership, Activity E

1. C
2. B
3. A
4. A
5. B
6. C
7. A
8. B

(Community examples are student response.)

Teacher's Resource Guide/Binder

Supply and Demand in Our Economic System,
reproducible master 21-2

1. Prices will go up because the supply is limited.
2. Prices will go up because of high consumer demand for the product. Also, the supply of dolls will be limited with no other product competition.
3. Prices will go down because of competition in the marketplace. Consumer demand for the old product will decrease.
4. Prices will go up because the supply is low while consumer demand is high.

5. Prices will go down because of a supply increase and more competition in the marketplace. (Remaining questions are student response.)

Review and Study Guide for Chapter 21,
reproducible master 21-3

1. needs, wants
2. limited, unlimited
3. profit
4. consumers
5. competition
6. limited (or silent)
7. capital
8. organization chart
9. B
10. G
11. I
12. D
13. A
14. E
15. F
16. C
17. H
18. In tall organizational structures, employees tend to be specialized and have fewer responsibilities. In flat structures, employees have a broader range of skills and more responsibilities.

Chapter 21 Test

1. B		13. T
2. G		14. T
3. I		15. F
4. D		16. T
5. A		17. T
6. E		18. F
7. F		19. T
8. C		20. A
9. H		21. B
10. T		22. D
11. F		23. C
12. T		24. B

25. It had natural resources, a patent system, skilled labor, good management, capital for investments, and a system of government that permitted the free enterprise system.
26. Limited partners, sometimes called silent partners, invest money or property into a business but do not work in it. They receive a percentage of the profits, and if the business fails, are only responsible for debts up to the amount of the investment.
27. private ownership and control of productive resources, a free market, the profit motive, supply and demand, competition, limited government involvement

Transparency Master 21-1

The Free Enterprise System

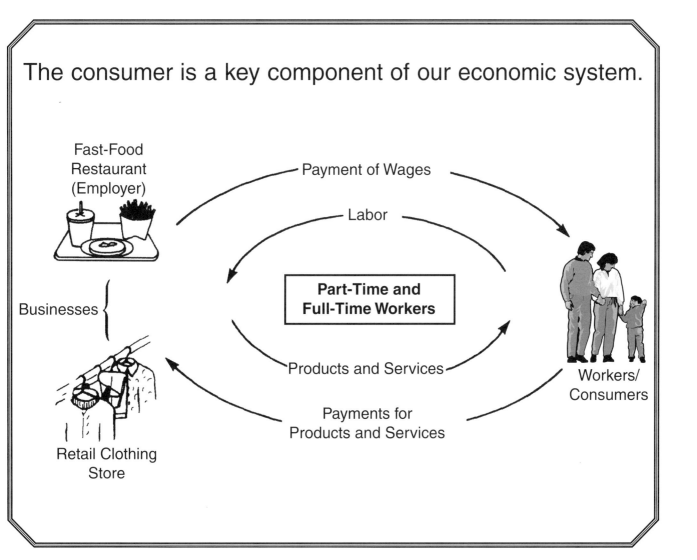

The consumer is a key component of our economic system.

Fast-Food Restaurant (Employer)

Payment of Wages

Labor

Businesses

Part-Time and Full-Time Workers

Products and Services

Payments for Products and Services

Retail Clothing Store

Workers/ Consumers

Reproducible Master 21-2

Supply and Demand in Our Economic System

Name_____ **Date** _____ **Period** _____

In the space provided, write what would happen to the price of five different items based on the situations described. Then choose one of the items and answer questions about how the free enterprise system affects the production, selling, and purchasing of that product. Explain your answers.

1. A new convertible auto, one of only 3,000 manufactured in the United States: _____
   _____
   _____

2. A new doll based on a cartoon character from the most popular children's television show: _____
   _____
   _____

3. A computer chip for a personal computer the week after a faster chip is marketed: _____
   _____
   _____

4. Oranges and grapefruit sold in grocery stores after a major frost in citrus groves:_____
   _____
   _____

5. Identical stereo systems with compact disc players offered at two different electronics stores in the same town:
   _____
   _____

Chosen product: _____

6. Who could own the business or industry that makes this product?

7. How would the production of this product be affected by a free market?

8. Describe how a company could use its resources to make a profit by selling this product.

9. What factors could affect the supply and demand of this product?

10. What kind of competition does the maker of this product have?

11. Describe the limited government involvement, if any, in the production or marketing of this product.

Reproducible Master 21-3

Review and Study Guide for Chapter 21

Name_____ **Date** _____ **Period** _____

Completion: Fill in the blanks with the correct terms.

1. _____ are the basics a person must have to live, while _____ are items a person wishes to have but can live without.

2. In our economy, resources are _____ while wants and needs are _____.

3. The main reason for operating a business is to make a(n) _____.

4. All businesses depend on _____ to buy their goods and services.

5. _____ encourages businesses to produce quality goods and services at low prices.

6. A(n) _____ partner invests money or property in a business in which he or she does not work.

7. _____ refers to the possessions and money used to increase business.

8. A(n) _____ _____ shows an organization's internal structure.

Matching: Match the following terms and identifying phrases.

_____ 9. Labor, land, capital, and equipment used to produce and provide goods and services.

_____ 10. A business owned by only one person.

_____ 11. A business owned by many people and formed by selling stocks.

_____ 12. The amount of products and services available for sale.

_____ 13. A situation in which people are able to make their own economic decisions.

_____ 14. The amount of products and services consumers want to buy.

_____ 15. A single company that controls the entire supply of a product or service.

_____ 16. The amount of money a business makes from selling goods and services that is greater than the cost of producing them.

_____ 17. A form of business organization in which two or more people go into business together.

A. free enterprise system
B. productive resources
C. profit
D. supply
E. demand
F. monopoly
G. proprietorship
H. partnership
I. corporation

Essay Question: Provide a complete response to the following statement.

18. Compare tall to flat organizational structures.

Succeeding in Our Economic System

Name_____

Date _____ **Period** _____ **Score** _____

Chapter 21 Test

Matching: Match the following terms and identifying phrases.

_____ 1. Labor, land, capital, and equipment used to produce and provide goods and services.

_____ 2. A business that has only one owner.

_____ 3. A business owned by many people and formed by selling stocks.

_____ 4. The amount of products and services available for sale.

_____ 5. A situation in which people are able to make their economic decisions.

_____ 6. The amount of products and services consumers want to buy.

_____ 7. A single company that controls the entire supply of a product or service.

_____ 8. The amount of money a business makes from selling goods and services that is greater than the cost of producing them.

_____ 9. A form of business organization where two or more people go into business together.

A. free enterprise system
B. productive resources
C. profit
D. supply
E. demand
F. monopoly
G. proprietorship
H. partnership
I. corporation

True/False: Circle *T* if the statement is true or *F* if the statement is false.

T F 10. American industries were born at the time of the Industrial Revolution.

T F 11. The U.S. government owns and controls business and industry.

T F 12. Resources are limited while wants and needs are unlimited.

T F 13. The relationship between supply and demand affects the prices of products and services.

T F 14. The main reason for operating a business is to make a profit.

T F 15. A product shortage can cause prices to drop.

T F 16. Competition encourages businesses to produce quality goods and services at lower prices.

T F 17. All businesses depend on consumers to buy their goods and services.

T F 18. Stockholders usually have a lot of input in business decisions.

T F 19. Managing a business requires careful planning, staffing, directing, marketing, and financing.

(Continued)

Name_____

Multiple Choice: Choose the best response. Write the letter in the space provided.

_____20. Which of the following differs from the free enterprise system?
     A. Socialism.
     B. Consumer economy.
     C. Capitalism.
     D. Market economy.

_____21. The supply and demand factor in the free enterprise system is based on the demands of _____.
     A. government
     B. consumers
     C. inflation
     D. All of the above.

_____22. One of the advantages of a partnership over a proprietorship is _____.
     A. only one person makes the decisions and manages the business
     B. the owner does most of the work
     C. partners may *not* agree on business decisions
     D. more money is available to finance the business

_____23. The promotion, selling, and distribution of goods and services is called _____.
     A. financing
     B. manufacturing
     C. marketing
     D. managing

_____24. Which is *not* an example of an unlimited need or want?
     A. Food.
     B. Time.
     C. Entertainment.
     D. Clothing.

Essay Questions: Provide complete responses to the following questions or statements.

25. Explain why the United States developed into a strong industrial nation.
26. Describe a limited partnership.
27. List the six major factors upon which the free enterprise system is based.

Entrepreneurship: A Business of Your Own

Objectives

After studying this chapter, students will be able to
- explain the importance of small business to the U.S. economy.
- list advantages and disadvantages of entrepreneurship.
- explain points to consider when planning a business, selecting a location, and pricing a product or service.
- discuss advantages and disadvantages of conducting a business from home.
- describe legal and financial issues associated with starting a business.
- build SCANS competencies in using resources, interpersonal skills, information, and systems.

Teaching Materials

Text, pages 401-421
   Terms to Know
   Facts in Review
   Applying Your Skills
   Developing SCANS Workplace Competencies
Student Activity Guide
   A. *Importance of Small Business*
   B. *Exploring Entrepreneurship*
   C. *Qualities for Success*
   D. *Planning a Business*
   E. *Entrepreneurship Terms*
Teacher's Resource Guide/Binder
   Business Expenses for an Entrepreneur,
      reproducible master 22-1
   Review and Study Guide for Chapter 22,
      reproducible master 22-2
   Chapter 22 Test, reproducible master
Teacher's Resource Binder
   Entrepreneur's Self-Quiz, color transparency CT-22

Introductory Activities

1. Ask students to pretend they own a business of their choice. Have them complete the statement "If I owned this business, I would…"

2. Poll students to see if any come from families who own businesses. Ask students to share their experiences.
3. Have students obtain brochures or pamphlets for would-be entrepreneurs from the local library, the state's labor/employment department, a community college, and the Small Business Administration (SBA). Have students share the information in class. Discuss the usefulness of each source.

Instructional Concepts and Student Learning Experiences

The Importance of Small Businesses

4. *Importance of Small Business,* Activity A, SAG. Students respond to true/false statements about the importance of small businesses, then rewrite any false statements.
5. Have students write an essay on the topic "Small Businesses: The Heart of the Free Enterprise System." Students should include at least two examples of local small businesses and explain how these businesses contribute to the community's economy.

Opportunities for Entrepreneurs

6. Poll students to see who would like to become an entrepreneur and who would not. Discuss reasons with students.
7. Have students brainstorm a list of hobbies and interests teens enjoy. Write responses on the board. What businesses could entrepreneurs create from each item listed?
8. *Exploring Entrepreneurship,* Activity B, SAG. Students interview an entrepreneur and discuss the interview in class.
9. Discuss the advantages and disadvantages of owning a franchise. What factors should an entrepreneur investigate prior to investing in a franchise?
10. Instruct students to list three local franchises with which they do business, then choose one and

research the requirements for buying a franchise from that company. Students can interview local franchise owners or contact companies directly.

11. Have students bring in classified newspaper ads which list existing businesses that are for sale. Select several examples and discuss the types of businesses and the advantages and disadvantages of buying an existing business. What questions would students ask before buying an existing business?

Planning Your Own Business

12. Have students define the term *self-starter.* List responses on the board. Discuss why this kind of person would make a good entrepreneur.

13. *Entrepreneur's Self-Quiz,* color transparency CT-22, TRB. Use the transparency to discuss what it takes to be entrepreneurs. Ask students if they possess these qualities and whether they will enjoy this role. After reviewing the questions in class, students may answer them on their own as a written assignment.

14. *Qualities for Success,* Activity C, SAG. Students choose the personal qualities they feel they possess for success as entrepreneurs and respond to questions about what it takes to succeed.

15. Ask students to brainstorm a list of decisions entrepreneurs must make. Then have students review the decision-making skills in Chapter 15 of the text. Have students explain how these skills relate to operating a business.

16. Have students independently review the checklist in Figure 22-5 of the text while considering a business that interests them. How feasible is their business idea? Students should write a description of their idea and share it with the class.

17. *Planning a Business,* Activity D, SAG. Students answer a series of questions that guide them in preparing for entrepreneurship and develop a business plan.

18. Have students search newspapers and magazines for ads offering business opportunities. Ask students to bring in ads appearing suspicious or too good to be true. What language in the ads alert students to the possibility of fraud?

19. Develop a case study based on a successful local entrepreneur. Have students provide an evaluation of the business, explaining why it is successful.

20. Ask students to think of good locations in the community for the following small businesses: a fast-food restaurant, copier service, gas station, franchise hair salon, full-service restaurant, and auto technician's shop. What factors are important to consider when choosing a business location?

21. Have students list businesses that entrepreneurs can operate from home. Organize a student debate about the advantages and disadvantages of working from home.

22. Have students visit an office supply store to price furniture and supplies that entrepreneurs might need to work at home. Have students discuss their estimates in class. Ask students if this expense might determine whether they would work at home.

23. Divide students into small groups. Ask each group to choose a business they might like to own. Have each group price their product or service, then compare it to the price of a similar product or service currently on the market. Each group should explain in class how they figured prices and how their prices compare to those of competitors.

Legal and Financial Issues

24. Have students review the advantages and disadvantages of proprietorships, partnerships, and corporations covered in Chapter 21.

25. Have students contact the local city or town hall to obtain information on local zoning laws and license requirements for small businesses. Using that information, students should determine whether they could open a pet grooming business in the following places: their home, a store next to the school, a store in the local mall, a store in an apartment building.

26. Have students obtain information from local banks about the requirements for opening business accounts.

27. Have students pretend they are applying for a business loan. Students should prepare a written business plan that includes a business description, list of financial needs, their assets and liabilities, and plans for future growth to present to a loan officer.

28. Have students write reports on how the services of lawyers, insurance agents, and accountants are beneficial for entrepreneurs. Suggest students get specific examples by interviewing local entrepreneurs, lawyers, insurance agents, or accountants.

29. Have students keep track of their personal expenses for one week by writing down *when, where,* and *for what* they spent money. Students should also save receipts. In class, compare this experience with the detailed record keeping that entrepreneurs must adhere to and discuss the importance of accurate financial record keeping.

30. *Business Expenses for an Entrepreneur,* reproducible master 22-1, TRG/B. Students imagine they are opening a florist shop to give examples for each type of expense listed.

31. *Entrepreneurship Terms,* Activity E, SAG. Students complete sentences about planning and operating a small business by using appropriate terms from the word bank.

Activities to Enrich Learning

32. Have students write a case study about a successful and an unsuccessful business entrepreneur. Discuss reasons for the entrepreneurs' success or failure in class.

33. Have students read the biographies of famous entrepreneurs, such as Ray Kroc (McDonald's), Debbie Fields (Mrs. Field's Cookies), or Sam Walton (Wal-Mart) and write biographical reports.

Activities to Extend Learning

34. Take students to visit two separately owned franchises of the same company. Have students observe the similarities and differences between the two franchises, such as the number of employees, customer service, product pricing, and working conditions. Have students write a report comparing and contrasting the two franchise locations. (Fast-food establishments are good examples to explore.)

35. Invite a panel of local entrepreneurs to speak to students about how to succeed in a new business.

36. Take the class to visit a local entrepreneur's business (not a franchise business). Have students note the location, equipment or materials required for operation, type of building, prices of the products and/or services sold, number of employees, and duties of the owner. Later in class, discuss these findings. Have students express their opinions about how well the business appears to be operating.

Answer Key

Text

Facts in Review, page 420

1. (List three:) local library, local chamber of commerce, Small Business Administration, state commerce department

2. opportunity to buy a business with a proven track record of success, exclusivity in a specific area, help in finding a good location and providing training and business advice

3. Federal Trade Commission

4. (List four:) be a self-starter, be innovative, have decision-making skill, take risks, set and achieve goals, be a good manager

5. financial, technical, and management assistance to help start, run, and enlarge a business

6. (List two of each:) advantages—no rent or lease payments, no wasted commuting time, opportunity to handle home responsibilities, possible tax advantages, possible interaction with telecommunities; disadvantages—family disruptions, possible objections from neighbors, possible conflicts with zoning laws, loneliness, isolation from other workers

7. total costs

8. corporation

9. to show that permission to run the business has been granted

10. (List three:) friends, family, personal savings, bank loan, Small Business Administration, outside investors

11. capital, fixed, variable (Examples are student response.)

12. by becoming familiar with basic terms and procedures, by recognizing whether hired accountants are doing a good job

13. dividing profit by receipts (or income, or revenues)

14. lawyer, accountant, insurance agent

Student Activity Guide

Importance of Small Business, Activity A

1. true
2. false (Small businesses compete against corporations of all sizes.)
3. true
4. false (Small businesses employ over half of U.S. workers not employed by government.)
5. true
6. false (The economy of the U.S. does rely on small business owners.)
7. false (Small businesses account for the majority of innovative products and services.)
8. true

Entrepreneurship Terms, Activity E

1. receipts
2. capital
3. assets
4. innovative
5. location
6. zoning laws
7. loan
8. franchise
9. commission
10. fixed
11. fraud
12. overhead
13. flexible
14. break-even point
15. liabilities
16. profit ratio

Teacher's Resource Guide/Binder

Review and Study Guide for Chapter 22,
reproducible master 22-2

1			L	I	C	E	N	S	E								
2						L	I	A	B	I	L	I	T	I	E	S	
3		Z	O	N	I	N	G	L	A	W							
4				F	R	A	U	D									
5	A	C	C	O	U	N	T	I	N	G							
6			A	S	S	E	T	S									
7	C	O	M	M	I	S	S	I	O	N							
8	O	V	E	R	H	E	A	D	E	X	P	E	N	S	E	S	
9			P	R	O	F	I	T	R	A	T	I	O				
10		F	R	A	N	C	H	I	S	E							
11				E	N	T	R	E	P	R	E	N	E	U	R	S	
12			I	N	N	O	V	A	T	I	V	E					
13			R	E	C	E	I	P	T	S							
14	E	N	T	R	E	P	R	E	N	E	U	R	S	H	I	P	

Down word (column through 1-SMALL, etc.): SMALLBUSINESS, DEMONSTRATOR

Chapter 22 Test

1.	B	13.	T
2.	F	14.	T
3.	C	15.	F
4.	I	16.	T
5.	D	17.	T
6.	A	18.	T
7.	E	19.	T
8.	G	20.	D
9.	H	21.	A
10.	T	22.	D
11.	T	23.	B
12.	F	24.	C

25. (List three of each. Student response. See pages 402-403 of the text.)
26. (Name five. Student response. See Chart 22-5 on page 405 in the text.)
27. (Name two of each. Student response. See pages 412-419 in the text.)

Reproducible Master 22-1

Business Expenses for an Entrepreneur

Name_____   **Date**_____   **Period**_____

An entrepreneur must carefully consider all the following expenses when starting a business. Imagine you are opening a new florist shop. Give examples of each type of business expense listed below.

1. Office or store space: _____

_____

2. Utilities: _____

_____

3. Security: _____

_____

4. Furniture and decorating: _____

_____

5. Equipment: _____

_____

7. Merchandise: _____

_____

8. Employees: _____

_____

9. Subcontractors: _____

_____

10. Transportation/delivery: _____

_____

11. Advertising: _____

_____

12. Taxes: _____

_____

Reproducible Master 22-2

Review and Study Guide for Chapter 22

Name_____ **Date** _____ **Period** _____

Solve the word puzzle by using terms from the chapter.

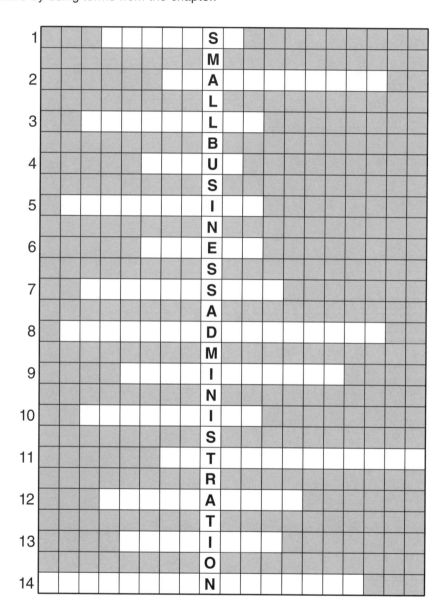

1. A certificate that shows a business owner has been granted permission to operate the business.

2. Any debts a person owes, such as a car loan.

3. A regulation as to what types of business activities can be performed in certain areas. (two words)

4. The act of deceiving or tricking.

(Continued)

Name _____

5. Aspect of record keeping that involves analysis of recorded data.

6. Items a person owns, such as cash, stocks, bonds, and property.

7. A percentage of sales paid to a salesperson.

8. Expenses beyond materials and labor such as rent and advertising that are figured into the price of a product. (two words)

9. The percentage of business receipts that are profit. (two words)

10. The right to market another company's product or service.

11. Another name for people who start and maintain their own businesses.

12. The ability to come up with new ideas for products, services, or sales techniques.

13. All the money business owners receive from their customers for cash or credit sales.

14. The organization and management of a business.

Entrepreneurship: A Business of Your Own

Name_____

Date _____ **Period** _____ **Score** _____

Chapter 22 Test

Matching: Match the following terms and identifying phrases.

_____ 1. The organization and management of a business.

_____ 2. A certificate showing that a person has been granted permission to practice a certain occupation.

_____ 3. Regulations as to what types of business activities can be performed in certain areas.

_____ 4. The percentage of business receipts that are profit.

_____ 5. A prime source of information for would-be entrepreneurs.

_____ 6. The money left from business income after paying all expenses.

_____ 7. Items that a person owns, such as cash, stocks, bonds, and property.

_____ 8. Any debts that a person owes, such as a car or home loan.

_____ 9. All the money received from customers in cash and credit sales.

A. profit

B. entrepreneurship

C. zoning laws

D. Small Business Administration (SBA)

E. assets

F. license

G. liabilities

H. receipts

I. profit ratio

True/False: Circle *T* if the statement is true or *F* if the statement is false.

T F 10. Some people think of small businesses as the heart of the free enterprise system.

T F 11. Businesses owned by entrepreneurs help keep the economy strong by creating jobs.

T F 12. Entrepreneurs are *not* their own bosses.

T F 13. Entrepreneurs have to be willing to do everything connected with a new business.

T F 14. Purchasing a franchise allows a person to buy a business with a track record of success.

T F 15. Buying an existing business is *not* an opportunity open to entrepreneurs.

T F 16. Optimism is one key quality for success.

T F 17. Fraud is the act of deceiving or tricking someone.

T F 18. Architects, writers, consultants, and insurance agents often work out of home offices.

T F 19. A person would be wise to take a class in small business accounting before starting his or her own business.

(Continued)

Name_____

Multiple Choice: Choose the best response. Write the letter in the space provided.

_____20. An entrepreneur can _____.
  A. sell products or services
  B. buy an established business
  C. buy a franchise
  D. All of the above.

_____21. A disadvantage of working at home is _____.
  A. family concerns may disrupt your business
  B. you can attend to home responsibilities throughout the workday
  C. you don't have to commute to work
  D. None of the above.

_____22. When applying for a business loan, the loan officer needs to know _____.
  A. your plans for future growth
  B. what assets and liabilities you have
  C. your credit history
  D. All of the above.

_____23. The law requires an entrepreneur to _____.
  A. sell only one kind of product
  B. keep thorough financial records
  C. advertise in local newspapers
  D. hire a lawyer

_____24. Which is an example of a capital expense?
  A. Advertising costs.
  B. Monthly rent payments.
  C. Machinery.
  D. All of the above.

Essay Questions: Provide complete responses to the following questions or statements.

25. List three advantages and three disadvantages of entrepreneurship.
26. What points should be considered in planning your own business? List five.
27. Name two legal and two financial issues associated with starting a business.

Part 6
Managing Your Income

23

Understanding Income and Taxes

Objectives

After studying this chapter, students will be able to
- describe the different forms of income and fringe benefits an employee can receive for doing a job.
- explain gross pay and net pay, and describe paycheck deductions.
- identify the various services and facilities provided by tax dollars.
- describe how consumers are taxed and the types of taxes they pay.
- explain how to file a federal income tax return.
- describe the purpose of and benefits provided by the social security program, medicaid, medicare, workers' compensation, and unemployment insurance.
- build SCANS competencies in using resources, interpersonal skills, information, and systems.

Teaching Materials

Text, pages 425-443
Terms to Know
Facts in Review
Applying Your Skills
Developing SCANS Workplace Competencies
Student Activity Guide
    A. *Forms of Income*
    B. *Understanding Your Paycheck*
    C. *Types of Taxes*
    D. *Tax Opinions*
    E. *Preparing Tax Returns*
    F. *Government Insurance Programs*
Teacher's Resource Guide/Binder
The W-4 Form, reproducible master 23-1
Filling Out a Tax Return Form, reproducible master 23-2
Review and Study Guide for Chapter 23, reproducible master 23-3
Chapter 23 Test, reproducible master
Teacher's Resource Binder
Federal Revenue and Spending, color transparencies CT-23 (two transparencies)

Introductory Activities

1. Poll students to see how many know what happens to the money taken from their paychecks. In addition to taxes and social security, are there other deductions (such as payroll savings plans) that are taken from their paychecks? Discuss the purpose of each deduction students mention.
2. Have students describe the ideal income for a job in their chosen career. Ask students to explain the process by which they determined how much their time and talents are worth.

Instructional Concepts and Student Learning Experiences

Forms of Income

3. *Federal Revenue and Spending,* color transparencies CT-23, TRB. Use both transparencies to show students the link between the taxes they pay and the government programs funded primarily through tax revenues. The "revenues" transparency shows the categories of taxes that are the government's primary sources of income. The "spending" transparency lists the key government programs funded by federal dollars.
4. Ask students to find out what the current minimum wage is and track its increases over the past 25 years.
5. Have students write a research report on the history of minimum wage laws.
6. Ask students to list the advantages and disadvantages of hourly wage work. Discuss the extra incentive of working overtime.
7. Have students find out the annual salary for different levels of managers in their chosen occupations. Discuss how the salaried managers' responsibilities differ from hourly wage earners in the same occupation.
8. Have students brainstorm occupations in which people earn commissions. For each occupation, discuss the advantages and disadvantages of earning a living by working on commission.

9. Have students write a description of the type of person who would excel at earning an income by doing piecework. Suggest that students interview individuals who do piecework in a factory or production company.
10. Ask students who work in the service industries to relate their experiences in receiving (or not receiving) tips as part of their income. Have them role-play incidents in which providing good service earns a tip.
11. Divide the class into two groups. Students should debate the usefulness of the two types of bonuses for motivating workers. Have one group discuss the advantages of an incentive bonus, while the other discusses the year-end bonus.
12. Have students determine what their ideal fringe benefits are. Then, have them assign monetary values to each benefit. Discuss how fringe benefits make up a significant part of income.
13. Have students bring to class several want ads that list fringe benefits for positions in their chosen occupation. Have students explain which fringe benefits appeal to them most.
14. Have students describe the fringe benefits, if any, they receive at their current part-time jobs.
15. *Forms of Income,* Activity A, SAG. Students complete a crossword puzzle using terms related to the various forms of income.

Understanding Your Paycheck

16. Have students bring copies of their paycheck stubs to class for comparison of formats and heading styles. Collect the stubs from students and photocopy several that display a wide range of styles. Return the originals to the students and, on your photocopied masters, blacken the payment amounts and social security numbers for privacy. Make handouts, distribute them to the class, and ask students to choose the most readable format.
17. Have students create posters or diagrams illustrating the purpose of each paycheck deduction. Display them in class.
18. *Understanding Your Paycheck,* Activity B, SAG. Students use an illustration of a paycheck stub to answer questions about a worker's paycheck.
19. Have students relate their experiences with filling out a W-4 Form. Students may list suggestions to help new workers complete the form correctly.
20. Use the sample W-4 Form in the text to explain to students how to correctly complete the form.
21. *The W-4 Form,* reproducible master 23-1, TRG/B. Students complete a W-4 Form as they would when starting a new job.
22. Ask students to give examples of jobs in which standard deductions are not taken from the paychecks. (For instance, a sole proprietor such as

a freelance writer or a plumber receive payments from customers, not a standard paycheck.) Discuss how these workers figure their taxes and thus contribute to their future retirement and medical needs.

Taxes

23. Have students contact a state or county authority to find out where local and state taxes are used. Have students make graphs or pie charts to illustrate their findings.
24. Ask students to refer to Chart 23-5 on page 432 of the text. Have students write a short paper on how they use, or will use, each of the government services and facilities listed.
25. Have students record the amount of sales tax they paid over a two-week period on goods and services purchased. Discuss their findings in class. Have students identify the merchandise subject to sales tax, such as food and clothing, and the percentage amount of sales tax paid. Discuss why the tax exists and how your city or state uses it.
26. *Types of Taxes,* Activity C, SAG. Students match various types of taxes to their descriptions.
27. *Tax Opinions,* Activity D, SAG. Students indicate whether they agree or disagree with statements about taxes.
28. Have students write a research report on the history and purpose of the Internal Revenue Service. What powers does the agency have to collect taxes?
29. Have students refer to the sample W-2 Form on page 433 of the text. Discuss how this form helps them prepare their federal tax return.
30. Provide students with samples of the most common federal tax forms (1040EZ, 1040A, and 1040). Explain the type of worker who would use each form. Then, give students some case studies about persons in various income situations (a single person who owns a business, a head of household who makes over $50,000 annually, etc.). Have the students determine which tax form should be used in each case.
31. Instruct students to complete a sample income tax return form, such as 1040EZ or 1040A.
32. Have students prepare a pamphlet or poster explaining to new workers how to file an income tax return form.
33. *Preparing Tax Returns,* Activity E, SAG. Students answer questions about preparing tax returns.
34. Obtain a copy of an income tax return form from your state (if your state has an income tax). Show students the similarities and differences between the state form and the federal form.

35. *Filling Out a Tax Return Form,* reproducible master 23-2, TRG/B. Students use given information to fill out a 1040EZ Form.
36. Have students research the penalties for tax evasion and report their findings in a class discussion.

Social Security

37. Have students write a research report on social security, focusing on the development of the Federal Insurance Contributions Act (FICA).
38. Have students research and discuss the purpose of the Social Security Administration.
39. Ask students to bring recent newspaper and news magazine articles related to social security matters to class. Have students give brief oral reports on their articles. Discuss the outlook for the future of social security.
40. Have students write an essay on the topic "What My Social Security Number Really Means." Have students discuss the various benefits they can receive through the social security system.
41. *Government Insurance Programs,* Activity F, SAG. Students complete statements about government insurance programs by filling in the blanks.
42. Ask students to compare the retirement benefits at their workplace to social security benefits. Have students share their findings with the class.
43. Have students write a report that compares and contrasts the benefits of medicare and medicaid.
44. Ask students to interview a retired person who gets medicare benefits about the pros and cons of using this health insurance program. Have students share interview results in class.

Workers' Compensation

45. Have students contact the state labor department to find out about workers' compensation laws in your state.
46. Have students find newspaper or news magazine articles reporting work-related injuries covered through the workers' compensation program. Have them share their articles in class. Discuss the benefits provided by the program and the safety issues involved.

Unemployment Insurance

47. Have students list at least five reasons why workers would lose a job through no fault of their own and be eligible for unemployment benefits. Then, have students list at least five reasons why persons would not be eligible for unemployment benefits.
48. Have students contact the local state unemployment office to learn the details of unemployment benefits, such as how to apply for them, what they total, and how long they last.

Activities to Enrich Learning

49. Have students write a case study about employees who earn income in several forms, such as wages, salary, commission, piecework, tips, and bonuses.
50. Instruct students to read a book on tax preparation tips and write a summary of the book's suggestions.
51. Have students interview a retired person on a fixed income to find out how the person uses social security benefits.

Activities to Extend Learning

52. Invite the human resources director of a local company to speak to the class about the importance of employer contributions to workers' compensation and unemployment insurance programs
53. Invite a professional tax preparer or accountant to demonstrate how to prepare tax return forms.
54. Arrange for students to visit the local state unemployment office to learn how to apply for unemployment benefits.

Answer Key

Text

Facts in Review, page 442

1. (List four) wage, salary, commission, piecework, tips, bonus, fringe benefits
2. Gross pay is total earnings. Net pay is gross pay minus deductions.
3. federal income tax, FICA; other paycheck deductions—state/local income tax, retirement plan, union dues, insurance premiums, savings plan, charitable contributions
4. to pay for government services and facilities
5. personal income, social security (FICA), property, sales, and excise taxes
6. an amount of income not subject to taxes
7. Direct taxes are charged directly to the taxpayer. Indirect taxes are included in the price of an item. (Examples are student response.)
8. Progressive taxes take a greater share of income from the rich than from the poor, while regressive taxes do the opposite. (Examples are student response.)
9. Wage and Tax Statement; summarizes the previous year's income and deductions
10. Forms 1040EZ and 1040A
11. Form 1040
12. to provide a basic level of income that people can supplement with savings, pensions, investments, or other insurance; retirement, disability, and survivors' benefits

13. the federal government's health insurance program for people age 65 or older, victims of permanent kidney failure, or certain people with disabilities
14. hospital insurance, medical insurance
15. medical care benefits, disability income, rehabilitation benefits, death benefits

Student Activity Guide

Forms of Income, Activity A

```
                    ¹P I E ²C E W O R K
                        O
                        M
                        M
                        I           ³P
                      ⁴S A L A R Y    O
                    ⁵T I P S          F
⁶W A G ⁷E   ⁸M          I            I
        A   I          O            T
      ⁹F R I N G E ¹⁰B E N E F I T S
        N   I          O            S
        E   M          N            H
        D   U          U            A
        I   M          S            R
        N   W                       I
        C   A                       N
        O   G                       G
        M   E
        E
```

Understanding Your Paycheck, Activity B

1. A. gross pay
   B. deductions
   C. net pay
2. $260.00
3. $58.28
4. $201.72
5. 40 hours
6. $6.50
7. The W-4 Form tells Stephen's employer how much tax to withhold from his paycheck.
8. No, Stephen cannot claim a personal exemption for himself on his W-4 Form because his parents claim him as a dependent on their tax return.

9. $13.40
10. insurance premiums, union dues, charitable contributions, and contributions to a retirement plan and/or savings plan

Types of Taxes, Activity C

1. A, B
2. E
3. A, C, D
4. D
5. A
6. A, B
7. E
8. D
9. E
10. D

Preparing Tax Returns, Activity E

1. No. Joel volunteers his time and is not a wage earner.
2. Cheryl will get a refund.
3. Larry will be required to pay additional money to the federal government.
4. (All answers should be checked.)
5. by claiming legitimate deductions, adjustments, and credits
6. tax evasion, which is a criminal offense
7. from post offices, most banks and libraries, and the Internal Revenue Service
8. records of income including wages, tips, and taxable benefits; records of interest earned and dividends received; canceled checks for expenses entered on tax returns as deductions; records of interest paid on a home mortgage; past tax returns

Government Insurance Programs, Activity F

1. social security
2. basic
3. credits
4. 62
5. 65
6. disability
7. survivors'
8. apply
9. percentage
10. Supplemental Security Income
11. Medicare
12. Medicaid
13. workers' compensation
14. rehabilitation
15. unemployment insurance

Teacher's Resource Guide/Binder

Filling Out a Tax Return Form, reproducible master 23-2

Department of the Treasury—Internal Revenue Service

Form 1040EZ Income Tax Return for Single and Joint Filers With No Dependents **20XX** OMB No. 1545-0675

Use the IRS label here

Your first name and initial: Joseph R. Last name: Lemont
Your social security number: 012 34 5678

Home address (number and street): 16 S. Park Avenue Apt. no.
City, town or post office, state, and ZIP code: Cincinnati, OH 45203

Presidential Election Campaign (See page 10.)
Note: Checking "Yes" will not change your tax or reduce your refund.
Do you want $3 to go to this fund? ▶ Yes ☐ No ☒
If a joint return, does your spouse want $3 to go to this fund? ▶ Yes ☐ No ☐

▲ IMPORTANT! ▲ You must enter your SSN(s) above.

Income
Attach Copy B of Form(s) W-2 here. Enclose, but do not staple, any payment.

Line	Description	Dollars	Cents
1	Total wages, salaries, and tips. This should be shown in box 1 of your W-2 form(s). Attach your W-2 form(s).	2,400	00
2	Taxable interest. If the total is over $400, you cannot use Form 1040EZ.		
3	Unemployment compensation, qualified state tuition program earnings, and Alaska Permanent Fund dividends (see page 11).		
4	Add lines 1, 2, and 3. This is your **adjusted gross income.**	2,400	00
5	Can your parents (or someone else) claim you on their return? ☒ Yes. Enter amount from worksheet on back. ☐ No. If single, enter 7,050.00. If married, enter 12,700.00. See back for explanation.	2,650	00
6	Subtract line 5 from line 4. If line 5 is larger than line 4, enter 0. This is your **taxable income.** ▶	0	

Payments and tax

Line	Description	Dollars	Cents
7	Enter your Federal income tax withheld from box 2 of your W-2 form(s).	55	00
8a	Earned income credit (see page 12).		
8b	Nontaxable earned income: enter type and amount below. Type		
9	Add lines 7 and 8a. These are your **total payments.**	55	00
10	**Tax.** Use the amount on line 6 above to find your tax in the tax table on pages 20–24 of the booklet. Then, enter the tax from the table on this line.	0	

Refund
Have it directly deposited! See page 15 and fill in 11b, 11c, and 11d.

Line	Description	Dollars	Cents
11a	If line 9 is larger than line 10, subtract line 10 from line 9. This is your **refund.**	55	00

11b Routing number
11c Type: ☐ Checking ☐ Savings
11d Account number

Amount you owe

Line	Description	Dollars	Cents
12	If line 10 is larger than line 9, subtract line 9 from line 10. This is the **amount you owe.** See page 17 for details on how to pay.		

I have read this return. Under penalties of perjury, I declare that the return is true, correct, and accurately lists all amounts and sources of income I received during the tax year.

Sign here Keep copy for your records.
Your signature / Date / Your occupation
Spouse's signature if joint return. See page 10. / Date / Spouse's occupation

For Disclosure, Privacy Act, and Paperwork Reduction Act Notice, see page 19. Cat. No. 11329W Form 1040EZ

Form 1040EZ page 2

Use this form if
- Your filing status is single or married filing jointly.
- You do not claim any dependents.
- You do not claim a student loan interest deduction (see page 7) or an education credit.
- You had **only** wages, salaries, tips, taxable scholarship or fellowship grants, unemployment compensation, qualified state tuition program earnings, or Alaska Permanent Fund dividends, and your taxable interest income was not over $400. But if you earned tips, including allocated tips, that are not included in box 5 and box 7 of your W-2, you may not be able to use Form 1040EZ. See page 11. If you are planning to use Form 1040EZ for a child who received Alaska Permanent Fund dividends, see page 11.
- You did not receive any advance earned income credit payments.
- You (and your spouse if married) were under 65 on January 1, 20XX, and not blind at the end of 1999.
- Your taxable income (line 6) is less than $50,000.

If you are not sure about your filing status, see page 10. If you have questions about dependents, use TeleTax topic 354 (see page 6). If you **cannot use this form**, use TeleTax topic 352 (see page 6).

Filling in your return
For tips on how to avoid common mistakes, see page 25.
Enter your (and your spouse's if married) social security number on the front. Because this form is read by a machine, please print your numbers inside the boxes like this:
9 8 7 6 5 4 3 2 1 0 Do not type your numbers. Do not use dollar signs.

If you received a scholarship or fellowship grant or tax-exempt interest income, such as on municipal bonds, see the booklet (see page 11). Also, see the booklet if you received a Form 1099-INT showing Federal income tax withheld or if Federal income tax was withheld from your unemployment compensation or Alaska Permanent Fund dividends.
Remember, you must report all wages, salaries, and tips even if you do not get a W-2 form from your employer. You must also report all your taxable interest, including interest from banks, savings and loans, credit unions, etc., even if you do not get a Form 1099-INT.

Worksheet for dependents who checked "Yes" on line 5
(keep a copy for your records)

Use this worksheet to figure the amount to enter on line 5 if someone can claim you (or your spouse if married) as a dependent, even if that person chooses not to do so. To find out if someone can claim you as a dependent, use TeleTax topic 354 (see page 6).

A. Amount, if any, from line 1 on front 2,400
+ 250.00 Enter total ▶ A. 2,650.00
B. Minimum standard deduction . . . . B. 700.00
C. Enter the LARGER of line A or line B here . . . . C. 2,650.00
D. Maximum standard deduction. If **single**, enter 4,300.00; if **married**, enter 7,200.00. . . . . D. 4,300.00
E. Enter the SMALLER of line C or line D here. This is your standard deduction . . . . E. 2,650.00
F. Exemption amount.
• If single, enter 0.
• If married and—
—both you and your spouse can be claimed as dependents, enter 0.
—only one of you can be claimed as a dependent, enter 2,750.00. F. 0
G. Add lines E and F. Enter the total here and on line 5 on the front . . G. 2,650.00

If you checked "No" on line 5 because no one can claim you (or your spouse if married) as a dependent, enter on line 5 the amount shown below that applies to you.
• Single, enter 7,050.00. This is the total of your standard deduction (4,300.00) and your exemption (2,750.00).
• Married, enter 12,700.00. This is the total of your standard deduction (7,200.00), your exemption (2,750.00), and your spouse's exemption (2,750.00).

Mailing return
Mail your return by **April 17,** 20XX Use the envelope that came with your booklet. If you do not have that envelope, see page 28 for the address to use.

Paid preparer's use only
See page 17.
Under penalties of perjury, I declare that I have examined this return, and to the best of my knowledge and belief, it is true, correct, and accurately lists all amounts and sources of income received during the tax year. This declaration is based on all information of which I have any knowledge.
Preparer's signature / Date / Check if self-employed ☐ / Preparer's SSN or PTIN
Firm's name (or yours if self-employed) and address / EIN / ZIP code

♻ Printed on recycled paper

Review and Study Guide for Chapter 23,
reproducible master 23-3

1. minimum wage
2. salaries
3. tips
4. taxes
5. profit sharing
6. net
7. gross
8. W-4
9. wage
10. social security
11. unemployment insurance
12. B
13. A
14. D
15. B
16. A
17. C
18. B
19. C
20. B
21. A

Chapter 23 Test

1. J	15. F
2. L	16. T
3. F	17. T
4. K	18. T
5. H	19. F
6. I	20. T
7. G	21. T
8. A	22. T
9. B	23. C
10. C	24. A
11. D	25. B
12. E	26. A
13. F	27. D
14. T	

28. personal income tax, social security tax, property tax, sales tax, excise tax (Descriptions are student response. See pages 430-432 of the text.)
29. (Student response. See pages 433-436 of the text.)
30. retirement benefits, disability benefits, survivors benefits (Explanations are student response. See pages 437-438 of the text.)

Reproducible Master 23-1

The W-4 Form

Name _____   Date _____   Period _____

Complete this W-4 Form as you would if you were starting a new job.

Form W-4 (20XX)

Purpose. Complete Form W-4 so your employer can withhold the correct Federal income tax from your pay. Because your tax situation may change, you may want to refigure your withholding each year.

Exemption from withholding. If you are exempt, complete only lines 1, 2, 3, 4, and 7, and sign the form to validate it. Your exemption for 1999 expires February 16, 2000.

Note: *You cannot claim exemption from withholding if (1) your income exceeds $700 and includes more than $250 of unearned income (e.g., interest and dividends) and (2) another person can claim you as a dependent on their tax return.*

Basic instructions. If you are not exempt, complete the Personal Allowances Worksheet. The worksheets on page 2 adjust your withholding allowances based on itemized deductions, adjustments to income, or two-earner/two-job situations. Complete all worksheets that apply. They will help you figure the number of withholding allowances you are entitled to claim. **However, you may claim fewer allowances.**

Child tax and higher education credits. For details on adjusting withholding for these and other credits, see **Pub. 919**, Is My Withholding Correct for 1999?

Head of household. Generally, you may claim head of household filing status on your tax return only if you are unmarried and pay more than 50% of the costs of keeping up a home for yourself and your dependent(s) or other qualifying individuals. See line **E** below.

Nonwage income. If you have a large amount of nonwage income, such as interest or dividends, you should consider making estimated tax payments using Form 1040-ES. Otherwise, you may owe additional tax.

Two earners/two jobs. If you have a working spouse or more than one job, figure the total number of allowances you are entitled to claim on all jobs using worksheets from only one Form W-4. Your withholding will usually be most accurate when all allowances are claimed on the Form W-4 prepared for the highest paying job and zero allowances are claimed for the others.

Check your withholding. After your Form W-4 takes effect, use Pub. 919 to see how the dollar amount you are having withheld compares to your estimated total annual tax. Get Pub. 919 especially if you used the Two-Earner/Two-Job Worksheet and your earnings exceed $150,000 (Single) or $200,000 (Married).

Recent name change? If your name on line 1 differs from that shown on your social security card, call 1-800-772-1213 for a new social security card.

Personal Allowances Worksheet

A Enter "1" for **yourself** if no one else can claim you as a dependent . . . . **A** _____

B Enter "1" if:
- You are single and have only one job; or
- You are married, have only one job, and your spouse does not work; or
- Your wages from a second job or your spouse's wages (or the total of both) are $1,000 or less.

. . **B** _____

C Enter "1" for your **spouse.** But, you may choose to enter -0- if you are married and have either a working spouse or more than one job. (This may help you avoid having too little tax withheld.). . . . . **C** _____

D Enter number of **dependents** (other than your spouse or yourself) you will claim on your tax return . . . . **D** _____

E Enter "1" if you will file as **head of household** on your tax return (see conditions under **Head of household** above) . . **E** _____

F Enter "1" if you have at least $1,500 of **child or dependent care expenses** for which you plan to claim a credit . . **F** _____

G **Child Tax Credit:** • If your total income will be between $20,000 and $50,000 ($23,000 and $63,000 if married), enter "1" for each eligible child. • If your total income will be between $50,000 and $80,000 ($63,000 and $115,000 if married), enter "1" if you have two eligible children, enter "2" if you have three or four eligible children, or enter "3" if you have five or more eligible children . . **G** _____

H Add lines A through G and enter total here. **Note:** This amount may be different from the number of exemptions you claim on your return. ▶ **H** _____

For accuracy, complete all worksheets that apply.
- If you plan to **itemize or claim adjustments to income** and want to reduce your withholding, see the Deductions and Adjustments Worksheet on page 2.
- If you are **single**, have **more than one job** and your combined earnings from all jobs exceed $32,000, OR if you are **married** and have a **working spouse or more than one job** and the combined earnings from all jobs exceed $55,000, see the Two-Earner/Two-Job Worksheet on page 2 to avoid having too little tax withheld.
- If **neither** of the above situations applies, **stop here** and enter the number from line H on line 5 of Form W-4 below.

------------------------- **Cut here and give the certificate to your employer. Keep the top part for your records.** -------------------------

Form **W-4**
Department of the Treasury
Internal Revenue Service

Employee's Withholding Allowance Certificate

▶ **For Privacy Act and Paperwork Reduction Act Notice, see page 2.**

OMB No. 1545-0010

20**XX**

1 Type or print your first name and middle initial	Last name	2 Your social security number

Home address (number and street or rural route)	3 ☐ Single ☐ Married ☐ Married, but withhold at higher Single rate. **Note:** If married, but legally separated, or spouse is a nonresident alien, check the Single box.
City or town, state, and ZIP code	4 If your last name differs from that on your social security card, check here. **You** must call 1-800-772-1213 for a new card . . . ▶ ☐

5 Total number of allowances you are claiming (from line H above or from the worksheets on page 2 if they apply) .   **5** _____

6 Additional amount, if any, you want withheld from each paycheck . . . .   **6** $ _____

7 I claim exemption from withholding for 1999, and I certify that I meet **BOTH** of the following conditions for exemption:
- Last year I had a right to a refund of **ALL** Federal income tax withheld because I had **NO** tax liability **AND**
- This year I expect a refund of **ALL** Federal income tax withheld because I expect to have **NO** tax liability.

If you meet both conditions, write "EXEMPT" here . . . . ▶ **7**

Under penalties of perjury, I certify that I am entitled to the number of withholding allowances claimed on this certificate, or I am entitled to claim exempt status.

Employee's signature
(Form is not valid unless you sign it) ▶

Date ▶

8 Employer's name and address (Employer: Complete 8 and 10 only if sending to the IRS)	9 Office code (optional)	10 Employer identification number

Cat. No. 10220Q

Reproducible Master 23-2

Filling Out a Tax Return Form

Name_____ Date _____ Period _____

Prepare this Form 1040EZ tax return for Joseph R. Lemont. He is 17 years old and single. He is claimed as a dependent on his parents' return. He does not want to contribute to the presidential election campaign fund. His W-2 Form shows $55 withheld for federal income tax, $2,400 earned for wages, and $183.60 withheld for social security tax. Joseph's address is 16 S. Park Avenue, Cincinnati, OH 45203. His social security number is 012-34-5678.

a Control number			
		OMB No. 1545-0008	
b Employer identification number		1 Wages, tips, other compensation 2,400.00	2 Federal income tax withheld 55.00
c Employer's name, address, and ZIP code		3 Social security wages 2,400.00	4 Social security tax withheld 183.60
Olde Town Garage 301 E. Main Street Cincinnati, OH 45203		5 Medicare wages and tips	6 Medicare tax withheld
		7 Social security tips	8 Allocated tips
d Employee's social security number 012-34-5678		9 Advance EIC payment	10 Dependent care benefits
e Employee's name, address, and ZIP code		11 Nonqualified plans	12 Benefits included in box 1
Joseph R. Lemont 16 S. Park Avenue Cincinnati, OH 45203		13 See instrs. for box 13	14 Other
		15 Statutory employee ☐ Deceased ☐ Pension plan ☐ Legal rep. ☐ Deferred compensation ☐	
16 State Employer's state I.D. no.	17 State wages, tips, etc.	18 State income tax 19 Locality name	20 Local wages, tips, etc. 21 Local income tax

Form **W-2** **Wage and Tax Statement**
Copy B To Be Filed With Employee's FEDERAL Tax Return

Department of the Treasury—Internal Revenue Service
This information is being furnished to the Internal Revenue Service.

Section 3—20XX Tax Table

For single persons with taxable income of less than $50,000

If line 5 is at least—	But less than—	Your tax is—	If line 5 is at least—	But less than—	Your tax is—	If line 5 is at least—	But less than—	Your tax is—	If line 5 is at least—	But less than—	Your tax is—	If line 5 is at least—	But less than—	Your tax is—	If line 5 is at least—	But less than—	Your tax is—
$0	$5	$0	475	500	73	**1,000**			1,550	1,575	234	2,100	2,125	317	2,700	2,725	407
5	15	2	500	525	77				1,575	1,600	238	2,125	2,150	321	2,725	2,750	411
15	25	3	525	550	81	1,000	1,025	152	1,600	1,625	242	2,150	2,175	324	2,750	2,775	414
						1,025	1,050	156	1,625	1,650	246	2,175	2,200	328	2,775	2,800	418
25	50	6	550	575	84	1,050	1,075	159	1,650	1,675	249				2,800	2,825	422
50	75	9	575	600	88	1,075	1,100	163	1,675	1,700	253	2,200	2,225	332	2,825	2,850	426
75	100	13	600	625	92							2,225	2,250	336	2,850	2,875	429
						1,100	1,125	167	1,700	1,725	257	2,250	2,275	339	2,875	2,900	433
100	125	17	625	650	96	1,125	1,150	171	1,725	1,750	261	2,275	2,300	343			
125	150	21	650	675	99	1,150	1,175	174	1,750	1,775	264	2,300	2,325	347	2,900	2,925	437
150	175	24	675	700	103	1,175	1,200	178	1,775	1,800	268	2,325	2,350	351	2,925	2,950	441
												2,350	2,375	354	2,950	2,975	444
175	200	28	700	725	107	1,200	1,225	182	1,800	1,825	272	2,375	2,400	358	2,975	3,000	448
200	225	32	725	750	111	1,225	1,250	186	1,825	1,850	276						
225	250	36	750	775	114	1,250	1,275	189	1,850	1,875	279	2,400	2,425	362	**3,000**		
						1,275	1,300	193	1,875	1,900	283	2,425	2,450	366			
250	275	39	775	800	118							2,450	2,475	369	3,000	3,050	454
275	300	43	800	825	122	1,300	1,325	197	1,900	1,925	287	2,475	2,500	373	3,050	3,100	461
300	325	47	825	850	126	1,325	1,350	201	1,925	1,950	291				3,100	3,150	469
						1,350	1,375	204	1,950	1,975	294	2,500	2,525	377	3,150	3,200	476
325	350	51	850	875	129	1,375	1,400	208	1,975	2,000	298	2,525	2,550	381			
350	375	54	875	900	133	1,400	1,425	212				2,550	2,575	384	3,200	3,250	484
375	400	58	900	925	137	1,425	1,450	216	**2,000**			2,575	2,600	388	3,250	3,300	491
						1,450	1,475	219							3,300	3,350	499
400	425	62	925	950	141	1,475	1,500	223	2,000	2,025	302	2,600	2,625	392	3,350	3,400	506
425	450	66	950	975	144				2,025	2,050	306	2,625	2,650	396			
450	475	69	975	1,000	148	1,500	1,525	227	2,050	2,075	309	2,650	2,675	399	3,400	3,450	514
						1,525	1,550	231	2,075	2,100	313	2,675	2,700	403	3,450	3,500	521

(Continued)

Name_____

Form **1040EZ**

Department of the Treasury—Internal Revenue Service

Income Tax Return for Single and Joint Filers With No Dependents   **20XX**   OMB No. 1545-0675

Use the IRS label here

Your first name and initial   Last name

If a joint return, spouse's first name and initial   Last name

Home address (number and street). If you have a P.O. box, see page 10.   Apt. no.

City, town or post office, state, and ZIP code. If you have a foreign address, see page 10.

Your social security number

Spouse's social security number

▲ **IMPORTANT!** ▲
You **must** enter your SSN(s) above.

Presidential Election Campaign (See page 10.)

Note: *Checking "Yes" will not change your tax or reduce your refund.*

Do you want $3 to go to this fund? ▶ Yes ☐ No ☐

If a joint return, does your spouse want $3 to go to this fund? ▶ Yes ☐ No ☐

Dollars   Cents

Income

Attach Copy B of Form(s) W-2 here. Enclose, but do not staple, any payment.

1 Total wages, salaries, and tips. This should be shown in box 1 of your W-2 form(s). Attach your W-2 form(s). **1**

2 Taxable interest. If the total is over $400, you cannot use Form 1040EZ. **2**

3 Unemployment compensation, qualified state tuition program earnings, and Alaska Permanent Fund dividends (see page 11). **3**

4 Add lines 1, 2, and 3. This is your **adjusted gross income.** **4**

Note: *You* **must** *check Yes or No.*

5 Can your parents (or someone else) claim you on their return?

Yes. Enter amount from worksheet on back. ☐

No. If **single,** enter 7,050.00. If **married,** enter 12,700.00. See back for explanation. ☐ **5**

6 Subtract line 5 from line 4. If line 5 is larger than line 4, enter 0. This is your **taxable income.** ▶ **6**

Payments and tax

7 Enter your Federal income tax withheld from box 2 of your W-2 form(s). **7**

8a **Earned income credit** (see page 12).

b Nontaxable earned income: enter type and amount below.

Type $ **8a**

9 Add lines 7 and 8a. These are your **total payments.** **9**

10 **Tax.** Use the amount on **line 6 above** to find your tax in the tax table on pages 20–24 of the booklet. Then, enter the tax from the table on this line. **10**

Refund

Have it directly deposited! See page 15 and fill in 11b, 11c, and 11d.

11a If line 9 is larger than line 10, subtract line 10 from line 9. This is your **refund.** **11a**

▶ **b** Routing number

▶ **c** Type: Checking ☐   Savings ☐

d Account number

Amount you owe

12 If line 10 is larger than line 9, subtract line 9 from line 10. This is the **amount you owe.** See page 17 for details on how to pay. **12**

Sign here ▶

Keep copy for your records.

I have read this return. Under penalties of perjury, I declare that to the best of my knowledge and belief, the return is true, correct, and accurately lists all amounts and sources of income I received during the tax year.

Your signature   Spouse's signature if joint return. See page 10.

Date   Your occupation   Date   Spouse's occupation

For Official Use Only

1 2 3 4 5

6 7 8 9 10

For Disclosure, Privacy Act, and Paperwork Reduction Act Notice, see page 19.   Cat. No. 11329W   Form **1040EZ**

(Continued)

Name_____

Form 1040EZ page 2

Use this form if	• Your filing status is single or married filing jointly. • You (and your spouse if married) were under 65 on January 1, 20XX, and not blind at the end of 1999.

Use this form if

- Your filing status is single or married filing jointly.
- You do not claim any dependents.
- You (and your spouse if married) were under 65 on January 1, 20XX, and not blind at the end of 1999.
- Your taxable income (line 6) is less than $50,000.
- You do not claim a student loan interest deduction (see page 7) or an education credit.
- You had **only** wages, salaries, tips, taxable scholarship or fellowship grants, unemployment compensation, qualified state tuition program earnings, or Alaska Permanent Fund dividends, and your taxable interest income was not over $400. **But** if you earned tips, including allocated tips, that are not included in box 5 and box 7 of your W-2, you may not be able to use Form 1040EZ. See page 11. If you are planning to use Form 1040EZ for a child who received Alaska Permanent Fund dividends, see page 11.
- You did not receive any advance earned income credit payments.

If you are not sure about your filing status, see page 10. If you have questions about dependents, use TeleTax topic 354 (see page 6). If you **cannot use this form,** use TeleTax topic 352 (see page 6).

Filling in your return

For tips on how to avoid common mistakes, see page 25.

Enter your (and your spouse's if married) social security number on the front. Because this form is read by a machine, please print your numbers inside the boxes like this:

9 8 7 6 5 4 3 2 1 0   Do not type your numbers. Do not use dollar signs.

If you received a scholarship or fellowship grant or tax-exempt interest income, such as on municipal bonds, see the booklet before filling in the form. Also, see the booklet if you received a Form 1099-INT showing Federal income tax withheld or if Federal income tax was withheld from your unemployment compensation or Alaska Permanent Fund dividends.

Remember, you must report all wages, salaries, and tips even if you do not get a W-2 form from your employer. You must also report all your taxable interest, including interest from banks, savings and loans, credit unions, etc., even if you do not get a Form 1099-INT.

Worksheet for dependents who checked "Yes" on line 5

(keep a copy for your records)

Use this worksheet to figure the amount to enter on line 5 if someone can claim you (or your spouse if married) as a dependent, even if that person chooses not to do so. To find out if someone can claim you as a dependent, use TeleTax topic 354 (see page 6).

A. Amount, if any, from line 1 on front _____
   + _____ 250.00 Enter total ▶ A. _____

B. Minimum standard deduction . . . . B. _____ 700.00

C. Enter the LARGER of line A or line B here . . . . C. _____

D. Maximum standard deduction. If **single,** enter 4,300.00; if **married,** enter 7,200.00 . . . . D. _____

E. Enter the SMALLER of line C or line D here. This is your standard deduction . . . . E. _____

F. Exemption amount.
   - If single, enter 0.
   - If married and—
     —both you and your spouse can be claimed as dependents, enter 0.
     —only one of you can be claimed as a dependent, enter 2,750.00.
   } F. _____

G. Add lines E and F. Enter the total here and on line 5 on the front . . G. _____

If you checked "No" on line 5 because no one can claim you (or your spouse if married) as a dependent, enter on line 5 the amount shown below that applies to you.

- Single, enter 7,050.00. This is the total of your standard deduction (4,300.00) and your exemption (2,750.00).
- Married, enter 12,700.00. This is the total of your standard deduction (7,200.00), your exemption (2,750.00), and your spouse's exemption (2,750.00).

Mailing return

Mail your return by **April 17, 20XX.** Use the envelope that came with your booklet. If you do not have that envelope, see page 28 for the address to use.

Paid preparer's use only

See page 17.

Under penalties of perjury, I declare that I have examined this return, and to the best of my knowledge and belief, it is true, correct, and accurately lists all amounts and sources of income received during the tax year. This declaration is based on all information of which I have any knowledge.

Preparer's signature ▶	Date	Check if self-employed ☐	Preparer's SSN or PTIN
Firm's name (or yours if self-employed) and address ▶		EIN	
		ZIP code	

✸ Printed on recycled paper

Reproducible Master 23-3

Review and Study Guide for Chapter 23

Name _____ **Date** _____ **Period** _____

Completion: Fill in the blanks with the correct terms.

1. _____ _____ is the lowest amount of money an employer is allowed to pay a worker per hour.

2. Workers who earn _____ do *not* receive extra pay when they work overtime.

3. Earning _____ from customers can encourage a hospitality worker to continue to provide good service.

4. Highways, public schools, and police and fire protection are services provided by the government through _____.

5. When employees' hard work results in greater company profits, the company returns some of the profits to employees through _____ _____.

6. _____ pay is take-home pay.

7. _____ pay is the total amount an employee earns for a pay period before any deductions are taken out.

8. A form that tells the employer how much tax to take out of an employee's paycheck is called the _____ Form.

9. A(n) _____ is a set amount of pay for every hour of work.

10. _____ _____ provides retirement, disability, and survivor benefits to eligible workers.

11. _____ _____ provides temporary benefits to workers who have lost their jobs.

Multiple Choice: Choose the best response. Write the letter in the space provided.

_____ 12. Earned income is _____.
   A. the same as tips
   B. the money you receive for doing a job
   C. the same as fringe benefits
   D. None of the above.

_____ 13. A percentage of money taken in from sales made is called _____.
   A. commission
   B. piecework
   C. wages
   D. salary

_____ 14. Earning a fixed amount for each piece of work done is called _____.
   A. minimum wage
   B. commission
   C. salary
   D. piecework

(Continued)

Name_____

_____ 15. A bonus is _____.
A. the same as a commission
B. an extra payment in addition to the worker's regular pay
C. the same as tips
D. None of the above.

_____ 16. Amounts of money subtracted from your total pay are called _____.
A. deductions
B. exemptions
C. fringe benefits
D. bonuses

_____ 17. The exemption amount on which a worker does *not* have to pay tax is set by _____.
A. the employer
B. the worker
C. Congress
D. None of the above.

_____ 18. FICA stands for the act that established _____.
A. fringe benefits
B. social security taxes
C. W-4 forms
D. All of the above.

_____ 19. Which of the following must be filed with all income tax returns?
A. W-4 Form.
B. Check stub.
C. W-2 Form.
D. All of the above.

_____ 20. Medicare is *not* available to _____.
A. people of any age with permanent kidney failure
B. people under 65 and in good health
C. people over 65
D. certain disabled people

_____ 21. The government health care program that provides services for people who cannot pay for them is called _____.
A. Medicaid
B. Medicare
C. FICA
D. Social security

Understanding Income and Taxes

Name_____

Date _____   **Period** _____   **Score** _____

Chapter 23 Test

Matching: Match the following terms and identifying phrases.

_____ 1. A form that tells the employer how much tax to withhold from an employee's paycheck.

_____ 2. Extra pay in addition to the worker's regular pay, usually taken out of the company's profits.

_____ 3. Amounts of money subtracted from an employee's total pay.

_____ 4. A form that states the amount the employee was paid in the previous year.

_____ 5. Take-home pay.

_____ 6. A set amount of money on which a person does *not* have to pay tax.

_____ 7. The total amount an employee earns for a pay period before any deductions are subtracted.

_____ 8. The money an employee receives for doing a job.

_____ 9. A set amount of pay for every hour of work.

_____ 10. A percentage of the money taken in from sales made.

_____ 11. When employees are paid a fixed amount of money for each piece of work done.

_____ 12. The federal government's insurance program for people over age 65 or for certain disabled people.

A. earned income
B. wage
C. commission
D. piecework
E. Medicare
F. deductions
G. gross pay
H. net pay
I. exemption
J. W-4 Form
K. W-2 Form
L. bonus

True/False: Circle *T* if the statement is true or *F* if the statement is false.

T   F   13. All the income a person earns is his or hers to spend or keep.

T   F   14. Minimum wage is the lowest amount of money an employer is allowed to pay a worker per hour.

T   F   15. Salaried workers receive extra pay when they work overtime.

T   F   16. Earning tips can encourage a worker to continue to provide good service.

T   F   17. Taxes enable the government to provide many services and facilities, such as parks, highways, public schools, and police and fire protection.

T   F   18. If too much tax was withheld during the year, a person can receive a refund from the federal government.

(Continued)

Name_____

T   F   19. The main purpose of social security is to replace all earnings lost after retirement.

T   F   20. Social security benefits must be applied for when a worker becomes eligible.

T   F   21. In most states, medicaid covers hospital, laboratory, and clinic services.

T   F   22. Unemployment insurance benefits are temporary, *not* permanent.

Multiple Choice: Choose the best response. Write the letter in the space provided.

_____23. Which of the following is *not* an example of an item that requires the payment of property tax?
   A. Houses.
   B. Expensive jewelry.
   C. Food and drugs.
   D. Cars.

_____24. A single person who rents an apartment and has a full-time job would probably *not* file _____.
   A. Form 1040
   B. Form 1040A
   C. Form 1040EZ
   D. All of the above.

_____25. Food servers or bellhops earn some of their wages through _____.
   A. commission
   B. tips
   C. piecework
   D. bonuses

_____26. Overtime pay is usually _____.
   A. 1½ to 2 times the worker's regular wage
   B. the same as the worker's regular wage
   C. less than the worker's regular wage
   D. an amount set by the employer

_____27. Workers' compensation plans usually cover _____.
   A. medical care
   B. disability income
   C. rehabilitation benefits
   D. All of the above.

Essay Questions: Provide complete responses to the following questions or statements.

28. List and describe the five most common taxes most citizens have to pay.
29. Explain how you would file an income tax return.
30. Describe three types of benefits provided by social security.

Managing Spending

Objectives

After studying this chapter, students will be able to
- prepare a budget to help them manage their money wisely.
- identify and use reliable sources of consumer information.
- explain the methods businesses use to promote goods and services.
- make wise shopping decisions about where and how to shop.
- describe their consumer rights and responsibilities.
- explain how their consumer rights are protected.
- build SCANS competencies in using resources, interpersonal skills, information, systems, and technology.

Teaching Materials

Text, pages 445-467
  Terms to Know
  Facts in Review
  Applying Your Skills
  Developing SCANS Workplace Competencies
Student Activity Guide
  A. *Managing Your Money*
  B. *Fixed and Flexible Expenses*
  C. *Preparing a Budget*
  D. *Advertising*
  E. *Where to Shop*
  F. *Comparison Shopping*
  G. *The Right Way to Complain*
  H. *Complaint Letter*
  I. *Complaint Form*
Teacher's Resource Guide/Binder
  Be an Informed Consumer, reproducible
    master 24-1
  The Pros and Cons of Advertising, reproducible
    master 24-2
  Advertising Evaluation Checklist, transparency
    master 24-3
  Review and Study Guide for Chapter 24,
    reproducible master 24-4
  Chapter 24 Test, reproducible master

Teacher's Resource Binder
  Balance Income and Expenses, color
    transparency CT-24

Introductory Activities

1. Poll students to find out how many use budgets to manage their money. Ask those who use budgets to describe how they prepare and manage their plans. Ask them to discuss the advantages of budgeting.
2. Ask students to discuss their favorite places to shop. Do students shop in these places because of price, selection, location, or customer service? Discuss students' roles as consumers in the economic system when they shop at their favorite stores.

Instructional Concepts and Student Learning Experiences

Budgeting Your Money

3. Discuss the disadvantages of "living from paycheck to paycheck" without a budget. Have students write a brief case study about a person who lives that way. Then, have students identify ways in which that person could change his or her spending habits.
4. *Managing Your Money,* Activity A, SAG. Students complete open-ended statements about budgeting and being an informed consumer.
5. *Preparing a Budget,* Activity C, SAG. Students prepare and evaluate a monthly budget.
6. Have students work in small groups to establish a set of long- and short-term financial goals for a recent high school graduate who is single with a full-time job. Compare the responses of each group, then discuss in class. Instruct students to keep their work for use in an activity to follow.
7. Have students list their personal long- and short-term financial goals. Invite students to share their goals with the class or discuss them with you privately.

8. *Balance Income and Expenses,* color transparency CT-24, TRB. Use the transparency to point out to students the importance of managing income by balancing it with spending. In order to do this, students need to keep track of their income and expenses and plan a budget.

9. *Fixed and Flexible Expenses,* Activity B, SAG. Students complete exercises in which they identify fixed and flexible expenses.

10. Instruct students to track all their expenses for a week. Have them prepare a written report that describes what they spent, where they spent it, and what they purchased. Discuss what part of the week's spending was budgeted spending and what part was impulse spending.

11. Have students work in small groups using the same budget prepared in Item 6. Tell students the person is now married and has a spouse who also has a full-time job. The couple want to buy a house and have a child within two years. Have the students revise the existing budget to reflect these changes.

12. Have students write an essay on how a budget is a benefit.

Managing Your Consumer Spending

13. *Be an Informed Consumer,* reproducible master 24-1, TRG/B. Students imagine they are shopping for car repair service, athletic shoes, and a personal computer. Students should list specific resources they used to make an informed buying decision.

14. Ask students to obtain three sources of consumer information to help them get the best buy for the following items: a CD player, a 35mm camera, a leather jacket, hairstyling services, and sports equipment. Have students share their findings in class.

15. Ask students to bring in the warranties for an item they or their parents own, such as a CD player, television, or appliance. Have students read the warranties aloud. Then ask them to identify the type of warranty, explain the coverage offered, and answer questions from the class.

16. Have students obtain copies of *Consumer Reports* or another consumer information publication. Students should read two articles, then prepare a written report on one article and an oral report on the other. Students should use the questions in Chart 24-5 of the text as guidelines in preparing the reports.

17. Have students bring different advertising materials for the same kind of item (for example, a retail ad and a direct mail package, each promoting a cookware set). Students should evaluate and compare the prices and features of the item advertised in each ad. Are any ads misleading? Discuss with students.

18. *The Pros and Cons of Advertising,* reproducible master 24-2, TRG/B. Students are to respond to given statements about advertising.

19. *Advertising Evaluation Checklist,* transparency master 24-3, TRG/B. Use the transparency to discuss with students ways consumers can evaluate advertising.

20. *Advertising,* Activity D, SAG. Students use the Internet, newspapers, and magazines to find advertisements for listed products and services. Students should identify the promotional method used in each ad and answer questions.

21. Have students investigate a celebrity-endorsed product by using consumer information to research the item's quality. Is the celebrity endorsement a cover-up for an inferior product? Students should summarize findings in a brief oral report.

22. Have students work in groups to create advertising campaigns for a product or service of their choice. Students should include buying incentives like coupons, prizes, and in-store games. Have each group present their campaign to the class for evaluation.

23. *Where to Shop,* Activity E, SAG. Students choose where to shop for several different products, then respond to questions about their choices.

24. Have students select an item they wish to buy, then decide where to shop for the item (retail store, direct sale, catalog, or Internet). In a brief report, students should describe factors that influenced their decision. Factors may include store type and location, price, and product selection.

25. Have students role-play what to do if a door-to-door salesperson comes to their home.

26. Bring different types of catalogs to class. Have students read and explain the ordering information. Students may also check the company's guarantee and return policy. Ask students to select several items and accurately complete the order form. On a separate sheet, students should make a written record of their order.

27. Have students write letters or pretend to call a catalog company inquiring about an order they didn't receive after 30 days. (Have them use the written record of their orders from Item 26.)

28. Using the catalogs from Item 26, discuss the procedures for returning catalog orders. Then have students pretend to return catalog orders following those procedures.

29. Discuss the advantages and disadvantages of shopping by mail, television, and the Internet using Chart 24-9 of the text.

30. *Comparison Shopping,* Activity F, SAG. Students complete a comparison shopping chart for an item they would like to purchase. Students should then explain where they would decide to purchase the item.

31. Ask students to comparison shop for two different brands of blue jeans at three different stores. Have students make charts comparing prices, quality, and features of the jeans at each store. In oral reports, have students use the charts to explain which jeans would best suit their budget and needs. Discuss whether comparison shopping helped them save money and get better quality.

Exercising Your Consumer Rights and Responsibilities

32. Discuss the importance of the consumer rights and responsibilities outlined in Chart 24-13 of the text.
33. *The Right Way to Complain,* Activity G, SAG. Students indicate whether given statements about consumer complaints are true or false.
34. Have students design a poster illustrating the procedures to follow when complaining about a product or service.
35. Have students role-play situations in which a consumer must return a defective item to a retailer. Have students portray both satisfactory and unsatisfactory results.
36. *Complaint Letter,* Activity H, SAG. Students write a complaint letter based on the situation in the case study. Have students read each other's letters and critique them in comparison to the sample letter in Figure 24-14 of the text.
37. Discuss with students reasons they would need to contact a consumer protection service.
38. Ask students to call or to write the local Better Business Bureau asking about the reputation of a local business. Have students share their findings with the class.
39. *Complaint Form,* Activity I, SAG. Students are to fill out a Better Business Bureau complaint form based on information provided in a case study.
40. If your local television station has an action line, have students watch the program for several evenings and report on the types of consumer complaints presented.
41. Ask students to locate state and local consumer protection agencies. Students should request consumer literature that describes each agency's functions.
42. Divide the class into groups to prepare panel reports on the federal agencies that protect consumer rights. These agencies include the Consumer Product Safety Commission, the Food and Drug Administration, the Federal Trade Commission, and the Federal Communications Commission.

Activities to Enrich Learning

43. Have students write an essay on the topic "An Informed Consumer Is a Smart Consumer."

44. Have students role-play a shopping trip taken by a person who budgets money and a person who lives from paycheck to paycheck without a budget.
45. Have students investigate advertising and consumer advocacy careers and prepare reports for the class.

Activities to Extend Learning

46. Invite a financial counselor to speak to students about the benefits of wise budgeting.
47. Invite an advertising executive to speak to students about different types of advertising. How does each type influence consumers to buy goods and services?
48. Invite representatives from consumer protection services to give a panel discussion of the rights and responsibilities of teenage consumers. Host a question-and-answer session afterward.

Answer Key

Text

Facts in Review, page 466

1. a written plan to help a person make the most of his or her money
2. Establish financial goals. Estimate monthly income and expenses. Balance the budget. Keep track of income and expenses. Evaluate the budget.
3. Fixed expenses are the same amounts that are paid regularly. Flexible expenses are varying amounts due at various times. (Examples are student response.)
4. Does income cover expenses? Is the budget flexible enough to handle unexpected expenses? Is my money doing what I want it to do? Is my budget helping me meet my goals on schedule?
5. by being informed, understanding advertising and other promotional methods, deciding where to shop, and developing shopping skills
6. (List three:) people, places, organizations, printed materials
7. (List five:) advertisements, product labels and tags, use and care guides, warranties, newspapers, books, magazines, pamphlets, bulletins
8. A limited warranty covers product repairs, but paying labor costs and handling charges may be the customer's responsibility. A full warranty includes free repair or replacement of a product or any defective part within a reasonable time.
9. A warranty is a promise guaranteeing that a product will meet certain performance and safety standards for a specified period. A service contract is an extended warranty for an additional cost.
10. to sell goods and services
11. by saving money on items they would purchase anyway

12. the intended purchase and the store's selection, prices, and location
13. fewer customer services, higher sales volume
14. (List three:) extra charges, shipping delays, merchandise-return hassles, delivery failures, can't examine merchandise
15. (List three:) time savings, money savings, wide selection, convenience
16. when spending too much, when buying something you don't need or can't use
17. to save money, get better quality, and find the product/service that best suits your needs
18. (List three:) Consumer Product Safety Commission, Food and Drug Administration, Federal Trade Commission, Federal Communications Commission

Student Activity Guide

Fixed and Flexible Expenses, Activity B

1. Fixed expenses are the expenses that must be paid regularly. They are payments you have contracted.
2. Flexible expenses are expenses you have for which you pay varying amounts.
3. fixed expenses—insurance premium, rent, car payment; flexible expenses—bus fare, books, car repair, doctor bill, groceries, medicine, movie, raincoat, savings, electric bill, bowling, summer school

The Right Way to Complain, Activity G

1. T	14. T
2. T	15. F
3. F	16. T
4. T	17. T
5. F	18. F
6. T	19. T
7. F	20. F
8. F	21. F
9. T	22. T
10. T	23. T
11. T	24. T
12. F	25. T
13. T	

Teacher's Resource Guide/Binder

Review and Study Guide for Chapter 24, reproducible master 24-3

Chapter 24 Test

1. F	12. F
2. G	13. T
3. A	14. F
4. D	15. T
5. B	16. F
6. E	17. T
7. C	18. A
8. T	19. C
9. T	20. D
10. T	21. B
11. T	22. C

23. Establish financial goals. Estimate monthly income and expenses. Balance the budget. Keep track of income and expenses. Evaluate the budget.
24. (List three of each:) Advantages are time savings, money savings, wide selection, and convenience. Disadvantages are possible extra charges, the need to rely on pictures, shipping delays, shipping charges, merchandise-return hassles, and possible failure to deliver.
25. (List three:) information, selection, performance, safety, recourse (Descriptions of responsibilities are student response.)

Reproducible Master 24-1

Be an Informed Consumer

Name_____ Date _____ Period _____

As you learn to improve your buying habits, you become a better consumer. Suppose you want to buy the following goods and services. Use the resources listed below to help you make an informed buying decision. In the space provided, list the specific resources you used.

1. **Car repair service**

   A. Consumer publication: _____
   _____

   B. Advertisements: _____
   _____

   C. A car dealer: _____
   _____

   D. Library resources: _____
   _____

   E. An automotive technology teacher: _____
   _____

   F. Another car owner: _____
   _____

   G. Warranty or guarantee: _____
   _____

2. **Athletic shoes**

   A. Consumer publication: _____
   _____

   B. Advertisements: _____
   _____

   C. A shoe salesperson: _____
   _____

   D. A coach or physical education teacher: _____
   _____

   E. An athlete:_____
   _____

(Continued)

Name_____

    F. Library resources:_____

    _____

    G. Warranty or guarantee:_____

    _____

3. **A personal computer**

    A. Consumer publication: _____

    _____

    B. Advertisements: _____

    _____

    C. A computer salesperson: _____

    _____

    D. A business teacher: _____

    _____

    E. Library resources:_____

    _____

    F. Another consumer who uses the product: _____

    _____

    G. Warranty or guarantee:_____

    _____

Reproducible Master 24-2

The Pros and Cons of Advertising

Name_____ Date _____ Period _____

Respond to the statements below, indicating your opinion about the pros and cons of advertising by checking *Agree, Disagree,* or *Unsure.* Then choose one statement from the checklist and explain why you agree or disagree with the statement.

Agree	Disagree	Unsure	
_____	_____	_____	1. Advertising is a reliable source of information about products and services.
_____	_____	_____	2. The main purpose of advertising is to sell goods and services.
_____	_____	_____	3. Billboards should be banned as an advertising method because they deface the environment.
_____	_____	_____	4. I should use advertising to compare prices of goods and services.
_____	_____	_____	5. Ads should tell only the good things about a product or service.
_____	_____	_____	6. Advertising can influence me to buy things that I don't really want or need or can't afford.
_____	_____	_____	7. All advertising is misleading.
_____	_____	_____	8. Advertising is good only when it introduces a new product to the marketplace.
_____	_____	_____	9. Advertising does not affect my buying behavior.
_____	_____	_____	10. An endorsement or testimonial by a celebrity means a product is the best quality you can buy.

I strongly agree/disagree with statement _____ because _____

_____

_____

_____

_____

_____

_____

_____

_____

_____

_____

_____

_____

Advertising Evaluation Checklist

A product ad should state the following:

- model or serial number

- key features (what it does)

- key benefits (what it does for you)

- extras or added features

- sale price versus regular price

- warranty information

- type of promotional offer (30% off, two for one, etc.)

- offer's expiration date

Reproducible Master 24-4

Review and Study Guide for Chapter 24

Name _____   **Date** _____   **Period** _____

Read each description below and decide which chapter term is being described. Write the correct term in the crossword puzzle.

© Goodheart-Willcox

Across

4. A fund that covers unexpected expenses, such as a new car or tire. (three words)
8. A written promise that guarantees a product will meet certain performance and quality standards.
10. The abbreviation for the organization that tries to settle consumer complaints against local business firms.
13. A service _____ extends a warranty for an additional time period for an additional cost.
16. A written plan to manage money is called a(n) _____.
17. _____ are any type of product bought by consumers.
18. The abbreviation for the agency that regulates the production, packaging, and labeling of foods, drugs, and cosmetics.
19. _____ stores sell a wide selection of one type of product or service.

Down

1. People who use their income to buy the goods and services they need and want are _____.
2. _____ _____ is an unplanned purchase made without much thought.
3. _____ involve work that consumers pay to have done, such as hairstyling.
5. Knowing your consumer _____ and responsibilities can help you make wiser buying decisions.
6. The abbreviation for the agency that ensures the safety of household products such as appliances and clothing.
7. Shopping by mail order or ordering from a(n) _____ offers convenient at-home shopping.
9. Businesses use radio, television, and newspapers to _____ their goods and services.
11. The right to _____ means a consumer has the right to complain about a product or service that is *not* satisfactory.
12. The abbreviation for the agency that handles complaints about radio and television broadcasts and cable TV services.
14. Looking at several brands at different stores to compare prices, quality, and features is known as _____ shopping.
15. The abbreviation for the agency that helps prevent unfair competition, deceptive trade practices, and false advertising.

Managing Spending

Name_____

Date _____   **Period** _____   **Score** _____

Chapter 24 Test

Matching: Match the following terms and identifying phrases.

_____ 1. Looking at several brands or models at several different stores.

_____ 2. The right to complain to a business and receive a response.

_____ 3. Persons who buy and use goods and services.

_____ 4. A written promise that guarantees that a product will meet certain performance and quality standards.

_____ 5. Any type of product that consumers buy, such as food or clothing.

_____ 6. An unplanned purchase.

_____ 7. Work that consumers pay to have done, such as hairstyling or repairs.

A. consumers
B. goods
C. services
D. warranty
E. impulse buying
F. comparison shopping
G. recourse

True/False: Circle *T* if the statement is true or *F* if the statement is false.

T   F   8. A budget is the first place to start managing money wisely.

T   F   9. Writing down long-range goals is part of the budget planning process.

T   F   10. When people figure their income, they should only count income they are certain to receive.

T   F   11. As a person's goals change, his or her budget will need to change as well.

T   F   12. Learning as much as possible about a product or service before buying it is *not* important.

T   F   13. Consumer information is published by government agencies and nonprofit organizations.

T   F   14. The main purpose of advertising is to inform consumers.

T   F   15. "Buy one, get one free" is an example of a promotion.

T   F   16. Price is always the best guide to a product's quality.

T   F   17. Checking the quality of an item is important if you plan to use it often or for a long time.

Multiple Choice: Choose the best response. Write the letter in the space provided.

_____ 18. Which of the following is a fixed expense?
A. Rent.
B. Food.
C. Clothes.
D. All of the above.

(Continued)

Name_____

_____ 19. Which of the following is a flexible expense?
      A. Installment payments.
      B. Mortgage payments.
      C. Recreation.
      D. Insurance premiums.

_____ 20. A full warranty _____.
      A. offers broad coverage of a product
      B. includes free repair or replacement of defective parts
      C. allows for replacement if the product can't be repaired
      D. All of the above.

_____ 21. Coupons, prizes, and in-store games are examples of _____.
      A. promotions
      B. buying incentives
      C. special sales
      D. advertising

_____ 22. Direct selling means that consumers buy from _____.
      A. a factory outlet
      B. a store in a shopping mall
      C. a door-to-door salesperson or an in-house party
      D. a specialty store

Essay Questions: Provide complete responses to the following questions or statements.

23. List the five major steps to developing a budget.
24. Name three advantages and three disadvantages of shopping by mail.
25. List three consumer rights and describe the related responsibilities.

Using Credit

Objectives

After studying this chapter, students will be able to
- discuss the advantages and disadvantages of using credit.
- identify the different types of credit.
- describe how to establish a credit rating.
- describe the laws that control credit use.
- explain the importance of using credit wisely.
- build SCANS competencies in using information and systems.

Teaching Materials

Text, pages 469-487
> *Terms to Know*
> *Facts in Review*
> *Applying Your Skills*
> *Developing SCANS Workplace Competencies*

Student Activity Guide
> A. *Understanding Credit*
> B. *Applying for Credit*
> C. *Cost of Credit*
> D. *Federal Credit Laws*
> E. *Using Credit Wisely*

Teacher's Resource Guide/ Binder
> *Parts of a Credit Card,* transparency master 25-1
> *Keeping Your Credit Card Safe,* reproducible master 25-2
> *Types of Credit,* reproducible master 25-3
> *Review and Study Guide for Chapter 25,* reproducible master 25-4
> *Chapter 25 Test,* reproducible master

Teacher's Resource Binder
> *Don't Get Trapped in the Revolving Credit Spiral!* color transparency CT-25

Introductory Activities

1. Ask students if they have ever borrowed money or bought an item on credit by making payments to family members or friends. Students may explain how they made sure they could repay the loan or make the payments on time. If they had to pay interest on the loan, students should explain how it affected their feelings about taking the loan.
2. Let the class brainstorm any images or phrases that come to mind when they hear the words *charge it*. From their responses, students should develop a list of reasons people use credit.
3. *Don't Get Trapped in the Revolving Credit Spiral!* color transparency CT-25, TRB. Use this transparency when discussing the risks in using credit. Tell students that with an 18.5 percent interest rate card, it will take more than 11 years to pay off a debt of $2,000 if you only pay the minimum balance due each month. During this time, you will pay interest charges of $1,934—almost doubling the cost of the purchase.

Instructional Concepts and Student Learning Experiences

Understanding Credit

4. Have students write a paragraph on what having credit means to them. Discuss responses in class. Point out any danger signs of future credit misuse.
5. Have students debate the pros and cons of using credit to take advantage of "buy now, pay later" promotions.
6. Have students role-play situations that illustrate the advantages and disadvantages of using credit. Have students role-play different people using credit, such as a student, single woman or man, single parent, husband and wife with five children, or retired person.
7. *Understanding Credit,* Activity A, SAG. Students answer questions about understanding credit.
8. Have students refer to the four major types of credit discussed in the text. Then, have them give examples of at least three situations in which consumers may use each type of credit. Discuss why the borrower in each situation would choose that specific credit type.

9. *Types of Credit,* reproducible master 25-3, TRG/B. Students decide a type of credit to use for each listed item and explain their choices.

10. Obtain a sample of a charge account bill, a monthly credit card statement, and an installment payment book or notice for students to review. Explain the information they can expect to find on each sample.

11. *Parts of a Credit Card,* transparency master 25-1, TRG/B. Use the transparency to show students the key information on a credit card.

12. *Keeping Your Credit Card Safe,* reproducible master 25-2, TRG/B. Use the reproducible to discuss with students how to protect their credit information.

13. Have students list the collateral they would use for a cash loan. How would students feel if they defaulted on the loan and lost the collateral?

14. Have students list persons who they believe would be willing to be their cosigner for a $1,000 loan. Have students approach these persons for their responses, then report their findings to the class. Discuss the risks involved for the cosigner and the borrower.

15. Have students write a case history of a young person who uses credit wisely. Contrast the case history with those of Eva and Kevin on pages 471 and 484 of the text. Ask students to explain why the person in their case study is a good credit risk.

16. Have students write a brochure for recent high school graduates with little or no established credit. The brochure may be entitled "How to Build Your Credit Rating."

17. Have students contact or visit a local credit bureau. What type of information is included in a credit record? What factors determine a good credit risk or a poor credit risk? How can consumers correct errors in their credit record? Have students find out answers to these questions and share information in class.

18. Refer students to the case studies on pages 471 and 484 of the text. Using information in the studies, ask students to evaluate Eva's and Kevin's credit rating. What might their credit records say about them to other lenders? Would either person be able to obtain more credit cards or loans?

19. Instruct students to obtain credit card applications from local retail stores. Have students read the credit agreements and explain the credit terms to the class. Why is reading and understanding a credit agreement before charging on a new card important?

20. *Applying for Credit,* Activity B, SAG. Students complete a credit application form.

21. Have students bring catalogs or department store ad flyers to class. After choosing one or two items,

students should calculate what each would cost to buy for cash (including tax, delivery charges, etc.). Then they should determine how much the items would cost if they charged them using 24 monthly installment payments at a monthly rate of 1.5 percent and an annual rate of 21 percent interest. Discuss the advantages and disadvantages of each method of purchasing the items.

22. *Cost of Credit,* Activity C, SAG. Students are to determine the cost of credit using a case study example.

23. Refer students to Eva's case history on page 471 of the text. Have students explain in writing how each federal credit law benefits or protects Eva as a borrower.

24. *Federal Credit Laws,* Activity D, SAG. Students match credit laws to the appropriate descriptions.

Using Credit Wisely

25. *Using Credit Wisely,* Activity E, SAG. Students compare credit costs on an item they wish to purchase by contacting three different creditors. They then respond to questions about using credit wisely for their purchase.

26. Discuss how the convenience of credit might influence teen shoppers to buy more items on impulse than they really want or need.

27. Have students evaluate whether or not to use credit to buy an item of their choice. To help them decide, students may write responses to the evaluation questions in the text. Discuss how evaluating whether or not to use credit can help students use credit wisely.

28. Divide the class into small groups. Have each group compare credit terms for a used car loan from three sources. First, ask each group to determine the loan amount. Second, on a separate sheet of paper, have groups make a chart to compare credit charges by using the format in Chart 25-8 of the text. Students should then contact three credit sources for information needed to complete the chart. Have the groups determine the best credit source, then explain their choice in class.

29. Refer to Kevin's case study on page 484 of the text. Discuss with students how Kevin could have avoided his credit problems by following the credit guidelines suggested in Chart 25-9 in the text.

30. Have students locate credit counseling services in the community. Students should request information about the types of services offered, then share the information in class.

31. In a written report, have students compare and contrast straight bankruptcy and Chapter 13 protection.

32. Discuss the types of credit problems that could lead a person to file for bankruptcy or Chapter 13

protection. Then have students develop a list of personal guidelines for responsible credit use to help them avoid credit problems.

Activities to Enrich Learning

33. Have students research and write a report on the origins of the major bank credit cards.
34. Role-play a situation in class in which students buy items such as pens or notebooks from you on credit. Use play money and set specific terms of repayment, such as interest on balances not paid in full by the due date. Repossess any items for which students cannot or will not pay.

Activities to Extend Learning

35. Invite a manager of a credit counseling service to speak to students about the dangers of abusing credit. Ask the manager to present actual case histories for illustration.
36. Invite an agent from a credit bureau to speak to students on the importance of credit ratings and credit reports. Ask the agent to focus on the borrower's rights.
37. Invite a credit manager from a bank or credit union to speak to students about establishing credit for the first time and using credit wisely.

Answer Key

Text

Facts in Review, page 486

1. When using cash for a purchase, money is exchanged. When using credit for a purchase, a promise to pay is exchanged.
2. (List four of each. See Chart 25-1 on page 470.)
3. (List four:) credit card account, charge account, installment account, vehicle leasing, cash loan, home equity loan
4. With a credit card account, customers have a credit card, use it to make purchases, then pay the entire bill when it arrives or minimum amounts for extended periods. With a charge account, a record of the purchase is kept on file and the full bill must be paid promptly when it arrives.
5. to protect the lender/creditor from the risk of nonpayment
6. Get a job; stay employed; open a checking account; open a savings account; buy a layaway item; apply to a gasoline company or a local store for a credit card.
7. to collect and maintain financial information on individuals
8. the information collected by credit bureaus

9. because they are legally binding and the borrower must fulfill the terms
10. amount of credit used, interest rate, repayment period
11. as a dollar amount and as an annual percentage rate
12. Truth in Lending Act
13. Equal Credit Opportunity Act
14. choosing not to make the purchase, paying for the purchase with savings, saving money to make the purchase later
15. by providing financial programs for repaying debt, by giving lessons in managing future debt, by restructuring payment schedules for people with serious debt
16. With straight bankruptcy, a debtor's assets are sold by the court to pay the debt. With Chapter 13 bankruptcy, debtors with regular incomes pay back some or most of their debts over a three- to five-year period.

Student Activity Guide

Understanding Credit, Activity A

1. the present use of future income that allows consumers to buy goods and services now and pay for them later
2. a business or individual that makes credit available to consumers by loaning money or selling goods and services on credit
3. to build a credit history as a person who is likely to repay debt
4. Creditors want evidence that any money loaned to a person will be repaid.
5. the creditor's evaluation of a person's willingness and ability to pay debts
6. It means the person can be trusted to pay their debts.
7. Good credit risks usually have steady incomes; make regular, on-time payments; own a car, home, stocks, or bonds; and have lived in the same community for a period of time.
8. allows you to buy and use expensive goods and services as you pay for them; convenience
9. expensive; may spend more money than you have; may encourage impulse purchases
10. (Name six:) credit card accounts, charge accounts, installment accounts, vehicle leasing, cash loans, home equity loans
11. Customers have the choice of paying for purchases in full each month or spreading payments over a period of time.
12. In a charge account, the business bills the customer once a month, and the customer is expected to pay in full by the assigned due date. In an installment account, the buyer pays for the merchandise according to a set schedule of payments.
13. If you are unable to repay the loan, the collateral serves as repayment.

14. Get a job and stay employed; open a checking account; open a savings account; buy an item on a layaway plan; apply to a gasoline company or a local store for a credit card.
15. (Student response. See page 476 of the text.)
16. to collect and keeps files of financial information on individual consumers
17. It is a legally binding contract.
18. Check your credit report for errors or missing information.
19. Notify creditors promptly and try to work out a temporary payment schedule.
20. Report the loss or theft immediately.

Cost of Credit, Activity C

1. the total amount a borrower must pay for the use of credit
2. $97.50
3. $156
4. $747.50 ($650.00 + $97.50 interest)
5. $806 ($650.00 + $156 interest)
6. The finance charge must be stated as a dollar amount and as an annual percentage rate.
7. (Student response.)
8. (Student response.)
9. She could have paid cash, paid cash with money from her savings account, or saved her money and bought the stereo later.
10. Nancy will need to pay off the stereo within the year. She will need to budget and pay monthly payments to enable her to have the amount paid within the year.

Federal Credit Laws, Activity D

1. B		5. D		8. A	
2. D		6. A		9. E	
3. A		7. C		10. E	
4. C					

Using Credit Wisely, Activity E

(Answers to all questions on page 181 and Question 3 on page 182 are student response.)
4. (See Figure 25-11 on page 483 of the text.)
5. Notify your creditors immediately and set up a repayment schedule to reduce the size of monthly payments.
6. They help debtors work out financial programs to repay debts; they help debtors learn to manage their money to prevent future debt; they help work out repayment schedules with creditors.
7. a legal proceeding for the purpose of stating a person's inability to pay debts
8. In straight bankruptcy, a person's assets, including car, house, and furniture, are sold by the court to pay the debts. In Chapter 13 bankruptcy, debtors pay back some or most of their debts over a three- to five-year period and keep all their possessions.
9. You must pay interest on the amount from the purchase date.

10. Budget monthly payments so the amount is paid in full before the expiration date.

Teacher's Resource Guide/Binder

Review and Study Guide for Chapter 25, reproducible master 25-4

Chapter 25 Test

1. M		11. H		21. T	
2. J		12. I		22. T	
3. A		13. F		23. F	
4. B		14. G		24. T	
5. E		15. F		25. B	
6. L		16. T		26. D	
7. K		17. F		27. C	
8. N		18. T		28. A	
9. C		19. T		29. C	
10. D		20. T			

30. (List three of each. Student response. See pages 470-471 in the text.)
31. (Name three:) Stay employed; open a checking account; open a savings account; buy an item on a layaway plan; apply to a gasoline company or local store for a credit card; pay bills on time; stay at the same address and employer.
32. (List four. See chart 25-9 on page 481 in the text.)

Parts of a Credit Card

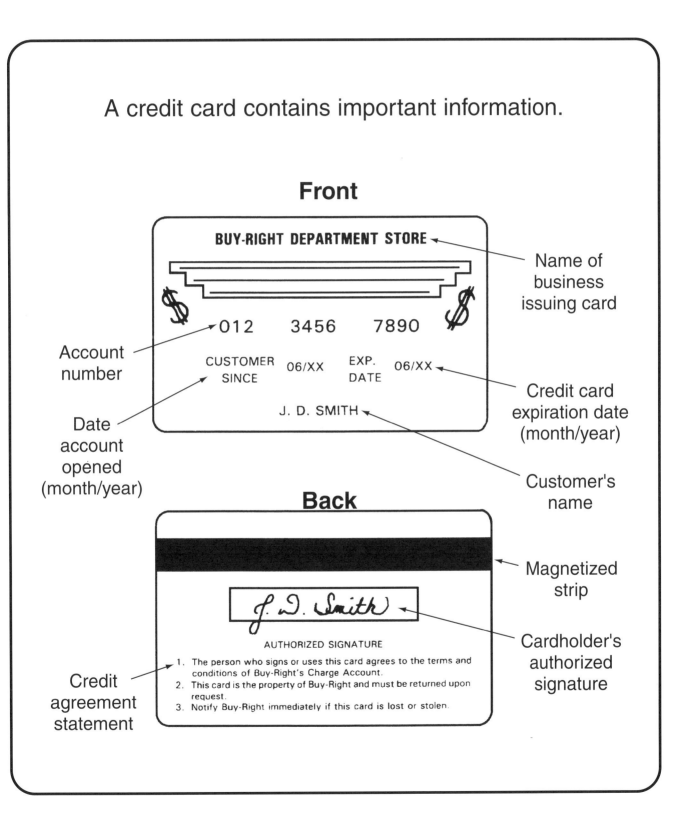

A credit card contains important information.

Front

BUY-RIGHT DEPARTMENT STORE — Name of business issuing card

012   3456   7890

Account number

CUSTOMER SINCE   06/XX

EXP. DATE   06/XX — Credit card expiration date (month/year)

J. D. SMITH — Customer's name

Date account opened (month/year)

Back

AUTHORIZED SIGNATURE

1. The person who signs or uses this card agrees to the terms and conditions of Buy-Right's Charge Account.
2. This card is the property of Buy-Right and must be returned upon request.
3. Notify Buy-Right immediately if this card is lost or stolen.

Magnetized strip

Cardholder's authorized signature

Credit agreement statement

Reproducible Master 25-2

Keeping Your Credit Card Safe

Name_____ **Date** _____ **Period** _____

Having or using a credit card is a big responsibility. Besides managing your credit spending, you must try to keep your credit card safe. That means making sure your credit card is not lost or stolen. You must also protect your credit card number. If someone obtains it, that person could use it illegally to make purchases on your account. Here are some more tips you can follow to keep your credit card safe.

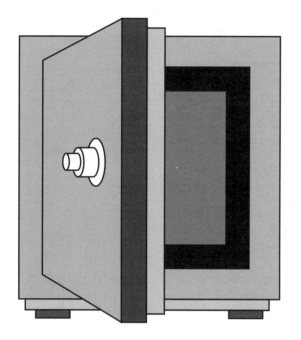

- *Check to see your name is spelled correctly on the front of the card.* Call the creditor's customer service number immediately if it is misspelled.

- *Sign the back of the card immediately.* If your card is lost or stolen and it is not signed, anyone could sign your name and use your card.

- *Keep your credit card in a separate case away from your wallet.* If your wallet is stolen, the thief will not get your credit card.

- *If your card is lost or stolen, notify the creditor immediately.* Otherwise, you may be responsible for some of the charges made on your card by the thief. Read your credit agreement to fully understand your creditor's policy on lost or stolen cards.

- *When you make a credit card purchase, be sure the clerk returns your card before you leave the store.* Also, ask for the carbon paper from the sales slip. Some dishonest person may take your credit card number from the carbons and use it to make telephone or mail purchases on your card.

- *When making a credit card purchase by telephone or by mail, be sure you are dealing with a reputable company.* This will help ensure that your number will not be misused.

- *Check your monthly billing statement to make sure that you made all the charges listed.* If you see a charge listed that you did not make, contact your creditor immediately.

Reproducible Master 25-3

Types of Credit

Name_____ **Date** _____ **Period** _____

Imagine you will buy the following products and services on credit. Select the type of credit you would use for each purchase from the list below. Then explain your choices and be prepared to report your decisions to the class.

Select from the following types of credit:

- cash loans
- charge accounts
- credit card accounts
- home equity loans
- installment accounts
- vehicle leasing

Item	Type of Credit Used	Explanation
1. New car		
2. Condominium		
3. Leather jacket		
4. Computer and printer		
5. A vacation		
6. CD player		
7. New work wardrobe		

(Continued)

Name_____

Item	Type of Credit Used	Explanation
8. Car repair		
9. College tuition		
10. Home improvement		
11. Concert tickets		
12. Doctor's office visit		
13. Sofa and chair		
14. Telephone bill		
15. Dinner at a restaurant		

Choose one of the 15 items and list three alternatives for using credit to purchase that item.

1. _____

2. _____

3. _____

Reproducible Master 25-4

Review and Study Guide for Chapter 25

Name_____ **Date** _____ **Period** _____

(Continued)

Name _____

Across

2. Commercial banks, savings and loan associations, and credit unions often make _____ _____.
5. A home equity _____ is based on the homeowner's equity in the house.
6. _____ _____ are the total amounts borrowers must pay for the use of credit.
7. _____ is a legal proceeding for stating a person's inability to pay back debts.
8. The price paid for the use of money over a period of time is called _____.
9. _____ allows a person to buy now and pay later.
10. _____ are businesses or individuals who make credit available to consumers by loaning money or selling goods and services on credit.
13. Customers who use _____ _____ are expected to pay their bills in full by the assigned due date.
14. A(n) _____ _____ is the creditor's evaluation of a person's willingness and ability to pay back debts.
16. _____ charge accounts allow customers the choice of paying for purchases in full each month or over a period of time.

Down

1. _____ is something of value held by the creditor in case a customer is unable to pay a loan.
2. A(n) _____ _____ collects and keeps files of financial information on individual consumers.
3. A(n) _____ _____ _____ is the actual rate of interest charged on a yearly basis.
4. Paying for merchandise according to a set schedule of payments is known as a(n) _____ account.
11. A(n) _____ is a responsible person who signs a loan agreement with the borrower.
12. The _____ period is the number of days allowed to pay for a new purchase before interest is charged.
15. _____ is determined by subtracting how much is owed on a house from the amount the house is worth.

Using Credit

Name_____

Date _____   **Period** _____   **Score** _____

Chapter 25

Matching: Match the following terms and identifying phrases.

_____ 1. The actual rate of interest charged on a yearly basis.

_____ 2. A legally-binding contract between the borrower and the creditor.

_____ 3. Allows a person to buy goods and services now and pay for them later.

_____ 4. Businesses or individuals that make credit available to consumers by loaning money or selling goods and services to them.

_____ 5. An account in which the buyer pays according to a set schedule of payments.

_____ 6. The price paid for the use of money over a period of time.

_____ 7. The total amount a borrower must pay for the use of credit.

_____ 8. A legal proceeding for the purpose of stating a person's inability to pay his or her debts.

_____ 9. An account that allows customers the choice of paying for purchases in full each month or spreading payments over a period of time.

_____ 10. The way businesses extend credit to customers without using credit cards.

_____ 11. A creditor's evaluation of a person's willingness and ability to pay debts.

_____ 12. An agency that collects financial information and keeps files on individual consumers.

_____ 13. The type of loan made by commercial banks and savings and loan associations.

_____ 14. Something of value held by the creditor in case a person is unable to repay the loan.

A. credit
B. creditors
C. revolving charge account
D. charge account
E. installment account
F. cash loan
G. collateral
H. credit rating
I. credit bureau
J. credit agreement
K. finance charges
L. interest
M. annual percentage rate
N. bankruptcy

True/False: Circle *T* if the statement is true or *F* if the statement is false.

T   F   15. Credit is *not* easily available to most consumers.

T   F   16. Credit is based on trust between the creditor and the credit user.

T   F   17. If a person has no collateral, it is *not* possible to get a loan.

T   F   18. Creditors want evidence that a person can and will pay his or her debts before they grant credit.

(Continued)

Name_____

T F 19. Buying an item on a layaway plan is a good way to build a credit rating.

T F 20. A person who has problems getting credit has the right to check his or her credit record.

T F 21. Job history, income, and bill-paying history are all parts of a credit record.

T F 22. To manage credit spending, a person should use credit sparingly and only after much thought.

T F 23. If a person has trouble making credit payments, he or she should stop paying the creditors.

T F 24. Making late payments is a sign of a credit problem.

Multiple Choice: Choose the best response. Write the letter in the space provided.

_____25. By signing a loan agreement, which person promises to pay the loan if the borrower fails to pay?
   A. Creditor.
   B. Cosigner.
   C. Investor.
   D. Banker.

_____26. To keep records of all credit transactions, be sure to include _____.
   A. payments and receipts
   B. contracts
   C. correspondence
   D. All of the above.

_____27. A credit user can keep a good credit record by _____.
   A. using a credit card weekly
   B. maintaining a high balance
   C. paying promptly
   D. None of the above.

_____28. The Truth in Lending Act _____.
   A. requires creditors to tell consumers the cost of using credit
   B. protects consumers against unfair billing practices
   C. provides for the accuracy of information in credit reports
   D. prohibits a creditor from denying credit for discriminatory reasons

_____29. Which is *not* a sign of credit problems?
   A. Using savings to pay off debts.
   B. Making late payments.
   C. Paying the balance in full each month.
   D. Running out of money before payday.

Essay Questions: Provide complete responses to the following questions or statements.

30. List three advantages and three disadvantages of using credit.
31. Name three ways to build a good credit rating.
32. List four ways to use credit wisely.

Banking, Saving, and Investing

Objectives

After studying this chapter, students will be able to
- select the financial institutions and banking services that will best meet their financial needs.
- endorse, deposit, write, and cash checks correctly.
- balance a checkbook.
- describe the special types of checks that can be used in place of personal checks and cash.
- evaluate the basic types of savings plans.
- compare different types of investments.
- build SCANS competencies in using resources, interpersonal skills, information, and systems.

Teaching Materials

Text, pages 489-515
Terms to Know
Facts in Review
Applying Your Skills
Developing SCANS Workplace Competencies
Student Activity Guide
  A. *Compare Financial Institutions*
  B. *Checks*
  C. *Using a Checking Account*
  D. *Safe-Deposit Boxes*
  E. *Investing Your Money*
  F. *Banking and Investment Terms*
Teacher's Resource Guide/Binder
  Writing Check Amounts Correctly, reproducible master 26-1
  Investment Terms, reproducible master 26-2
  Review and Study Guide for Chapter 26, reproducible master 26-3
  Chapter 26 Test, reproducible master
Teacher's Resource Binder
  Precautions for ATM Card Users, color transparency CT-26

Introductory Activities

1. Poll students to see what kind of banking services they use, such as checking or savings accounts,
   cashier's checks, money orders, or other services. Have students explain which banking services they find most useful.
2. Ask students how they cash their paychecks. How many students opened a checking account for this purpose?

Instructional Concepts and Student Learning Experiences

Types of Financial Institutions

3. Have students bring in brochures from at least one commercial bank, one savings and loan association, and one credit union. (If your community has more than one of each establishment, instruct students to bring in brochures from two of each type of institution.) Students should compare and contrast the features and benefits of each type of financial institution.
4. Which financial institution is most conveniently located to each student's home or workplace? Instruct students to write a report on their closest financial institution, identifying the available types of accounts, fees, and services it offers.
5. Have students write reports on the origins and the functions of FDIC and NCUA.
6. *Compare Financial Institutions,* Activity A, SAG. Students survey local financial institutions about the services they offer.
7. Have students design a poster showing how to choose a financial institution. Display posters in the classroom.

Electronic Banking

8. Have students note the locations of ATM terminals in your community. Discuss how these locations are convenient for bank customers.
9. *Precautions for ATM Card Users,* color transparency CT-26, TRB. Use the transparency to reinforce the need for exercising care and caution when using ATM terminals.

10. Have students brainstorm the advantages and disadvantages of having an ATM card. Discuss situations like the danger of impulse spending and the importance of recording each ATM transaction in the checkbook register.
11. Ask students if their workstation offers automatic deposit of paychecks. Have students brainstorm ways that automatic deposit would benefit them.
12. Have students write a case study in which two friends go shopping—one with a debit card and the other with a credit card. Instruct students to include in their case study a description of how each card works. Also, have students explain which method of purchasing is most advantageous.

Checking Accounts

13. Instruct students to write an instruction guide for individuals opening their first checking account.
14. Set up the classroom to model a bank. Have students role-play the following situations: opening a new checking account, writing a check correctly, endorsing a check, and depositing a check.
15. Ask students to compare and evaluate the three types of checking accounts described in the text. Have them research this information at a local bank, then prepare oral reports describing which account would best meet their needs.
16. Using a photocopy of a blank check, students should practice writing checks. Then, have students exchange the checks with each other. Students must show signed identification so the recipient can verify the signature. (This exercise can help prepare students to work in retail stores.)
17. *Checks,* Activity B, SAG. Students identify the information given on checks.
18. Have students discuss the pros and cons of opening a joint checking account with a relative.
19. *Using a Checking Account,* Activity C, SAG. Students complete sample transactions, including making a deposit, writing a check, filling out a check register, and balancing a bank statement.
20. Have students research the laws against and penalties for check forgery. Students should share findings in a written report.
21. Have students role-play the consequences of not balancing a checking account, such as bounced checks, calls from collection agencies, and not having enough money to pay bills.
22. *Writing Check Amounts Correctly,* reproducible master 26-1, TRG/B. Students practice converting numbers into written dollar amounts.
23. Have students define the expression *to bounce a check.* Students should research the penalties for bouncing checks and report orally to the class.

Special Types of Checks

24. Obtain samples of the following types of checks: cashier's check, certified check, traveler's check, and money order. Have students practice filling out traveler's checks and money orders. In which situations would students use each type of check?

Safe-Deposit Boxes

25. *Safe-Deposit Boxes,* Activity D, SAG. Students describe the purpose of safe-deposit boxes and identify items that are usually kept inside. Students also visit a bank to find out policies regarding safe-deposit boxes.
26. Ask students what items of theirs should be kept in a safe-deposit box.

Savings Accounts at Financial Institutions

27. Have students bring in the business section of the local newspaper. In class, have students read ads for financial institutions and discuss the rate of interest and other advantages each institution offers for savings plans. Have students clip the ads for the best savings opportunities and display them on a bulletin board.
28. Have students imagine they have successfully saved $1,000. Ask them to examine their short- and long-term financial goals, then decide which type of savings plan would be best for their purposes: a regular savings account, a money market deposit account, or a certificate of deposit.

Investing Your Money

29. Ask students to write down what they think *to play the stock market* means. Students should compare their answers to the factual information about investments in the text.
30. Have students check the library for reference materials on investing. Then, have students write a report on what they learned. How would they use the information to make an investment of $5,000?
31. *Investing Your Money,* Activity E, SAG. Students complete a crossword puzzle using investment terms.
32. Have students check consumer business magazines in the library to find the rate of return on stocks, bonds, mutual funds, and money market funds in the previous calendar year. Then, have students diagram the return on a $1,000 investment in each of the securities.
33. Have students determine what would be the best investment choice for each of the following: a recent high school graduate with $500 in savings; a newly married couple with $5,000 in wedding gift money; and a single, 28-year-old person with $10,000.

34. Have students research and write a report on the history of savings bonds.
35. Have students follow the status of one stock for two weeks by checking the stock report in a daily newspaper or through a financial program on TV or the Internet. Have students discuss the performance of the stocks in class and determine whether they are good investments. Can this be determined from only a two-week monitoring period?
36. Instruct students to write an essay on the topic "How I Can Benefit from an Individual Retirement Account."
37. Have students list the kinds of self-employed persons who could have a Keogh plan for retirement.
38. *Banking and Investment Terms,* Activity F, SAG. Students complete statements about banking services.
39. Divide the class into two groups. Have one group give a panel presentation on traditional IRA plans while the other presents Roth IRA plans. List the similarities and differences between the two plans.
40. Have students suggest savings or investment plans for a person who wants to invest in real estate and needs a down payment.
41. Divide the class into pairs. Have students imagine they are real estate agents who must explain to prospective buyers how to benefit from a real estate investment.
42. Discuss the risks of buying income property. Have students brainstorm best-case and worst-case scenarios for a landlord.
43. Have students find reference books at the library on real estate investing. Instruct them to report on the advantages and disadvantages of a limited partnership.

Making Investments

44. Have students pretend they have $1,000 to invest. Students should make a personal investment plan by following text guidelines for investing. (Instruct students to consider all the savings and investment plans discussed in the text.) Students should explain their plans with supporting facts from the text or their library research.
45. *Investment Terms,* reproducible master 26-2, TRG/B. Students research and write the definitions of financial terms and bring a newspaper article containing as many terms as possible to class.

Activities to Enrich Learning

46. Have students investigate careers in banking by interviewing personnel from financial institutions and conducting library research. Have students discuss their findings in class.

47. Instruct students to investigate careers in real estate by interviewing real estate professionals and conducting library research. Have students write a report on their findings.

Activities to Extend Learning

48. Take students on a field trip to a local financial institution to learn about banking procedures, careers in banking, and money management opportunities.
49. Invite the president of a local financial institution to speak to students about savings opportunities for young adults.
50. Invite a real estate broker to speak to the class about the risks and benefits of investing in real estate.
51. Invite a financial planner to speak to the class about different ways of planning for retirement.

Answer Key

Text

Facts in Review, page 514

1. (List three:) convenient location, convenient hours, financial safety of the institution, service fees
2. 24-hour access to your money
3. (List five. See Chart 26-3 on page 492.)
4. regular (budget), minimum-balance, and interest-bearing accounts
5. It must be endorsed, which is signing your name on the back along the left end.
6. restrictive endorsement
7. debit card
8. Your bank and the bank of the party that cashed the check both charge fees. After several overdraws, your poor banking practices may be reported to the local credit reporting agency.
9. the record of checks, deposits, and service charges to your account
10. cashier's check
11. Simple interest pays money only on the deposit. Compound interest pays money on both the deposit and interest earned.
12. money market deposit account
13. (List four:) stocks, bonds, mutual funds, money market funds, retirement accounts, real estate
14. A bond is a certificate of debt or obligation issued by a corporation or government. A stock is a share in a corporation's ownership.
15. early in his or her career

Student Activity Guide

Checks, Activity B

A. name and address of bank
B. name and address of person (or persons) authorized to use this check

C. bank's identification number
D. check number
E. check routing symbol (used by Federal Reserve Banks)
F. bank's identification number
G. account number
H. payee's name
I. date
J. amount in numbers
K. reason for writing check
L. check amount written out in words, with a line drawn through the remaining space
M. signature that matches bank signature card

Using a Checking Account, Activity C

Making a Deposit: Total deposit is $172.62.
Writing a Check:

Filling Out a Check Register: After recording the deposit and the check, the balance is $323.02.

Balancing a Bank Statement: Total deposits not credited in this statement are $172.62. Total of checks outstanding is $149.27. Balance is $323.02.

Safe-Deposit Boxes, Activity D

(The following items should be checked:) 1, 4, 5, 7, 8, 10, 12, 13, 14
16. to protect and safely store your valuables from fire and theft
17. (Student response.)

Investing Your Money, Activity E

Banking and Investment Terms, Activity F

1. commercial
2. FDIC
3. loan
4. credit union
5. NCUA
6. regular (or budget)
7. minimum-balance
8. interest-bearing
9. joint
10. blank
11. restrictive
12. bank statement
13. traveler's
14. cashier's
15. certified
16. money order
17. regular
18. certificate of deposit
19. safe-deposit boxes
20. automated teller machine
21. personal identification
22. automatic transfer
23. debit card

Teacher's Resource Guide/Binder

Writing Check Amounts Correctly, reproducible master 26-1

1. Fifty-five and 50/100
2. Three hundred forty-nine and 00/100 (or no/100)
3. Forty-five and 95/100
4. Seven and 49/100
5. Fourteen and 53/100
6. One thousand fifty and 75/100
7. Ninety-nine and 99/100
8. 75/100
9. Seven hundred and 00/100 (or no/100)
10. Six hundred sixty-one and 25/100

Review and Study Guide for Chapter 26, reproducible master 26-3

1. bank statement
2. credit union
3. smart
4. debit
5. restrictive
6. cashier's check
7. canceled
8. online banking
9. common
10. minimum-balance

11. F
12. T
13. F
14. T
15. T
16. T
17. T
18. F
19. T
20. F

Chapter 26 Test

1. J
2. H
3. A
4. D
5. M
6. F
7. I
8. B
9. G
10. E
11. C
12. L
13. K
14. F
15. T
16. F
17. T
18. T
19. T
20. F
21. T
22. T
23. F
24. A
25. A
26. C
27. D
28. A

29. Consider the services offered, the convenience of hours and location, the safety of your money, and the cost of services.
30. When writing a check, include the following: date, including day, month, and year; name of payee; amount of check in numbers; amount of check in words; purpose of check; and your signature.
31. Set an investment goal; do not invest money you cannot afford to lose; examine your investment plans; find reliable professionals to help.

Reproducible Master 26-1

Writing Check Amounts Correctly

Name_____   **Date** _____   **Period** _____

Writing a check accurately so that the correct amount is deducted from your account is important. Write out the following dollar amounts as you would on a check. Pay special attention to spelling and hyphenation.

1. $55.50

   _____Dollars

2. $349.00

   _____Dollars

3. $45.95

   _____Dollars

4. $7.49

   _____Dollars

5. $14.53

   _____Dollars

6. $1,050.75

   _____Dollars

7. $99.99

   _____Dollars

8. $.75

   _____Dollars

9. $700.00

   _____Dollars

10. $661.25

   _____Dollars

Reproducible Master 26-2

Investment Terms

Name_____ **Date** _____ **Period** _____

Research and write the definitions of the following investment terms. Find articles in a consumer business magazine or the business section of a newspaper to show how the terms are used. Bring the articles to discuss in class.

1. High-risk investment: _____

_____

2. Low-risk investment:_____

_____

3. Yield:_____

_____

4. Returns: _____

_____

5. Blue chips: _____

_____

6. Dow Jones Industrial Averages: _____

_____

7. S&P 500: _____

_____

8. Diversification: _____

_____

9. Cyclicals: _____

_____

10. AAA-rated: _____

_____

11. Assets: _____

_____

12. Prospectus: _____

_____

13. Price/earnings ratio: _____

_____

14. Maturity: _____

_____

15. Market indicators: _____

_____

Reproducible Master 26-3

Review and Study Guide for Chapter 26

Name_____ Date _____ Period _____

Completion: Fill in the blanks with the correct terms.

1. A record of the checks, deposits, and charges on your account for a specific length of time is called a(n) _____ _____.

2. The financial services of a(n) _____ _____ are for its members only.

3. A(n) _____ card has an embedded computer chip to track certain information.

4. A(n) _____ card allows you to withdraw funds from your checking account without writing a check.

5. "For deposit only" is an example of a(n) _____ endorsement.

6. A(n) _____ _____ is drawn on the bank's own funds and signed by a bank officer.

7. _____ checks have been processed by your bank.

8. _____ _____ allows you to use your computer to communicate with your bank by sending and receiving electronic messages via the telephone.

9. _____ stock involves more risk because the value of the stock depends on company earnings and economic conditions.

10. A(n) _____-_____ account requires a person to keep a minimum amount of money in the account at all times to avoid paying a service charge.

True/False: Circle *T* if the statement is true or *F* if the statement is false.

T   F   11. A mutual fund is a certificate of debt or obligation issued by a corporation or a government.

T   F   12. Savings and loan associations provide many of the services of a commercial bank.

T   F   13. It is usually safe to carry checks made out to "Cash."

T   F   14. Saving money in a financial institution provides a safe place to keep the money, and it pays interest.

T   F   15. A Keogh plan is a tax-deferred retirement plan for self-employed people or employees of unincorporated companies without pension plans.

T   F   16. Banks and savings and loan associations are insured by the FDIC.

T   F   17. ATMs are remote computer terminals customers can use to make financial transactions.

T   F   18. Your signature is an example of a restrictive endorsement.

T   F   19. If your checking account is overdrawn, you cannot write checks against it.

T   F   20. A certificate of deposit pays a lower interest rate than a regular savings account.

Banking, Saving, and Investing

Name_____

Date _____   **Period** _____   **Score** _____

Chapter 26 Test

Matching: Match the following terms and identifying phrases.

_____ 1. A type of mutual fund that deals only in high-interest, short-term investments.

_____ 2. A tax-deferred retirement plan available in two types—traditional and Roth.

_____ 3. Remote computer terminal customers can use to make financial transactions.

_____ 4. A check drawn on the bank's funds and signed by a bank officer.

_____ 5. *For deposit only* is an example.

_____ 6. A personal check with the bank's guarantee that the check will be paid.

_____ 7. A tax-deferred retirement plan for self-employed people or employees of unincorporated companies without pension plans.

_____ 8. A record of checks, deposits, and charges on an account for a specific length of time.

_____ 9. A method in which savings earn interest on any interest already earned.

_____ 10. A savings method in which money is deposited for a specific period of time and earns a set annual rate of interest.

_____ 11. A certificate of debt or obligation issued by a corporation or a government.

_____ 12. A company that collects money from a number of investors and invests the money in securities.

_____ 13. An order for a specific amount of money payable to a specific payee.

A. automated teller machine (ATM)

B. bank statement

C. bond

D. cashier's check

E. certificate of deposit (CD)

F. certified check

G. compound interest

H. individual retirement account (IRA)

I. Keogh plan

J. money market fund

K. money order

L. mutual fund

M. restrictive endorsement

True/False: Circle *T* if the statement is true and *F* if the statement is false.

T   F   14. A cash card is sometimes called a check card.

T   F   15. Commercial banks are often called full-service banks.

T   F   16. Savings and loan association do *not* provide any of the services of a commercial bank.

T   F   17. The services of a credit union are for its members only.

T   F   18. When two or more people share an account, it is called a joint account.

(Continued)

Name_____

T   F   19. Avoid carrying checks made out to *Cash.*

T   F   20. Most places of business do *not* ask for identification when a person wants to cash a check.

T   F   21. Saving money in a financial institution provides a safe place to keep money that also pays interest.

T   F   22. Securities, retirement accounts, and real estate are examples of investments.

T   F   23. A certified check is drawn on a bank's own funds and is signed by a bank officer.

Multiple Choice: Choose the best response. Write the letter in the space provided.

_____24. Most savings and loan associations are insured by the _____.
A. FDIC
B. FSLIC
C. NCUA
D. NOW

_____25. When you write a check, sign your name _____.
A. the same way you did on the bank signature card
B. by printing it
C. in pencil only
D. None of the above.

_____26. If you write a check for an amount more than what you have in the account, your account is _____.
A. balanced
B. unbalanced
C. overdrawn
D. registered

_____27. Which of the following items should be kept in a safe-deposit box?
A. Jewelry.
B. Wills and deeds.
C. Stocks and bonds.
D. All of the above.

_____28. A regular savings account _____.
A. pays the lowest rate of interest of all savings accounts
B. requires that money be deposited for a set amount of time
C. pays a slightly higher interest rate than other savings plans
D. is available only through a credit union

Essay Questions: Provide complete responses to the following questions or statements.

29. Describe how to choose a financial institution.
30. Describe how to correctly write a check.
31. What four guidelines are important to follow when making investments?

Insurance

Objectives

After studying this chapter, students will be able to
- determine the types of auto insurance coverage they need.
- describe the types of health insurance coverage.
- summarize the two basic types of life insurance and the purposes of each.
- describe the different types of life insurance and the purposes of each.
- build SCANS competencies in using resources, interpersonal skills, and information.

Teaching Materials

Text, pages 517-531
  Terms to Know
  Facts in Review
  Applying Your Skills
  Developing SCANS Workplace Competencies
Student Activity Guide
  A. *Auto Insurance*
  B. *What Do You Do If You're in an Accident?*
  C. *Health Insurance*
  D. *Home Insurance Possessions Inventory*
  E. *Insurance Terms to Know*
  F. *Life Insurance*
Teacher's Resource Guide/Binder
  Comparing Types of Life Insurance, reproducible
    master 27-1
  Choosing the Right Insurance, reproducible
    master 27-2
  Review and Study Guide for Chapter 27,
    reproducible master 27-3
  Chapter 27 Test, reproducible master
Teacher's Resource Binder
  Insurance—The Umbrella of Protection, color
    transparency CT-27

Introductory Activities

1. Ask students to consider the costs they would encounter if they wrecked their car; required

surgery and a long hospital stay; had their home destroyed by fire; or had their apartment burglarized. How would students handle these unexpected financial losses?
2. *Insurance—The Umbrella of Protection,* color transparency CT-27, TRB. Use this transparency to introduce the concept of insurance as a way to protect people from unexpected financial losses. Ask students to explain what is protected by each type of insurance.
3. Discuss with students how insurance protects consumers. Ask students to refer to television commercials, magazine ads, or instances in which their family made claims.

Instructional Concepts and Student Learning Experiences

Automobile Insurance

4. Have students investigate and report on the laws in your state regarding uninsured motorists and their liability.
5. Ask students to give examples of claims that could be made through property liability coverage.
6. Have students prepare panel reports on different factors that influence auto insurance rates. Have them include case studies, reference material from the library, and news articles.
7. Have students pretend they own new cars and must obtain insurance. Students should contact several insurance companies to compare rates and coverage, then report their findings to the class.
8. Have students write an essay on why auto insurance is essential for all drivers.
9. Discuss in class safe driving methods and how safe driving can decrease auto insurance costs. Following the discussion, show students a videotape on safe driving.
10. *Auto Insurance,* Activity A, SAG. Students read case studies about auto insurance and answer related questions.

11. Have students write a case study of an auto accident in a state that has no-fault auto insurance.
12. Ask students to describe an auto accident that involves no injuries. Obtain insurance claim forms and have students complete them. Discuss the importance of accuracy when completing claim forms.
13. Have students investigate and report on the financial responsibility laws in your state. Discuss how these laws protect drivers in case of accidents.
14. Have students create posters that depict the procedures to follow in case of an auto accident.
15. *What Do You Do If You're in an Accident?* Activity B, SAG. Students explain the procedures to follow if they are involved in an accident, then answer related questions.

Health Insurance

16. Divide the class into groups to discuss the advantages of each of the following insurance types: basic medical, major medical, disability, group health insurance, HMOs, PPOs, and POSs.
17. Have students prepare charts comparing the costs, benefits, and deductibles of three different health insurance plans.
18. *Health Insurance,* Activity C, SAG. Students answer questions about health insurance.
19. Have students describe how the following persons would use an HMO or a PPO: a single person in good health, a married couple with three children, and a 55-year-old person with high blood pressure.
20. Ask students if they are a part of a group health insurance plan. Have students share the details of the plan in class and discuss how they have benefited from the group plan.

Home Insurance

21. *Home Insurance Possessions Inventory,* Activity D, SAG. Students prepare an inventory of their household possessions with estimated values for home insurance purposes, then answer related questions.
22. Instruct students to describe a plan in which they would obtain home insurance for a home valued at $150,000.
23. Have students brainstorm reasons renters should have renter's insurance. Which possessions would students find most difficult to replace?
24. Obtain a copy of a home owner's insurance policy and a renter's insurance policy to show to students. Read both policies and compare coverage.

Life Insurance

25. *Comparing Types of Life Insurance,* reproducible master 27-1, TRG/B. Students contact a local insurance company to find information on whole life, term, and universal life insurance. Based on their findings, students should explain which type they think is best.
26. Divide the class into small groups. Each group should describe people who should have life insurance. Have each group role-play each person they describe.
27. Have students list the life insurance needs of the following persons: a single person with no dependents; a single person with one dependent; the head of a household of four; a married senior citizen; and a single senior citizen.
28. Break the class into groups to debate which type of life insurance offers the best benefits: whole life, term, or universal life. Have students prepare for the debate by referring to outside research material about these types of insurance, including their findings from reproducible master 27-1.
29. Have students write case studies describing how people benefit from life insurance policies.
30. *Insurance Terms to Know,* Activity E, SAG. Students complete a crossword puzzle of insurance terms.
31. *Life Insurance,* Activity F, SAG. Students complete a true-or-false exercise that tests their knowledge of life insurance, then answer related questions.

Employer-Sponsored Insurance Programs

32. Ask students to report on insurance fringe benefits offered by their employers for full-time employees. Have students compare their employers' plans to other companies in the same field.
33. Have students write a description of the ideal insurance fringe benefit package they would like to have when working full-time.
34. Have students read want ads for jobs in their chosen occupation and circle the ads that offer the best insurance fringe benefits. Have students present their findings to the class.

Choosing an Insurance Company, Agent, and Policy

35. *Choosing the Right Insurance,* reproducible master 27-2, TRG/B. Students read case studies and work in groups to determine the types of insurance needed in each case. Groups should review their answers with a local insurance company representative, then report their findings in class.
36. Have students prepare a small brochure or checklist that gives guidelines for choosing an insurance company, agent, or policy. Have students write the brochure for an audience of high school graduates new to the workforce.

37. Have students interview their family's insurance agent as if they were shopping for an agent of their own. Students may tape the interview or sum up the interview in a written report.
38. Have students write a description of the type of auto, health, and life insurance they would need if they were living on their own and working full-time. Also have students explain how they would go about shopping for the best policies, agent, and company for each type.
39. Have students write a research report on a major insurance company, such as Blue Cross or Prudential. Have them focus on the company's history and reputation for settling claims fairly and promptly. As part of their report, have students include an interview with a local agent from the company.

Filing an Insurance Claim

40. Have students pretend they must file an insurance claim. Students may prepare an oral report and describe the type of claim and the steps they would take to file it.
41. Bring in sample insurance claim forms for students to examine and read. Discuss what kind of information they should have on hand in order to complete the forms.
42. Have students refer to Juanita's case study on page 527 of the text. Have students determine what kind of insurance Juanita's parents should have.

Activities to Enrich Learning

43. Have students contact an insurance company or their family agent to investigate reasons the company would (1) refuse to renew an auto insurance policy; (2) deny a health insurance applicant; and (3) cancel any type of policy.
44. Have students research and write a report on the origin of insurance, focusing on health and life insurance policies.

Activities to Extend Learning

45. Invite an insurance agent to speak to the class about the benefits of the types of insurance described in the text.
46. Invite an insurance company representative to give the class the same presentation he or she would give to employees at a company.
47. Host a career day in which students explore career opportunities in the insurance field. Invite speakers from local insurance companies, career counselors, and insurance agents to speak to the class.

Answer Key

Text

Facts in Review, page 530

1. when a person has something of value that would be costly or difficult to replace
2. automobile, health, home, life
3. property damage liability
4. The deductible is the amount a policyholder must pay before the insurance company will begin to cover an expense.
5. a type of insurance that eliminates the legal process of proving who is at fault in the accident
6. (List five:) age of driver, year and model of car, completion of a driver education course, good grades, nonsmoker status, insurance coverage on more than one car, mileage driven, owner's driving record, installation of anti-theft device, amount of deductible
7. Basic medical insurance covers the costs of hospitalization. Major medical insurance picks up where basic coverage ends. Disability insurance provides regular income payments to a person unable to work because of injury or illness.
8. provides more coverage at much lower cost to the individual
9. health maintenance organization (HMO), preferred provider organization (PPO), point-of-service plan (POS)
10. protection against damage or loss of the dwelling and/or personal property due to fire, lightning strikes, burglary, theft, vandalism, and explosion; payment of living expenses while the homeowner lives somewhere else due to property damage
11. protection against financial loss if: others are injured on or by your property, you or your property damages another's property; you are sued for injuries to others or damage to their property, you are held legally liable for injuries or property damage
12. property protection does not cover the dwelling itself
13. to protect against the loss of income due to death
14. Whole life insurance provides death benefits for a lifetime and is a form of savings. Term insurance provides death benefits for a set period specified in the policy. Universal term insurance provides death benefits for a set period as well as a savings and investment account.

Student Activity Guide

Auto Insurance, Activity A

Case 1:

1.	B	4.	F
2.	E	5.	A
3.	D	6.	C

(Cases 2-5 are student response.)

What Do You Do If You're in an Accident?, Activity B

1. (Student response. See Chart 27-3 on page 521 of the text.)

2-4. (Student response.)

Health Insurance, Activity C

1. hospitalization, laboratory tests, medicine, and possibly doctor visits and surgical procedures
2. It pays the largest share of expenses resulting from a major illness or injury.
3. two-thirds of a person's gross income
4. his primary care physician associated with the HMO; either no charge or a minimal fee
5. She must use a doctor or a hospital from the approved PPO list or pay higher fees. The fees charged for medical services, which are negotiated with the PPO by Tawanda's group or insurance carrier, are usually discounted 10 to 20 percent.
6. A POS member may get care outside the network, but an HMO member cannot. Nathaniel's benefits will be reduced.
7. (Student response.)

Insurance Terms to Know, Activity E

Life Insurance, Activity F

1. false	8. true
2. true	9. false
3. false	10. true
4. true	11. false
5. true	12. true
6. true	13. false
7. false	

14-17. (Student response.)

Teacher's Resource Guide/Binder

Review and Study Guide for Chapter 27, reproducible master 27-3

1. insurance
2. universal life
3. no-fault
4. term insurance
5. premium
6. whole life
7. coinsurance
8. major medical
9. beneficiary
10. cash value
11. disability
12. financial responsibility
13. health maintenance
14. liability
15. property
16. D
17. A
18. B
19. D
20. C

Chapter 27 Test

1. L	10. H	19. T
2. A	11. I	20. F
3. G	12. F	21. T
4. J	13. T	22. T
5. K	14. F	23. C
6. D	15. T	24. D
7. E	16. F	25. A
8. C	17. T	26. A
9. B	18. F	27. B

28. Stop immediately. Notify the police immediately. Do not admit fault. Avoid discussing the accident with anyone except the police. Exchange information with the other driver. Notify your insurance agent. Notify the State Motor Vehicle Department as required by law.

29. Basic medical insurance covers the costs of hospitalization, all related services, and possibly some doctor visits and surgical procedures. Major medical insurance covers the costs of bills not covered by basic medical insurance. Disability insurance provides regular income payments when a person is unable to work because of injury or illness.

30. Make sure the company has a reputation of settling claims fairly. Buy from a company that has the most benefits and options that are important to you. Select an experienced, honest, and reliable agent. Choose a policy that provides the coverage you need.

Reproducible Master 27-1

Comparing Types of Life Insurance

Name_____ **Date** _____ **Period** _____

Contact a local insurance company for the information needed to fill in the chart. Then complete the statement below by explaining which type of life insurance you would recommend for a 22-year-old college graduate who is single and has a good job with a promising future. She also has a life insurance policy worth the value of one year's salary, paid by her employer so long as she remains an employee.

Type of Life Insurance	Definition	Cost	Benefits	Disadvantages
Whole life				
Term				
Universal life				

After comparing the types of life insurance, I think _____

is the best because _____

_____

_____

_____

_____

Reproducible Master 27-2

Choosing the Right Insurance

Name_____ **Date** _____ **Period** _____

Work in small groups to determine the types of insurance needed in the case studies below. Review your answers with a local insurance company representative. Then share your findings with the class.

1. Avery is a 23-year-old single person with no dependents. He plans to marry his fiancee, Jacqueline, within a year and start a family right away. Avery drives a two-year-old car and rents an apartment. Because he earns a good salary, Avery has been able to buy a personal computer. This item would be expensive to replace if stolen. Next week, Avery must decide what type of health insurance to select from several types offered by his employer.

   What insurance does Avery need? Explain your answer. _____

   _____

   _____

   _____

   _____

2. Jim and Liz, both 28 years old, are married. They have one child, Sam, who is two years old. Jim and Liz want to send Sam to a good college when he graduates from high school. They drive a late-model four-door sedan, although they are saving for a new car. Jim and Liz own a condominium they have furnished with expensive furniture. Jim is self-employed as a construction worker; Liz is employed by a small business that offers health insurance.

   What types of insurance do Jim and Liz need? Explain your answer. _____

   _____

   _____

   _____

   _____

3. Will and Marnie are a married couple in their late fifties. They have three children. One daughter will get married next year, one is in college, and the youngest is still in high school. Will and Marnie pay half of their children's college tuition and want to pay for their daughter's wedding. Will drives a current model passenger van and Marnie drives a compact car. They have a mortgage on a four-bedroom home that will be paid off in five years. Will is a federal government employee. Marnie is a homemaker. They have been planning for retirement and want to increase their savings as retirement gets closer.

   What types of insurance do Will and Marnie need? Explain your answer. _____

   _____

   _____

   _____

   _____

Reproducible Master 27-3

Review and Study Guide for Chapter 27

Name_____ **Date** _____ **Period** _____

Completion: Fill in the blanks with the correct terms.

1. Most people need _____ to recover financially from accidents, serious illnesses, and other misfortunes.

2. _____ _____ insurance is a policy combined with a savings and investment account that earns current market rates.

3. _____–_____ auto insurance eliminates the legal process of proving who is at fault in an accident.

4. _____ _____ covers the policyholder for a set period of time as specified in the policy.

5. The _____ is the set amount that the policyholder pays the insurance company on a regular basis.

6. Insurance that covers the policyholder for a lifetime is called _____ _____ insurance.

7. _____ is a plan in which the insurance company pays a high percentage of medical costs, such as 80 percent, while the insured pays the rest.

8. _____ _____ insurance is sometimes called catastrophic insurance because it protects people from huge medical bills.

9. The _____ is the person named by the policyholder to receive the death benefit of a life insurance policy.

10. _____ _____ is the amount a policy is worth in cash upon surrender of the policy.

11. _____ insurance provides regular income payments when a person is unable to work because of injury or illness.

12. _____ _____ laws are designed to assure that motorists can pay for any damages or injuries they may cause while driving their cars.

13. A(n) _____ _____ organization is a group of medical facilities and personnel who provide health care services to its members.

14. Property damage _____ coverage pays for damages your car causes to the property of others if you are responsible for the accident.

15. _____ coverage on a homeowner's policy insures the policyholder against such dangers as fire, theft, or vandalism.

(Continued)

Name_____

Multiple Choice: Choose the best response. Write the letter in the space provided.

_____16. Auto insurance premiums are usually based on which of the following?
   A. Driving record.
   B. Year and model of the car.
   C. Amount of the deductible.
   D. All of the above.

_____17. Having life insurance is especially important to persons who _____.
   A. have children who depend on their income
   B. have no dependents
   C. are single
   D. are unemployed

_____18. When filing an insurance claim, a person should *not* _____.
   A. report any accident, burglary, or theft to the police
   B. wait a few days to phone the insurance agent or company
   C. follow up with a written explanation of what happened
   D. cooperate with the company as it investigates, settles, or defends any claims

_____19. When choosing an insurance company, _____.
   A. compare the policies at various companies
   B. research the company's reputation of settling claims fairly and promptly
   C. buy from the company that offers policies with the benefits and options wanted
   D. All of the above.

_____20. This automobile insurance coverage protects persons who are legally liable for accidents in which others are injured or killed.
   A. Comprehensive physical damage.
   B. Collision.
   C. Bodily injury liability.
   D. Property damage liability.

Insurance

Name_____

Date _____   **Period** _____   **Score** _____

Chapter 27 Test

Matching: Match the following terms and identifying phrases.

_____ 1. A policy combining death benefits with a savings and investment account that earns current market rates.

_____ 2. The set amount a policyholder pays the insurance company on a regular basis.

_____ 3. A plan in which the insurance company pays a large percentage of the medical costs, such as 80 percent, and the insured pays the rest.

_____ 4. The amount the policy is worth in cash upon surrender of the policy.

_____ 5. Insurance that covers the policyholder for a set period of time as specified in the policy.

_____ 6. Sometimes called catastrophic insurance because it protects individuals and families from huge medical bills.

_____ 7. Provides regular income payments when a person is unable to work because of injury or illness.

_____ 8. Insurance that eliminates the legal process of proving who is at fault in an accident.

_____ 9. An amount the policyholder must pay before the insurance company will begin to cover the expense.

_____ 10. The person named by the policyholder to receive the death benefit of a life insurance policy.

_____ 11. Insurance that covers the policyholder for a lifetime.

_____ 12. An organization of medical personnel and facilities that provides health care services to its members.

A. premium
B. deductible
C. no-fault auto insurance
D. major medical insurance
E. disability insurance
F. health maintenance organization (HMO)
G. coinsurance
H. beneficiary
I. whole life insurance
J. cash value
K. term insurance
L. universal life insurance

True/False: Circle *T* if the statement is true and *F* if the statement is false.

T   F   13. People need insurance to recover financially from accidents, serious illnesses, theft, fire, and other misfortunes.

T   F   14. Only people with a lot of money or possessions should have insurance.

T   F   15. Anyone who owns or drives a car takes certain financial and personal risks.

T   F   16. Property damage liability does *not* cover damages to lampposts, telephone poles, or buildings.

T   F   17. A person with a good driving record usually pays lower insurance premiums.

(Continued)

Name_____

T   F   18. *Not* everyone needs to be covered by some form of health plan.

T   F   19. Some companies may exclude certain illnesses or treatments from their policies.

T   F   20. Homeowner's insurance provides only property protection.

T   F   21. The main purpose of life insurance is to provide income for anyone who depends on the insured person's income, such as a spouse.

T   F   22. A good insurance agent will advise people honestly about the type and amount of coverage they need.

Multiple Choice: Choose the best response. Write a letter in the space provided.

_____23. This automobile insurance coverage protects persons who are legally liable for accidents in which others are injured or killed and is called _____.
A. comprehensive physical damage
B. collision
C. bodily injury liability
D. property damage liability

_____24. Auto insurance premiums are usually based on _____.
A. the driving record
B. year and model of the car
C. amount of the deductible
D. All of the above.

_____25. Having life insurance is especially important to people who _____.
A. have children who depend on their income
B. have no dependents
C. are single
D. are unemployed

_____26. Financial responsibility laws are related to _____.
A. auto liability insurance coverage
B. home owner's insurance
C. disability insurance
D. major medical insurance

_____27. When filing an insurance claim, a person should *not* _____.
A. follow up with a written explanation of what happened
B. wait a few days to phone the insurance agent or company
C. report any accident, burglary, or theft to the police
D. supply any information needed by the insurance company

Essay Questions: Provide complete responses to the following questions.

28. Explain the steps a person should take if involved in a car accident.
29. Describe the three types of health insurance coverage.
30. Explain the guidelines for choosing an insurance company, agent, and policy.

Managing Family, Work, and Citizenship Roles

Objectives

After studying this chapter, students will be able to
- explain their responsibilities in the role of family members.
- describe several strategies for balancing family and work roles.
- list factors that contribute to a family-friendly workplace.
- explain the responsibilities of citizenship.
- describe the two major categories of law.
- explain how to select and deal with a lawyer.
- build SCANS competencies in using resources, interpersonal skills, information, and systems.

Teaching Materials

Text, pages 533-555
- *Terms to Know*
- *Facts in Review*
- *Applying Your Skills*
- *Developing SCANS Workplace Competencies*

Student Activity Guide
- A. *Your Family Role*
- B. *Managing Your Time*
- C. *Support Systems*
- D. *Legal Terms*
- E. *Consulting a Lawyer*
- F. *Examining the Court System*

Teacher's Resource Guide/Binder
- *Citizenship Rights and Responsibilities,* reproducible master 28-1
- *The Court System,* transparency master 28-2
- *Review and Study Guide for Chapter 28,* reproducible master 28-3
- *Chapter 28 Test,* reproducible master

Teacher's Resource Binder
- *Using Time Well,* color transparency CT-28

Introductory Activities

1. Ask students what is meant by the term *role.* Then ask them if they fulfill any roles in their lives. This will help you determine how much they know about their roles as children, siblings, students, workers, etc. List as many roles as possible on the board. Then ask them if they ever have any problems fulfilling all these roles. If they answer yes, tell them that this chapter should help them handle the challenge.

2. Ask students to describe themselves as citizens of their community, state, and country. Discuss the similarities and differences in each role.

3. Have students brainstorm and compare the rights and responsibilities they have as U.S. citizens to the rights and responsibilities of citizens of other countries.

Instructional Concepts and Student Learning Experiences

Family Roles

4. *Your Family Role,* Activity A, SAG. Each student interviews another person in the class about his or her family roles.

5. Ask students to name various family roles and write these on the board. Look at these roles one at a time, and ask students to name the responsibilities that go along with each role. Then ask them what rights might go along with each of these roles.

6. Honesty and commitment are discussed in the text as ways to build strong relationships. Ask students to name other factors that help build strong families, such as love, trust, and respect.

7. Discuss the importance of communication in family relationships. What methods do families use to communicate with each other? Have the new methods of electronic communication helped families stay in contact with each other better? Have these improved relationships within the family or hindered them?

8. Ask students to share their reactions when they are told to do something by their parents as opposed to being involved in deciding how household tasks can be shared and managed. Which is likely to lead to better feelings and results?

Balancing Family and Work Roles

9. *Using Time Well*, color transparency CT-28, TRB. Use this transparency as you review the three strategies for managing time. Ask students to add other strategies that have helped them manage their time, such as assignment notebooks, pocket calendars, having a scheduled study time, etc.

10. *Managing Your Time*, Activity B, SAG. Students list the tasks they have to complete during the day, rank them in order of priority, and check them off as they are completed. At the end of the day, they are to answer questions about their use of time.

11. Ask students how goal setting can help them with time management.

12. Bring in samples of weekly and monthly planners that are available commercially. Discuss the advantages of using a weekly/monthly time plan. Have students make their own weekly time plans. Evaluate their helpfulness at the end of a week.

13. Poll the class to see how many students use to-do lists. Discuss the advantages of using to-do lists. Then ask each student to create a to-do list for the following week. After the week is over, have students write paragraphs about how effective the lists were in helping them manage their time.

14. Have students list their most common time-wasters. Brainstorm solutions to avoid these time-wasters.

15. Have students role-play *procrastination* in completing homework assignments or household chores. Then have them replay the same scene showing effective time management.

16. *Support Systems*, Activity C, SAG. In small groups, students are to research, identify, and describe five support programs available in your community. They should be prepared to share their findings with the class.

17. Discuss how the Internet can be a support for families (easy source of current information, a way to communicate with distant family members, a way to "chat" with people who have similar problems, a source of advice for parents, etc.). Also discuss cautions in the use of the Internet.

The Family-Friendly Workplace

18. Have students discuss this statement: "The demands of work should always come ahead of family demands." Do students agree that fewer employers hold this view today than in previous years?

19. Have students point out the advantages and disadvantages of the Family and Medical Leave Act for both the employee and the employer. Do they know anyone who has benefited from the provisions of this Act?

20. List the various types of work arrangements on the board. Have students describe each and brainstorm possible advantages and disadvantages to each arrangement.

21. With the help of the class, find workers who have flextime, job sharing, and telecommuting work arrangements. Have pairs of students interview these individuals to find out how they view their work arrangement. Ask students to report back to the class.

Citizenship Responsibilities

22. *Citizenship Rights and Responsibilities*, reproducible master 28-1, TRG/B. Students are asked if they agree or disagree with statements about citizenship rights and responsibilities.

23. Some schools require students to complete a community service project as a requirement for graduation. Discuss the pros and cons of this requirement.

24. Ask students if they have ever voted in a school election, for a club officer, or on family matters. Have students describe the voting process they experienced and explain how their vote influenced the outcome.

25. Have students obtain the names and addresses of places in their community where they can register to vote when they turn 18.

26. Have students write an essay on the topic "The Importance of My Role as a Voter."

27. Instruct students to debate whether the voting age should remain at 18 years or be raised to the previous requirement of age 21.

Obeying the Law

28. Have students consider the laws they obey every day. Discuss with students how these laws protect their personal safety and rights as well as society's as a whole.

29. Have students research and list specific laws in each of the following categories: international, administrative, criminal, and constitutional.

30. Bring in copies of your state's driving laws for students to read. Ask students to analyze the laws and express why they think some of the laws were enacted. How might voters influence the changing of these laws?

31. Have students bring in newspaper articles that describe criminal laws that have been broken, including felonies and misdemeanors. Discuss the degree of seriousness and resulting penalties for each type of crime.

32. Ask students to interview their employers to find out how a criminal record can affect a job applicant's chances of being hired. Students may report findings in class.

33. Have students research and report on three civil laws that have been enacted in your state.
34. Ask students if they have ever signed a contract. How did students uphold the provisions of the contract?
35. Have students list their legal rights and responsibilities as a minor in your state. Discuss the laws that protect them as minors.
36. Write a contract in which all students agree to adhere to a specific classroom behavior in exchange for specific compensation. After students read it, poll them to see how many are willing to sign it. Ask those who don't want to sign the contract to explain why.
37. Have students role-play incidents that can be classified as torts.

Consulting a Lawyer

38. Have students role-play the various situations in the text that require the services of a lawyer.
39. *Consulting a Lawyer,* Activity E, SAG. Students answer questions about consulting a lawyer.
40. *Legal Terms,* Activity D, SAG. Students complete a fill-in-the-blank exercise using chapter terms.
41. Have students develop and write guidelines for finding a lawyer. Have them write for an audience of high school graduates who work full-time.
42. Have students research and report on how to obtain legal aid in your community if they cannot afford a lawyer.

The Court System

43. *Examining the Court System,* Activity F, SAG. Students answer questions about the court system.
44. *The Court System,* transparency master 28-2, TRG/B. Use this transparency to help students understand the state and federal court systems.
45. Have students research and list the types of cases handled in each type of court described in Chart 28-18 in the text.
46. Have students write research reports on the topic "The Responsibilities of a Juror."
47. Record and play back for the class one of the half-hour television shows that depict small claims court. Discuss the similarities and differences between these portrayals and everyday cases.
48. Organize a "Day in Court" in which students role-play cases in a mock small claims court.
49. Have students write a research report on the role of the justices in the Supreme Court.

Activities to Enrich Learning

50. Assign students to search the Internet for companies that offer excellent family-friendly services for their employees. Find out information about the services provided and how company management feels the company benefits from offering these services to their employees. Prepare a written report.
51. Have students form panels to discuss the following topics: laws that should be eliminated, laws that should be changed, and new laws that should be enacted.
52. Have students contact several lawyers to find out about the services they perform and the fees they charge. Have students report findings to the class.
53. Have students investigate career opportunities in the legal field. Discuss the educational requirements of each career.
54. Have students give a talk on the topic "Why I Would (or Would Not) Want to Run for Public Office."

Activities to Extend Learning

55. Invite a member of a community support group to your class to speak about the benefits of participating in such groups.
56. Invite a local political figure to speak to the class about the power of voters.
57. Invite a law enforcement officer to speak to students about crime prevention and the court process that awaits those who commit crimes.
58. Take students on a field trip to a session of small claims court. Arrange for the students to meet with the judge for a brief question-and-answer session.

Answer Key

Text

Facts in Review, page 554

1. building relationships, maintaining the home, using leisure time effectively
2. because it builds strong relationships and people are more likely to believe and trust you
3. because it effectively uses the time and talents of each member to pursue a common goal
4. It helps in deciding what is important.
5. (List three:) Identify time wasters and avoid them; avoid postponing unpleasant work; set realistic deadlines; stay motivated by keeping your goals in mind; be flexible.
6. (List four:) a support system, community programs, extended programs in school, care centers, professional help, family counseling services
7. having and caring for a baby; adopting a child or adding a foster child to the family; caring for a sick child, spouse, or parent; being unable to work because of serious illness
8. (List three:) flextime, job sharing, telecommuting, a home-based business

9. must be a citizen and at least 18 years old
10. international, administrative, constitutional, and criminal laws
11. A misdemeanor is a less serious crime, punishable by a fine or imprisonment for less than a year. A felony is a serious crime, punishable by imprisonment or even death.
12. intentional or unintentional
13. legal aid offices or clinics; public defenders appointed by the state
14. The case may be appealed, after which, the first court decision is either upheld or overturned.
15. less formal, lower filing fees, no lawyers

Student Activity Guide

Legal Terms, Activity D

1. register
2. public laws
3. international laws
4. administrative laws
5. constitutional laws
6. criminal law
7. felony
8. misdemeanor
9. civil laws
10. contract
11. valid
12. tort
13. parties
14. competent
15. consideration

Consulting a Lawyer, Activity E

1. before you make the decision or a serious problem arises
2. (List six:) buying or selling real estate, writing or entering into a contract, getting divorced, experiencing financial problems, writing a will, being charged with a criminal action, facing a civil suit, having trouble obtaining satisfaction in regard to a consumer complaint
3. Ask a trusted teacher, friend, or family member to suggest a lawyer, or call the Lawyer Referral Service.
4. a service sponsored by local bar associations whose phone number can usually be found in the Yellow Pages under Attorneys or Lawyers
5. a legal aid office, a legal aid clinic at a law school
6. small claims for wages; disputes between the client and a lender, an installment seller, or a landlord; domestic matters, such as divorce, child custody, or the contesting of a will

Examining the Court System, Activity F

1. to try and punish people who have committed criminal offenses, to interpret laws, to settle legal problems between people involved in civil disputes
2. criminal and civil cases involving people within the state
3. cases involving federal laws, people from more than one state, or cases previously tried at the state level

4. type of case, type of criminal offense, value of a civil claim, or whether an original ruling or a review of a previous ruling is being sought
5. trial court
6. panel of citizens selected to help decide a case in a trial court
7. The case goes to a panel of justices in a higher court who review the case and either uphold or overturn the trial court's decision.
8. to be more accessible to more people for cases involving small amounts of money
9. Tyrone is the plaintiff. Kate is the defendant.

Teacher's Resource Guide/Binder

Review and Study Guide for Chapter 28, reproducible master 28-3

1. roles
2. commitment
3. cooperation
4. leisure time
5. goals
6. procrastinate
7. support system
8. family-friendly
9. flextime
10. citizens
11. public laws
12. contract
13. plaintiff
14. defendant
15. felony
16. tort
17. public defender
18. criminal

Chapter 28 Test

1. K	12. D	22. T
2. B	13. F	23. F
3. J	14. T	24. T
4. E	15. F	25. T
5. C	16. F	26. T
6. A	17. T	27. C
7. I	18. T	28. C
8. L	19. T	29. A
9. H	20. F	30. D
10. F	21. T	31. B
11. G		

32. (Describe three:) Identify time wasters and avoid them; avoid postponing unpleasant work; set realistic deadlines; stay motivated by keeping goals in mind; be flexible.
33. A person must be a citizen of the United States and at least 18 years old to register to vote. A person can register at the county commissioner's office, the election supervisor's office, the municipal clerk's office, or in some states the department of motor vehicles.
34. Public laws govern the association between citizens and the government. Civil laws outline citizens' rights in relation to one another.
35. Choose the best lawyer for the situation. Ask a trusted family member, friend, or teacher to suggest one. Call the Lawyers Referral Service for assistance. For people who cannot afford one, call a legal aid office in the community.

Reproducible Master 28-1

Citizenship Rights and Responsibilities

Name_____   **Date** _____   **Period** _____

Respond to the statements below about citizenship rights and responsibilities. Then choose a statement from the checklist. Explain why you agree or disagree with the statement.

Agree	**Disagree**	**Unsure**	
_____	_____	_____	1. Our taxes provide revenue for keeping our communities clean and our citizens safe, so volunteer help should not be needed.
_____	_____	_____	2. It is the responsibility of every citizen to be involved in their community in some way.
_____	_____	_____	3. What you give in your volunteer work can be more personally rewarding than what you receive.
_____	_____	_____	4. Tax-supported government agencies should not need volunteer help.
_____	_____	_____	5. Citizens should have the right to choose their leaders.
_____	_____	_____	6. Citizens should not have to register to vote.
_____	_____	_____	7. The voting age should be lowered to age 16.
_____	_____	_____	8. Noncitizens in this country should be allowed to vote.
_____	_____	_____	9. As a citizen, I need to be aware of the many laws that may affect me.
_____	_____	_____	10. The death penalty should not be imposed for felonies.
_____	_____	_____	11. I would hire a person with a criminal record.
_____	_____	_____	12. Minors should be legally bound by written contracts.
_____	_____	_____	13. I would consult a lawyer immediately if I needed help with a legal problem.
_____	_____	_____	14. All court cases should be tried by a jury.
_____	_____	_____	15. Being a U.S. citizen has important responsibilities.

I strongly agree/disagree with statement _____ because _____

_____

_____

_____

_____

_____

_____

_____

_____

_____

Transparency Master 28-2

The Court System

State Courts

Supreme Court
- Cases involving state constitutional law
- Review cases previously appealed in appellate courts

Appellate Courts
- Review cases previously tried in a lower court

Trial Courts of General Jurisdiction
- More serious criminal and civil cases for larger geographic area

Also known as:
- Circuit
- County
- Superior
- Common pleas
- District

Trial Courts of Limited Justice
- Local misdemeanor cases
- Minor civil cases

Federal Courts

Supreme Court
- Original jurisdiction in cases involving a state
- Review cases from state and federal courts involving constitutional law

Circuit Court of Appeals
- Appeals of cases originally tried in district courts

District Courts
- Cases involving federal laws and/or citizens of different states

Reproducible Master 28-3

Review and Study Guide for Chapter 28

Completion: Fill in the blanks with the correct terms.

1. You perform many _____ in your life as a student, family member, and worker.

2. When you make a _____ to someone, you are promising to fulfill certain duties and responsibilities.

3. A spirit of _____ is very important in families where all adult members work outside the home.

4. _____ _____ plays an important role in helping people maintain a balanced lifestyle and feel refreshed.

5. Having _____ can help you see the big picture so you can focus your time and effort on what is really important.

6. People who _____ keep postponing unpleasant tasks.

7. A(n) _____ _____ of friends, relatives, and neighbors can offer you help in times of need.

8. A(n) _____-_____ workplace is one that offers options for employees for handling family matters.

9. _____ allows employees to set work hours that meet both their needs and their employers' needs.

10. In the United States, _____ can choose their leaders by voting.

11. _____ _____ govern the association between citizens and the government.

12. A(n) _____ is a legally binding agreement between two or more people.

13. The person who files a lawsuit and takes the case to court is called the _____.

14. The person accused of a wrongdoing in a court case is called the _____.

15. A(n) _____ is punishable by imprisonment or even death.

16. A(n) _____ is a wrongful act committed against a person, independent of a contract.

17. If an accused person cannot afford a lawyer, the state will appoint a(n) _____ _____.

18. A(n) _____ record can handicap a person's future.

Managing Family, Work, and Citizenship Roles

Name_____

Date _____   Period _____   Score _____

Chapter 28 Test

Matching: Match the following terms and identifying phrases.

_____ 1. Laws that govern the association between citizens and the government.

_____ 2. The most serious type of crime punishable by imprisonment or even by death.

_____ 3. The person accused of a wrongdoing in a court case.

_____ 4. A legally binding agreement between two or more people.

_____ 5. A less serious crime, such as disorderly conduct or speeding.

_____ 6. Laws that outline citizens' rights in relation to one another.

_____ 7. The person who files a lawsuit and takes the case to court.

_____ 8. Workers can arrange to work hours that are more suited to their individual needs.

_____ 9. A panel of 12 citizens that may be selected to help decide a case in trial court.

_____ 10. A wrongful act committed against another person, independent of a contract.

_____ 11. A single job is split between two or more employees.

_____ 12. Working away from a central office using a computer and modem.

A. public laws
B. felony
C. misdemeanor
D. telecommuting
E. contract
F. tort
G. job sharing
H. jury
I. plaintiff
J. defendant
K. civil laws
L. flextime

True/False: Circle *T* if the statement is true or *F* if the statement is false.

T   F   13. Each person can fulfill only one role at a time.

T   F   14. An individual's roles change throughout his or her lifetime.

T   F   15. Burnout is a feeling of intense delight, such as accomplishing something few others can do.

T   F   16. The number of employers who believe that the demands of work should always come ahead of family demands is increasing.

T   F   17. The cost-effectiveness of family-friendly programs in the workplace has been well-documented.

T   F   18. U. S. citizens can choose whom they want their leaders to be by voting.

T   F   19. Elected candidates are responsible for passing laws that are used to govern the people.

T   F   20. Voters are never given the opportunity to vote directly *for* or *against* laws.

(Continued)

Name_____

T   F   21. Voters can elect leaders on three levels—local, state, and national.

T   F   22. A crime is an offense against the public or state.

T   F   23. A criminal record cannot handicap a person's future.

T   F   24. Mutual agreement is one criterion needed to make a contract binding.

T   F   25. Contracts can often be spoken agreements.

T   F   26. If an accused person cannot afford a lawyer, the state will appoint a public defender.

Multiple Choice: Choose the best response. Write the letter in the space provided.

_____27. Which of the following does *not* fall under the provisions of the Family and Medical Leave Act?
   A. Having and caring for a baby.
   B. Adopting a child or adding a foster child to the family.
   C. Caring for a sick brother or sister.
   D. Being unable to work because of serious illness.

_____28. Being convicted of a crime means that a person automatically _____.
   A. must go to prison
   B. is fined
   C. has a criminal record
   D. is fired from his or her job

_____29. The best time to consult a lawyer is _____.
   A. before you make an important financial or legal decision
   B. when you are in serious trouble
   C. as a last resort
   D. when you have no money

_____30. Which court system has original jurisdiction in local misdemeanor and minor civil cases?
   A. The Supreme Court.
   B. Appellate courts.
   C. District courts.
   D. Trial courts of limited jurisdiction.

_____31. If a small-business employer refused to pay the wages owed a worker, the worker could take his or her case to _____.
   A. trial courts of limited justice
   B. small claims court
   C. the Supreme Court
   D. a circuit court of appeals

Essay Questions: Provide complete responses to the following questions or statements.

32. Describe three strategies that can help a person manage time.
33. State the conditions under which a person is allowed to vote and explain how to register to vote.
34. Explain the difference between public laws and civil laws.
35. Explain how to select a lawyer.